'This second edition introduces students to the organizational life and behaviour of cultural organizations. The authors have added new topical chapters and have reorganized others and in doing so have provided an updated and even more specialized text concerning organizational behaviour in the creative and cultural industries. This book addresses the idiosyncrasies of these industries that are generated by the creative/aesthetic autonomy of the artist. The uniqueness of cultural organizations stems from their subordination to artistic creativities and the fact that such symbolic creativities are not bound to set rules. This means that effective leaders of such organizations are the ones who are able to manage an output or product that is extremely uncertain. This book is a "must read" for those who aspire to become such leaders'.

Guy Morrow, *University of Melbourne, Australia*

'I've long thought that Saintilan and Schreiber's book couldn't be surpassed. But it has been. The second edition is even better!'

Stephen Brown, *Ulster University Business School, Belfast*

'The second edition builds upon the substantial strengths of topic coverage and real world applications of the first edition to include opportunities and challenges posed by technology-based innovations in content creation and evolving forms of engagement with social media. Additionally, the new volume addresses evolving sensibilities of cultural sector stakeholders toward the environment, diversity and inclusion'.

Robert DoFillippi, *Sawyer Business School, Suffolk University*

'This second edition helpfully updates the structures and methodologies currently in practice within the creative industries, taking into account the increased influence of social media and digitization. Two new chapters on diversity and mental health & wellbeing are included, both even more pertinent after the Covid-19 pandemic. As before each chapter begins with a summary of what the student will study for each topic, questions on the chapter and relevant case studies for analysis. Overall an informative reference book for any Creative Industries student wishing to understand how this sector operates with examples of operational and personnel issues it might encounter and how to overcome them'.

Marius J Carboni, *University of Surrey and Morley College, London*

Managing Organizations in the Creative Economy

The creative and cultural industries represent a growing and important sector in the global economy. Thriving in these industries is particularly tough and organizations face unique challenges in the digital age. This textbook provides a vivid initiation into the creative industries workplace.

Managing Organizations in the Creative Economy is the first textbook of its kind, introducing organizational behaviour theories and applying them to the creative world. The text is underpinned by the latest research and theoretical insights into creative industries management and organizational behaviour, covering key topics such as structure, culture and the management of change and creativity as well as contemporary issues such as diversity, sustainability, managing stress, wellbeing and self-care, and remote working. The authors bring theory to life through practical examples and cases provided by industry experts, supported by specially created companion videos featuring managerial responses to the cases.

This second edition textbook provides readers with an updated applied theoretical understanding of organizational behaviour that will be of particular benefit to those looking to work in the creative and cultural industries. Students on courses such as arts business, arts management and music business, and even students within the broader study of the entertainment and creative industries, will find this to be a vital read.

Paul Saintilan has established an international career and reputation in creative industries management and teaching, and is currently CEO at the Australian Performing Arts Conservatory (APAC) in Brisbane, Australia.

David Schreiber is Chair of Creative & Entertainment Industry Studies and Associate Professor at Mike Curb College of Entertainment and Music Business, Belmont University, USA.

Discovering the Creative Industries

Series Editor: Ruth Rentschler

The creative and cultural industries account for a significant share of the global economy. Gaining and maintaining employment and work in this sector is a challenge and chances of success are enhanced by ongoing professional development.

This series provides a range of relatively short, student-centred books which blend industry and educational expertise with cultural sector practice. Books in the series provide applied introductions to the core elements of the creative industries. In sum, the series provides essential reading for those studying to enter the creative industries as well as those seeking to enhance their career via executive education.

Arts and Cultural Leadership
Creating Sustainable Arts Organizations
Kenneth Foster

Fundraising for the Creative and Cultural Industries
Leading Effective Fundraising Strategies
Michelle Wright, Ben Walmsley and Emilee Simmons

Managing the Arts and Culture
Cultivating a Practice
Edited by Constance DeVereaux

Managing Organizations in the Creative Economy, 2nd edition
Organizational Behaviour for the Cultural Sector
Paul Saintilan and David Schreiber

For more information about this series, please visit: www.routledge.com/Discovering-the-Creative-Industries/book-series/DCI

Managing Organizations in the Creative Economy

Organizational Behaviour for the Cultural Sector

Paul Saintilan and David Schreiber

2nd Edition

MEIEA® Music & Entertainment Industry Educators Association

Mike Curb College of Entertainment and Music Business, Belmont University

Routledge
Taylor & Francis Group
LONDON AND NEW YORK

Designed cover image: Jag_cz

Second edition published 2023
by Routledge
4 Park Square, Milton Park, Abingdon, Oxon, OX14 4RN

and by Routledge
605 Third Avenue, New York, NY 10158

Routledge is an imprint of the Taylor & Francis Group, an informa business

First edition published by Routledge 2018

British Library Cataloguing-in-Publication Data
A catalogue record for this book is available from the British Library

Library of Congress Cataloging-in-Publication Data
Names: Saintilan, Paul, author. | Schreiber, David, 1975– author.
Title: Managing organizations in the creative economy: organizational behaviour for the cultural sector / Paul Saintilan and David Schreiber.
Description: 2nd edition. | Abingdon, Oxon; New York, NY: Routledge, 2023. |
Series: Discovering the creative industries |
Includes bibliographical references and index.
Identifiers: LCCN 2022049175 (print) | LCCN 2022049176 (ebook) |
ISBN 9781032202594 (hardback) | ISBN 9781032202532 (paperback) |
ISBN 9781003262923 (ebook)
Subjects: LCSH: Cultural industries—Management. | Organizational behavior.
Classification: LCC HD9999.C9472 S25 2023 (print) |
LCC HD9999.C9472 (ebook) | DDC 658—dc23/eng/20221013
LC record available at https://lccn.loc.gov/2022049175
LC ebook record available at https://lccn.loc.gov/2022049176

ISBN: 978-1-032-20259-4 (hbk)
ISBN: 978-1-032-20253-2 (pbk)
ISBN: 978-1-003-26292-3 (ebk)

DOI: 10.4324/9781003262923

Typeset in Calvert
by codeMantra

Access the Support Material: www.routledge.com/9781032202532

Contents

List of figures

Preface

In preparing this book, we have attempted to write a practical teaching tool rather than a theoretical treatise. We have tried to bring the topics and concepts to life for students through case studies and practical examples from many creative industries practitioners (see Acknowledgements section below for a summary of these industry experts). Naturally, we see this as underpinned by scholarship and research, and we do cite academic literature, but our focus is on providing students with a vivid initiation into the creative industries workplace. The authors of this book have both experienced difficulties getting students engaged with traditional, generic management and organizational behaviour texts, and both believe that a customized resource like this will be of help to students interested in creative industries management. There are of course many issues that are of heightened significance in the creative industries which deserve special treatment.

Although the book adopts some of the characteristics of a traditional organizational behaviour text, we have also attempted to introduce creative and cultural industry research. Chapter 1 sets the premise for the book, defining the characteristics of creative industries that then sets up the context for subsequent chapters. Chapter 2 describes the inevitability of change and the implications this has for creative industries managers. The remainder of the book is structured into three broader sections, the first focusing on individual aspects of human behaviour, followed by aspects that may affect a group or team, before closing on larger organizational topics such as structure and culture. Ethical integrity is fundamental to authentic management in any sector, and this subject concludes the book. We point out its practical relevance to creative industries management.

We should acknowledge that we are both music business academics who have extended the scope of our work to arts, entertainment, film production, design and advertising. We both began our careers working in industry before actively seeking a life in academia. We are able to bring a perspective that can help close the gap between theory and practice, between academic researchers and industry practitioners. Although examples from the music industry loom large, we do hope that these illustrations bring to life practical aspects of the theory which have implications for other creative industries.

Integrated into the text are features and cases that relate real-life scenarios we may encounter in the creative industries. There are end-of-chapter questions and exercises, and six of the cases have companion videos which are available to instructors via the Routledge website. These videos provide managerial perspectives on the conflict scenarios presented in the cases. Five of these six cases have been previously published as *Collarts Music Organisation Case Studies* and have been used by many institutions worldwide (accessed via The Case Centre website). The videos would be best played at the end of class discussion on the cases.

Notes on changes made to the second edition

A number of changes have been made to the second edition to bring it into alignment with some of the transformational changes that have impacted the creative industries since the first edition was published, such as the increased impact of digitization and social media, the rise of the #MeToo movement, concerning research on mental health issues facing creative industries workers, and the growing attention being paid to sustainability, carbon footprint and climate change. The new chapter 'Diversity, Equity and Inclusion in Creative Organizations' (Chapter 11) takes material that was included in the Ethics chapter of the first edition and gives it renewed focus and weight. The new chapter 'Stress, Wellbeing and Self Care in Creative Organizations' (Chapter 6) helps students build a strong psychological platform for success in these industries. It provides analysis and recommendations which are useful at both an organizational and individual level. The analysis of 'bad work' and challenging environments is founded on the characteristics of the creative industries defined in Chapter 1. The importance of Teams (Chapter 10) has also been given its own chapter, rather than sitting within 'Leadership'. It emphasizes the importance teams play in organizations while dedicating discussion on remote and flexible work environments and the future of the creative industries workplace. The chapter on Power and Politics (Chapter 8) takes material on the abuse of power and sexual harassment formerly in the Ethics chapter and gives it renewed focus and weight. The Ethics chapter (Chapter 14) is retained and places greater focus on the need for sustainability given the pressures of accelerating climate change. There has been some restructuring to streamline content such as consolidating the chapters on Attitude and Motivation into one cohesive chapter.

Acknowledgements

There are a number of people who deserve to be acknowledged for their important support of this project. We would like to thank the Routledge team who worked on this book for their expertise, principally Terry Clague, Naomi Round Cahalin, Izzy Fitzharris, Katie Hemmings and Sinead Waldron. Thanks to technical contributors such as Dipak Durairaj at Codemantra, Ersen Sen (graphic design), Sam George-Allen and Henry Solomon (proofreading assistance), Karla Henwood (video) and Callum Birch (videography).

In writing an 'industry-integrated' text, we are indebted to the practitioners and senior managers we know who have given their time so generously and contributed to case studies. This includes figures who have made a major international impact on the music industry such as Michael Smellie (former Chief Operating Officer of Sony BMG worldwide) and J. F. Cecillon (former Chairman and CEO of EMI Music International). Very talented marketers currently working in the major labels such as Cindy James and Simon Cahill have helped update key cases to ensure they're aligned with contemporary language and practice.

Beautiful stories and insights into creative industries management have been provided by: Moffatt Oxenbould AM (former Artistic Director of Opera Australia); Phil Towle (renowned for his work with Metallica); Shae Constantine (former major label A&R guru and Founder/Managing Director of Intersection); Kevin Grosch (CEO of Made In Network); Andrew Kautz (COO of Big Machine Records); Rob Cannon (who has extensive experience in entertainment management and entertainment education and has held international record company roles); and Nadine Waran-Perrero (who has international experience in entertainment and higher education). Guy Morrow from The University of Melbourne and his colleague Abe Watson have also enhanced this second edition with interesting cases (we should also thank Guy for his enthusiasm and unfailing support of this title since its first publication). Furthermore, we would like to thank songwriters, musicians and recording artists who were willing to share their stories so that others can learn from them, such as Louisa Wendorff, Devin Dawson, Dean Fields and Ashlyne Huff.

Fredric Dannen, Crown Books (an imprint of Random House, a division of Penguin Random House LLC) and McIntosh & Otis, Inc. should be thanked for consenting to the publication of the Casablanca Records case study excerpt in Chapter 13, drawn from the book *Hit Men*.

We are grateful to MEIEA (the Music & Entertainment Industry Educators Association) Belmont University for providing funding support for some of the project's bells and whistles such as the online companion videos available in the instructor resources. Mary Jo Capps (former CEO of Musica Viva Australia) made an excellent contribution to these videos, as did Thomas Heymann (artist manager and former streaming music industry leader), Shaun James (previous Foxtel and major record label head), Moffatt Oxenbould AM (former Artistic Director of Opera Australia), Michael Smellie (former COO of Sony BMG worldwide) and Jeremy Youett (former New York Theatre Producer and General Manager and now a senior creative executive at Microsoft). Finally, we would also like to extend a thank you for the support from Diversity, Equity and Inclusion initiative from the Mike Curb College of Entertainment and Music Business at Belmont University, the financial contribution to helping us broaden our insight and understanding of diversity and inclusion practices in the creative industries is more salient than ever. In particular, a special shout out to Jennifer Duck and Sara Wigal, as they provided broader context and perspective on these important matters in the creative economy.

Paul

On a personal level, I need to acknowledge the profoundly important support I received from my wife Carolyn and family. My career in the entertainment industry benefitted from the insights of many wonderful people, and they were in my thoughts while writing this book: the late, great George Blake, Nöel Pelly, Philip Henry and Tim Roberts, UK friends such as Bill Holland and Chris Pollard and contributors to the Australian scene such as Richard Evans, Wendy McCarthy AO, Donald McDonald AC, Shane Simpson AM and Kim Williams. Finally, Dave proved to be the most wonderful co-author, bringing endless positivity and energy, as well as teaching me things along the way.

David

I would first and foremost like to thank my beautiful wife Kate and my lovely daughters Eliana and Teagan for their love and patience as their dad spent countless hours in front of the computer writing. This text would not be possible without their unwavering support! I love you!

I would also like to express my gratitude to those who supported this work along the way, whether through administrative assistance, moral support or the time to provide insight and expertise: Marissa Begin, Dean Fields, Louisa Wendorff, Devin Dawson, Ashlyne Huff, Brooke Webster, Andrew Kautz, Kevin Grosch, Mike Harris, Jennifer Duck and Sara Wigal, Nadine Waran-Perrero Doug Howard and Cheryl Slay-Carr, the entire MV2 team and of course my co-author Paul Saintilan. Without his willingness to reach out in December 2014, this would likely still be a thought in our minds – thank you!

About the authors

Paul Saintilan

Dr Paul Saintilan is a creative industries 'pracademic', author, teacher and industry consultant, and is currently CEO of the Australian Performing Arts Conservatory (APAC) in Brisbane, Australia. He possesses senior international experience in entertainment management, qualifications such as a music degree, MBA and PhD, and experience as a College Dean and educational leader. He brings an international perspective, having lived in Sydney, London, Geneva and New York. As an international marketing director for EMI Music and Universal Music in London, he directed international campaigns for major recording artists. In the 1990s, he rose to become one of the most influential executives in the international classical music industry. He has held senior non-profit sector roles such as CEO of Music Australia and Director of Marketing & Development at Musica Viva Australia. He subsequently entered higher education as a teacher, with a mission to make it more industry-integrated. As head of arts and entertainment management at the Australian Institute of Music he expanded the department and its qualifications and established the Master of Arts Management program at Sydney Opera House, which presented a range of Australia's foremost experts in the Boardroom of

Sydney Opera House. As Dean of the Australian College of the Arts ('Collarts') he took over a college very much in its infancy and supervised its dynamic growth over the next five years. He has presented courses in Switzerland at the Glion Institute and Webster University. Since 2007, he has helped to prioritize good mental health and advocated the use of mindfulness meditation in the creative industries. Prior to the pandemic, he published meditation guides for creative industries students, and in 2020 edited the critically acclaimed book *Musicians & Addiction: Research and Recovery Stories* published by Music Australia. In 2013, he published case studies which became individually distributed via The Case Centre in London. They led to the publication of this textbook and remain available separately in updated form, promoting this textbook to a wide audience of academics and teachers.

David Schreiber

Dr David Schreiber is an Associate Professor and a Chair of the Creative & Entertainment Industries program at Belmont University in Nashville, TN. He has written textbooks on organizational behaviour in the creative economy and innovation in the creative industries and has published on topics related to symbolic capital and its role in decision-making in the music industry and the use of sub-cultural capital in artist branding. Furthermore, David is a member of the Academy of Management (AOM), European Group of Organization Studies (EGOS), the Music and Entertainment Industry Educator's

Association (MEIEA), International Music Business Research Association; served as Associate Editor and served on the board of MEIEA for nearly a decade.

David received a Bachelor of Arts from the University of Wisconsin-Stevens Point, but after working in the music industry for seven years, he realized his true passion was found in teaching. He returned to University of Miami for a Master of Music and subsequently a Doctor of Philosophy from University of Westminster in London, England.

Prior to accepting his current position at Belmont University, Dr Schreiber taught at Greenville College, Minnesota State Mankato and Albright College. He has worked in multiple areas of the music industry, including Regional Manager at Schmitt Music, Marketing and Business Development Manager for Shiny Penny Productions, in the licensing and royalty department of Miami Records, Business Development Manager at Pivot Entertainment and managed artist Dean Fields.

What is organizational behaviour and why write a specialist text for creative and cultural industries?

Chapter 1

CHAPTER LEARNING OBJECTIVES

After studying this chapter, you should be able to:

- Define organizational behaviour and identify the disciplines which have contributed to its development as a field of study;

DOI: 10.4324/9781003262923-1

- Present and argue the case for why formal study of organizational behaviour is important and has value;
- Explain the importance of 'people skills' to creative industries management;
- Define the cultural and creative industries and identify special characteristics of these industries which have implications for organizational behaviour;
- Describe the creative industry manager's roles and skills.

Let's be clear. We have nothing against sand mining, automotive repairs, insurance underwriting or most other products and services on which modern society relies. But we are far more excited by arts, music, entertainment and industries built on creative expression and creative ideas (Figure 1.1). We find deeper meaning for ourselves in these industries, we find studying them not so much a burden as an enjoyment and, if you are studying a related degree programme, it is likely you feel the same way. We also believe that 'there is an art to managing art': that there are idiosyncrasies of creative industries which call for a specialized text (Figure 1.2). Let us explain.

WHAT IS 'ORGANIZATIONAL BEHAVIOUR'?

When we use the term 'creative organization' in this book, we use it to denote both small and large entities, from an individual who has started a new online venture, to the Walt Disney Company, though it implies some ongoing collective attention towards achieving creative outcomes. 'Organizational behaviour' (often abbreviated as 'OB') is a field of study which investigates human behaviour in organizations, for the purpose of improving organizational effectiveness and performance, and the satisfaction of those working within the organization. It studies the roles, functions and skills of managers, including important topics such as motivation, attitudes, perceptions, leadership, communication, organizational culture, structure, conflict, negotiation and organizational change. This book aims to provide a vivid initiation into the organizational life of creative

Figure 1.1 Helsinki headquarters of advertising agency Havas Worldwide, designed by Joanna Laajisto. Photo: Mikko Ryhänen.

Figure 1.2 Large concert crowds can increase audience appreciation (not true of all products and services). Photo credit: dwphotos/Shutterstock.com.

and cultural organizations and will explore each of the above topics within this context.

OB is a hybrid discipline, which means it draws inspiration and insight from many larger, more established disciplines, such as management, psychology, sociology, social psychology, anthropology, political science and economics. This makes it a fascinating area of study.

WHY FORMALLY STUDY 'OB'?

There are many reasons why formal study of OB will benefit those wishing to work in the creative industries:

Developing important people skills

If you have an aspiration to be a senior leader and contribute at a high level, 'people skills' and understanding the human dimension of management actually become more important than technical skills (e.g. statistics, accounting, and marketing). 'People skills' is the very area that OB focuses on. All large creative projects are collaborative, and the more senior you are, the more you need to achieve your objectives through other people. When someone manages staff for the first time, they may believe that their own work, their own emails, working through their own in-tray, should be the focus of their efforts. Yet, if someone manages six people, who work 40 hours each per week, that manager controls 240 hours of human resource every week. A manager who is properly managing that resource will achieve far more through others than they will ever achieve through themselves. Being able to successfully work with others, motivate others and achieve organizational objectives through others are vital skills for successful career advancement.

Becoming a more sophisticated manager

You will become more sophisticated at reading organizational situations, analysing the underlying drivers of organizational developments and predicting how events will unfold, and you will possess a greater repertoire of potential approaches and responses to situations that arise. You will become more socially aware and politically skilled, helping you to tackle challenges in the workplace. You will understand the importance of developing an ethos of integrity and respect in the process of building trusting relationships. Education helps you to be a professional and not an amateur, to pursue excellence, to avoid the reputational risks of managerial dilettantism and a 'fake it until you make it' ethos, which can result in disaster, such as the infamous Fyre Festival.

Taking things less personally

If you have studied common organizational conflicts, you will be less likely to interpret these as a 'personal' conflict when they happen to you and more likely to see them as normal conflicts that play out in workplaces everywhere, every day, all over the world, due to different roles, responsibilities and personality types.

Becoming a more effective leader

If you understand what motivates people and how to build effective teams, you are able to produce more useful change in an organization. You will enable creative processes to flourish and provide the tools for change to happen. You can set the vision for your organization's aims and provide the resources and motivation necessary for your team to achieve that vision.

WHAT ARE THE CREATIVE AND CULTURAL INDUSTRIES?

Routledge's Mastering Management in the Creative and Cultural Industries series adopts a broad understanding of the 'creative and cultural industries', which expands beyond traditional arts such as music, ballet, opera, theatre, painting and sculpture, to creative industries such as advertising, architecture, design, fashion, software, publishing, TV and film/movies (Chong, 2010). There have been many attempts to define the creative and cultural industries, and the concentric circles model (Figure 1.3) will provide further clarity as to what we mean when we speak of the 'creative and cultural industries'. It helps to explain why we place a strong focus on 'core' industries such as music, performing arts and visual arts. Those more distant but related industries such as advertising, architecture, design and fashion are introduced by way of example but feature less centrally than the core industries.

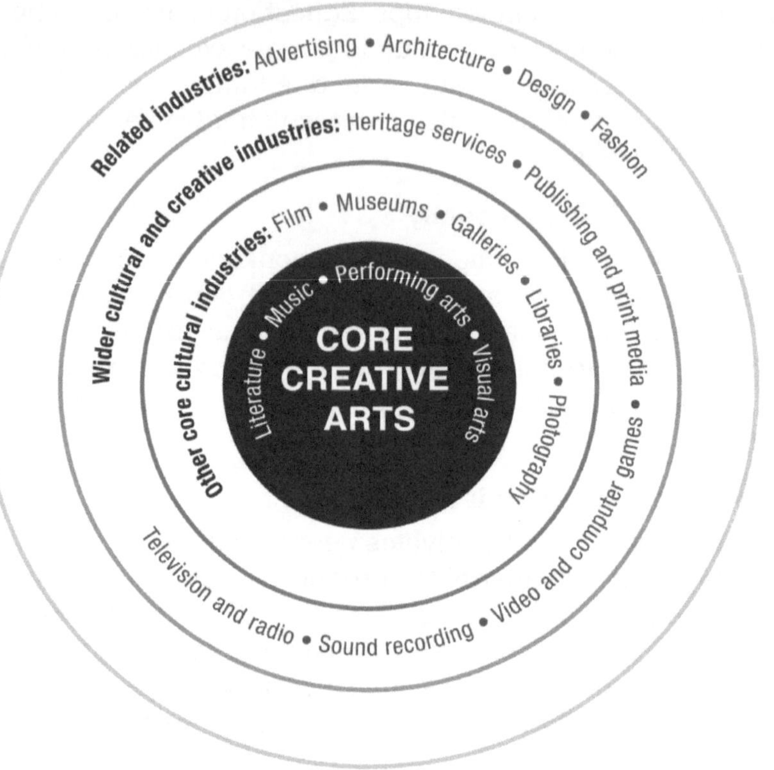

Figure 1.3 Concentric circles model of the cultural industries. Reproduced with permission from David Throsby (Throsby, 2008).

WHAT'S DIFFERENT ABOUT THESE INDUSTRIES?

The study of OB commenced with an aspiration to identify 'the best way' of doing things (see for example Frederick W. Taylor's 1911 *Principles of Scientific Management*). However, while reducing work to inflexible principles and processes may work in a military or manufacturing context, it may not be the best approach for creative organizations. It would be concerning if workers at a car plant arrived each morning and asked 'what colour will we paint the Teslas today?' It would raise the question of whether their approach should be more researched and scientific. Yet, if creative workers were placed in such an environment, they would find it stifling (Amabile,

1998). So, OB theory no longer believes in one best way, or one size fits all; rather, it posits that we need to look carefully at the context and the conditions that prevail before determining the most appropriate course of action. Different conditions and circumstances call for different approaches and when working with creative individuals, you must allow them the space and freedom to invest their own ideas and expertise in the project (referred to in this text as 'creative autonomy'), while providing the focus necessary to achieve their own or the organization's goals. This is a key reason why the creative and cultural industries need special treatment through specialized texts.

Early managerial studies did not differentiate creative and cultural firms from manufacturing firms. This did not occur until Theodore Adorno and Max Horkheimer (1944) proposed the concept of 'culture production', which was understood as similar to the mass production of 'things', but in the context of music, radio programmes and film. Later, Peterson's (1975) work on the 'production of culture' led to more research attention being devoted to the cultural industries.

Creative and cultural firms routinely enter into a complex system of joint ventures and partnerships, span international boundaries and are predominately comprised of small- to medium-sized enterprises (Hesmondhalgh, 2013). With the advent of new technologies, the creative industries are now capable of influencing societies and culture more than ever before, while consumers of these products and experiences are increasingly able to collaborate in the creation of productions. 'Co-creation' is increasing, where audiences participate in the creative development process (an example of co-creation is provided in Chapter 12 featuring the musician Imogen Heap). Cultural tastes and habits change quickly, which impacts the way creative managers run their businesses and make decisions. When an artist can become an overnight sensation via a social network, the artist's label needs to react quickly and must not be bogged down by bureaucratic red tape. In order for creative and cultural firms to be effective in this environment, they must be agile, flexible and adaptive and provide space for creative autonomy. This influence must be taken into consideration when studying how work is shaped in these organizations and ultimately how work is then produced.

There is now a significant body of academic research which demonstrates that cultural and creative organizations possess certain characteristics, which impact on the best approach to take (Baumol, 1967; Bourdieu, 1984; Caves, 2000; Hesmondhalgh, 2013; Peterson, 1975; Power & Scott, 2004; Negus, 2013; Vogel, 2015). These specific characteristics, which are idiosyncratic to creative and cultural firms, impact the workplace in unique ways. We acknowledge the work of Richard Caves (2000) and David Hesmondhalgh (2013), who have done much work on these distinctive features. Throughout this book, we assume that the workplace we are looking at is one based on these characteristics. We list below the most significant of these creative and cultural industries characteristics:

Uncertainty of demand and elevated risk

Demand is uncertain and producers of creative products never really know if people will commit to purchase. Uncertainties exist before and after the release of product to the public. Managers usually need to commit to projects before the creative work has been completed, and so there is uncertainty over what the final version will look like. There is uncertainty over how audiences will respond to the work. This uncertainty means decision-making is often based on 'gut feel' and 'instinct' even though these industries increasingly rely on more rational decision-making and the use of 'big data' to limit exposure to risk. Uncertainty leads to doubt and fear, and so managers need to actively build trust, confidence, belief and conviction in their projects. People working within creative organizations can experience heightened feelings of insecurity, which can have negative psychological effects. Self-management skills to mitigate these challenges are discussed in Chapter 6. Risk and insecurity have been ever present in creative organizations. Even in previous eras of 10% annual growth, major entertainment organizations would have periodic 'restructures' that threw out employees and cultivated a culture of insecurity (Forde, 2019).

Shae Constantine, a former Creative and Marketing head at Sony Music Entertainment and Warner Music, describes belief building as an important skill in creative organizations:

> An A&R Manager or Artist Marketer is in the belief building business. You're never 100% sure how a project will creatively work out, or how the audience will respond to it, yet you're trying to build a coalition of support around it. More projects commercially fail than succeed in music, and so you will come across doubters, people who criticize your project, people who are trying to kill your project. You need to hold your nerve and fight for it, lead them to be a believer also and be emotionally invested. If you don't believe in it, why should anyone else? You need to radiate belief and bring people into that. And people want to believe, they want to be part of something. People want to rally to causes; everyone in this country [Australia] loves the underdog but they have to believe the underdog can succeed. Most of the time the difference between success and failure is the belief that pushes it across the line. Belief drives that extra hour of work at night, the extra agenda point in a meeting and the 'prove them all wrong' factor.

Failure management

As Vogel (2015) observes, and as Shae Constantine notes above, in entertainment businesses, due to the uncertainty of demand and the excess of supply over demand, many more products lose money than make money. This is true in movies, television, toys, video games, book publishing and recorded music. Thus, managers in these companies need to be experts in risk and failure management.

Connection to the product

Creative work is rarely a detached, distant product for those who create it (Caves, 2000; Hirschman, 1983). It can be the product of enormous personal and emotional investment and can become wrapped up in the creator's whole identity. In fact, for some artists, their creative work and the success of their artistic career can become the meaning of their life. This places enormous pressures and responsibilities on those who work with them, and because the product has a voice and has this emotional investment, it calls for an entirely different approach compared to industries that deal with inanimate objects such as fast moving consumer goods (FMCG).

Creativity versus commerce

There is an inherent tension between 'authentic creative self-expression' and satisfying the demands of the marketplace (Caves, 2000; Hesmondhalgh, 2013). The movie *Wayne's World* is a modern parable of authentic music making being seduced and exploited by rapacious capitalists. While the 'art versus commerce' debate has flagged, suspicion of bureaucratically controlled creative processes lives on.

Creative autonomy

As mentioned earlier in the chapter, there is a belief within the creative and cultural industries that giving space to key creative personnel is important for them to create truly original work. Being granted autonomy in the workplace is known to lead to job satisfaction and positive feelings towards work (Amabile, 1998), but for producers, artists and others, this freedom is critical to the creative process and necessary for artists and audiences to believe the final product possesses authenticity.

Subjectivity

Aesthetic products are 'more abstract, subjectively experienced, non utilitarian, unique and holistic' (Hirschman, 1983, p. 50). This means that managers need to be stronger at shaping, interpreting, curating and advocating meaning, relative to other industries. Communication and advocacy skills are vital.

Managing criticism

Arts and entertainment products receive formal and institutionalized 'criticism' from cultural critics in a way that few industries do (Eliashberg & Shugan, 1997). The use of social media by artists leads to them experiencing the best and worst of community affirmation and criticism. Emotional support is needed for creative talent, as they are 'putting themselves out there', which makes them vulnerable to attack, criticism and even humiliation. The more they are intimately connected to the product they create and see it as an extension of themselves, the more vulnerable they become. The subjective nature of creative and cultural industries also means that negative opinion can't necessarily be 'proven' wrong.

Diversity of skills

The relatively complex products produced within the creative and cultural industries require the integration of diversely skilled specialists, many of whom will have strong opinions on the merit of the work that is being created, which has been referred to as the 'Motley Crew' principle (Caves, 2000). Such specialists in the case of a film could include the creative expertise needed in directing, the budgeting and forecasting of its financial success, sound editing and music supervision and the marketing and distribution expertise to maximize its promotion.

Infinite variety

The endless supply of creative and substitute products available to the public for consumption, each slightly or substantially different, creates an 'infinite variety' principle (Caves, 2000). Our leisure time is limited, and as consumers of cultural products – music, art, film or television – we have the ability to choose how we want to spend that time, either going out to the movies or going to our favourite artist's concert. If we don't like a certain song on the radio or a streaming service, we can always find another that is more suitable to our tastes or choose another movie to watch on our subscription service.

Generating and juggling a large quantity of disparate products

The experience of working in entertainment organizations is often about juggling multiple products at different stages of development, rather than focusing on one major product or service at a time (Hesmondhalgh, 2013). For many companies this arises from using a 'portfolio strategy' to offset the high risk levels and high failure rate. Generating more products and marketing 'back catalogue' (successful historical products) offsets the risk of newer products failing. This can make working in a creative or cultural organization more pressured and complex than if employees focused on a smaller number of products.

High production costs and low reproduction costs

It can be very expensive to make some creative and cultural products from scratch (e.g. a movie or an album), but it can cost hardly anything to replicate them using digital technology. This is why piracy hits cultural industries harder than manufacturers of products like screws and nails, for example, and why intellectual property protection has become a defining issue of the twenty-first-century creative industries.

Semi-public goods

Consuming a creative or cultural product does not diminish or destroy its use for another person in the way that consuming some other products does, such as eating food, or wearing out a car through usage. In fact, the more people who share the experience of an entertainment product (such as a concert), the higher the satisfaction can be for all consumers (Hesmondhalgh, 2013). So huge concert crowds can actually increase audience appreciation, which is not true of all products and services.

Increasing expense of live entertainment

Two economists, Baumol and Bowen, argued that live entertainment suffers from a 'cost disease' as labour-intensive processes don't benefit from the same improved productivity through technological transformation that other industries experience. As a consequence, they become relatively more expensive than other products over time (Baumol, 1967). For example, a symphony orchestra employs the same number of people to perform a symphony as it was performed two hundred years ago, but the number of workers needed to make a car drops over time through technological advancements.

Higher marketing costs

In entertainment organizations, per unit marketing costs tend to be large relative to the total production cost, compared to other industries (Vogel, 2015). The marketing budget for a movie can be 50 per cent of its production cost. Even a marketing budget of 15 per cent of production cost would be considered excessive in some industries (e.g. financial services). This increases the human resource that needs to be devoted to marketing and promotional activity.

Vertically differentiated skills

There is enormous diversity in the level of quality that occurs among cultural products (Caves, 2000). With this comes artists with varying skill levels who provide the creative input. Caves (2000) refers to this as the 'A-list' and 'B-list', two tiers of creative professionals who are called upon to provide services. Professionals within the field are able to differentiate between the A- and B-list, with the assumption that those on the 'A-list' are more proficient in their craft and therefore bring less unpredictability. Often within the music industries session musicians or producers will be drawn from different levels, based on their professional reputation. This can be the case for screenwriters in film as well.

Time flies

Creative and cultural products often intersect with media in a way that results in short-term interest and the need for fast response times. So a media spotlight on an entertainment project requires an immediate reaction from those involved in the project, as the story is liable to be buried by other stories within a short time frame. The time-sensitive nature of relevance in this case creates the need for strong temporal coordination of production and marketing activities (Caves, 2000). Not only media stories but also entertainment products themselves customarily have short life cycles (Vogel, 2015). The ascendancy of social media has only accelerated this phenomenon, meaning that an enormous amount can change in audience perception over a short period of time.

It is not that these distinctive features are entirely unique to creative and cultural firms; rather, they are of elevated significance compared to other contexts. This in turn has implications for management and OB in these organizations.

So, what do these distinctive features mean for the management of cultural and creative enterprises, and how do they impact OB in these companies? The following list summarizes some of the skills which are of greater significance in this managerial context:

- *Communication and advocacy skills*, to be able to build coalitions of support around your projects and shape and interpret meaning.
- The *ability to manage creative people* who have a high emotional and personal investment in the project, who can be both egotistical and vulnerable and who need to be given space and autonomy in the creative process.
- The ability *to reconcile art and commerce*, to ensure projects work commercially and are financially viable and accountable while retaining authenticity and respect for creative workers. This also involves mediating between business focused and artistically focused contributors. Michael Smellie, the former Chief Operating Officer of Sony BMG worldwide, commented to one of the authors: 'If you can give me a graduate who can have a conversation with a Chief Financial Officer and not freak them out, and have

Figure 1.4 Photo by LOOP Digital Agency.

a conversation with an artist and not freak them out, then you will be doing the world a great favour, because this is comparatively rare'.

- The *ability to manage diverse teams*, comprising people from different business and creative specializations, across different companies and countries.
- The ability to manage multiple projects simultaneously, each at a different stage of development (Figure 1.4).
- The ability to work in a fast moving, competitive environment which is open to criticism and public comment.

WHAT DO MANAGERS IN CREATIVE ORGANIZATIONS DO?

There has been a commendable striving for 'scientific' approaches to the study of management and OB, from authors who would like to see 'gut feel' and intuitive approaches resting more firmly on facts and evidence (Robbins & Judge, 2022). There is evidence that far more analysis is applied now to the development of creative products than has historically been the case. Yet, even one of the fathers of the OB discipline, Henry Mintzberg, has argued that while managers can apply science, managing is a combination of art, science and craft (Mintzberg, 2013). People are complex and the 'laws' that govern human behaviour are a long way from the law of gravity. The physical sciences can tell us that in over 900 years' time, on 7 September 2993, at 11:43 am, there will be a total eclipse of the sun in Alabama, but an OB theorist will have difficulty predicting the behaviour of Jenny in Accounts next Monday. One of the criticisms of management consultants and analysts let loose on arts and creative organizations is that they try to 'apply logic to something that is at the mercy of too many variables' (Forde, 2019, p. 191). Thus, reducing creative work to simplistic formulas (i.e. 'this type of movie with these types of actors will generate this sort of commercial return') through the eyes of creative industries specialists will appear incredibly unsophisticated because the modelling is unable to accommodate the larger number of considerations they routinely need to juggle.

Being able to work with various organizational stakeholders, to see different perspectives and speak their language, is a key factor in successfully integrating into, and performing well in, creative organizations. If you're working within a record label, while the advertising agency might want to talk about brands and products, perhaps the idealistic young artist who has just joined your label will be less comfortable with those terms. Knowing your audience, and tailoring your pitch to that audience, is important to mediating between artists and business managers and navigating the terrain between art and commerce.

Communicating with, and overseeing the needs of, 'creatives' becomes the focus of many culture producing firms and their managers. As a leader, it becomes imperative that you understand that the creative process takes time and that you must strike a balance between the economic interests of the firm and the creative process. The artist, songwriter or producer needs the time, space and freedom to do what they do best, and as a future creative leader, you must provide an atmosphere conducive to this. If you step into a 'writing room' in a music publishing company, you're introduced to a living room atmosphere. It's comfortable, relaxing and designed purposefully for the songwriter to feel at ease and allow for creative expression. It is not 'corporate' or an anonymous office lined wall-to-wall with cubicles. Designing a workplace where your people want to come in and work from and can be productive is something to which you should contribute. Knowing this and effectively cultivating this type of culture is at the heart of your day-to-day responsibilities. The implications of the global pandemic on workplaces and the rise of remote working are covered in Chapter 12.

Not only must you understand and manage the creative process, but also you will ultimately need to lead a team to do the same. Frustrations can set in and stress levels skyrocket if challenges arise such as your forecasted sales not being met. The continuous 'uncertainty of demand' and other challenges outlined above require a skilled manager who is comfortable working in a high-risk, turbulent environment.

Furthermore, intermediaries such as managers, agents, executives and artists can have healthy egos that need to be managed carefully. Traditional managerial responsibilities such as 'planning, organizing, leading and controlling' are absolutely essential, but must be taken into a local, regional, national and international context along with the 'power struggles' that come with them. As any manager in the creative and cultural industries understands, at times of success can come destructive behaviours, not only for an individual, but also for the entire team. Going beyond mere 'controlling' to approach and resolve conflict head-on is critical for employees and managers working within the cultural field. Because of the emotional investment that people make in the creative industries, these industries can also place a spotlight on the full messiness of human behaviour. Ethical dilemmas such as conflicts of interest also arise and need to be identified and resolved.

APPLYING THESE PRINCIPLES AND SCOPE OF THE TEXT

As stated at the outset, the objective of this text is to provide students with a vivid initiation into the organizational life of the creative and cultural firm. Although the content is relevant to the broader study of creative and cultural industries, the specific focus will be on the commercial and non-profit music, arts and entertainment fields.

In the first section, we will cover individual behaviours that are common in the firm. Because the creative and cultural industries operate within a turbulent environment where managers are often confronted with regular and consistent change, it is how we react and work with change that is first discussed. We then take a look at how the personality of individuals may impact the work environment, with specific attention paid to the personality of a creative individual. Later, we look at meaningful work, job satisfaction and being committed to the company we work for. The chapter 'Stress, Wellbeing and Self Care in Creative Organizations' (Chapter 6) addresses the need identified by many studies for greater focus on the mental health of those working in the creative industries.

Having looked at individual behaviour, we then turn to group and social processes in chapters on conflict, group decision-making, power and politics, diversity, equity and inclusion, teams and leadership. The final chapters examine organizational structure, organizational culture and ethics (tackling ethical dilemmas that arise in the creative industries). We are proud that we have been able to attract a variety of cultural and creative industries managers to contribute insights to this book, which we will use in the hope of bringing issues and theories to life.

Professional practice– Things *Not To Do* at a commercial record company: Some practical tips (which may also be relevant for other creative industry workplaces)

Discussions with human resources directors at major record companies indicate there are a few practical issues which interns and new employees need to bear in mind when they commence employment. To be specific, here are some things new recruits should avoid doing when they walk through the front door of a music or entertainment company:

1. *Fail to respect the confidentiality of artist or company information*, by posting it on social media, being indiscrete, gossiping, etc. It is natural for new recruits to get excited when they are in meetings that discuss confidential aspects of an artist's release plans, touring schedule or marketing campaign. They will also come in contact with creative work at various stages of development. Nothing could do more damage to one's prospects in the industry than destroying the trust the organization has placed in you to handle confidential information.
2. *Being disrespectful to artists or of creative work supported by the company, based on your own opinion of its artistic merits.* Large entertainment organizations develop product for many different audiences, involving many different genres. This breadth means you're not necessarily going to like all of the music you're involved with, and nor should you. These companies are creating music for diverse audiences, not for one member of staff. This is covered further in Case Study 7.1: 'The Taste Case'.

3. *Behaving inappropriately with artists.* Despite their celebrity, artists are real people who appreciate natural, friendly, relaxed interactions. They have highly pressured lives, and companies try to provide a supportive, safe haven for artists in the midst of these pressures. So, asking for 'selfies', getting them to sign posters and generally behaving like a crazed fan creates two problems. It means that instead of behaving like yourself, the nice person they hired, you've morphed into a crazed fan. Secondly, by behaving like this, you've punctured the protective bubble surrounding the artist, and it's like they're being chased down the street outside the building.
4. *Behaving inappropriately in the office, such as allowing phones and tablets to interfere with meetings, or allowing dress to become too casual.* The fact that creative organizations have a more relaxed and informal office environment than, for example, a bank can be taken too far. It is disrespectful to other staff to be focused on your phone or tablet when they're talking in meetings. Dress codes tend to be comparatively relaxed, managers do wear jeans and t-shirts, but that doesn't mean they will come in looking like they're heading off to the beach. Entertainment companies still appreciate people making an effort and looking stylish and professional.
5. *Making no effort to understand the culture and the people of the company.* Fortunately this is rare, because entertainment companies tend to attract very committed people, but they are usually proud of their culture, their artists and their people, and they expect new employees to study these things on an ongoing basis.
6. *Bringing unreasonable expectations to the relationship.* Expectations are best aligned prior to commencing with the company, and most companies make an effort to do that. But it only frustrates HR managers when recruits want to press the fast forward button

and accelerate their responsibilities beyond what can be accommodated. A lot of the time the HR manager won't know when positions will arise and, thus, when an intern might move beyond the intern programme, and so can't give an honest answer. People also need to build trust before they can be given progressively more responsible work. While many companies strive for an open and inclusive culture, a culture where 'the best creative idea wins' even if it comes from an intern who has been there 5 minutes, not every idea can 'get up', and not every wish can be accommodated, and so people shouldn't become disillusioned if that happens.

7 *An excess of exuberance with regards to alcohol at a company event.* This can be highly damaging. It is natural to be excited attending company events where artists will be present, at exciting venues, where free food and alcohol will be served. However, drinking too much can end in professional disaster if you lose yourself and embarrass yourself in front of media partners and other stakeholders. The music industry is a very social, people-driven business. People notice things and gossip about things. So, protect your own professional reputation.

To switch the tone from negative to positive, here are also some things to positively develop on an ongoing basis:

- *Work on bringing positivity and energy to the workplace* – Entertainment companies generally enjoy working with positive, passionate, vital people, not negative people who will drag everyone down.
- *Work on being solution-focused rather than problem-focused* – People who focus on finding solutions rather than identifying problems are valuable. Even if you have a problem you need to bring to a supervisor, what would be your advice on how it could be solved? Sometimes the person closest to the problem is you, and so your ideas on how best to solve it are important.

- *Work on being forward-looking rather than backward-looking* – The past is gone, but we can impact the present and future, so put your focus there.
- *Work on taking initiative, being proactive and continually look for learning opportunities.* If a company requires an employee to spend time on reception, and he or she considers this a demotivating detour from where they would like to be, and they put someone else there who views it as a fantastic way to get to know all the people who work in the company, and do business with the company, it is obvious who is going to get the most out of the experience.
- *Work on matching the tone to the audience.* You shouldn't talk to a hip hop artist the same way you would talk to the Finance Vice President, or vice versa. Different audiences require a different tone of voice. The more time you invest understanding artists, the music and the business, the greater your knowledge and vocabulary will be to drive these conversations. Different executives also have different responsibilities, different lenses, and different priorities, and you should be mindful of these.
- *Work on your ongoing self-education.* Read the trade press, read the key resources used by senior managers, read books about the company you work for. All of this is valuable in getting the most out of your employment and making yourself more employable for the future.
- *Work on your 'personal brand'.* Cultivating your own 'personal brand' in the workplace means looking at the way you communicate, the way you conduct yourself, the way you dress, your efforts at professional development and the way you use all of these things to express who you are and where you're heading. The creative industries are a highly competitive environment, and they can also be an environment where theatre and style have heightened importance,

and so time spent on the way you present to others, and how others see you, is time well spent.

It should be stressed that this book has been consciously designed to tackle many of these issues, such as: understanding and working with artists; examining resilience and staying committed to the organization; communicating effectively; knowing when it is appropriate to introduce your own personal taste to decision-making; and managing your personal brand and reputation in the workplace.

Discussion questions and class exercises

1 Define organizational behaviour, and identify the disciplines which have contributed to its development as a field of study.
2 Present and argue the case for why formal study of organizational behaviour is important and has value.
3 Explain the importance of 'people skills' to creative industries management.
4 Define cultural and creative industries and identify special characteristics of these industries which have implications for organizational behaviour.
5 Describe the creative industry manager's roles and skills.

References

Adorno, T. & Horkheimer, M. (1944). *Dialectic of Enlightenment*. Trans. John Cumming. Reprinted 1979. London: Verso.

Amabile, T. M. (1998). 'How to kill creativity', *Harvard Business Review*, Vol. 76, no. 5, pp. 76–87.

Baumol, W. J. (1967). 'Performing arts: The permanent crisis', *Business Horizons*, Fall, pp. 47–50.

Bourdieu, P. (1984). *Distinction: A Social Critique of the Judgement of Taste*. Cambridge, MA: Harvard University Press.

Caves, R. E. (2000). *Creative Industries: Contracts between Art and Commerce*. Cambridge, MA: Harvard University Press.

Chong, D. (2010). *Arts Management*, 2nd Edition. London: Routledge.

Eliashberg, J. & Shugan, S. M. (1997). 'Film critics: Influencers or predictors?' *Journal of Marketing*, Vol. 61, no. 2, pp. 68–78.

Forde, E. (2019). *The Final Days of EMI: Selling the Pig*. London: Omnibus Press.

Hesmondhalgh, D. (2013). *The Cultural Industries*, 3rd Edition. London: Sage.

Hirschman, E. C. (1983). 'Aesthetics, ideologies and the limits of the marketing concept', *Journal of Marketing*, Vol. 47, pp. 45–55.

Mintzberg, H. (2013). *Simply Managing*. San Francisco, CA: Berrett-Koehler Publishers.

Negus, K. (2013). *Music Genres and Corporate Cultures*. New York: Routledge.

Peterson, R. A. & Berger, D. G. (1975). 'Cycles in symbol production: The case of popular music', *American Sociological Review*, Vol. 40, no. 2, pp. 158–173.

Power, D. & Scott, A. J. (2004). *Cultural Industries and the Production of Culture*. London: Routledge.

Robbins, S. P. & Judge, T. A. (2022). *Organizational Behavior*, 18th Edition. Global Edition. Essex: Pearson Education Limited.

Throsby, D. (2008). 'The concentric circles model of the cultural industries', *Cultural Trends*, Vol. 17, no. 3, pp. 147–164.

Vogel, H. L. (2015). *Entertainment Industry Economics: A Guide for Financial Analysis*, 9th Edition. New York: Cambridge University Press.

Change in creative organizations

Perceiving and dealing with change

Chapter 2

CHAPTER LEARNING OBJECTIVES

After studying this chapter, you should be able to:

- List and explain the factors that are driving change within the creative and cultural industries;
- Define organizational change;
- Effectively apply different theories of change to the creative and cultural industries workplace;
- Describe the external and internal drivers that influence change within the creative and cultural organization;
- Identify how employees within these firms react to external changes in the environment;

DOI: 10.4324/9781003262923-2

- Explain why employees resist change;
- Apply managerial concepts to help facilitate people adapting to change.

INTRODUCTION

Mergers, layoffs, bankruptcies, re-structuring, technological transformation and obsolescence and regular shifts in consumer behaviour: we receive a constant stream of evidence that the creative industries are dealing with enormous turbulence. Often this transformative change is portrayed as negative or it's implied that 'doom and gloom' is upon us (Figure 2.1). However, change can also bring opportunities and be seen as the catalyst for good things to come. It can lead to turnover in bad management while paving the way for innovative or inspirational leadership. Overcoming challenges can positively stimulate organizational culture and teams in the workplace. In the chapter's first case study, two college students show how changes caused by technology proved to be enormously positive when a 'one'-word tweet by Taylor Swift took their career to a new level (see Case Study 2.1). When change is thrust upon you, perceived as positive or negative, how will you react to it?

HOW A ONE-WORD 'TWEET' CAN CHANGE AN ORGANIZATION FOREVER

US musician Louisa Wendorff and her friend and artistic collaborator Devin Dawson had their lives turned upside down in one day, and confronted transformational change at both an organizational and personal level.

Louisa Wendorff, a singer–songwriter from southern California, who loved entertaining and connecting with audiences, had long set her sights on achieving commercial success as a professional musician. She took voice and dance lessons and participated in every musical that she could, before heading off to a well-known university in Nashville, Tennessee. There, she would connect with her friend and writing partner, Devin Dawson. Devin, also from California, taught himself

Figure 2.1 Change can often make you think things are going to hell in a hand basket! Photo credit: Fer Gregory/Shutterstock.com.

guitar at a young age and always felt compelled to write songs. Like many musicians his age, Devin also aspired to be a rock star, but unlike most players, he achieved early success after signing a two-album deal with a record label. He recorded his first album with his band and then set out on a four-year tour. With each subsequent release experiencing only modest success, he stepped back to re-evaluate his position and enrolled in culinary school for a brief period. However, he realized that it would never be the best fit for him. After having an epiphany that he should abandon the familiar and head to Nashville, he found himself at the same university as Louisa, where they would soon partner as songwriters and friends.

Change can be difficult for many of us and impact us in different ways. It occurs in organizations and impacts industries. In industries that experience transformative change, organizations must rapidly evolve to keep pace with that change. The music industry's digital transformation and the rise of social media have driven the development of new and evolving skills and practices, which have allowed new possibilities to emerge (which will be illustrated by this feature). Further to this alignment between the industry and the organization, there also needs to be alignment between the organization and the individual. For Devin and Louisa, and many organizations in the creative industries, they are unable to adequately separate who they are as individuals from the business they've become. They are brands that are intimately connected to the product they create. So, when change happened to their business, it impacted Louisa and Devin directly and personally. Most Do-It-Yourself (DIY) musicians continuously write, record and release music to organically grow a fan base, in the hope of one day making a living at their craft. Devin and Louisa were doing just this when they decided to release a 'mash-up' of two songs by one of the world's leading pop stars, Taylor Swift. After combining two of Taylor's hits from her album '1989', *Blank Space* and *Style*, they decided to upload it to YouTube in the hope of fostering continued engagement with their fans. Unbeknownst to them, it wasn't but a few hours later that Taylor took a liking to this new creation, so much so that she tweeted to her 60 million followers at the time, one word – 'OBSESSED!'. In an instant, Devin and Louisa's careers changed forever. Transformational change can bring excitement and great uncertainty. This is often because the future state is unknown and managing it is often impossible through 'planned' or linear means. Strategy 'emerges' and decisions are often made emotionally and quickly with little information (Eisenhardt, 1989). This is exactly what began to transpire for these two young artists. Within a few hours, the calls began for interviews – the video went viral, and in just a few days the YouTube views went from a few hundred to millions. They were invited to play the 'Red Carpet' at the 57th Grammy Awards, the industry's biggest event and conversations about record deals began. When management and publishing interests and other opportunities started pouring in, they realized that the organizational and personal approaches and resources that had worked up to that point would no longer suffice. The video was featured on each stop of Taylor's worldwide '1989' tour, with the video itself achieving tens of millions of views.

Whether transformational change is intended or unintended, the organization must become drastically different to respond to the new demands being placed upon it. For creative organizations, this results in changes to both structure and culture, but when the organization IS the brand that IS the artist/ entrepreneur starting the business, this culture shift needs to become a behavioural one with a new attitude about the change. The role of an individual's personality and dispositions become critical. As a self-proclaimed 'hater' of change throughout her life, Louisa knew she was in for a possibly anxiety-riddled, yet exciting, transformation.

Immediately following the holiday break, both Louisa and Devin noticed a drastic impact on how they were perceived by friends, close acquaintances and those they didn't know, which in turn impacted how they perceived and reacted to the change that was happening to them and their business. Their closest friends pushed them away (likely in fear and uncertainty of how this development would impact their relationship), while they became closer to their acquaintances, and people they didn't know thought they were famous. Fascinated by how they were being perceived, they became more confident in what they were doing, bolder, and more willing to take risks. Instead of fearfully clinging to a past sense of themselves, or staying within their comfort zone, they needed to embrace the change, and the opportunities that it provided. Organizations have stories that define them, we as individuals have stories that define us, but sometimes it's time to write new stories. This is cultural change. As part of this transformational change to their careers, Devin and Louisa have also realized the importance of strengthening the organizational infrastructure that supports them.

After being thrown into the spotlight, Louisa built a strong creative team to help drive this change process, bringing on a manager, creative director and producer. She was having discussions about recording and publishing agreements and was flying between New York, LA and Nashville every few weeks to maximize the potential of this newfound fame and success. She was 'living the dream' and thought it was everything she wanted. Since then, however, she has taken time to work on her physical and mental wellbeing while choosing to take a hiatus on her musical career.

Devin, after the success of the Blank Space mash-up, signed a publishing deal to help manage the administration and licencing of his songs. He went on to sign a multi-album record deal with Warner Music in Nashville and has since written Number 1 songs and has gone multi-platinum as a recording artist, while touring nationally and international with the likes of the Zach Brown Band, Hunter Hayes, Blake Shelton and many more.

The two of them ultimately pursued very different paths as a result of this catalytic moment, and whether it was towards music or not, each required a shift in attitude and behaviour. Each of them needed to define where they wanted this momentum to take them, to communicate this to others, and to let others in and trust them, in order to develop their personal brand and organizational structure. It seems crazy to reflect on the fact that all of this transformational change to their careers and their personal lives was sparked by one word: 'OBSESSED!'

***

Whether it's a life-changing, transformational opportunity, or an incremental change (such as moving into an office with a colleague who plays his 70s classic rock a bit too loud for everyone's liking), change affects all of us in different ways. It is often met with resistance and responses to it will differ depending on how it's perceived, the environment in which it occurs and the characteristics of the person it affects.

As we explore the concept of 'change' in this chapter, we will first explain the propensity for change in the creative and cultural industries, and why the environment is so turbulent. We will look at what 'organizational change' is before moving on to why it happens and how we perceive and react to it. Change in a creative and cultural organization can affect a single employee, a department or an entire organization. No one theory of change can accommodate all these perspectives; rather we draw on multiple theories from disciplines such as psychology, sociology, management and economics to help explain what is happening and how we respond to it. One thing we do know is that people, organizations and circumstances *will* change; in fact change is the only constant. Therefore, it requires effective people management skills to navigate the emotions and reactions that come with change, which in turn will make us better leaders and followers in our organizations. Before concluding, we will explore the options managers have to successfully steer their employees through changing organizational circumstances.

THE CREATIVE INDUSTRIES AND THE PROPENSITY FOR CHANGE

Within the creative industries there can be 'causal ambiguity' in terms of what is responsible for success or failure (Ordanini *et al.*, 2008), and a pervasive belief that 'nobody knows' what will be successful (Caves, 2003). As we saw in Chapter 1, 'nobody knows' does not simply refer to the fact that we can never be certain of the audience response and that tastes and preferences change, but also that organizations often need to commit to a project before the artistic vision is fully realized (Caves, 2000). By the time the product is finally unveiled, the costs are sunk and non-recoverable. In the non-profit sector (comprising organizations such as galleries, museums and classical music) there is also demand uncertainty, causal ambiguity over what creates success and inherent risk (Crealey, 2003). We can attempt to extrapolate past data to predict the future, but managers often have little confidence in that, due to differences in the artworks being compared, the unpredictability of audience preferences, and changing audience tastes (Childress, 2012). Some researchers have even suggested that 'gut' intuition can be a very appropriate basis for decision-making in certain circumstances (Hayashi Alder, 2003; Lank & Lank, 1995; Sadler-Smith & Shefy, 2004).

When trying to understand how change works, especially in the context of the creative industries, we can use different perspectives to help us explain what happens. For example, if we use the lens of 'semiotics' (the study of 'signs and symbols') we can see change operating in two dimensions with creative and cultural products (Jones *et al.*, 2015). Change can take place at the level of *semiotic codes* – the symbols and cues by which artists give meaning and which audiences use to interpret and make sense of the work that is being created. 'Genre' in music and 'style' in the visual arts rely on these codes, which allow us to understand and classify songs as 'country', 'blues' or 'Tejano'.

In the visual arts, it enables us to perceive and classify a painting as 'surrealist' or 'impressionist'. The second dimension of creative products is what is known as the *material base* (Jones *et al.*, 2015). The material base allows us to create (or in a sense 'deliver') the creative product to the consumers. In music, this could be the instruments, the human voice or recording equipment. In the visual arts, the media used to convey artistic expression changes and evolves, from the use of canvas and paint to cameras and sets in film. The delivery format by which we enjoy, listen, observe or interact with that product also changes, such as the shift from going to the cinema to watching on-demand TV services such as Netflix (Jones *et al.*, 2015). These dimensions, unique to the creative and cultural industries, are important because the dimensions themselves undergo change, and this change ultimately impacts the businesses in which we work, and how they are structured. This change can also encourage entrepreneurial activity and the creation of new business models that stimulate economic activity and cultural production.

Jones *et al.* (2015) identified four primary types of change based on these dimensions and the pace at which change takes place (Figure 2.2). They are: Preserve, Ideate, Transform and Recreate. We will discuss each in turn.

Preserve

This type of change is characterized by slow change in semiotic codes and material base. It is often the most stable or conservative of these four change types and is often characteristic of industries such as classical music, ballet, opera, art museums or galleries. They tend to maintain the characteristics that traditionally define these genres and attempt to preserve the products they offer and the techniques that help produce them.

Ideate

This type of change is defined by fast changes in semiotic codes while maintaining the material form in which they are created. These products include fashion, theatre or fine art. Fashion, for example, is created through similar products using denim or

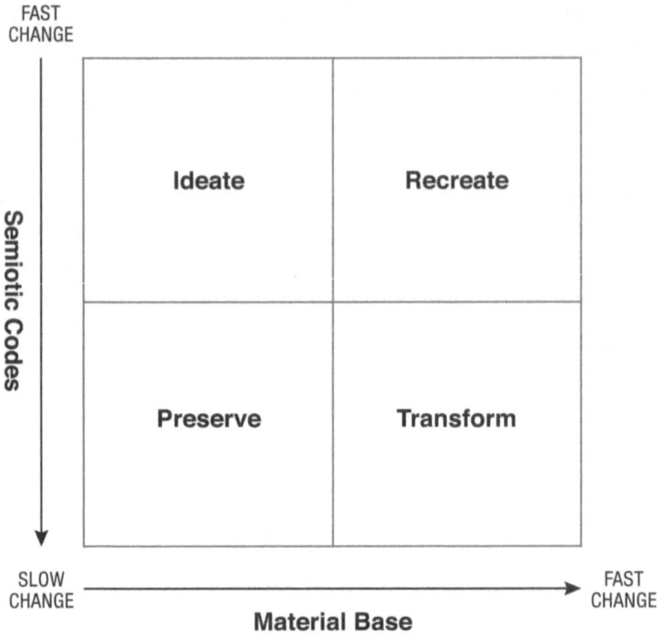

Figure 2.2 Typology of change in the creative industries. Reused and adapted by permission from Oxford University Press.

Source: Jones, C., Lorenzen, M. & Sapsed, J. (2015). *The Oxford Handbook of Creative Industries*. Oxford: Oxford University Press.

cotton, but the 'trend' or semiotic code will evolve from season to season. We see this in Electronic Dance Music (EDM) as well. The equipment used to produce this genre of music has not evolved as quickly as the varying sub-genres it encompasses – from 'ambient' to 'breakbeat' and 'drum and bass'.

Transform

This category of change is exemplified by rapid alterations in material base but slow changes in semiotic codes. For example, technological innovation is often the catalyst that allows for new ways to create or consume creative products, while the codes in which they are embedded will remain relatively stable. So a classic movie like *Casablanca* will be stable as it moves through the rise and fall of a succession of formats such as Video Home System (VHS) tape and Digital Versatile Discs (DVD). Similarly, a classic song will be the same as it moves from vinyl through to cassette tape, to Compact Disc (CD), to digital download or streaming. Each of these changes may be minor in terms of the recognition and enjoyment of the music but will be potentially cataclysmic for parts of the industry attached to the dismantled technology. The recording studio industry went through profound change as it needed to retool from analogue studios to digital studios. Many went out of business. In a process called 'disintermediation' an entire intermediary in the supply chain can be eliminated, causing massive job losses and bankruptcies. The dismantling of old-fashioned record stores is an example of disintermediation. After the 1990s, their numbers dwindled as other parts of the supply chain, such as artists, labels and digital wholesalers, started to distribute directly to consumers, bypassing traditional retail outlets and thereby cutting them out of the process.

Recreate

This category is represented by fast change in both semiotic codes and material base. They are the most dynamic of the creative industries. In design, for example, the introduction of new plastics and materials allowed for new types of products in furniture design. This is then amplified by new consumer trends, tastes and responses, which add further change and dynamism to the industry (Figure 2.3).

WHAT IS ORGANIZATIONAL CHANGE?

With the high propensity for change in the creative industries being driven by stylistic variations, transformations in materials and technology and ever-evolving tastes and preferences, organizations need to anticipate change as best they can to remain competitive and relevant. 'Organizational change' is a process that occurs when a company alters its working methods or aims to deal with new situations or market conditions. When changes occur in organizations, they can be intended or unintended. With 'intended change', a deliberate decision is made which effects the organization. For example, a production company may decide to move forward with the filming of a new 'pilot' of a sitcom, or may choose to enter into new distribution

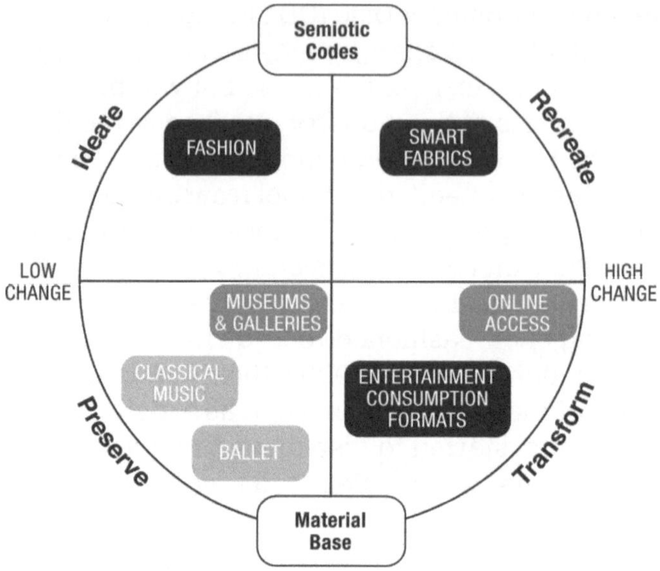

Figure 2.3 Examples of change in fashion, galleries, music, performing arts, film and video games. Reused and adapted by permission from Oxford University Press.

Source: Jones, C., Lorenzen, M. & Sapsed, J. (2015). *The Oxford Handbook of Creative Industries*. Oxford: Oxford University Press

agreements for its existing programmes. 'Unintended change' occurs in response to unforeseen circumstances and can occur at any moment. Change can be driven by external factors and internal factors, which will be discussed next.

EXTERNAL DRIVERS FOR CHANGE

We have alluded to external factors that can drive change, such as: competitive or market conditions; technology; shifts in the legal or regulatory landscape; and evolving social and cultural tastes (Aguilar, 1967). We will now look at each of these in greater detail.

COMPETITIVE OR MARKET CONDITIONS

One of the main drivers for change in creative and cultural organizations is changes to the competitive landscape and market conditions. In the late 1990s, the advent of MP3 technology and the controversial start-up Napster enabled consumers to begin sharing music files online. Because the majority of this activity was illegal, it caused great disruption in the marketplace. This destruction of the once-dominant CD format caused major labels to rethink their business models to remain competitive. The term 'creative destruction' has been applied to format and product destruction, which is driven by competition. The term is attributed to the economist Schumpeter (1942, 1975), and the destruction is characterized as 'creative' because it forces new solutions and new possibilities, which manifests for consumers as product improvements and lower prices. Evolving from a business reliant on the sales of recordings from artists, record companies began to reconceptualize their businesses and their roles, offering contracts that engaged them in 'all rights details'. They sought to be involved in every aspect of commercially developing an artist and their brand, whether that be recording, publishing, brand partnerships and endorsements, concerts and events, touring, artist management, merchandizing and synchronization deals (TV and film licencing) (Karubian, 2008; Marshall, 2013). This began to offset the declining sales that were causing massive layoffs and downsizing in major label groups.

TECHNOLOGY

As alluded to earlier, technology has brought about substantial changes to the creative industries that impact firm behaviour and performance. The music industry, for example, has seen enormous change since it was launched with the invention of movable type in 1450, being constantly re-invented through the introduction of myriad formats: sheet music; the phonograph; music 'cylinders'; the jukebox; 78 rpm (revolutions per minute) shellac pressings; the launch of radio; the introduction of magnetic tape; the 33 rpm microgroove LP (long play) record; the 45 rpm record; the introduction of black and white, and then colour, TV; the launch of FM radio; the cassette tape; the rise of the music video as a format; the launch of the Compact Disc (CD); the launch of Digital Audio Tape (DAT); the MiniDisc; the Sony Walkman; the iPod; the rise of MP3 digital downloading and subsequent download and streaming services (Garofalo, 1999). Each transition was accompanied with nervousness and doubts as to whether the world as we knew it would survive the change. Would the recorded music industry survive the introduction of radio, blank cassette tapes and the home taping of radio shows? It did. Taking this mountaintop view gives us confidence that the creative industries can overcome the technological and copyright challenges they currently face while providing further opportunities for growth. Certainly, the money now being generated from streaming has made the music industry economically much stronger in recent years.

SHIFTS IN THE LEGAL OR REGULATORY LANDSCAPE

The legal frameworks which govern and protect the creative industries are vital to their long-term viability. In fact, the creative industries couldn't exist in the way we know them without intellectual property (IP) laws, which have been undergoing complex change since the first copyright law was enacted in Britain in 1710 (Garofalo, 1999). It is critical that creative and cultural firms proactively drive and negotiate changes to copyright legislation. They must understand how these changes will affect their business, assets and stakeholders. Their structure, employees and culture must be willing to embrace and change accordingly as legal protections are altered. For example, the legal and regulatory changes that impacted the US commercial radio industry in 1996 had a profound impact, not only on the consolidation of broadcasting stations but in terms of the musical diversity on the airwaves. There was less diversity in programming, limitations to local content laws and generally less competition within the radio markets (Coalition, 2006).

EVOLVING SOCIAL AND CULTURAL TASTES

Forever at the forefront of shifting sociological and cultural trends, the creative and cultural firm's very existence sits within the unpredictability that is 'consumer taste'. When companies have a huge success that takes everyone by surprise, their competitors quickly mobilize resources to introduce similar products in an attempt to emulate that success. The rise of rap, or hip hop, YouTube parody artists and even the viral nature of TikTok short-form videos, forces record companies to modify their artist rosters and talent acquisitions. The TV sitcom *Seinfeld*, the 'show about nothing', proved so successful that it led to a number of shows emulating the quirky chemistry between key characters within a Manhattan backdrop (such as *Friends*, *Will & Grace* and *30 Rock*).

Whether it responds to taste trends or is a 'taste maker' that influences trends, the creative and cultural firm sits at the cornerstone of that unpredictability and is vulnerable to the change that accompanies it. How unpredictable is consumer taste? Let's look at the case of Clive Davis, arguably the music industry's greatest artists and repertoire exponent, supposedly gifted with supreme abilities to tap into popular taste and the cultural zeitgeist. His autobiography (Davis, 2013) recounts a number of examples of great artists failing to generate audience interest: Bob Dylan's first album *Bob Dylan* did not sell well (Davis, 2013, p. 37); Simon and Garfunkel's first album *Wednesday Morning, 3AM* did not make much impact and the duo split up (p. 50); the revamp of Fleetwood Mac's initial album disappointed (p. 232); the initial results of Aretha Franklin fell well below the level she would later achieve (p. 278); Whitney Houston's self-titled album took 50 weeks to reach number one (p. 311); the band Air Supply's first US-released album flopped, they were rejected by ten US record companies and were on the verge of breaking up (p. 344–345); and Sarah McLachlan's success was slowly built up over time (p. 416–417). In addition to these examples, it is well known that the Beatles were famously 'passed on' by Decca Records, and Elvis Presley's initial attempt at performing was a failure. Given that much of the initial creative work of these artists was similar to what would eventually become successful, it can be argued that the unfamiliarity of it required some audience adjustment.

INTERNAL DRIVERS FOR CHANGE

In addition to events occurring outside the organization's control, there can be a number of internal drivers of change, such as: workplace demographics; growth; and poor performance (Weick & Quinn, 1999). Let's examine each of these in turn.

WORKPLACE DEMOGRAPHICS

The workforce is becoming more culturally and racially diverse, and women now account for more than 50% of the creative and cultural industry workforce (Women in the Creative Industries: Key Conclusions, 2022, Burns *et al.*, 2012). When it comes to education, the workforce in the creative industries is similar to other professional industries. How individuals become employed is often dependent on the social network and reputation of those being hired, rather than credentials or accreditation (Florida, 2003). Chapter 11 delves into the challenges and advantages of increasing diversity. For example, the 2016 Oscars were marred by complaints that all 20 contenders in the Best Actor category were white, for the second consecutive year. It led to criticism and boycotts and resulted in The Academy of Motion Picture Arts and Sciences overhauling its processes to increase diversity (Child, 2016). The creative industries have made progress on diversity, equity and inclusion (DEI) efforts, but there is certainly further progress to be made in recruiting and developing overall organization strategies that support a welcoming and inclusive work environment.

GROWTH

The success of an organization is often a catalyst and driver of change. Growth can necessitate new business practices and drive the business into new products and markets. With expansion comes the need to hire new employees or find new offices. In one particular social media firm, the need to accommodate the growing demand for their services forced them to find a new home. This new location provided an opportunity to not only re-imagine their ideal working environment but also use the move to make a statement about their success as a firm.

POOR PERFORMANCE

Unexpected losses or under-performance of a creative product or service by a company can often contribute to pressures that result in change. If the weekend box office numbers are well under forecast, or if sales from an album release of a record labels' number-one-selling artist aren't what was expected, this can ultimately result in layoffs or re-structuring of departments

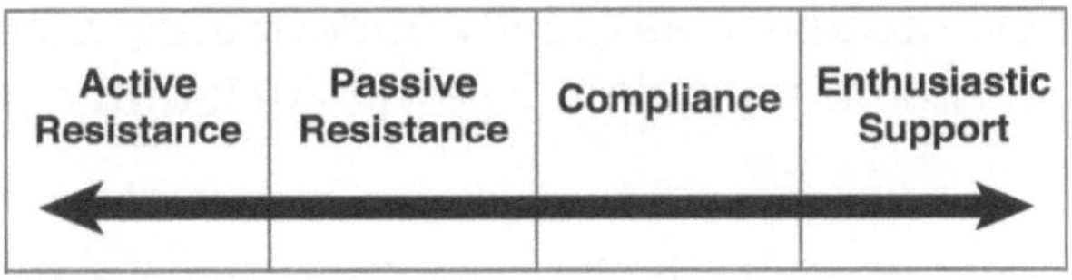

Figure 2.4 Illustration of the range in which we may respond to change when we are confronted with it.

and divisions. A crisis may also stimulate change. The recent wave of internship litigation involving entertainment companies in the United States (Zillman, 2015) has caused many of the major corporations to revise their policies and procedures.

HOW WE REACT TO CHANGE

When confronted with change, people react in different ways: we may perceive the change as negative and thereby *actively resist* the change; we may also choose to *passively resist* change or merely *comply*; or if an employee perceives the new changes as positive they may provide *enthusiastic support* (Carpenter *et al.*, 2009). These responses are depicted in Figure 2.4 and will be discussed in turn.

Active resistance

The most negative reaction to a change attempt comes in the form of active resistance. In these more extreme cases, those who feel most strongly about the change may actively sabotage or be more outspoken about it. If a controversial staff appointment causes ripples amongst employees, they may appeal to direct reports for their firing or be vocal about their dissatisfaction to other employees.

Passive resistance

In a 'passive resistance' reaction, the person may be upset by the changes, but may not voice their position or perspective on the issue. They bear their dislike quietly and may 'bottle up' stress and unhappiness. Feelings of uncertainty may cause employees to seek other job opportunities without consulting direct reports (Dex *et al.*, 2000). Furthermore, employees who respond with passive resistance are also more likely to engage in deviant behaviour such as quietly undermining other staff and the organization (Agboola & Salawu, 2011; Duffy *et al.*, 2002).

Compliance

When an employee reacts to change with compliance, they are willing to embrace the new situation, but will likely do so with little support or enthusiasm. They understand that change is inevitable and are willing to accept it. They may be committed to seeing it through due to a sense of personal or professional obligation.

Enthusiastic support

If new change initiatives are instituted, some employees may embrace them by being advocates for the new direction. They may defend the new way and embrace the challenges that may lie ahead. They are likely to believe that the new vision benefits the organization and themselves.

WHY PEOPLE RESIST CHANGE

Why do employees often struggle with change? As a leader within a creative organization, you must contend with ever-evolving circumstances within the firm and respond to the challenges that come externally. As we just discussed, the reactions to these conditions can be wide-ranging, from enthusiastic support to outright rebellion. However, understanding the 'whys' of these reactions will help mitigate and better prepare you to manage through the most damaging reactions (Kanter, 2012; Quast, 2012). With almost two-thirds of all change initiatives failing (Ewenstein *et al.*, 2015), we must do our best to increase our chances of success. People resist change for many reasons, but will naturally oppose it when they don't believe the change is in their best interests. Being asked to take on more work projects, or take the lead on a project in which they don't believe, are examples of changes that are likely to be resisted. Other reasons for resisting change include: the fear of uncertainty or the unknown; mistrust; loss of control; status or job security; bad timing; and the personal characteristics of the individual (Nelson & Quick, 2015). We will discuss each of these in turn.

FEAR OF THE UNKNOWN AND UNCERTAINTY

When people are confronted with significant change in the workplace, it creates a sense of ambiguity, which leads to uncertainty. If they are highly significant, strategic or transformative changes, this fear of the unknown can also become highly elevated. Will these changes lead to more or less work for me? Will I lose my job? This kind of thinking can lead people to be sceptical of change.

MISTRUST

If a new manager is the instigator of change, or the 'change agent', often employees will begin by mistrusting him or her (Quast, 2012). Trust in the workplace is earned and it often takes time to acquire. If the manager has not established themselves as competent in their position, has not led in a consistent fashion, or is not seen as one who acts with integrity and loyalty, then employees will be less likely to embrace the change (Schindler & Thomas, 1993). They will greet it with scepticism and may react negatively to it. In such a circumstance, managers must lead people with integrity and focus on developing trust.

LOSS OF CONTROL/STATUS/JOB SECURITY

When people see a lot of change, with a number of new employees and positions being introduced, they can begin to doubt their capabilities and where they stand within the organization. They may see this as challenging their status, power base and positioning within the firm, which can in turn lead to resistance.

BAD TIMING

If the right amount of change isn't introduced with empathy at the right time in the right place, it can lead to resistance. People often feel threatened if they perceive that the change is 'thrown on them' without proper warning. Of course, this can't always be avoided, but in circumstances where it can, providing time to anticipate what is to come can help mitigate some resistance. When it can't be avoided, being sensitive to people's reactions and demonstrating proper empathy can help to establish necessary trust.

PERSONAL CHARACTERISTICS AND DISPOSITION

Individuals with a strong internal locus of control or who have a generally positive disposition are more likely to embrace change (Avey *et al.*, 2008). Someone who has a strong internal locus of control believes that they can influence external events or outcomes. Therefore, in the face of change, they feel able to influence how they will be affected by them. Furthermore, if the individual being affected by the change doesn't feel as if he or she is being supported by their supervisors, they will be less likely to see the change as positive. Creative personalities often welcome change, as they often perceive 'routine' as mundane and uninteresting. Since personal characteristics and dispositions of creative people are important to understanding organizational behaviour in the creative and cultural industries, these personality traits will be further discussed in Chapter 3.

HOW TO MANAGE CHANGE RESISTANCE

There are a number of ways managers can address resistance to change, such as: communication; participation; and empathy and support. We will discuss each in turn.

Communication

It is vital that senior managers provide information about the changes that are about to occur or are occurring, and why they are occurring. Not all employees will appreciate the details of the process, but for those who do, they will see this as an act of respect and support. The number one reason why change is resisted is because employees are not provided with the details of why the change is occurring in the first place. Communicating these details will help alleviate some of the uncertainty they may be feeling.

Participation

Having employees participate in the change agenda can help in establishing a sense of ownership in the process. Having ownership or 'skin-in-the-game', so to speak, gives employees the choice of how to respond. This sense of control enables them to feel that they can influence the outcome instead of having outcomes imposed upon them. Buy-in and involvement can go a long way towards building a sense of teamwork and camaraderie that can help to alleviate negative perceptions of change. For example, management may tell employees that they need to deliver certain key outcomes for a project. Having them participate in defining what those outcomes should be or putting them in charge of the process of delivering those outcomes will help them to embrace this change. If you need 10% cut from your budget, allow them to choose which 10% to cut. Or, if you need to dismantle your internal capability in a certain technical area and outsource it to independent companies or freelance producers, allow them to choose which companies and freelancers are engaged. If you need to build your presence in a new genre category, allow the team to choose which genre will play to the organization's strengths and how the outcomes will be achieved.

Empathy and support

Showing empathy for people who are having difficulties dealing with change can help ease some of the negative feelings towards the change process. Empathy, the ability to understand and imagine what someone else might be thinking or feeling, can help to 'meet them where they're at' or relate to how this change may be personally perceived and felt (Loisel, 2015). Knowing this will help to address these concerns in the change process and allow the manager to support the employee in the most meaningful way to them. In the case of change that requires re-skilling and re-structuring, at the extreme end this may require personnel changes. Companies have a responsibility to invest in staff training to prevent staff skills becoming redundant, but in the case of transformative industry change, brand new skills may need to be brought in from outside. In this case, severance packages may be required to provide economic support to those whom the company may need to let go. For example, Netflix had a policy that rewarded under-performance with generous severance packages (McCord, 2014). They felt that being honest with their employees and having frank conversations about not having the skill-set needed for the position is better to do sooner rather than later. It not only saves the company time and money, but also it doesn't do the employee any good if they are in a job where they lack the qualifications to perform effectively (Nisen, 2013) and are likely to fail. Attempts to show empathy and put yourself in the position of the person being affected by the change can help to mitigate the negative feelings and reactions that may result.

IN CONCLUSION: CHANGE, RESISTANCE AND THE CREATIVE PROCESS

At the heart of all new product development in the creative and cultural industries is the creative process. It is the engine that drives creative and cultural industries, but with the creative process comes change, lots of it, as well as uncertainty and turbulence. As managers and leaders of the process of delivering these products and experiences to market, we must understand how change affects our organizations and the people who serve them. The more you understand how and why employees react to change, the more prepared you will be to lead your team into the challenges that the creative and cultural industries will face in the coming years. From the continued uncertainty of demand, ever-expanding global cultural influences, changes to technology and regulation, and the cultural trend towards more personalized experiences, will come changes to how we do business. Those who are ready to adapt and lead their people through this uncertainty will be the ones better equipped to survive and flourish.

Discussion questions and class exercises

1. List and explain the factors that are driving change within the creative and cultural industries.
2. Are there other examples that can be discussed that were not listed within this text?
3. Discuss why most initiatives in organizations aren't successful.
4. As a manager, what are some ways to encourage your employees to be more accepting of change initiatives that may come from your supervisor or the corporate office?
5. Discuss what change circumstances have affected you and how.

References

Agboola, A. A. & Salawu, R. O. (2011). 'Managing deviant behavior and resistance to change', *International Journal of Business and Management*, Vol. 6, no. 1, p. 235.

Aguilar, F. J. (1967). *Scanning the Business Environment*. New York: Macmillan.

Avey, J. B., Wernsing, T. S. & Luthans, F. (2008). 'Can positive employees help positive organizational change? Impact of psychological capital and emotions on relevant attitudes and behaviors', *The Journal of Applied Behavioral Science*, Vol. 44, no. 1, pp. 48–70.

Burns, C., Barton, K. & Kerby, S. (2012). *The State of Diversity in Today's Workforce*. Washington, DC: Center for American Progress, p. 2. Available at https://www.americanprogress.org/issues/economy/reports/2012/07/12/11938/the-state-of-diversity-in-todays-workforce/ (accessed 7 August 2017).

Carpenter, M. A., Bauer, T. & Erdogan, B. (2009). *Principles of Management*. Washington, DC: Flat World Knowledge.

Caves, R. E. (2003). 'Contracts between art and commerce', *The Journal of Economic Perspectives*, Vol. 17, no. 2, pp. 73–83.

Caves, R. E. (2000). *Creative Industries: Contracts Between Art and Commerce*. Cambridge, MA: Harvard University Press.

Child, B. (2016). 'Spike Lee to boycott the 2016 Oscars over lack of nominee diversity'. *The Guardian*. Available at https://www.theguardian.com/film/2016/jan/18/spike-lee-boycott-2016-oscars-nominations-academy-awards-lack-of-diversity (accessed 5 August 2017).

Childress, C. C. (2012). 'Decision-making, market logic and the rating mindset: Negotiating BookScan in the field of US trade publishing', *European Journal of Cultural Studies*, Vol. 15, no. 5, pp. 604–620.

Coalition (2006). 'Radio Station Ownership Consolidation Shown to Harm Musicians and the Public, Says FMC Study'. Available at https://futureofmusic.org/press/press-releases/radio-station-ownership-consolidation-shown-harm-musicians-and-public-says-fmc- (accessed 7 August 2017).

Crealey, M. (2003). 'Applying new product development models to the performing arts: Strategies for managing risk', *International Journal of Arts Management*, pp. 24–33.

Davis, C. (2013). *The Soundtrack of My Life*. New York: Simon and Schuster.

Dex, S., Willis, J., Paterson, R. & Sheppard, E. (2000). 'Freelance workers and contract uncertainty: The effects of contractual changes in the television industry'. *Work, Employment & Society*, Vol. 14, no. 2, pp. 283–305.

Duffy, M. K., Ganster, D. C. & Pagon, M. (2002). 'Social undermining in the workplace', *Academy of Management Journal*, Vol. 45, no. 2, pp. 331–351.

Eisenhardt, K. M. (1989). 'Making fast strategic decisions in high velocity environments'. *Academy of Management Journal*, Vol. 32, no. 3, 543—576.

Ewenstein, B., Smith, W. & Sologar, A. (2015). *Changing Change Management*. [online] McKinsey & Company. Available at: https://www.mckinsey.com/featured-insights/leadership/changing-change-management (accessed 24 June 2022).

Florida, R. (2003). 'Cities and the creative class', *City & Community*, Vol. 2, no. 1, pp. 3–19.

Garofalo, R. (1999). 'From music publishing to MP3: Music and industry in the twentieth century', *American Music*, Vol. 17, no. 3, pp. 318–354.

Hayashi Alder, M. (2003). 'Where to trust your gut', *Harvard Management Review*, May, pp. 1–10.

Jones, C., Lorenzen, M. & Sapsed, J. (2015). *The Oxford Handbook of Creative Industries*. Oxford: Oxford University Press.

Kanter, R. (2012). 'Ten reasons people resist change', *Harvard Business Review*. Available at https://hbr.org/2012/09/ten-reasons-people-resist-change (accessed 7 August 2017).

Karubian, S. (2008). '360 deals: An industry reaction to the devaluation of recorded music', *Southern California Interdisciplinary Law Journal*, Vol. 18, p. 395.

Lank, A. G. & Lank, E. A. (1995). 'Legitimizing the gut feel: The role of intuition in business', *Journal of Managerial Psychology*, Vol. 10, no. 5, pp. 18–23.

Loisel, H.(2015). 'Empathy and Accountability When Leading Change', *Sirius Decisions*. Available at https://www.forrester.com/blogs/empathyandaccountabilitywhenleadingchange/ (accessed 18 July 2022).

McCord, P. (2014). 'How Netflix Reinvented HR', *Harvard Business Review*, Vol. 92, no. 1, pp. 71–76.

Marshall, L. (2013). 'The 360 deal and the "new" music industry', *European Journal of Cultural Studies*, Vol. 16, no. 1, pp. 77–99.

Nelson, D. & Quick, J. (2015). *ORGB 4*. Stamford, CT: Cengage Learning.

Nisen, M. (2013). 'Legendary ex-HR Director from Netflix Shares 6 Important Lessons', *Business Insider*. Available at http://www.businessinsider.com/netflix-corporate-culture-hr-policy-2013-12 (accessed 7 August 2017).

Ordanini, A., Rubera, G. & Sala, M. (2008). 'Integrating functional knowledge and embedding learning in new product launches: How project forms helped EMI music', *Long Range Planning*, Vol. 41, no. 1, pp. 17–32.

Quast, L. (2012). 'Overcome the 5 Main Reasons People Resist Change'. *Forbes.com*.

Sadler-Smith, E. & Shefy, E. (2004). 'The intuitive executive: Understanding and applying "gut feel" in decision-making', *The Academy of Management Executive*, Vol. 18, no. 4, pp. 76–91.

Schindler, P. L. & Thomas, C. C. (1993). 'The structure of interpersonal trust in the workplace', *Psychological Reports*.

Schumpeter, J. A. (1942, 1975). 'Creative destruction'. In *Creative Destruction: Capitalism, Socialism and Democracy*. New York: Harper, pp. 82–85.

Weick, K. E. & Quinn, R. E. (1999). 'Organizational change and development', *Annual Review of Psychology*, Vol. 50, no. 1, pp. 361–386.

Zillman, C. (2015). 'Unpaid interns have their day in court—Again'. *Fortune*. Available at http://fortune.com/2015/01/29/unpaid-internships-legal-battle/ (accessed 7 August 2017).

Personality in creative organizations

Personality of 'the creative' and those who manage them

Chapter 3

CHAPTER LEARNING OBJECTIVES

After studying this chapter, you should be able to:

- Explain the Big Five personality traits and apply them to a creative industry context;
- Identify and describe the differences between various personality profiles used in the workplace;
- Identify key personality traits that affect job performance in the creative industries;
- Explain characteristics of someone who may be perceived as 'creative';

DOI: 10.4324/9781003262923-3

- Define personality characteristics such as locus of control, self-efficacy, self-monitoring and affect;
- Apply concepts and research-backed recommendations on how to best manage creative individuals.

WHAT DOES IT MEAN TO BE CREATIVE?

What it means to be creative has been debated since ancient times. Even with decades of research, it is often difficult to reach consensus on what is creative output and who is a creative individual. However, there has been some consensus with regard to a working definition of creativity. Creativity can be defined as a process through which we generate something new by combining elements that already exist (Jones *et al.*, 2015; Walia, 2019). Creative ideas 'must be of high quality' and 'novel, good and relevant' (Kaufman & Sternberg, 2015). These subjective characteristics by their very nature make creativity hard to measure. Being creative is often limited by a person's willingness to try new things or 'think outside the proverbial box' and can be a product of individuals (Kaufman & Sternberg, 2015), teams (Gilson, 2015) or networks (Cattani *et al.*, 2015).

Figure 3.1 The original... the eccentric ... certainly not the mundane. The dynamics of the creative individual can bring new opportunities and unique challenges to any organization. Photo credit: CREATISTA/ Shutterstock.com.

The novelty of new ideas in the creative industries can be rejected or seen as 'ahead of their time' by audiences. Rejection of new ideas or products isn't always done purposefully, nor is it necessarily representative of the quality of work. Consumers, by their very nature, are slow to adopt innovative new trends, and appreciation can be latent. Recall from Chapter 2 the number of successful musicians whose initial projects failed. Creativity has become a testament to 'outside the box' thinking and management practices, from creative marketing (Fillis & Rentschler, 2006; Titus, 2007) to creative management (Bilton & Leary, 2002), to creative strategy (Bilton, 2007; Bilton & Cummings, 2015). As we explore the concept of creativity and being a creative person, we'll examine the 'personality' that corresponds with this type of thinking and being. How does this person see the world and the tasks of producing something creative? Do they exhibit different personality traits than someone who struggles to be 'creative'? How do these personality differences affect the workplace and production of creative product if you are the creator or seek to manage those who create? What, if any, are those differences and how do you better manage the process? For example, artists could lack conscientiousness (a personality trait to be discussed further in this chapter) and still be enormously employable, but creative managers/cultural intermediaries who lacked conscientiousness would have a tougher time, as they are more embroiled in the organization of activities where this attribute may be needed for outcome delivery.

Although contemporary management has been proactive in understanding workplace behaviours, as we take into consideration the characteristics of the cultural industries, it is particularly important to address the specifics of creative personalities and the creative process. The creative personality is unique, driven by characteristic traits, behaviours and interactions with others. Furthermore, when working with creative personalities, everyone brings their own skills, abilities, personalities, emotions and attitudes into the workplace, so when a clash of character and disposition occurs, we need ways to navigate through them while remaining committed to organizational objectives. Working through personality differences as an employee or manager provides unique challenges. The more they are understood, the better equipped you will be to manage the various personalities and motivations you might encounter.

PERSONALITY

'Personality' refers to individual characteristics that relate to the way we think, feel and behave. Psychologists have studied these characteristics within two broad areas: trait theory and interactional psychology (Association, 2015a). Much has been learnt about people and how we relate to each other in the workplace, which has led to improved ways of managing and leading people.

One way in which psychologists have tried to understand people and their behaviour is through the study of personal traits. Trait theory refers to the relatively stable characteristics that cause people to behave in certain ways. We may describe someone as 'outgoing', 'moody' or 'willing to experience new things'. These descriptions help to identify 'who' a person is while contributing to the perception of an identity.

Interactional psychology, on the other hand, sees differences in people as a function of the way they engage with the environment or situation in which they find themselves. Artists such as Britney Spears and Woody Allen can comfortably perform at a large venue in front of thousands of people, but be described as 'shy' (Lazaro, 2011; Miller, 2013). This may be indicative of how the situation can influence the performance of an actor or musician.

The definition of creativity is complex and includes the concept of domains: ideas and categories that we can relate in our mind to help solve problems or come up with relevant and original solutions. Situational information helps to trigger these ideas which act as a starting point to the creative process. How we are able to take our knowledge and skill to combine categories that result in new solutions is at the centre of being 'creative' (Kilgour, 2006). Creative thinking is the 'process of merging thought categories, or mental images, either across or within domains, in ways that have not been done before, in order to develop an original and appropriate solution to a situation or problem' (Kilgour, 2006, p. 82). For example, developing a sofa in the shape of a woman's lips (Figure 3.2).

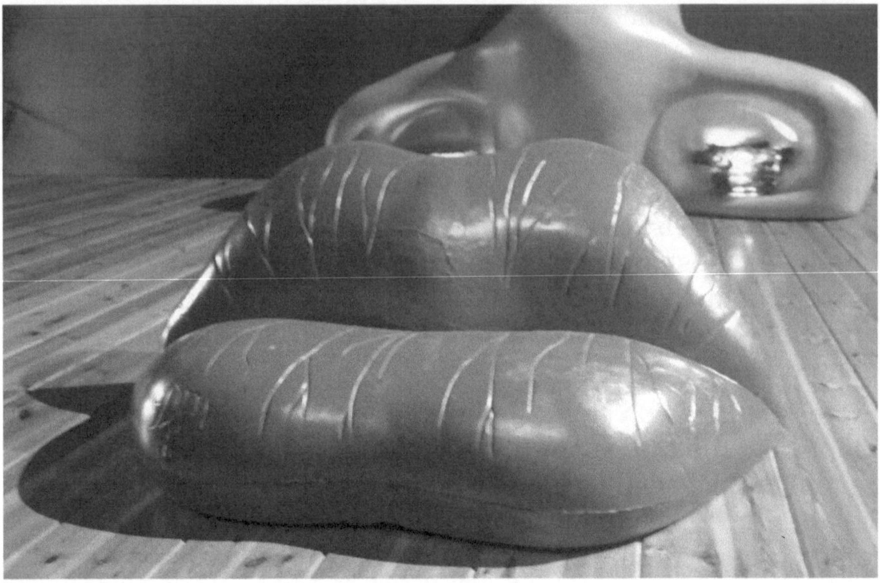

Figure 3.2 The Mae West Lips Sofa by Salvador Dalí. Photo credit: Photo_Traveller/Shutterstock.com.

Organizations that produce cultural product often attract and employ individuals who are drawn to the creative process and its outputs (DeFillippi *et al.*, 2007; Gelade, 2002). They tend to enjoy working around other creative individuals and are invigorated by the excitement and potential uncertainty of the work's day-to-day requirements. They are passionate about the product or service being offered and may come from a similar background to the people they are supporting. They can bring the technical expertise that may be needed to support the production of the creative product (e.g. sound engineers, lighting designers) while being able to interpret the semiotic codes needed for consumer and cultural relevance. Creative managers working for a music publisher may be songwriters themselves, or in the case of movie directors, the individual may have studied to be an actor. For example, Tom Hanks, an American actor, started his career on screen before becoming a critically acclaimed filmmaker.

Many employees in the creative industries are also outgoing, as the need to develop a professional network is critical to both their success and their clients. Two qualities highly sought after by employers in the creative and cultural industries are being open to new ideas and experiences, and dealing with diverse values, ideas and personalities with an assertive yet positive disposition. Having these personality traits is a great start to a potentially successful career within these industries.

THE 'BIG FIVE' PERSONALITY TRAITS

The 'Big Five' personality traits, otherwise known as the 'Five Factor Model', are broad characteristics psychologists use to describe human personality (Figure 3.3). They help to distinguish individuals and their behaviours from one another. Although the premise is that most people can be identified with these traits, the model has attracted criticism from people who

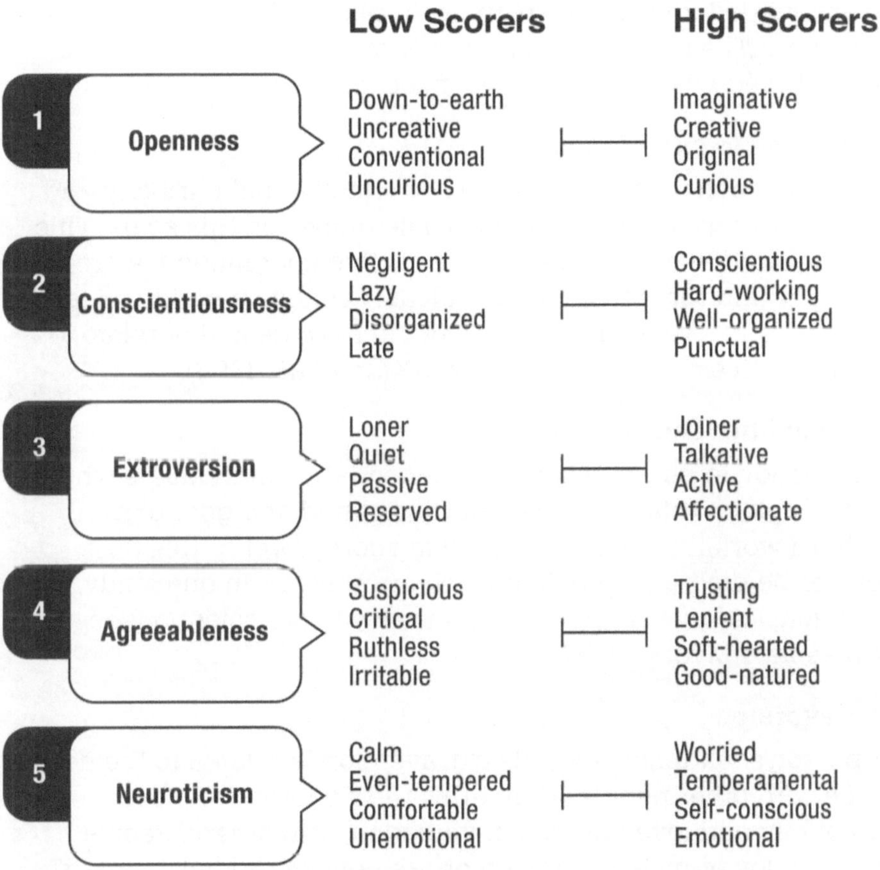

Figure 3.3 The 'Big Five' personality traits and corresponding personality characteristics.

believe that these preconceived labels can limit and restrict human potential (Boyle, 2008). Each of us has what Brian Little describes as 'fixed' or 'free' tendencies towards these characteristics (Porter, 2014). Fixed traits are the ones that come to us naturally. Free traits are those that we can identify with temporarily or 'turn on' as needed. For example, if it feels natural to try new things, you may rate high on 'openness to experience', which would be considered 'fixed'. However, if you are more reserved by nature, you can temporarily identify with this trait by knowing the behaviours that are associated with it; you can be 'open' to a particular experience that you are comfortable with if the right situation arises. In the case of extraversion and introversion, you may have a tendency to be introverted, but when needed you can 'turn on' the typical behaviours of an extrovert. The five characteristics of the Five Factor Model that are outlined below can each be 'fixed' or 'free'.

Openness to experience

When someone is willing to embrace intellectual curiosity and try new things, they tend to associate higher on this scale. This person will have wide interests, an active imagination, a creative capacity and receptivity to new ideas. Creative individuals tend to be much more open to experiencing new ideas that relate to their creative ability and curiosity (King *et al.*, 1996).

Conscientiousness

A tendency to be organized and dependable. Individuals who score high on this scale are self-disciplined and goal-driven or hard working. Those who tend to score lower in this trait tend to be disorganized, impulsive or careless. In one study, rock musicians were found to score low in conscientiousness (Gillespie & Myors, 2000).

Extraversion

A person's tendency towards extraversion is related to the desire to be with other people. They draw their energy from social situations and love having conversation with others. People who are lower on extraversion or are considered 'introverted' personality types draw their energy from being alone; they love to recharge through personal reflection and personal activity.

At times this can be perceived as being aloof or self-absorbed (Toegel & Barsoux, 2012). Some of the most famous creative people who would be perceived to score high on extraversion are self-described introverts, such as Audrey Hepburn, Christina Aguilera, J. K. Rowling and Emma Watson (Schocker, 2015).

Agreeableness

People who are sympathetic, kind, affectionate and trusting score high on agreeableness, but creative individuals often score lower in this trait, being seen as uncooperative, suspicious or less trustworthy (King *et al.*, 1996).

Neuroticism

The tendency towards emotional instability; this person may experience high anxiety, may anger more easily or may experience a wide range of emotions less consistently. High neuroticism has been demonstrated to be a common factor in many creative personalities, especially those who find a career within the field of popular music (Gillespie & Myors, 2000; Cooper & Wills, 1989).

MYERS-BRIGGS TYPE INVENTORY (MBTI)

Carl Jung, a Swiss psychiatrist and psychoanalyst whose work tapped into the unconscious mind, had a deep appreciation for our creative life and the journeys it takes us on (Hollis, 2013). In the documentary *Avicii: True Stories* the Swedish DJ and producer Avicii said that after reading Carl Jung he realized for the first time he was an introvert feeling the pressure of being made to behave like an extrovert.

Jung's work and it's ascendancy in the twentieth century, not only influenced the field of psychology but also writers and artists such as abstract expressionist painters Jackson Pollock and Mark Rothko (Sedivi, 2009). Jung, known for his psychological theories of how we take in and process information, was one of the foremost thought leaders on the concept of introversion and extraversion. His work led to the development of a personality test that is now well known as the Myers-Briggs Type Indicator inventory (MBTI). This self-report questionnaire measures how people perceive the world and make decisions. It measures four dimensions: people's tendencies to be more extroverted or introverted (Extraversion or Introversion); how they perceive their surroundings (Sensing or Intuition); their decision-making tendencies (Thinking or Feeling); and how they interpret their environment (Judging or Perceiving). Let's examine each in turn.

EXTRAVERSION (E) AND INTROVERSION (I)

As discussed above with regard to the Five Factor Model, interacting and engaging with others energizes someone who falls within the spectrum of extraversion. Their energy is often directed outwards and they enjoy interacting with others. Someone who shows a tendency towards introversion directs his or her energies inwards. They are energized by internal reflection and are motivated by concepts and ideas.

SENSING (S) AND INTUITION (N)

The second area that the MBTI addresses is that of 'perceiving or data collection' – Sensing (S) or Intuition (N). Those people who indicate a preference for Sensing rely on actual data and pay attention to details. Those who indicate a preference for Intuition rely on inspiration and look at the 'big picture'.

THINKING (T) AND FEELING (F)

The third area addresses the decision-making process that people use. Those people who prefer Thinking (T) base their decisions on logic and principles. On the other hand, those who prefer Feeling (F) base their decisions on human values and harmonious relationships.

PERCEIVING (P) AND JUDGING (J)

The final area that the MBTI addresses is that of lifestyle. Here, people indicate their preferred and most often used mental preference Perceiving (P) or Judging (J). Those who prefer Judging indicate that decisiveness and task or project completion are important. Those who prefer Perceiving indicate that curiosity and starting a task or project is of value (Foundation, 2015).

Participants who complete the MBTI questionnaire will receive a letter for each of the four dimensions at the end of the exercise (e.g. 'INTJ'). The psychological type denoted by INTJ has its own commentary and literature on what these preferences mean for the individual, and what it means for their relationships with other types.

ENNEAGRAM

Similar to Myers-Briggs, the Enneagram is a personality profile that describes patterns in how people interact with and view the world. It helps people interpret how they manage their emotions and is often used in spiritual circles while being widely promoted in business management. Although Myers-Briggs has been well-established in modern culture since its creation in the 1940s (Haslem, 2018), the Enneagram has found more recent success since its creation in the 1990s (Riso & Hudson, 1996). It is based on a nine personality types ranging from 'The Reformer' to the 'The Peacemaker'– each of which helps to describe a person's perspectives while understanding those around them. When you have greater clarity on what motivates yourself and others, it's often easier to empathise with people while knowing how to better respond to stressful situations in and out of the workplace (The Enneagram Institute, 2021).

DISC

The DiSC personality assessment tool is also widely used in organizations to help employees improve workplace relationships by improving teamwork, communication and productivity. Similar in aim to the previous tools, the DiSC is used to better understand yourself and others in the workplace.

The DiSC model of behaviour was developed by William Moulton Marston in the 1920s and has since been adapted into practical application. Similar to that of the Myers-Briggs and Enneagram, the DiSC is a type indicator test that assesses an individual's 'primary emotions' and associated behavioural responses that align with eight scales in which a person may be described.

DiSC is an acronym that stands for the four main personality profiles described in the DiSC model: (D)ominance, (i)nfluence, (S)teadiness and (C)onscientiousness:

People with D personalities tend to be confident and place an emphasis on accomplishing bottom-line results.

People with i personalities tend to be more open and place an emphasis on relationships and influencing or persuading others.

People with S personalities tend to be dependable and place the emphasis on cooperation and sincerity.

People with C personalities tend to place the emphasis on quality, accuracy, expertise, and competency (DiSCprofile.com, 2022)

CRITICISMS OF PERSONALITY PROFILES

As popular and readily available as the Enneagram, DiSC and Myers-Briggs are, they certainly don't come without their critics. With the Enneagram, for example, some believe, because its story involves a claim to antiquity and an element of mysticism, that it can be considered pseudoscience and 'vague' (Fayard, 2019). In each profile, questions of 'reliability' concern some psychologists (Fayard, 2019), especially since many of its test takers and consumers put so much emphasis on their results. They argue that it doesn't appear to describe some people very well, while others feel they could fit into as many as 2, 3 or 4 categories. Everyone is so different and unique from each other, that attempting to categorize and label individuals in this way is limiting. Furthermore, the reliability and accuracy can be put into doubt when tests such as these (and even the Myers-Briggs) are given in a forced choice format.

Fayard (2019) has also discussed issues with these type-indicator tests, simply that

> research shows that personality types miss a lot of information; by characterizing someone as an introvert OR an extrovert, we miss a lot of the personal nuances of people who, like most of us, actually land somewhere in the middle.
>
> (page 1)

We should recognize that everyone's lived experiences vary greatly and that those experiences affect each of us differently, forming who we are as a person.

WHAT TRAITS PREDICT JOB PERFORMANCE

Understanding personality isn't only beneficial for your own self-awareness, but as a manager, it can help you discern your employee's needs and wants. What drives people to behave or perform in certain ways is a culmination of who they are and their experiences in that environment. In order for managers to better understand their employees, the use of personality tests to determine 'fit' for an organization has increased over the years. This is especially true for organizations in the creative and cultural industries, where information sharing through social networks has traditionally carried more weight than any analytical assessment of prospective employees (Godart & Mears, 2009).

Furthermore, researchers have found that important factors in job performance such as creativity, leadership and integrity are related to personality, not intelligence. Analytical intelligence was at one point considered the key predictor of a person's performance capabilities in the workplace, but no longer (Association, 2015b). In the creative and cultural industries, in particular, certain personality characteristics are sought and seen as better predictors of success than analytical intelligence, even though some studies have shown at least a modicum of intelligence correlates with creativity (Kaufman & Sternberg, 2015). In other industries, the idea of being highly conscientious, responsible, dependable or organized is generally associated with success, but when judging or hiring creative personalities, assumptions that such traits will lead to superior job performance may be misguided. Some research shows that conscientiousness can actually 'impede success in investigative, artistic and social jobs that require innovation, creativity and spontaneity' (Association, 2015b; King *et al.*, 1996).

Personality tests can and do enable employers in these situations to help identify personality traits that they know will 'fit' with the performance expectations of the job and the culture of the firm. For example, some talent agencies are purposeful in their selection of employees to ensure their personality will be a good fit with the demands of the job and set them up for success. The leaders of one performing arts organization, Australia's Circus Oz, in conversation with one of the authors reflected on the employees over the years who had successfully made a home at the Circus, and those who had quickly moved on. A key determinant was whether they were comfortable with uncertainty and ambiguity. This was necessary because of the somewhat perilous financial circumstances the company faced for much of its early life. Those staff who didn't stay long often gravitated to organizations that were more stable, structured and predictable.

Thus, if a company knew that managers possessing certain traits fared better than others who didn't possess those traits, identifying and screening on the basis of those traits could select individuals with a higher chance of success. This is in the employee's interests as well as the company's, as it clearly is not ideal for an employee to join a company and feel uncomfortable and unhappy.

The role of personality testing and profiling in the creative industries

Although a more common practice for firms outside the cultural sector, the use of personality testing and profiling in creative companies is on the rise. Organizational psychologists and human resource departments often rely upon these valuable tools to select good employees and ensure a better 'fit' within their organization. Personality tests are designed to help facilitate the hiring process by making an appropriate match between the person and the position they are applying for. They measure the dimensions of an individual's personality and their related characteristics. However, keep in mind that personality testing in creative organizations and the three tools discussed earlier in the chapter demonstrate the principles involved, but they are not designed for the purposes of screening job applicants.

For one Nashville-based music company, MV2 Entertainment, the use of testing plays an important role in leadership development and talent selection decisions for their songwriters and artists. The company is driven by a 'values-based leadership' philosophy which means all decision-making needs to be run through the lens of their core values and mission. This begins with management's approach to the hiring and signing process – 'hire hard and manage easy'. In order for company leaders to conduct the best assessment possible of applicants, not only do they mandate an extensive behaviour-focused interviewing process, but they also use the DiSC® and Flippen profile to obtain a better understanding of their potential employees and their talents.

MV2ENTERTAINMENT

Figure 3.4 MV2 Entertainment logo. Reprinted by Permission, MV2 Entertainment, Nashville, Tennessee.

Not only does the DiSC® personality assessment tool give MV2 Entertainment a snapshot of the characteristics and dispositions of an individual, but also it allows them to assess the potential success and productivity of those they hire and the talent they sign to their rosters. Tony Harrell, General Manager of MV2, is a strong advocate of its use: 'It really helps us to better understand what drives our potential songwriters and whether this is the right place for them. We look for talent that is motivated by similar values as we seek as a business'. If there is a 'fit', the organization's leaders can be better coaches and advocates for their songwriter's work, which in turn provides a safe and comfortable place for them to create. The transparency that this testing provides enables them to be honest and straightforward with their songwriters, which can be an asset compared to the ambiguous and tumultuous relationships that exist in some organizations.

The Flippen Profile is an additional tool used by MV2 Entertainment that allows management to assess the leadership characteristics of their employees and potential hires. The Flippen profile allows for an essential 'awareness' with each employee. If they understand how others perceive them in the workplace relative to where they see themselves or within the targeted behaviour, it provides an opportunity to refine their interpersonal and leadership skills. It is now integrated so intimately into MV2 Entertainment's culture, it is often a topic of conversation and provides an opportunity for employees to hold each other accountable for behaviour while aiming for continuous improvement. This awareness provides a deep connection with each employee that helps reinforce a tight culture within the firm.

MV2 Entertainment is at the forefront of using tools that other companies in other industries have used for decades. There is much to be learned in the creative industries regarding the usefulness of these measures, but for this Nashville company, it's what drives their decision-making and what they believe to be at the core of their success.

PERSONALITY OF THE CREATIVE INDIVIDUAL

Creative individuals often show a multiplicity of characteristics, leading to an array of emotions and behaviours that at times can be quite unpredictable. They are remarkable at adapting to situations easily and can be resourceful; yet, they are complex. They are able to integrate and synthesize concepts in ways others are unable to (Selby *et al.*, 2005). Because of this complexity, it's been difficult for scholars to 'pigeon hole' them into a 'personality' type, but the one trait that has been shown to be the most consistent is openness to experience (Baer, 2014). It is indicative of embracing ideas and getting excited about new information. They genuinely value intellectual and cognitive matters as well as their own independence and autonomy. They can be verbally fluent and express ideas in ways that others cannot. They enjoy aesthetic experiences and respond favourably to them.

When given their space, creative individuals can be productive, get things done and tend to have a stronger internal locus of control (Roy & Gupta, 2012). As previously mentioned in Chapter 2, 'locus of control' refers to the idea that people believe that they can control the events that affect them. People who believe that they have greater control over what happens to them are considered to have an internal locus of control; they tend to believe they are in control of their success. Those individuals who feel that they have little control over their circumstances or that people control their fate are said to have a stronger external locus of control. In the workplace, individuals who exhibit an internal locus of control tend to be happier and take greater ownership of their experience and situation. Those with an external locus of control will often feel they are being treated unfairly and take less ownership of their experience and situation.

Creative personalities also exhibit high aspirations for themselves and their creations. They feel they can be productive and contribute to the world in which they create and offer new ideas. We can consider them as having high self-efficacy. 'Self-efficacy' is an individual's belief that they can perform effectively in a variety of situations. Generally, creative individuals who have achieved a level of recognized success are confident in their skills and would be considered to have high self-efficacy. Those with low self-efficacy may be riddled with doubt in their abilities and may second-guess themselves. If artists aren't being offered deals or dancers are being overlooked for places within companies, this can lead to self-doubt and low self-efficacy.

Furthermore, creative personalities tend to think and associate ideas in unusual ways; they have unconventional thought processes and can make unusual connections to unrelated ideas or things (Kilgour, 2006; Wilson, 2016). Frustration can set in with co-workers when creative thinkers, with a focus on divergent thinking, 'spark off' seemingly unrelated ideas or possibilities, while someone who is a convergent thinker might want to strip it all back to one clear, linear direction. Creative processes can be fraught when, after an idea generation process has occurred, decisions need to be made while the 'creative' thinker still wishes to further complicate and multiply possibilities, rather than choosing and prioritizing.

If they are not careful with properly managing the creative process, companies within the creative industries can easily find themselves cultivating an environment that undermines rather than supports creative personnel. Company leaders are often faced with the practical challenges of day-to-day activities where their time and attention are focused on business requirements such as managing and controlling, and the need to perform and report results, which can become a challenge for developing a creative culture (Amabile, 1998). This has become even more evident in recent decades as some creative industries, such as the US commercial radio industry and global recording industry, have witnessed an onslaught of corporate consolidation and a move towards tighter oligopolies. However, it is imperative that within the creative and cultural firm, a balance is struck so that the creative process is seen as core to the business, and not marginalized by these other activities. What makes our industries unique (i.e. the creativity) can be undermined if we don't try to understand the people who are most critical to delivering the company's creative output. Creative culture at an organizational level rather than an individual level is discussed further in Chapter 13.

THE CREATIVE PROCESS

The creative process

1 This is awesome,
2 This is tricky,
3 This is shit,
4 I am shit,
5 This might be OK, and
6 This is awesome.

Modelling the creative process in this way, albeit comically, could at least anecdotally be considered representative of its chaotic nature and the neurotic tendencies for those who engage in it. Empirically however, this process has been modelled since the 1920s (Wallas, 1926) and has since been further developed by many prominent scholars (Hennessey & Amabile, 2009, Finke *et al.*, 1992; Mumford *et al.*, 1991). Early depictions of a model attempt to describe a four-stage process (Lubart, 2001; Wallas, 1926) or a sequence of thoughts and actions that lead to novel, adaptive products, ideas and services (Lubart, 2001). Wallas' (1926) four stage model of the creative process included:

Preparation – Defining the problem while relying on your knowledge, education and experience.

Incubation – Setting it aside. Allowing your mind to work on finding a creative solution to the issue.

Illumination – Occurs when the promising idea breaks through to conscious awareness.

Verification – Involves evaluating, refining and developing your idea.

In the world of the creative and cultural industries, creativity and innovation are at work every day and are often not as linear or sequential as depicted by Wallas. When creativity is at its best, ideas and thoughts interact and may take on many different iterations over time. Some ideas are thrown out, some are further refined, while others lead to new ideas until an outcome is achieved. Amabile (1983) understood the complexities of the process and developed a model that more accurately represents how people move back and forth throughout the phases in different combinations and sequences. With close examination, you will notice similarities between her work and Wallas', but the main difference lies in the belief that the creative process is more iterative.

Problem or task recognition – The initial trigger to create something; those more intrinsically motivated may start easily in this stage, while those that rely on external motivation may have a more difficult time getting started.

Preparation – This stage in the creative process occurs before any ideas are generated. The individual will draw upon or reactivate information they already know that may be relevant to the task.

Response generation – Ideas are generated in response to the problem or task.

Response validation – In the fourth stage of the process, validation determines the appropriateness, usefulness and quality of the response. The creator(s) determine whether it is correct and holds value.

Outcome – The final stage of the process that has three possibilities. Does the creation: 1) achieve the goal that was set; 2) fail to achieve the outcome; or 3) make progress towards the goal? At this point, the creator(s) may go back to a different phase if more work is determined or needed.

As previously discussed, defining creativity can be a challenge, but we do know that uncreative people tend to latch onto the first idea that comes to mind (Petty, 2009), whereas more creative people will bounce back and forth between these phases, giving the 'idea' more thought and criticism. In the craft of song writing, whether individually or as a co-writer with at least one other writer, we can see this process play out. The less creative person will toss out a lyric, phrase or melodic structure and be content, while the more creative individuals may talk through the original idea as appropriate or not – what Amabile considers the 'validation' phase. The lyric or melody is treated as a starting point for incorporating different words or harmonic structures. Refining will continue until progress is made towards the goal or until the song is written. If the song isn't complete after reaching the 'outcome' stage, the songwriters may go back to preparation and draw upon new information, or generate a new response.

WORKING THROUGH IDENTITY: THE CREATIVE PERSONALITY AND THE CREATIVE INDUSTRIES

Understanding the personality characteristics of a creative individual is one thing, but understanding the individuals who are drawn to manage them is also important. The manager who works with or represents the creative individual must possess the ability to relate to that individual and coach appropriately so that the creative individual's goals and the company's goals are aligned. The simultaneous roles that we play within an organization can often complement our work, but also create inter-role conflict. When an agent is asked to play the role of business manager and 'in-house' psychologist while pursuing the professional needs and demands of his or her artist or client, it can often create tension in priorities and role expectations.

Often in these industries, employees seek to legitimize themselves within these roles and often do so through self-aggrandisement (Schreiber, 2014). By portraying 'larger' images of themselves, individuals will often inflate credentials, drop names or try to associate themselves and their work 'loosely' with others who have achieved more success. This identity projection is an attempt by the creative individual or management representing them to be seen as capable in doing their work, even though they may not yet have attained much in terms of symbolic meaning or reputation. Creative people may draw on these patterns of speaking to help draw out what they do and their place within the work they are doing (Coupland, 2015). Being perceived by others as 'authentic' and one to do business with is the aim of this type of behaviour and is done often because of the importance that the development of the professional network has in the industry. The search for identity and the willingness to aggrandize is rooted in the personality of the individual. It is important however for those working in the industry to be aware of such behaviours. Managers or agents that are responsible for guiding careers should be aware of these insecure dispositions and how they may impact the brand they are representing.

MANAGING THE CREATIVE INDIVIDUAL

Coaching and managing creative people requires certain considerations and a degree of sensitivity. Their skill-set and personality characteristics warrant and appreciate a certain respect. They like to push emotional and physical boundaries, are open new ideas and experiences and seek innovation. Our objective is to help creative people succeed – to provide the tools and support necessary for them to do their job and limit the frustrations inherent in the creative process. If you are a more linear thinker and fall on the more conscientious end of the spectrum, the creative process may be very frustrating for you.

Or maybe you were part of the creative team yourself and now find yourself leading it. You are now faced with the challenges of being responsible for more than your own creative work, but the output of other people. When managing people, they will inevitably be concerned about how their new leader will affect them and their own opportunities for growth and development. It's a fine balance between getting what you need from your creative team while keeping them motivated and satisfying their needs.

On one level, managing creative people isn't unlike leading anyone else in the workplace, but because we know that a creative mindset and the creative process exhibit certain characteristics, there a few things that can be kept in consideration to better ensure that the creative process, and ultimately creative output remains as unencumbered as possible. We should also ensure we listen to the team's needs and enable them to grow and provide feedback. However, there a few actions worth emphasizing when you find yourself at the helm of a talented and driven group of creatives.

Embrace failure

Show your creative people unconditional support and encourage them to do the absurd and fail. Innovation comes from uncertainty, risk and experimentation. Tell them what needs to be done and then let them do it in their own way. It may not always be the most efficient, or how you would like to approach the problem, but you need to give them the time and flexibility to experiment with different outcomes and solutions. Your job is to provide the tools and support they need to do theirs. There is no place for micro-managing creative people. It is always better to provide the framework and allow them to complete the project in their own way. This relates to the concept of 'creative autonomy' introduced in Chapter 1.

Involve them in meaningful work

Showing people the bigger picture, so they understand why things are being done, and that what they are doing matters, are important aspects in motivating any employee, but this is especially true for the creative individual. Creative workers are often intrinsically motivated, with their behaviour driven by internal rewards such as 'the love of the work' (discussed further in Chapter 4). Creative people draw satisfaction from meaning and can have a relentless drive towards finding meaning through art and making their lives meaningful. They will be more excited about what they are doing if they know what they are doing has meaning.

Don't pressure them

Creativity is enhanced by giving creative individuals room to think and create, providing flexibility to do their work. Time constraints are important in any business, but the creative process does not always methodically adhere to rules and procedures. Finding an appropriate balance between the process and when the product or service is to be delivered should always be considered. Flexibility and patience are often needed. Allow them time to recharge and to find a process that enables them to do their best work.

Provide them with appropriate space

Having an appropriate space in order for the creative person to generate ideas is often critical. The most ingenious ideas often occur when the creative person is at their most relaxed. Providing the appropriate atmosphere for this to occur is essential. Many of the music publishing companies in Nashville, for example, are located on 'music row', which consists of renovated homes. The warm, cosy feeling of these offices provide writing rooms for songwriters that are often complete with couches and warm lights, similar to the ambience of one's living room.

Keep them challenged and engaged

Boredom is aggravating to the creative individual. The creative person is often welcoming of change and willing to try new things. Creativity is linked to higher tolerance of ambiguity, so providing new opportunities or problems often will keep them more engaged.

Value ideas and creations

Because creatives can be emotionally connected to their product and ideas, they become more vulnerable to criticism. They bare their soul when they create or generate ideas. Making them feel like their ideas are valuable and that they are contributing to the overall aim of the company is key to keeping them productive and motivated.

Don't engage them in monotonous tasks or assignments

A quick way to kill a creative person's productivity is to assign them many monotonous tasks. Creative individuals will often embrace fast paced environments and welcome new experiences and opportunities. They love variety, originality and individual effort, which is in direct opposition of clerical tasks or administrative matters.

CONCLUSION

Understanding the complexities of the creative personality can be challenging, but the importance of doing so cannot be underestimated, as creative inspiration is the foundation of the creative industries. As we discussed in this chapter, personality can be described through trait (the Big Five) or integrative (Myers-Briggs Type Indicator) theoretical perspectives. The field of psychology now has decades of research into human personality and behaviour which allows us to develop and apply tools to manage behaviour. Appreciating the characteristics and behavioural tendencies of creative people in particular can help us better manage the often delicate and non-linear creative process. Furthermore, as the creative industries and its leaders are refining their management practices, we are noticing an increased use of personality profiles to assess talent and future leaders. The more we know about the people we bring into our organizations, the better prepared we will be. The recommendations we've provided here will assist productivity and improve interpersonal relations within the creative industries workplace.

DISCUSSION QUESTIONS AND CLASS EXERCISES

1 Discuss why the creative process can be a challenge for organizations and their objectives.

2 Do you feel the creative models illustrate the creative process effectively? What are their strengths and what might they be missing in terms of accuracy?

3 Discuss ways in which as a potential manager can help manage the creative person. How might they keep them motivated through the fits and starts of writing songs, recording albums, designing logos, painting portraits or writing papers?

CASE STUDY 3.1: CRISIS IN THE OPERA HOUSE

The tempestuous operatic soprano Valerie Vesuvius erupts, nearly killing an intern and a member of the artistic administration team, and engulfing the national opera company in crisis. The CEO convenes a meeting in the boardroom for senior management to discuss the situation. Senior executives adopt conflicting positions, encouraging class debate on the appropriate course of action.

Valerie Vesuvius had an international reputation for being 'difficult' and her backstage tantrums were legendary within the House. Up to this point, the company had tried to 'manage' the issue, retaining a relationship with its publicly adored and 'bankable' star, while trying to appease disgruntled cast members and staff.

On this occasion the diva had flown in late for rehearsals, and by the end of her first day in the building had missed a number of crucial appointments and insulted most of the people working in the makeup and costume departments. She was supposed to be performing the role of Mimi in Puccini's *La Bohème*, which was due to open in only three days' time.

The CEO, Imogen Impresario, had convened a meeting in the boardroom for senior management to discuss the situation. Impresario looked around the table. She had joined the company only one month earlier and found

Figure 3.5 Leading and managing difficult personalities is essential in the creative industries. Photo credit: tugol/Shutterstock.com.

herself ascending a steep learning curve. Prior to this position she had been CEO of a private foundation which disbursed grants to arts organizations.

Marc Monet, the artistic director, was the last to arrive. He glided into the room, immaculately dressed, apparently unruffled by the morning's tumult. The CEO turned towards him. 'OK, Marc, perhaps you could start by talking us through your understanding of exactly what happened'.

> Certainly. I think we all know the long, tortured history of this saga, but in terms of what triggered the last convulsion... the sequence of events appears to be that yesterday Vesuvius finally turned up around 10 am, two days late, and thus in breach of her contract. She attended one music call, momentarily, but then insulted the production's Musetta and left. She fleetingly attended

a fitting but insulted the wig master and left. She didn't attend a press call that had been scheduled for her. Instead, she roamed the building, creating a firestorm of ill will in a number of departments. Both our Musetta and the wig master were later seen leaving the building in tears. This morning Michelle from artistic administration went to see Vesuvius, and privately questioned her professionalism. This triggered a second explosion, where the artist threw a bust of Puccini at her, narrowly missing an intern, but taking out an empty vase. Michelle claims she was hit by shrapnel from the vase, which drew blood. Vesuvius then marched into my office, demanding Michelle's dismissal. I declined her request. She then stood in my doorway spewing molten lava, before storming out of the House, leaving a trail of sulphurous gases. To my knowledge she is currently uncontactable. We have a full dress rehearsal commencing in four hours.

'Thanks very much, Marc', said Impresario. 'What on earth was Michelle doing taking an intern on a mission like that?'

The meeting was scheduled to take place anyway on quite a different matter – Vesuvius sends them scurrying all over the place on personal errands – but apparently Michelle felt that she had no alternative but to be drawn into a discussion about it.

'Given yesterday's events, of which she would have undoubtedly been aware, it showed a distinct lack of judgement', Impresario responded drily.

Is it a mistake to feel that one is entitled to work in an environment without bullying and intimidation? Michelle is a superb member of our team and was doing what she felt to be in the best interests of the company and her colleagues.

She had every right to bring this to our attention. But she made a mistake in taking everything upon herself.

While we would all agree that there *is* conduct that is unprofessional and unacceptable, before starting down a path that can lead to explosions, we first need to fully understand the implications of that step, which is a complex calculus. She is not in the best position to make that calculation. And secondly, we also need to determine the most effective way of dealing with the situation. Someone at her level has fewer options than we have as a team, which is why difficult artist relations issues need to be brought to my attention, or your attention. We might feel it is sufficient to have a quiet word with the manager or agent, and let them deal with it. We might design a scenario whereby a staff member the artist trusts brings it up at an appropriate moment. We might call a formal meeting with the artist and the manager, and invite a number of staff along to lend it more gravity. We might issue her with a formal written warning. We might advise that we refuse to offer her any future engagements beyond those already contracted. We might terminate her agreement due to unprofessional conduct. There are a range of options.

Monet played ostentatiously with his cufflinks.

Refusing to offer any future engagements might provoke Vesuvius to withdraw, in which case the audience would see her withdrawal as her fault and not ours. It would also send a clear signal to the company as a whole that her behaviour is unacceptable … It's worth us considering …

The CEO nodded. 'Before we leave the subject of Michelle, I also believe she got emotional, raised her voice and became abusive to Vesuvius'.

'That's true. It was highly regrettable but she was provoked'.

'She shouldn't sink to the same level as the person we're condemning. I respect you standing up for members of

> your team, but I expect more professionalism. In this business you need a thick skin. We all know that'.

Colin Cash, the financial controller, chimed in.

> I would just like to add in terms of the "complex calculus" that we have her performing in the tour we're running through Asia next year. We're pretty handsomely subsidized for that tour, and so it contributes financially to our year end targets. She has an enormous following out there, and the tour is somewhat built around her involvement. If she pulls out or feigns illness it may jeopardize the tour.

Monet adjusted his cravat. 'I don't see why this is such a big deal. We've had artist blow-ups before, and we just deal with them. That is what we do. That is what ***I*** do. This is an artistic decision'.

'Certainly, but it's also a corporate decision', responded the CEO. 'There's too much at stake in terms of revenue, risk, reputation ... It impacts on too many other things'.

'Everywhere I've worked we've always had Vesuviuses', Monet continued.

> Perhaps not as damaging, but there's always been one. Do we want to work with creative people? Great artists aren't normal. Great artists are extreme, and extreme people do extreme, mad, crazy things. This is what working in the arts is all about. If you want to work with boring, normal people, go and work in a bank, or for a toothpaste company. Vesuvius is a perfectionist – she's no harder on the people around her than she is on herself. We need to work with people like her or we shouldn't be in this business. It is just a case of me going back to her with a stronger line. And I am perfectly capable of doing that.

The head of marketing, Betty Blacktown, spoke up. 'Opera is about big personalities. And the media and public love drama; it makes artists interesting. Otherwise she would be some boring, vanilla singer. She's a prima donna, which is a good thing'.

The human resources director, Sharon Shield, was the next to wade in.

> Well, as I understand it, "prima donna" simply means "first lady", or the best person for a role – it doesn't give someone a licence to abuse, intimidate and humiliate staff. This is workplace bullying. Pure and simple. It opens up the company to legal risks. If we ignore or excuse this sort of behaviour, we send a clear message to staff that we consider bullying to be acceptable. We send a clear message to the other, admittedly few, difficult artists that they can get away with virtually anything while they're here. It can result in stress leave, allegations of harassment, a hostile work environment and discrimination. Vesuvius is sick, she's an organizational sociopath or psychopath. She needs help.

Monet continued the pro-artist line.

> I think we need to recognize that stars are often insecure, vulnerable and under enormous pressure. They spend half their lives jetlagged, hearing about catty reviews or negative blogs that have been written about them. Most artists don't actually understand the connection they have with an audience and live in perpetual fear that one night the magic just won't happen. There is also "creative conflict" in rehearsal situations, which is normal. Sometimes sparks of genius fly off in creative confrontations.

'The conflict here has nothing to do with the creative process', Shield replied.

> She wasn't remotely near a rehearsal room. My view, for what it's worth, is that she's a predatory, narcissistic

> bitch, and if we don't put our foot down, we'll just refuel her belief that she is entitled to get away with it.

Impresario turned again to Monet. 'Is there any way we can keep her more isolated and stop her from poisoning everyone?'

Monet shook his head. 'I don't see how in a collaborative art form like opera you can quarantine someone. Particularly the star of the show. Collaborative and collegial attitudes are necessary for the whole ensemble to flourish'.

'In terms of fallout, what's the conductor saying?' continued Impresario.

Monet smiled and attempted his thickest Eastern European accent: 'She is bitch. Big, crazy bitch. She no good for health, like Chernobyl. But very good singer, like Callas. Callas also bitch. They make big, angry experiences. Vot to do?'

'And the director?'

'The same'.

'I know I'm the boring finance guy' interjected Cash,

> but what we need to do at some point is a quick "back of the envelope" cost-benefit analysis. If we can't afford to lose her, dealing with the aggravation may just be a cost of doing business. We need to explore the financial and practical implications of replacing her. We need to define the parameters in which we can work and know the long term cost before we do anything drastic. What are we actually deciding here? And who is deciding? Is this something that should be decided by the management team, or left to the CEO and artistic director after we have all been consulted?

There was a pause. The CEO looked uncertain.

Shield continued.

> It goes deeper than a cost-benefit analysis. It comes down to culture and values. What sort of company

are we? What do we actually stand for? What do we expect of ourselves and others? Let's look at our mission statement. From memory it says something like "we are committed to our values of cooperative teamwork and mutual respect". I have heard it said in these corridors that "our job is to provide an environment in which an artist can give of his or her best". Can we honestly say that the environment at the moment is conducive for the other artists in this production to "give of their best"? Of course not. The bottom line is that Vesuvius has no respect for her colleagues. What price do we put on values like respect and integrity? Sure, do your cost-benefit analysis, but at some point you will be trying to price the priceless.

Monet retorted, 'May I remind people that 'excellence' is also a value, and that despite her undoubted flaws, she is capable of delivering artistic excellence at an unparalleled level'.

'Yes', Shield responded, 'but if she compromises the work of others, and opera is a collaborative art form, as you say, then the total excellence diminishes'.

Impresario reasserted her authority on the meeting with renewed vigour. 'OK. There are a couple of practical points I need to go over with you, Marc. What does her contract say?'

'I believe that there is a pro forma clause around conduct that would serve as adequate grounds for termination'.

'And if we were to sit her down and strongly intervene, what would be her reaction?'

'I don't think she would respond constructively'.

'And what about her cover? How well covered are we?'

'Artistically, very strongly. But of course the cover has a much lower profile from an audience perspective'.

Betty Blacktown jumped in. 'Vesuvius is a big draw, but *Bohème* is *Bohème*. I think I could sing Mimi and we'd still get an audience'.

'If we do dismiss her', said Impresario, 'what sort of language should we use in the announcement?'

Monet paused.

> Well, the normal language is that the artist is "indisposed", whatever that means, or has some cold or flu. But I don't think that would work in this case. I think tensions have filtered out sufficiently for a few critics and bloggers to know ... In which case the clichéd line is that we are parting company on this production due to "irreconcilable creative differences".

'Is there any other additional leverage we have over her? Is there anything else that we are supporting that we could look to withdraw?'

'Nothing out of the usual. I'll check'.

OK. To wrap up here, Marc, I would be grateful if your Department could construct a highly detailed timeline of recent events, with an accuracy down to the minute, and against each event list the people who witnessed it. Please bring me the bust of Puccini and the broken vase. Also, please check the relevant clauses in the contract plus any other favours we may be doing for her. Finally, at least attempt to track down the diva for the dress rehearsal this afternoon and check on the readiness of the cover. Betty, we need our publicist on standby in case we need to draft a media release. Colin, please work up a draft cost-benefit analysis we can discuss after lunch. Let's meet back here at 2pm sharp. Marc, would you stay behind? Thank you.

The meeting broke up. Impresario pondered the dilemma. If they did act, how strongly should they intervene? A gift for handling temperamental artists is seen as an asset in this business. If she is seen to terminate the agreement, would she look like a naïve newcomer who doesn't understand opera and handling superstar artists? Would a failure to act undermine her authority with the whole company? Would refusing to delegate the decision to Monet alienate the two of them? Could she be complicit in supporting a culture of bullying?

Discussion questions

1. Which Big Five personality traits best describe Valerie Vesuvius? Give examples of behaviour from the case to support your observations.
2. Do you think this is a typical personality of a creative individual? Why/why not? Or are her behaviours a reflection of something else? Would trait or behavioural psychology better explain her actions?
3. Did Valerie exhibit a typical internal or external locus of control?
4. Would Valerie be considered a high or low self-monitor? Provide examples.
5. Which Big Five personality traits best describe the CEO, Imogen Impresario? Provide evidence from the case to support your ideas.
6. Do you think this is a typical personality 'type' that you would find in the creative and cultural industries? Why or why not?

The textbook authors would like to thank Moffatt Oxenbould AM, former Artistic Director of Opera Australia, for extremely helpful suggestions which undoubtedly improved the case. Dr Guy Morrow also provided generous advice on resources and angles.

A video of managerial responses to this case study is available to instructors from the companion website: www.routledgetextbooks.com/textbooks/MMCCI

References

Amabile, T. M. (1983). 'The social psychology of creativity: A componential conceptualization', *Journal of Personality and Social Psychology*, Vol. 45, no. 2, p. 357.

Amabile, T. M. (1998). 'How to kill creativity', *Harvard Business Review*, Vol. 76, no. 5, pp. 76–87.

Association, A. P. (2015a). 'Personality'. Available at http://www.apa.org/topics/personality/ (accessed 7 August 2017).

Association, A. P. (2015b). 'Which traits predict job performance'. Available at http://www.apa.org/helpcenter/predict-job-performance.aspx. (accessed 7 August 2017).

Baer, D. (2014). 'This personality trait is the most important driver of creative achievement'. *Business Insider*. Available at http://www.businessinsider.com/the-personality-trait-that-drives-creative-achievement-2014-7 (accessed 7 August 2017).

Bilton, C. (2007). *Management and Creativity: From Creative Industries to Creative Management*. Oxford: Blackwell Publishing.

Bilton, C. & Cummings, S. (2015). 'Creative strategy: notes from a small label'. In *Organising Music, Theory, Practice, Performance*. Cambridge: Cambridge University Press Edited by: Nic Beech & Charlotte Gilmore.

Bilton, C. & Leary, R. (2002). 'What can managers do for creativity? Brokering creativity in the creative industries', *International Journal of Cultural Policy*, Vol. 8, no. 1, pp. 49–64.

Boyle, G. J. (2008). 'Critique of the five-factor model of personality', *The SAGE Handbook of Personality Theory and Assessment*, Vol. 1, pp. 295–312.

Brands, W. (2017). *Everything DiSC*. Available at http://everythingdisc.com/ (accessed 7 August 2017).

Cattani, G., Ferriani, S. & Colucci, M. (2015). 'Creativity in social networks: A core-periphery perspective'. In C. Jones, M. Lorenzen & J. Sapsed (eds.), *The Oxford Handbook of Creative Industries*. Oxford: Oxford University Press, pp. 75–95.

Chamorro-Premuzic, T. (2013). 'Seven rules for managing creative-but-difficult people', *Harvard Business Review*. Available at https://hbr.org/2013/04/seven-rules-for-managing-creat/ (accessed 7 August 2017).

Cooper, C. L. & Wills, G. I. D. (1989). 'Popular musicians under pressure', *Psychology of Music*, Vol. 17, no. 1, pp. 22–36.

Coupland, C. (2015). 'Identity work – organising the self, organising music'. In N. Beech & C. Gilmore (eds). *Organising Music, Theory, Practice, Performance*. Cambridge: Cambridge University Press, pp. 72–82.

DeFillippi, R., Grabher, G. & Jones, C. (2007). 'Introduction to paradoxes of creativity: Managerial and organizational challenges in the cultural economy', *Journal of Organizational Behavior*, Vol. 28, no. 5, p. 511.

DiSC Profile.com (2022). 'What is the DiSC assessment?', Available at: https://www.discprofile.com/what-is-disc#:~:text=DiSC%20is%20an%20acronym%20that, on%20accomplishing%20bottom%2Dline%20results (accessed 1 June 2022).

The Enneagram Institute. (2021). 'The Enneagram Institute'. Available at: https://www.enneagraminstitute.com/ (accessed 1 June 2022).

Fayard, J. V. (2019). 'Your favorite personality test is probably bogus', *Psychology Today*. Available at: https://www.psychologytoday.com/us/blog/people-are-strange/201909/your-favorite-personality-test-is-probably-bogus (accessed 1 June 2022).

Fillis, I. & Rentschler, R. (2006). *Creative Marketing: An Extended Metaphor for Marketing in a New Age*. New York: Palgrave Macmillan.

Finke, R. A., Ward, T. B. & Smith, S. M. (1992). *Creative Cognition*. Cambridge, MA: MIT Press.

The Myers & Briggs Foundation. (2015). *MBTI Basics*. Available at http://www.myersbriggs.org/my-mbti-personality-type/mbti-basics/ (accessed 29 October 2015).

Gelade, G. A. (2002). 'Creative style, personality, and artistic endeavor', *Genetic, Social, and General Psychology Monographs*, Vol. 128, no. 3, p. 213.

Gillespie, W. & Myors, B. (2000). 'Personality of rock musicians', *Psychology of Music*, Vol. 28, no. 2, pp. 154–165.

Gilson, L. (2015). 'Creativity in teams: Processes and outcomes in creative industries'. In C. Jones, M. Lorenzen & J. Sapsed (eds). *The Oxford Handbook of Creative Industries*. Oxford: Oxford University Press, pp. 50–74.

Godart, F. C. & Mears, A. (2009). 'How do cultural producers make creative decisions? Lessons from the catwalk', *Social Forces*, Vol. 88, no. 2, pp. 671–692.

Hollis, J. (2013). 'A brief note on Carl Jung', *The Jung Page: Reflections on Psychology, Culture and Life*. Available at http://www.cgjungpage.org/learn/about-jung (accessed 7 August 2017).

Haslem, S. A. (2018). *The Self Made Women Who Created the Myers Briggs*. Accessible at: https://www.nature.com/articles/d41586-018-06614-8#:~:text=Introduced%20by%20Isabel%20Briggs%20Myers, I)%3B%20sensing%20(S)%20t (accessed 1 June 2022)

Hennessey, B. A. & Amabile, T. M. (2009). 'Creativity', *Annual Review of Psychology*, Vol. 61, pp. 569–598

Jones, C., Lorenzen, M. & Sapsed, J. (2015). *The Oxford Handbook of Creative Industries*. Oxford: Oxford University Press.

Kaufman, J. C. & Sternberg, R. J. (2015). 'The creative mind'. In *The Oxford Handbook of Creative Industries*. Oxford: Oxford University Press.

Kilgour, M. (2006). 'Improving the creative process: Analysis of the effects of divergent thinking techniques and domain specific knowledge on creativity', *International Journal of Business and Society*, Vol. 7, no. 2, p. 79.

King, L. A., Walker, L. M. & Broyles, S. J. (1996). 'Creativity and the five-factor model', *Journal of Research in Personality*, Vol. 30, no. 2, pp. 189–203.

Lazaro, C. (2011). 'Why Woody Allen is the most shy yet one of the most popular icons in Hollywood', *International Business Times*. Available at http://www.ibtimes.com.au/why-woody-allen-most-shy-yet-one-most-popular-icons-hollywood-1289708 (accessed 7 August 2017).

Lubart, T. I. (2001). 'Models of the creative process: Past, present and future', *Creativity Research Journal*, Vol. 13, no. 3/4, pp. 295–308. Available at http://teach.belmont.edu:2048/login?url=http://search.ebscohost.com/login.aspx?direct=true&db=aph&AN=5673213&site=ehost-live (accessed 7 August 2017).

Miller, H. (2013). 'Britney Spears opens up about anxiety and shyness in E! documentary'. *The Huffington Post.* Available at http://www.huffingtonpost.com/2013/12/23/britney-spears-anxiety-shy_n_4492885.html (accessed 7 August 2017).

Mumford, M. D., Mobley, M. I., Reiter-Palmon, R., Uhlman, C. E. & Doares, L. M. (1991). 'Process analytic models of creative capacities', *Creativity Research Journal*, Vol. 4, no. 2, pp. 91–122.

Norcross, J. C., Koocher, G. P. & Garofalo, A. (2006). 'Discredited psychological treatments and tests: A Delphi poll', *Professional Psychology: Research and Practice*, Vol. 37, no. 5, pp. 515–522. https://doi.org/10.1037/0735-7028.37.5.515

Owens, M. (2021). *What Is the Enneagram of Personality?* Available at https://www.truity.com/enneagram/what-is-enneagram (accessed 1 June 2022).

Petty, G. (1997). *How to be Better at... Creativity.* Raleigh, NC: Kogan Page.

Petty, G. (2009). *Teaching Today. A Practical Guide.* Cheltenham: Nelson Thornes Limited.

Porter, J. (2014). 'The Science of Personality in the Workplace'. *Fast Company.*

Riso, D. R. & Hudson, R. (2000). 'Understanding the Enneagram: The Practical Guide to Personality Types'. *Houghton Mifflin Harcourt.*

Riso, D. R. & Hudson, R. (1999). *The Wisdom of the Enneagram: The Complete Guide to Psychological and Spiritual Growth for the Nine Personality Types.* New York: Bantam.

Riso, D. R. & Hudson, R. (1996). *Personality Types: Using the Enneagram for Self-discovery.* New York: Houghton Mifflin Harcourt.

Roy, R. & Gupta, S. (2012). 'Locus of control and organisational climate as predictors of managerial creativity', *Asia-Pacific Journal of Management Research and Innovation*, Vol. 8, no. 4, pp. 525–534.

Schocker, L. (2015). '16 super successful introverts', *The Huffington Post.* Available at http://www.huffingtonpost.com/2015/08/15/famous-introverts_n_3733400.html (accessed 7 August 2017).

Schreiber, D. (2014). *An Investigation of Influences on Strategic Decision-making in Popular Recorded Music Industry Micro-enterprises*, Doctoral Dissertation, University of Westminster.

Sedivi, A. E. (2009). *Unveiling the unconscious: The influence of Jungian psychology on Jackson Pollock and Mark Rothko*, undergraduate thesis. Available at http://publish.wm.edu/cgi/viewcontent.cgi?article=1293&context=honorstheses (accessed 7 August 2017).

Selby, E. C., Shaw, E. J. and Houtz, J. C. (2005). 'The creative personality', *Gifted Child Quarterly*, Vol. 49, no. 4, pp. 300–314.

Titus, P. A. (2007). 'Applied creativity: The creative marketing breakthrough model', *Journal of Marketing Education*, Vol. 29, no. 3, pp. 262–272.

Toegel, G. & Barsoux, J. L. (2012). 'How to become a better leader', *MIT Sloan Management Review*, Vol. 53, no. 3, pp. 51–60. Available at http://teach.belmont.edu:2048/login?url=http://search.proquest.com/docview/963962182?accountid=8570 (accessed 7 August 2017)

Wallas, G. (1926). *The Art of Thought*. London: Cape.

Wallia, C. (2019) 'A dynamic definition of creativity', *Creativity Research Journal*, Vol. 31, no. 3, pp. 237–247, doi: 10.1080/10400419.2019.1641787

Wilson, O. (2016). 'Characteristics of highly creative individuals', *The Second Principle*. Available at http://thesecondprinciple.com/creativity/creativetraits (accessed 7 August 2017).

Attitude and motivation in creative organizations

Chapter 4

CHAPTER LEARNING OBJECTIVES

After studying this chapter, you should be able to:

- Identify and compare the various components that influence attitude formation;
- Recognize attitudes associated with successful and damaging outcomes in the creative industries;
- Describe how to manage attitudes towards risk, failure and criticism of the products they create;
- Compare and contrast the sources of job satisfaction and commitment;
- Assess how attitudes influence workplace deviance;
- Explain the differences between intrinsic and extrinsic motivation;
- Describe the role of 'grit' and perseverance in long-term motivation;

DOI: 10.4324/9781003262923-4

- Compare and contrast the different 'need theories' and how they influence motivation;
- Summarize how to best motivate individuals in an organization;
- Explain the role of 'organizational space' and how it can affect motivation in the creative process.

Figure 4.1 Your attitude not only shapes how you view your day or your circumstances, but is directly related to how happy you are with your job as well! Photo credit: Aysezgicmeli / Shutterstock.com

INTRODUCTION

Attitude is everything

As seen in a range of studies (Maynard & Parfyonova, 2013; Vough & Caza, 2017), attitude affects every aspect of success, from the possibility of promotion to how people treat you on a day-to-day basis. The perception people form and their reactions to those perceptions can make the difference between whether you love what you do or hate what you do, and whether people even want to be around you. If you come to work with a smile on your face and a willingness to embrace challenges, you will be welcomed. People will *want* to work with you. If you come in with a negative or defeatist attitude, you will be avoided or worse yet 'managed out' (i.e. made redundant or fired!). There are virtuous and vicious circles in the workforce, and your own positivity can inspire positivity in others (virtuous circle), or your own negativity can encourage negativity in others (vicious circle).

A person's attitude is 'a relatively enduring organization of beliefs, feelings, and behavioural tendencies' towards his or her environment (Hogg & Vaughan, 2005, p. 150). It can be influenced by a number of factors, beginning with who they are, how they've been raised and the values, goals or social interactions that shape their perspectives (Albarracin & Shavitt, 2018). Inherent dispositions and cultural influences can also affect how we feel. In the workplace, an employee's attitude can be determined by how they perceive and feel about the work they are doing (Saari & Judge, 2004), the feedback they receive from supervisors, as well as the management style and emotional intelligence of the organization's leaders (Trofimov *et al.*, 2019). As you would expect, a positive attitude can often be linked to job satisfaction whereas a negative attitude is often associated with job dissatisfaction that leads to deviant behaviours (Reisel *et al.*, 2010).

The first half of this chapter explores the attitudes we formulate in the workplace and how a deeper understanding allows us to better manage people in the workplace to achieve objectives. The latter half of the chapter will focus on what motivates employees before discussing best practices in keeping oneself and one's team motivated in their work. We will draw on a range of motivational theories.

JOB SATISFACTION AT CIRQUE DU SOLEIL

Cirque du Soleil is a great company to study from a human resources perspective because all the employees have run off to join the circus! It attracts staff who don't want to work in a stodgy, bureaucratic environment, but in an exciting, creative one. So how does the company keep its workforce satisfied? In findings that have relevance to both satisfaction and motivation, the creative artists at Cirque, while appreciating things like a competitive salary, excellent food and travel, were most 'set on fire' and committed to the organization by factors such as: receiving opportunities for creative professional development, such as learning from famous clown artists; being allowed to participate in the creative and technical development of their acts; being given the time, resources and encouragement to take pride in their workmanship and perfect their craft; being part of a culture that celebrates and focuses on creativity and excellence; and receiving appreciation and recognition for a job well done. These factors are identified within the company as contributing to staff satisfaction and motivation (DeLong & Vijayaraghavan, 2002).

INFLUENCES ON ATTITUDE FORMATION

ABC model

Attitudes exercise a vast influence on behaviour, so much so that the two are often closely linked (Ajzen & Fishbein, 2005). How an individual perceives his or her situation, and the attitudes formed because of these perceptions, will determine how the employee ultimately responds. This is termed the 'theory of consistency', in that we expect people's behaviour to be consistent with their attitudes (McLeod, 2014). In the workplace, this can have an impact on the performance of employees and the interaction they have with one another. For example, if an employee has a positive attitude towards others in the workplace, you would generally expect them to treat others with respect and be a positive influence on them. If an employee has a negative attitude towards events or others in the workplace, you would likely expect them to behave in a manner that is off-putting or counterproductive to the organization's goals. In order to better understand attitudes, psychologists developed the 'ABC Model of Attitudes' (Figure 4.2), which represents three components that make up a person's attitude. 'A' embodies the 'Affective' component; 'B' signifies the 'Behavioural'; and 'C' stands for 'Cognitive'. So, what does this all mean and how does this impact what you do at work?

All attitudes contain these three components, but which component is the most significant can vary (Figure 4.3).

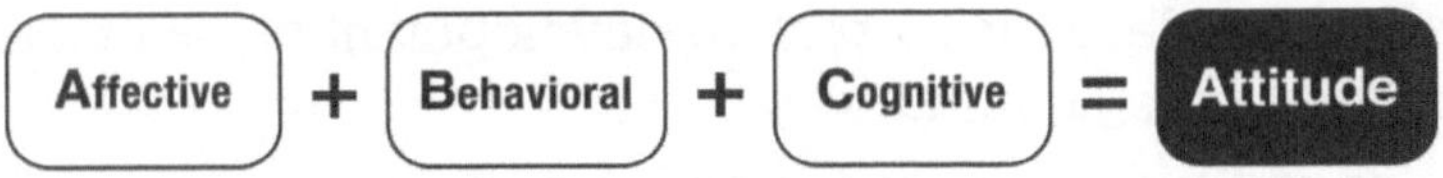

Figure 4.2 ABC model of attitudes: Emotions, behaviour and beliefs all contribute to your attitude.

Component	Where Does the Attitude Come From?	What is it?	Example
A Affective	Emotionally Based	Can be controversial, based on a person's values	*I love that new song you just played me, it has a great feel to it.*
B Behavioral	An Individual's Behavior	How someone behaves towards an attitude object	*I'd love to sign that to a deal with our company, I know just the artist looking for something like this.*
C Cognitive	Thoughts or Beliefs	Based on your beliefs	*The song exhibits characteristics that seem related to commercial success.*

Figure 4.3 The above examples demonstrate how each component of the model may alter your thinking and perspective.

Adapted from: ABC Model (Ellis, 1991).

When you are said to have an attitude based on an affective component, it is considered to be emotionally based. When someone responds with an 'I like it when …' or 'I hate it that …', it is an emotionally laden response and often based on an individual's value system. This can result in conflict and controversy. For example, Jack, a creative manager at a music publishing company, acknowledges his preference for a song, 'I love that chorus, it has the right hook and creates a beautiful sense of imagery'. His attitude towards the song is based on an affective component. We encounter affective-influenced attitudes every day in the creative industries that often drive talent selection decisions, creative development decisions and other larger strategic initiatives.

When an individual bases his or her attitude on a 'behavioural' component, it influences the way the individual acts or behaves. In the case of our creative manager's (Jack's) attitude towards the song we just mentioned, since he felt that he was dealing with a good song, he may try to offer this songwriter a contract to try and promote it. His behaviour is being dictated by his attitude about the song, therefore aligning with the 'behavioural' component of the model.

When an employee's thoughts or beliefs drive their attitude (an intellectual response, not emotional), it involves the 'cognitive' aspect of the model. We have already discussed how Jack felt about the new song and his willingness to sign a deal with that songwriter, but he may have developed beliefs, more intellectual and analytical in nature, that songs with certain characteristics have a higher chance of commercial success than others.

ATTITUDES AND THE CREATIVE INDUSTRIES

The attitudes we carry into the workplace can also be influenced by industry trends. Decreases in revenue and industry contraction can create uncertainty and insecurity. As an employee, uncertainty over the future influences how you perceive the value of your work and how you think your managers perceive it. It can be a challenge to build employee commitment in an environment facing economic pressures, especially those centred on the subjective nature of creative work. Such an environment can produce a whirlwind of employee attitudes and behaviours that are difficult to corral while attempting to provide leadership and direction.

Film production, for example, can be a hot bed of crazy 'what if' scenarios that can influence attitudes along the way. Cast injuries or illnesses, equipment malfunctions, and even threats of terrorism can slow or halt a production and influence how risk is perceived. These uncertainties create environments of high stress that can often challenge people's attitudes and motivation towards the work they are doing. If they fall out of line with company expectations or create hostile or toxic work environments, management must be able to manage through or persuade workers to uphold attitudes that are favourable to productivity. One thing that managers often seek to uncover is whether employees are satisfied with their jobs or whether they are ready to quit. This can often be determined through their attitude toward the work, the employees and the organization.

ATTITUDES TOWARDS RISK AND MANAGING FAILURE

When dealing with an excess of supply of creative products and challenging experiences typical of the creative and cultural industries, we must be able to manage risk and uncertainty. Needing to be flexible, innovative and ideas-driven are hallmarks of these organizations. Individuals working in them will generally have a different attitude towards risk and a higher tolerance for taking on risk (Banks *et al.*, 2000; Carr, 2009). This attitude influences in two ways; either through dealing directly with high-risk projects or by social learning and imitating others (Abun *et al.*, 2021; Olson & Fazio, 2001; Zimbardo & Leippe, 1991). We will discuss these in turn.

Attitudes can be formed either through directly experiencing something or by indirect influence, such as observing others. When we form an attitude through direct experience, it tends to be more strongly held, and not as easily influenced by change or other types of persuasion (Fazio & Zanna, 1981; Glasman & Albarracín, 2006). Let us look at attitudes within creative workplaces that have arisen from the brutal reality of watching projects live and die. In Chapter 1, Shae Constantine, a former creative and marketing head at Sony Music Entertainment and Warner Music described belief building as an important skill in creative organizations in advocating and fighting for projects.

His comments illustrate two points of relevance to this chapter. The first is that attitudes which are borne of direct experience on projects living and dying before one's eyes are passionately held. It also shows the 'virtuous circle' notion that if your manager 'radiates belief' and gives his or her all to the project, this will inspire others to do the same, while helping shape positive workplace attitudes which increase the chances of success.

When attitudes are learned socially, they are often picked up through observing the behaviours of others and imitating them

(Rosenthal & Zimmerman, 2014; Zimbardo & Leippe, 1991). For example, reflect for a moment about the new BTS release or the new *Avengers* movie. Is your enthusiasm coming from a genuine place or are you riding a wave of social and public opinion that these products must be great if everyone else is getting involved? Or conversely, do you 'thumb your nose' at anything that is popular, since it is created for mass audience appeal rather than being grounded in authentic artistic endeavour? Social learning does not have to be reinforced to be learned (Zimbardo & Leippe, 1991), but it must come from a trustworthy or credible source to the person who adopts it in order for them to see the value of it and mimic it. If that enthusiasm (or lack thereof) for the new BTS single comes from an eight-year-old girl, and you are a mid-twenties male, there is a good chance that you will approach that enthusiasm with caution.

The attitudes that we form towards risk in the creative and cultural industries are rooted in the 'belief' that the products and experiences being offered will be successful, while attempts at risk mitigation are sought by seeking advice or expertise from 'trusted' advisors or networks. Soliciting expert advice and feedback from other professionals that we trust helps to move forward product decisions in the hope of reducing uncertainty. Belief, trust and risk are embedded within the unique working relationships in the creative and cultural industries (Banks *et al.*, 2000; Cattani *et al.*, 2015) and facilitated by social networks.

ATTITUDES TOWARDS THE PRODUCT YOU CREATE

Those who manage or represent artists, musicians, arrangers, cartoonists and other 'creators' are constantly needing to manage the attitudes and the behaviours that accompany them, especially when there is enormous personal and ego investment by those who create the products we sell (Caves, 2000). As we established in Chapter 1, these creative products are closely connected to the meaning of the creator's life; they often see these products as an extension of who they are as a person. With that comes self-imposed personal pressures to continue delivering a high level of creative output on a consistent basis. As we also established in Chapter 3, the personality of the creative individual in these circumstances can often lead to self-doubt. This self-doubt can be seen in artists as they attempt to 'commercialize' what they create. A gap can emerge between what they believe to be the most creative, authentic, high-quality work they can create, versus what may stand the highest chance of commercial success. This can create 'cognitive dissonance' within the creative, where two beliefs and aspirations collide. This can be seen quite often in pop music. Pushing artists into creative directions with which they are uncomfortable is problematic, because it is the artist who needs to 'pull it off' as the advocate and spokesperson for the project. It is possible that with inauthentic projects, the artist becomes damaged no matter whether the project succeeds or fails. They become damaged if it is successful by having to live a lie, and they become damaged if it is unsuccessful by being associated with failure. As one former president of a major label observed:

> I've seen artists pushed into things before, where they end up not liking the record very much, you know, and that's really a shame. And what's really a shame is if you're pushed into a crossover record as an artist, then the real damage can be that if it does sell like crazy, and you hate it, then you live with it forever as your big moment, and then if it doesn't sell, then it's just kind of thrown aside, but then it can hurt your career, too.
>
> (Saintilan, 2019)

Projecting a public image is something an artist should develop carefully, as they may end up living with it for a long time. From a creative organization point of view, ignoring the artist's voice in the process can result in problems arising further down the line. This was specifically the case for a Nashville-based female pop artist who recently signed a record deal. Her first album captured authentically who she felt she was as an artist, with songs that spoke to her life experiences. Her 'brand' was 'down-home' and sweet, yet flirted with a sense of rebellion and cutting edge. The album was a moderate regional success, but kept true to her writing and image as an artist. With the release of her second album, the record label felt they needed to push the boundaries of this image, so they moved her to Los Angeles and went all-in to compete in the solo pop female market. Given the intensity and frenetic pace of the industry, her career became a whirlwind of activity – consistently putting her at odds with who she was as an artist and what the day-to-day expectations would be of her. She was being asked to dress in ways that she felt were inappropriate and produce videos that portrayed her as scandalous and sexual. The consistent tension she was feeling between her artistic intentions and commercial exploitation created self-doubt and a negative attitude towards what she was doing. So how do you best manage this tension? We will explore options below.

ATTITUDES TOWARDS CRITICISM

The creative and cultural industries open themselves up for criticism in a way seen in few industries. Historically, entertainment promoters have invited critics to criticize their work, giving them free tickets and samples. The social media world has only intensified this in ways that can be spiteful. One major label vice president described the dangers of social media criticism for artists:

> It is very useful to stick a cup to the internet and listen to the chatter at the aggregate level, and we've spent a lot of time looking at buzz metrics, so looking at what the wider patterns in the data tell you about where something is in the public sentiment or not. Looking at specific comments is a hiding to nowhere, and then doing things based on those comments, for every one person you please, 20 trolls pop up... and it's a very hurtful and painful process for an artist. I mean I see it, and it's horrible.
>
> (Saintilan, 2019)

Managers in the creative industries need to manage criticism, to know when to take it on board, and when to quarantine and protect the creative team. What might be sport for a social media troll, can be highly personal, and a life's work for a creative artist. If the criticism is unproductive and can't be shielded, how can it be framed differently, or contextualized for the creative team, what kind of emotional support can be provided, and what are the best ways to manage them through it?

As we will see in the chapter on conflict, criticism which is constructive and well intentioned is designed to help the creative team get better, aspire to higher standards and improve their craft. It is actually a gift, because its application is designed to yield positive outcomes. Yet in an area as subjective and personal as creative work, it will often be perceived as a hurtful attack on the creative personnel involved.

SOURCES OF JOB SATISFACTION, COMMITMENT AND MOTIVATION

How employees feel about their job has long been studied by organizational behavioural theorists (Ealias & George, 2012; Pinder, 2014) and is a reflection of their attitude towards their work and organization (Imran *et al.*, 2014; Saari & Judge, 2004). Job satisfaction can be defined as the level of contentment employees feel about their work, which can affect their performance (Spector, 1997).

A survey conducted by Major Players, a creative recruiting firm in the United Kingdom, asked their clientele how they and their employees in the creative industry felt about their jobs and the places they worked. They found that

> 75% think stimulating work and having a good atmosphere in the office is more important than getting paid a high salary; an overwhelming 60% don't feel overworked at all; the majority of respondents feel that they are fairly remunerated for the job they do, with scarcely 20% feeling strongly that they are undervalued in terms of salary.
>
> (Iannella, 2010, p. 1)

This provides a positive indication that many individuals who work in the creative and cultural industries are satisfied with the jobs they are doing and the companies they are working for, although care should be exercised generalizing this study to post-pandemic creative and cultural industry firms in all countries. Although work hours per week tend to be high for jobs in the creative and cultural industries (Vogt, 2007), the fact that the majority of respondents in the Major Players survey didn't feel overworked may be due to the enjoyment they find in the work they do. For many of them, their 'work' feels more like a glorified hobby.

Job satisfaction can be influenced by a number of factors, such as: a person's ability to do a job well or complete the required tasks; the level of communication within an organization; the way management treats its employees through supervision policies and the amount of control and autonomy it gives them; their relationships with co-workers; their current pay; the nature of their work; and opportunities for employment (Rast & Tourani, 2012).

SUPERVISION AND PERCEIVED CONTROL

As discussed in Chapter 1, many employees desire autonomy in their work and the ability to be involved in the decision-making process. This has been found to be important in design work (Spector, 1986), but this is especially the case for creative individuals. Having the freedom to create without feeling as if someone is constantly checking your work is highly valued among creative employees (Rast & Tourani, 2012).

CO-WORKERS AND JOB SATISFACTION

Job satisfaction is also linked to the relationships you have with co-workers. It is often said that 'it is not the job you do, but the people you work with' that make the difference. A feeling of camaraderie and belonging is held in high regard for those in the workplace, especially given the prominence relationships and networks play in the creative industries (Rast & Tourani, 2012). Often the informal interpersonal fit and compatibility, where you have shared interests and enthusiasms and can relate to someone personally, proves more important to securing entry level positions than technical skills. Despite corporate models that favour defining tight specifications and recruiting people who tick all the boxes, employers in the creative industries can be more relaxed about hiring the 'person' and not the experience or educational training (particularly for early career positions). Thus, to secure employment, it is advisable to not only learn how certain parts of an industry work through internships and mentorships, it is also critically important to learn the professional and informal etiquette found within the company and/or creative industry in which you wish to work. Learning these skills and developing the appropriate behaviours early on will only better prepare you to win the ongoing support and confidence of co-workers as you develop your career.

PRESENT PAY

Although the relationship between pay and job satisfaction has been highly researched (Rast & Tourani, 2012), the findings have proved controversial (Robbins & Judge, 2022). There is some evidence of a positive correlation between what an individual gets paid and how satisfied they are with their work, but it isn't as strong as one might initially believe. Many professionals believe that you might be better off weighing other factors in your job search, apart from pay. 'Interesting work' or 'opportunities to learn' may contribute more towards some people's satisfaction than high salaries. This will be covered further in the section on motivation, under 'intrinsic' and 'extrinsic' motivators.

NATURE OF WORK

If you enjoy the nature of the work you do, you are likely to be more satisfied with your work situation. Those who seek employment in the creative sector are often presumed to seek 'self-actualization' and 'self-realization' at work. Work in the creative industries is often ranked by quality level, reputation and market value. Fashions and trends that dictate success are 'talent' driven, where those who experience initial success also experience a steep learning curve and further opportunities for success (Menger, 2015). However, this does not necessarily equate to how you are compensated through your pay. Salaries and 'talent' levels aren't always aligned.

The very nature of creative work is often seen as a 'shared ethos between work and life' (Menger, 2015, p. 1). The lines can blur between what he or she considers 'work' and a 'hobby'. In some circumstances artists discover a true passion for what they do and have figured out ways to get paid for it. Unfortunately, this can also have an undesired effect for the creator. Often what they loved about their craft turns into relentless commercial and production pressure, where it becomes more 'work' than pleasure.

OPPORTUNITIES FOR PROMOTION

When an employee feels that there are opportunities for promotion, they tend to show more positive feelings towards their job and employer. They become motivated to do their best work knowing that at some point it will be recognized and subsequently rewarded when the time is right. Employees who feel there is little or no room to learn and grow within their organization are less likely to commit as fully as they could. As managers, making sure that these opportunities exist should be a priority.

Attitude and a culture of winning

In life, attitude is everything, at Big Machine a winning attitude is essential ...

Unlike any other company on Nashville's iconic Music Row, Big Machine Label Group (BMLG) (Figure 4.4) has made a name for itself with some of the world's top selling recording artists. Since its beginnings in 2005, Scott Borchetta, the company CEO, has grown the label group from 13 employees to over 100. Working closely with Scott, Chief Operating Officer (COO and one of the company's original employees), Andrew Kautz oversees all operations of the label – spearheading the company's financial, legal, administrative and business development processes. Big Machine Label Group is one of the largest independent record labels across all genres. Home to some of the world's top recording artists, Rascal Flatts, Cheryl Crow, Tim McGraw and many others, Big Machine has developed a reputation and culture unique to the 'row'.

BIG MACHINE LABEL GROUP

Figure 4.4 Big Machine Label Group: Reprinted by permission, Nashville, Tennessee, USA.

Since its inception, Scott has fostered a strong 'winning culture'. A passion for success and a competitive drive has permeated through the organization while shaping the attitudes of its employees. Here, employees are often known as 'machinists' and are commonly greeted with 'welcome to the machine', where 'precision' and being a 'specialist' vs. a 'generalist' is the expectation. Stemming from Scott's passion for racing, these metaphoric mantras speak to the intentional focus on quality, while providing a sense of team and belonging.

Over the years, Scott and Andrew have purposely developed a structure with limited middle management and a philosophy of independence. They don't micro-manage and are intentionally not corporate. They don't have a long list of policies that might stifle creativity and innovation, rather they continue to rely on the espoused values of hard work, a winning attitude and sense of purpose to shape behaviour. This mentality of independence drives autonomy. 'Everyone has their lane' and that approach enables employees to have a great deal of flexibility and leeway in doing their job. Of course, at times people swerve or change lanes on occasion. This is when it's critical to quickly establish the rule of the road and get everyone back in the right lane, to ensure a focused mission.

Developed over the years, this strong culture lends itself to a natural 'attrition' of employees who need a lot of direction. Autonomy is expected ... and it's important that employees perceive a critique of their work as constructive and an opportunity to improve, not as a negative. This kind of environment can only work with a self-confident employee and a 'get-it-done' attitude. A culture of intensity and passion towards a common desire to win is at the heart of Big Machine's success. And although this type of attitude is critical for any employee at the label, it is also important for leadership to recognize the team when it 'has gotten it done'. At Big Machine, celebrations of that success are important, whether it's a #1 party or celebrating their artists and staff during CMA (Country Music Association) or Grammy week. It is an opportunity to pay tribute and recognize everyone who has played a part in the success of the organization. Although some positions are more public than others, it is always a delicate balance of 'who gets the light shined on them' and it is important for the leaders to especially recognize outliers, while also acknowledging the entirety of the team's efforts that contribute to the success. Fostering a strong sense of purpose and teamwork is important in contributing to employees feeling good about their work and having a positive attitude and influence every day.

When it comes to organizational citizenship, it is expected that all employees feel compelled to go above and beyond. The strong culture shapes this behaviour and it runs deep. Employees are purposefully selected and remain dedicated at Big Machine, as there has been very little attrition over the past 12 years. As Andrew recalls, 'I can count on one hand the number of people we've had to displace since we opened our doors'. It's a testament to the attitudes that Big Machine's employees bring to the workplace and the strong virtuous cycle of positivity that is reinforced by its culture. Being satisfied with your work and fostering a positive attitude starts with finding the right people. Big Machine's focus has always been on mission-focused versus money-focused employees. If money is the most important thing to an employee, Big Machine is probably not the right place for them. Whether employees or artists, they've always kept their focus on success and in doing so the money follows. Success allows them to attract employees and artists focused on the right things internally and artistically.

Discussion questions

1 Knowing what can drive employees to feel positively about their jobs, what specifically are BMLG's leaders doing to foster a culture of citizenship?

2 Is this culture and attitude of winning one that can be successfully replicated across any creative organization? Why or why not?
3 How do organizational rituals such as #1 parties or celebrating successes during CMA and Grammy week contribute to workplace satisfaction? Why is this so important in the creative industries?

Figure 4.5 A person's motivation can often depend on the environment they work in and the people they work with. Photo credit: Dean Drobot / Shutterstock.com

MOTIVATION AND COMMITMENT TO YOUR CRAFT AND THE CREATIVE ORGANIZATION

Many creative workers struggle with a lack of ambition and motivation in the workplace. When we are dependent on external sources of motivation to remain productive, it can be an uneven source of inspiration, as the workplace is a dynamic environment that will throw at us both motivating and demotivating experiences. As managers, it is important to understand what drives our employees and what behaviours may derail progress for people or cause them to lose sight of the organization's goals. This can be especially important as we grapple with the personality characteristics of creative people that we discussed in Chapter 3. Knowing what motivates them to create and develop new and novel ideas, concepts, products and experiences will help you as a future manager and leader of creative and cultural organizations to maintain a productive, desirable place of work.

MOTIVATION IN THE WORKPLACE

Motivation is a force that influences people to act or not act on something and helps to explain why we do things (Lai, 2011). These influences may come from internal drives or desires, external influences, or as a result of a process. In organizations, motivation is often influenced by senior leadership or management and is often directed towards completing tasks that are in-line with the organization's goals. However, it can also be driven by a personal identification with the mission of the organization or an intrinsic love of the creative project workers are developing. Keeping employees motivated and 'lighting the fire' within them has long been a challenge for managers in organizations. When employees are unmotivated, they are more likely to miss work, leave the organization or put in as little effort as possible to get by (Amabile, 1996). In the uncertain and turbulent environment of the creative industries, motivation in organizations can be fleeting. For creative individuals, especially for those who work independently or are self-employed, it can be challenging to keep their 'eye on the ball'. People like Sarah must rely much more on intrinsic factors, drawing motivation from within to keep themselves focused when deadlines need to be self-imposed. The following sections will explore different theories related to motivation that have proved useful in studying human behaviour in organizations. Like previous concepts, we will also apply these theories to creative workers, in terms of overcoming motivational barriers to help them realise their full creative potential.

INTERNAL (OR 'INTRINSIC') MOTIVATION

Intrinsic motivation is an internal state that impels one to act towards achieving a certain goal (Ryan & Deci, 2000). It can involve the natural human propensity to learn. Earlier in the chapter we saw that creative artists at Cirque du Soleil were most 'set on fire' and committed to the organization by factors such as: receiving opportunities for creative professional development, like learning from famous clown artists; being allowed to participate in the creative and technical development of their acts; being given the time, resources and encouragement to take pride in their workmanship and perfect their craft; being part of a culture that celebrates and focuses on creativity and excellence; and receiving appreciation and recognition for a job well done (DeLong & Vijayaraghavan, 2002). These are all 'intrinsic' motivators because we find our own enjoyment in the work through learning and a sense of accomplishment.

The main characteristics in intrinsic motivation are self-determination, competence, task involvement, curiosity, enjoyment and interest (Amabile *et al.*, 1994). These qualities are often found in the independent artistic community. Artists, sculptors and photographers are often internally driven to achieve the highest standards in their craft, knowing they must develop a level of competence to remain competitive. Often the economic support for their work is meagre and sporadic, which drives them to create for more personal reasons. Their love and curiosity for their work and the interest and enjoyment they find in practising it sustains them over time, as opposed to external or outside forces that may encourage them to create (Stohs, 1992). In order for these fine artists to hone their skills with limited external incentive, they must be driven by an internal passion and desire for their craft. The 'artist' in this sense is motivated by the need to achieve self-fulfilment through their creativity. The work has personal value as self-expression; its value doesn't just arise from the economic or functional utility that their work may create (Hirschman, 1983).

EXTERNAL (OR 'EXTRINSIC') MOTIVATION

Extrinsic motivation is behaviour driven by external rewards. It may be influenced by the need to be competitively successful or recognized. It may be driven by the pursuit of money or other tangible incentives. Or it may be an external force that constrains one's behaviour, such as a fear of punishment or an unwanted outcome (Amabile *et al.*, 1994). External incentives that may drive an individual include a salary, a bonus, a commission owed to an agent, a record contract, an award or even achieving a chart position.

In the creative industries, the long hours and hard work put in by many employees are often driven by an internal passion for the product they find themselves assisting in producing and distributing to the market. Often, coordinators, assistants and other support staff are driven less by the tasks they must perform day-to-day, and more by the external rewards they receive through this work. The 'sexiness' that often draws people to these industries comes through associating and working with well-known artists, actors and musicians. Supporting acts who influence popular culture, being publicly associated with the mission of a non-profit organization, or even being able to attend '#1 parties', release shows, award ceremonies, screenings and showcases can, for some people, be better motivators than achieving a firm's financial goals.

Perseverance and the concept of 'grit'

Do you think you have what it takes to succeed? To develop your craft over 'the long haul'? To sustain the ups and downs of cultural trends? To weather constant evaluation and criticism such as regular assessment by executives and managers of whether your 'product' is relevant and currently marketable?

Do you have what it takes to succeed as a manager? Leading, confronting and motivating the creative to be innovative and productive can have its rewards, but is also not without its challenges. Can you endure the instability of working with the creative and the process of creation?

How we tackle these 'longer-term' motivational challenges has been at the forefront of recent studies. Angela Duckworth, through her experiences as an educator and psychologist, was struck by the underperformance of some of her students with high IQs, and the talent and achievement of others with lower IQs. She looked more deeply into it and found that success came down to a student's 'GRIT' factor (Duckworth *et al.*, 2007).

Grit is perseverance and the passion for long-term goals, and is characterized by your desire to stick with your future, for years, not simply to get through the next task (Duckworth *et al.*, 2007; Duckworth & Quinn, 2009). It's looking at how you stay motivated for the long haul. Talent, or measures such as IQ, don't necessarily make a person 'gritty'. These phenomena are unrelated or even inversely related, but grit is strongly correlated with the personality trait of conscientiousness (Duckworth *et al.*, 2007). Since we know that many creative individuals tend to rate lower in conscientiousness on the 'Big Five' (George & Zhou, 2001; Gillespie & Myors, 2000), we can see this perseverance shine through in others as they 'grind' their way to success and recognition, even though their creativity level may not be as high. It is the ballerina who decides to train eight hours a day with a major company while finishing high school by taking online courses. She auditions every weekend for a chance at another 'intensive' the following year in the hope of one day making the company. It is this 'grit' that allows her to work hard and make her aspirations a reality; in the words of Angela Duckworth, 'it is a marathon for her, not a sprint' (Duckworth, 2013). In order to be successful in your career, especially in the creative industries where the environment of uncertainty and subjectivity persists and competition is intense, you must be able to sustain your ambitions through the inevitable adversity that will be encountered. Whether it's the ballerina we just discussed, a classical violinist, a songwriter or a sculptor who is trying to make a living with their talent, they work long and hard to persevere. It is a mindset grounded in the pursuit of growth and development. The ability to learn is not fixed but connected to effort. It involves grit!

NEED THEORIES

Need theories help to identify what motivates people. Some of the most popular examples of these theories are Maslow's Hierarchy of Needs, McClelland's Need Theory and the concept of Theory X and Theory Y, a two-factor model that has been developed to look at needs, motivation and job satisfaction. In the following sections, we will take a closer look at these theories, compare and contrast them, and discuss how they can help to manage or improve motivation in the creative workplace.

MASLOW'S HIERARCHY OF NEEDS

Maslow's Hierarchy of Needs was developed in the 1940s and 1950s, but remains relevant today in understanding personal motivation in the context of management training. Abraham Maslow developed this model to describe the different stages of development that people go through in life. Its increasing importance in management training and consultancy over the years has helped leaders to develop employee potential while pursuing organizational goals.

Maslow's Hierarchy depicts each of our needs, broken down into five categories that help to explain what motivates us.

Physiological

The hierarchy begins with our basic survival needs (physiological needs). This includes our motivations for water, sleep, food and oxygen, and even sex as a fundamental procreation need. These are the needs we must meet to satisfy our most fundamental drives and even to continue to exist.

Safety needs

The second step in the hierarchy is our need for safety. These needs include protection, security, order, laws or morality. In practical terms in the context of organizational behaviour, it is our need for employment so we can support our families and own property, which in turn provides a safe and secure home to go to at the end of the day.

Belongingness and love

Once we feel safe, we are typically motivated to meet the need of belonging, to be loved. We may seek romantic relationships with others or join groups with similar interests. Families, friends, fraternities or sororities all help us to feel as if we are part of a group and have a place where we belong.

Esteem

The fourth step within Maslow's hierarchy of needs is esteem. When we develop high self-esteem, we feel comfortable enough to be on our own and seek independence, achievement, status, prestige or respect from others. We have found a place in which we are comfortable and will build the confidence necessary to begin managing or leading others. This is the first step in what Maslow considered to be 'higher-order' needs.

Self-actualization

The original and final 'higher-order' need within Maslow's hierarchy is self-actualization. Only when all other needs have been met are we able to free our minds to seek self-fulfilment, purpose and realize our own personal potential. Maslow believed that being fundamentally aware of who we are and what we can contribute through our own potential, can only happen through honest self-assessment and having trust in oneself (Shostrom, 1968).

Maslow believed that each need must be met before someone will be motivated or concerned about reaching a higher-order need. This particular contention has been the subject of some debate, however (Rouse, 2004). The complexity of the human condition does suggest that our motivation to acquire these needs may be less rigid and we may be concerned about more than one at any given moment. Someone who is motivated to achieve a higher-order need may also be simultaneously concerned about a lower-order need, but not dominantly so. For example, if you are a self-actualizer, you will also be concerned about eating and sleeping. The fluidity of moving between steps in the hierarchy is part of our life experience.

MCGREGOR'S THEORY X AND THEORY Y

Douglas McGregor at the MIT Sloan School of Management developed another prominent set of theories of motivation in the 1960s called Theory X and Theory Y. These theories look at how managers can better perceive the motivations behind a worker's behaviour and adjust their management styles to be more effective (McGregor, 1960). Note the focus of these theories is on the manager's assumptions about employees, not the employee's views on motivation.

Theory X

Theory X managers assume that workers generally dislike work and require a more authoritative supervisory style to keep them on task. The assumption is that employees are more motivated by lower-order needs in Maslow's hierarchy. Theory X managers believe employees try to avoid responsibility and need to be told what to do regularly. Incentives such as fear of punishment may be required. McGregor recognized that this perspective tends to be in the minority (McGregor, 1960).

Theory Y

In contrast, Theory Y managers assume that workers are self-motivated and happy to work. It is a more trusting and optimistic perspective on human nature and more aligned with the pursuit of higher-order needs in Maslow's hierarchy, including self-actualization. Theory Y managers assume that employees wish to be creative and active participants in the workplace, and will benefit from a participative and inclusive supervisory style. They assume employees will respond positively to trust, freedom and autonomy.

MCCLELLAND'S NEED THEORY

McClelland's Need Theory, otherwise known as 'three-need' theory, proposes that people develop needs over time and are motivated by their life experiences (Steers *et al.*, 2004). A person's effectiveness in the workplace is influenced by these three needs:

Achievement

People with a high need for achievement look to challenging goals and a standard of excellence (McClelland, 1971). They love to set benchmarks for themselves and receive feedback along the way while seeking constant improvement (Nelson & Quick, 2015). They need less supervision and are also motivated by Maslow's higher-order needs.

Affiliation

People with a high need for affiliation value relationships and seek acceptance. They love personal interaction, prefer not to cause conflict and will more easily conform to organizational norms.

Power

People who are in need of power will seek it through either individual (personal) or institutional (social) means. The need for individual power is achieved through managing others, and they may seek to influence in ways that benefit them personally. Those who seek institutional power engage with others in the pursuit of organizational goals. They use their power to achieve goals greater than themselves and not for personal gain (Nelson & Quick, 2015).

McClelland's theory, although broader in scope than McGregor's Theory X and Theory Y, or Maslow's Hierarchy of Needs, is better able to account for individual motivations as they relate to power acquisition and use. Power and political skill – ways in which we attempt to influence others through non-authoritative means – will be discussed in greater depth in Chapter 8.

HERZBERG'S TWO-FACTOR THEORY

Yet another prominent theorist who developed a model explaining motivation in work was Frederick Herzberg. Herzberg looked at the experiences of employees and related them to lower and higher order needs and job satisfaction. When he asked employees about what makes them dissatisfied with work, many of the respondents listed things such as supervision, salary, status, security and working conditions. He termed these 'hygiene factors'. Hygiene factors are work conditions that generate dissatisfaction due to discomfort or pain. When employees were asked about what satisfies them, they listed things such as achievement, recognition, responsibility, possibilities for advancement and growth, and work itself. He termed these 'motivation factors'. Motivation factors are work conditions that satisfy the need for psychological growth (Nelson & Quick, 2015). Of the two, hygiene factors can only bring an employee to a level of 'no dissatisfaction'. They won't necessarily light a bonfire within them, but they do fulfil their lower-order needs. Herzberg found that to motivate employees, managers should focus on the motivation factors such as providing opportunities for professional growth and development.

MOTIVATING EMPLOYEES IN CREATIVE ORGANIZATIONS

Why are these theories important when managing people in organizations in general, and in particular in the creative and cultural industries? Keeping your employees on task is especially challenging in an industry that is experiencing constant flux and restructuring. Changing reward systems, work roles and responsibilities, as well as often limited feedback systems (Amabile, 1996) all contribute to the challenges of keeping employees motivated. The creative and cultural industries also lie at the heart of the knowledge economy where meaning in the work is more important than efficiency.

MOTIVATING THE CREATIVE INDIVIDUAL

Motivating the creative individual or fostering an environment of productive creativity has caught the attention of researchers in recent years. Empowering employees through appropriate, non-authoritative leadership can have a positive impact on employees' perceptions of autonomy and foster the intrinsic motivation that powers the creative process (Fischer *et al.*, 2019). This can come in complete contrast to the brutal extrinsic motivators that drive the creative and cultural industries in terms of sales, awards and other marks of achievement. To commercialize and incentivize creative work through economic means can be a powerful extrinsic motivational tool, either for good or bad. But it contrasts with the intrinsic motivation that drives many creative people. We will explore each in turn, the positive and limiting aspects of both intrinsic and extrinsic motivational tools on creativity and those who 'create'.

INTRINSIC AND EXTRINSIC MOTIVATIONAL STRATEGIES

Having 'connection to the product' and a 'need for autonomy', the artist or creator is intimately connected through self-expression to the product they create. As we previously established, intrinsic motivation comes from within, an internal state that drives you to accomplish what you are seeking. Many artists pursue authenticity and search for creative work that is 'true to the heart'. When creative people create for the love of what they do, driven by an internal state, their work tends to be perceived as more creative and less mundane (Amabile, 1985). This is what Amabile calls the 'Intrinsic Motivation Principle of Creativity'. When people are motivated by the personal enjoyment of the creative process (for artists, musicians and dancers) or the strong desire to learn something new or solve a problem (for those who manage them and other employees), it often comes from a drive or passion within them.

This can be a challenge for managers who are responsible for the creative process or for fostering an atmosphere of creativity and innovation in the firm. How do you motivate a person who does their best work when driven internally to do so within an industry that customarily rewards their work through external factors? Conflict can arise when the company is focused on the profitability and return on investment, while the creator is focused on the authentic self-expression of the creative output.

This can certainly be challenging for managers and intermediaries, but for the creator this speaks to Cave's (2000) 'art for art's sake' concept. 'Art for art's sake' involves the creation of art for its own sake, free from any other purpose. Artisans who create products or services often care deeply about what they create. Because it is their creation, *meaning* becomes more innate, *ownership* is natural and *identity* is ingrained. To understand what motivates the creator, you must see the value of their work through their eyes. Why have they created what they've created? What meaning or value have they attached to this output? The challenge for managers with regard to this attachment is avoiding false expectations of potential economic value or commercial success for the creator. Because they are the 'creator', they will have the tendency to place greater value on that creation and personally identify with it as an extension of themselves. Therefore, your task as a manager is to assess and maximize its commercial value without diminishing the creator's motivation to create.

'Time is of the essence', yet another of Cave's (2000) creative industries characteristics, demands the need for efficient, dynamic and flexible work teams and an environment that encourages speed and fast response times. Operating within the dynamic and turbulent environment of the creative industries demands a sense of urgency and efficiency, and paradoxically patience and long-term vision for cultural trends and aesthetic preferences. Keeping your creative team motivated yet focused through this uncertainty is critical. Although strong intellectual property laws place a 'ceiling' on rights which encourages timely exploitation, the window of opportunity can run into the decades. Keeping product relevant in spite of evolving tastes and trends requires resilience.

Ultimately, our understanding of motivating the creative person and successfully applying those concepts to the creative process is dependent on the organization itself and its management. It results from having an organizational culture that encourages creativity through: the fair, constructive judgement of ideas; reward and recognition for creative work; mechanisms for developing new ideas; an active flow of ideas; and a shared vision of what the organization is trying to accomplish (Amabile, 1996). Furthermore, having a supervisor who serves as a good work model, who sets goals appropriately, supports the work group, values individual contributions and shows confidence in the group as a whole, will foster a culture of productivity and commitment (Amabile, 1996). It's also important to have a diversely skilled work group in which people communicate well, are open to new ideas, constructively challenge each other's work, trust and help each other, and feel committed to the work they are doing (Amabile, 1996). External support such as access to resources, including funds, materials, facilities and information, will also go a long way to supporting creative and non-creative staff to fulfil their potential.

Creativity and the concept of flow

The concept of 'flow' arose in the work of Csikszentmihalyi, who observed an artist so immersed with painting that, despite fatigue and hunger, he continued until he was finished. When an artist, designer or a top chef is in 'flow' it is comparable to being 'in the zone' and completely lost in the experience. It involves intrinsic motivation as the satisfaction is derived from the work itself, where the feeling of an energized focus is enjoyed throughout the activity (Nakamura & Csikszentmihalyi, 2014).

The concept of flow was found to exist in both work and play settings, which allowed Csikszentmihalyi to explain which conditions lend themselves to the state of 'being in it' (Csikszentmihalyi, 2000). For example, those who were interviewed about being 'in flow' described that the activities were manageable challenges, where feedback on the process and 'adjusting as you go' creates an experience 'that seamlessly unfolds from moment to moment, [as] one enters a subjective state' (Nakamura & Csikszentmihalyi, 2014, p. 90). Csikszentmihalyi went further to describe what these characteristics entail.

Characteristics of flow

- intense and focused concentration on what one is doing in the present moment;
- merging of action and awareness;
- loss of reflective self-consciousness (i.e. loss of awareness of oneself as a social actor);
- a sense that one can control one's actions; that is, a sense that one can in principle deal with the situation because one knows how to respond to whatever arises;
- distortion of temporal experience (typically, a sense that time has passed faster than normal);
- experience of the activity as intrinsically rewarding, such that often the end goal is just an excuse for the process.

Achieving flow is an inherently fragile process and one which is sensitive to imbalances if your skills exceed what is required to do the activity or are not yet developed. If a marimba player is learning a new Bach étude, but has not yet mastered the technical skills needed, she may at first feel challenged, but then may grow anxious and frustrated. If the same marimbist is learning a simple piece of music, she may feel relaxed as it comes easily, but will quickly become bored. These mental shifts that occur can cause a person to stop the activity. Feeling anxious or bored can be a stimulus for the person to adjust their activity so they can then feel flow once again.

Since Csikszentmihalyi's early work, there has been plenty of research of its effects on creativity. Amabile (2005) found that people are not only more creative in flow, but that they also report they are more creative the day after as well. Regularly being in this state could help individuals train themselves to be more creative over time (Kotler, 2014). Furthermore, the Flow Genome Project has been conducting research specifically related to neuroscience. In one particular instance,

> 40 research subjects were presented with an exceptionally tricky brainteaser—the kind that requires a deep creative insight to solve. No one solved it. But when flow was induced artificially through transcranial magnetic stimulation, 23 subjects got the answer right and in record time.
>
> (Kotler, 2014)

So what does this all mean for organizations and encouraging the creative process? Being in this optimal state of consciousness, where you feel and do your best, has led to scientific breakthroughs, sports championships and creative achievements in the arts. It can be one of the largest drivers of innovation and breakthroughs. If you can encourage your songwriters, designers, writers and painters to more consistently engage in flow states, the creative output may lead to innovative products, or new trends in fashion, music or video.

Questions for discussion

1 What is flow and how is it achieved? Have you ever experienced being in a flow state? Describe.
2 Does environment influence whether you are able to experience flow? If so, what kind of environment could you provide to your creative team, artists or writers in order to encourage entering 'flow states'?
3 Provide a specific example of a creative person that you know or are close to. What kind of projects would be appropriate for him or her in order to increase their chances of experiencing flow when working on the project?

SUPPRESSING CREATIVITY: CAUSES OF MOTIVATIONAL PROBLEMS IN THE WORKPLACE

On the other end of the motivation spectrum are activities seen as impediments to creativity (Amabile, 1985). Not only can it be challenging to maintain motivation in the creative organization, but there are barriers that can actually impede it as well. Managers should avoid these to maintain a healthy and productive workplace:

Organizational impediments

These include an organizational culture that impedes creativity through internal political problems, harsh criticism of new ideas, destructive internal competition, and an avoidance of risk or overemphasis on the *status quo*. Political behaviour is prevalent wherever there are groups of people who work closely together. Although managing through the negative impacts of political behaviour will be discussed in greater detail in Chapter 8, it is important to note here that it can have a negative impact on the creative process. Keeping your mind open to new ideas and not being quick to judge or assess, can also aid in keeping the creative process productive. Negative internal competition can be a particular challenge. For example, you often find very competitive environments in major label A&R (Artist and

Repertoire) departments, where managers are often trying to find the 'next big act', not as a team process, but individually. The emphasis that is placed on the 'next big thing' becomes an internal personal agenda. Information isn't shared and often held close to the individual. This creates suspicion among others tasked with the same goal. It erodes trust among co-workers and can impede the creative process in finding new talent for the music company.

Workload pressure

These include extreme time pressures, unrealistic expectations for productivity and distractions from creative work. Although 'time is of the essence' (Caves, 2000) in creative product, it is important to allow the process to happen. Implementing extreme time pressures will no doubt impede and stress the creative process. As we've learned, in order to be creative, creative workers need time and space. They must have the appropriate workspace with limited distractions if you want them to perform in the time-frame the market demands.

Motivation and organizational space in the creative and cultural industries

Nashville songwriters and needs beyond the merely functional

When you speak to a creative person who is making a living from their craft, one of the most important things you will hear them speak about is the 'space' in which they do their work. The importance of workspace as it applies to motivation should not be underestimated, especially for many Nashville songwriters. When 'penning' the next big country song or material to be used in television or film, the need to have a writer's room that is almost spiritual goes a long way towards productivity. While in terms of pure 'functionality' they can work almost anywhere as long as they have their guitar, a pencil and paper, it's the more natural warm feeling of a room that will make them most comfortable and ultimately the most creative and productive.

One such singer-songwriter, Dean Fields, recalls one of the 'saddest places' he ever had to write. '

> It felt so much like a dungeon, the company stuck my co-writer and I in a room that was essentially abandoned office space, nothing on the walls, it was sterile and had such a shitty feel to it. I don't how we got anything written that day.

On the contrary, he and many of his co-writers often find the warmth and natural character of a house the most creatively productive. Couches, chairs, tables and curtains all help to make the songwriter feel 'at home' and more relaxed when doing their work. The feeling of cleanliness, no clutter and a comfortable couch and table to write on goes a long way to making the place 'feel good'. 'It often feels much better when it's someone's house, their personal "professional" space as opposed to a random room in an office somewhere'. Another thing that is often overlooked in the business environment is the use of natural light or, at the very least, warm lights as opposed to incandescent or fluorescent lighting. When this latter type of lighting is used, it can distract artists or create a psychologically oppressive environment. In contrast, 'a window ... you'd be surprised how far a window can go in stimulating the creative mind' (Fields, 2016).

Many of the music publishing companies on legendary 'music row' in Nashville make consistent and regular use of writers' rooms. 'Naturally, when two or three writers are holed up in a small space for an extended period of time, a natural, less pleasant odour can creep in' (Fields, 2016). Making sure these 'distractions' are avoided is also helpful in maintaining focus and motivation for these songwriters. Even the availability of small essentials like coffee, water or tea and even breath mints go a long way in setting the tone for productivity in Nashville writers' rooms and music studios.

Motivating your creative team – Made-In and the desire for 'shared experience'

Made-In Network is a 'video first' media company that 'operates on the belief that creating original content on YouTube is the future of Entertainment' (Grosch, 2016). In broadcasting, OTT refers to watching video or other media programming over a broadband Internet connection rather than through existing cable or satellite providers (Hansell, 2009). Made-In Network is headquartered in Nashville, Tennessee. It has developed strategic partnerships with Google, YouTube and some of the world's greatest creators. The company works alongside some of the world's top consumer brands for custom video integration and other OTT solutions. Made-In is led by entrepreneur and visionary Kevin Grosch, and with a team of more than 20 creative individuals, keeping motivation high is often at the forefront of his thinking.

As is the case for most companies, motivation starts with the hiring process for Kevin. When staffing his team, he looks for smart, driven individuals that are 'seeking more'. He intentionally seeks those who perceive working at Made-In as not just any job, but who are looking to take on a role as an important contributor to the development of creative projects and the long-term growth of the company.

Kevin seeks employees that are motivated by a 'shared work experience' – people who have a desire to be a part of something. He has been purposeful about this concept since stumbling upon it out of necessity early on in the company's existence. Initially he couldn't afford to pay for employee parking in downtown Nashville, which is increasingly costly, so it forced the small team to car pool into work. The unintended outcome of this was that it helped to foster a strong culture that has carried on through the company's growth. The development of 'stories' has built a team that reminisces, 'when we first started, we all had to carpool'. They grabbed coffee and shared stories together, creating a sense of camaraderie and belonging, hallmarks of a strong team. They created a 'shared experience' together, which has provided a 'second home' for many of them. They still joke about 'when they first started' but this sense of togetherness keeps them driven to produce quality programming. Since the early days, this shared work experience has grown more intentional with Quarterly Fun Days, which are inclusive and led by the team. These days are more than just 'forced fun' (although they run the risk of being perceived as such); they allow them to integrate new employees into the culture.

One of the constant challenges that Kevin finds in keeping creative people on task is the classic 'how much freedom to give' versus 'how much direction'. He believes that all people are, or can be, creative in some capacity, and in his view it is incorrect to say that his team is a group of 'creatives'. However, he does believe that individuals who seek employment at Made-In are dedicating their lives to an artistic career and often see their work as an extension of themselves. This mentality relates back to Caves (2000) 'art for art's sake' principle where employees seek originality and self-expression in their work. They seek decision-making that can be personally fulfilling, and in essence, they seek to put their 'creative stamp' on projects that allow them to become intimately attached to their work. This is the key to keeping them motivated (!): providing enough flexibility for them to be creative, yet enough direction to influence the outcome. When you try to force a 'vision from the client on them, they will shut down, you MUST give them room to create within those boundaries so that their "personality" or their creative vision can become a part of it' (Grosch, 2016). Kevin firmly believes that in other industries, employees can be creative, although they are often more task-motivated to 'get the job done', as opposed to exhibiting the fundamental desire to feel fulfilled in their creative work.

In the end, working in the creative industries is a job by which a company provides a product or service to a client, and even in the most creative of environments, this can become routine. Like others before Made-In, Kevin also provides his employees with the opportunity to break the routine by exploring novel ideas or projects. However, there are some boundaries: one, the concepts must positively impact the company; and two, *the employees* are the ones who need to make it happen. He calls them 'creative labs' and, as long as the set expectations of their jobs are being met, he sets no time limit on this 'free time'. All of this was a direct result of his employees reaching out to him about this option for them. He thought it was a great idea and officially instituted the concept of the creative lab. However, nothing really happened for about five or six months. The team felt listened to and *that* was the key. Sometimes it's not the result we seek that provides contentment, but just knowing we've been heard. Ultimately, they did start using the creative lab concept and the team began working on their own ideas. There have not been any results yet, but it does provide another outlet for staff to put their creative 'stamp' on things.

Overall, Kevin seeks to have his employees enjoy their time at Made-In Network, that is, their actual experience of the work, not just the function that they perform. He also institutes benefits like 'unlimited time-off days', giving the perception of autonomy to the team. Although he can't make the case that productivity has increased because of it, he does want them to feel more empowered and fulfilled. No one has quit after three years and the average range per employee who has taken this time off is between a few days to four weeks. This is no longer than many workplace time-off policies after a few years of employment. It builds goodwill and loyalty while motivating the team to feel pride in the work they do for Made-In. They work with friends and when these tactics are used, it becomes a place where they want to work in the hope of creating this 'shared experience'.

ORGANIZATIONAL CITIZENSHIP AND WORKPLACE DEVIANCE

Someone who experiences positive feelings towards work and is satisfied with their job may show what is called organizational 'citizenship behaviour'. Organizational citizenship behaviour goes above and beyond job roles and expectations. These employees may create special committees, work extra hours or take on extra work because they feel highly committed to the organization's goals, mission and values. Employees satisfied with their work situation speak more favourably about their employer, which can lead to lower staff turnover (Currivan, 2000; Schwepker, 2001). Even how the company is perceived by competitors and stakeholders has an impact on how employees feel about their work (Fuller *et al.*, 2006). If there is a perceived external prestige about the company in which one works, it can augment an employee's affective commitment to the organization (Carmeli, 2005).

When employees are dissatisfied with their job, they may engage in 'workplace deviance'. Workplace deviance is any voluntary, counterproductive behaviour that violates organizational norms and adversely affects organizational function (Bennett & Robinson, 2000). Examples of workplace deviance may include gossiping, workplace theft and using work time or equipment for personal gain. These types of behaviours are often triggered by negative events within the firm or if an employee feels they are being treated unfairly by managers. In the creative industries, the uncertainty of success and constant management of risk can lead to high levels of stress in the workplace. If employees aren't satisfied with their circumstances, they are more likely to engage in destructive behaviour. When digital distribution impacted the recorded music industry it led to a significant decline in sales and consequently significant staff layoffs. This in turn resulted in internal disengagement, criticism and outright contempt towards the companies among a segment of workers. When times turn bad, this creates even greater pressure on managers to keep employees motivated.

SUMMARY AND KEY POINTS

This chapter commenced by exploring the various ways in which we form attitudes, whether through affective, cognitive or behavioural means. Knowing how attitudes are formed can help us navigate the emotional landscape of the creative office environment. As a creative industries manager, you need to manage the attitudes generated by the products you create, the criticisms that come with their development and the high risks involved in potential product failures after launch. The way you do this will either damage or forge your reputation in the workplace and broader industry. In order to serve your employees better, as managers it's important to identify and put into action tactics that can help maintain job satisfaction and commitment to the organization. Doing so will maintain the creative environment needed to successfully produce and launch new product offerings. Providing opportunities for promotion and granting staff the flexibility and autonomy to be creative is at the centre of keeping the creative employee satisfied with their work; so is appealing to a higher order sense of what employees are seeking from work beyond merely doing a task for pay, such as the quest for meaning and fulfilling one's potential.

The chapter concluded with a discussion of key theories that help to explain what motivates us. From external motivators to an individual's internal drive, what we do know is that motivation can be a complex phenomenon. Over the years, management and organizational scholars have successfully used 'need' theories to help explain workplace behaviour and motivation. These needs range from the fundamental need to earn a salary and maintain good working conditions, to higher-order needs such as having autonomy and finding meaning in work.

One of the challenges we face as managers in organizations today is the ability to lead our employees through the uncertainty and turbulence that characterizes the creative and cultural industries. In particular, focusing on the higher-order needs for creative individuals will help management keep employees focused, but the complex creative process can nonetheless be a challenge. Management must consistently provide enough flexibility and protection of creative workers to allow the creative process to occur, while simultaneously managing the demands and pressures of the marketplace.

Discussion questions and class exercises

1. What are the factors that influence motivation?
2. Knowing these, how can we motivate the creative individual to work or produce in a meaningful way? Provide specific managerial examples.

3 How can the 'uncertainty of demand' principle influence motivation for the creative firm?
4 How does the intimate 'connection to the product' principle influence motivation in a creative individual?
5 How might we design a firm to encourage the maximization of these motivating factors?

References

Abun, D., Ubasa, A. L. A., Magallanes, T., Encarnacion, M. J. & Ranay, F. B. (2021). 'Attitude toward the work and its influence on the Individual work performance of employees: basis for attitude management', *Technium Social Sciences Journal*, Vol. 18, p. 378.

Ajzen, I. & Fishbein, M. (2005). 'The influence of attitudes on behavior', *The Handbook of Attitudes*, Vol. 173, p. 221.

Albarracin, D. & Shavitt, S. (2018). 'Attitudes and attitude change', *Annual Review of Psychology*, Vol. 69, pp. 299–327.

Amabile, T. M. (1985). 'Motivation and creativity: Effects of motivational orientation on creative writers', *Journal of Personality and Social Psychology*, Vol. 48, no. 2, p. 393.

Amabile, T. M. (1996). *'The motivation for creativity in organizations'*, Harvard Business School Background Note 396-240, January.

Amabile, T. M., Barsade, S. G., Mueller, J. S. & Staw, B. M. (2005). 'Affect and creativity at work', *Administrative Science Quarterly*, Vol. 50, no. 3, pp. 367–403.

Amabile, T. M., Hill, K. G., Hennessey, B. A. & Tighe, E. M. (1994). 'The work preference inventory: assessing intrinsic and extrinsic motivational orientations', *Journal of Personality and Social Psychology*, Vol. 66, no. 5, p. 950.

Ariely, D. (2012). '*What makes us feel good about our work*'. *Ted Talks*. Available at https://www.ted.com/talks/dan_ariely_what_makes_us_feel_good_about_our_work (accessed 7 August 2017).

Ariely, D., Kamenica, E. & Prelec, D. (2008). 'Man's search for meaning: The case of Legos', *Journal of Economic Behavior & Organization*, Vol. 67, no. 3, pp. 671–677.

Banks, M., Lovatt, A., O'Connor, J. & Raffo, C. (2000). 'Risk and trust in the cultural industries', *Geoforum*, Vol. 31, no. 4, pp. 453–464.

Bennett, R. J. & Robinson, S. L. (2000). 'Development of a measure of workplace deviance', *Journal of Applied Psychology*, Vol. 85, no. 3, p. 349.

Carmeli, A. (2005). 'Perceived external prestige, affective commitment, and citizenship behaviors', *Organization Studies*, Vol. 26, no. 3, pp. 443–464.

Carr, J. (2009). 'Creative industries, creative workers and the creative economy: A review of selected recent literature'. Available at http://www.gov.scot/Resource/Doc/289922/0088836.pdf (accessed 7 August 2017).

Cattani, G., Ferriani, S. & Colucci, M. (2015). 'Creativity in social networks: A core-periphery perspective'. In C. Jones, M. Lorenzen & J. Sapsed (eds). *The Oxford Handbook of Creative Industries*. Oxford: Oxford University Press, pp. 75–95.

Caves, R. E. (2000). *Creative Industries: Contracts between Art and Commerce*. Cambridge, MA: Harvard University Press.

Csikszentmihalyi, M. (2000). *Beyond Boredom and Anxiety*. San Francisco, CA: Jossey-Bass.

Currivan, D. B. (2000). 'The causal order of job satisfaction and organizational commitment in models of employee turnover', *Human Resource Management Review*, Vol. 9, no. 4, pp. 495–524.

Delong, T. J. & Vijayaraghavan, V. (2002). *Cirque du Soleil*. Boston, MA: Harvard Business School.

Duckworth, A. L. (2013). 'The key to success? Grit'. *Ted Talks*. Available at https://www.ted.com/talks/angela_lee_duckworth_the_key_to_success_grit?language=en (accessed 17 July 2017).

Duckworth, A. L. & Quinn, P. D. (2009). 'Development and validation of the Short Grit Scale (GRIT–S)', *Journal of Personality Assessment*, Vol. 91, no. 2, pp. 166–174.

Duckworth, A. L., Peterson, C., Matthews, M. D. & Kelly, D. R. (2007). 'Grit: Perseverance and passion for long-term goals', *Journal of Personality and Social Psychology*, Vol. 92, no. 6, p. 1087.

Ealias, A. & George, J. (2012). 'Emotional intelligence and job satisfaction: A correlational study', *Research Journal of Commerce and Behavioral Science*, Vol. 1, no. 4, pp. 37–42.

Ellis, A. (1991 (1991). 'The revised ABC's of rational-emotive therapy (RET)', *Journal of Rational-Emotive and Cognitive-Behavior Therapy*, Vol. 9, no. 3, pp. 139–172.

Fazio, R. H. & Zanna, M. P. (1981). 'Direct experience and attitude-behavior consistency', *Advances in Experimental Social Psychology*, Vol. 14, pp. 161–202.

Fischer, C., Malycha, C. P. and Schafmann, E. (2019). 'The influence of intrinsic motivation and synergistic extrinsic motivators on creativity and innovation', *Frontiers in Psychology*, Vol. 10, p. 137.

Fuller, J. B., Hester, K., Barnett, T., Frey, L., Relyea, C. & Beau, D. (2006). 'Perceived external prestige and internal respect: New insights into the organizational identification process', *Human Relations*, Vol. 59, no. 6, pp. 815–846.

George, J. M. & Zhou, J. (2001). 'When openness to experience and conscientiousness are related to creative behavior: An interactional approach', *Journal of Applied Psychology*, Vol. 86, no. 3, p. 513.

Gillespie, W. & Myors, B. (2000). 'Personality of rock musicians', *Psychology of Music*, Vol. 28, no. 2, pp. 154–165.

Gino, F., Ayal, S. & Ariely, D. (2013). 'Self-serving altruism? The lure of unethical actions that benefit others', *Journal of Economic Behavior & Organization*, Vol. 93, pp. 285–292.

Glasman, L. R. & Albarracín, D. (2006). 'Forming attitudes that predict future behavior: A meta-analysis of the attitude-behavior relation', *Psychological Bulletin*, Vol. 132, no. 5, p. 778.

Hansell, S. (2009). 'Time Warner goes over the top', *The New York Times*. Available at https://bits.blogs.nytimes.com/2009/03/03/jeff-bewkes-goes-over-the-top (accessed 21 March 2016).

Hirschman, E. C. (1983). 'Aesthetics, ideologies and the limits of the marketing concept', *The Journal of Marketing*, Vol. 47, pp. 45–55.

Hogg, M. A. & Vaughan, G. M. (2005). *Social Psychology*. New York: Prentice Hall.

Iannella, M. (2010). 'Creative industry job satisfaction survey'. *Major Players*. Available at http://www.majorplayers.co.uk/news-events/news-events/creative-industry-job-satisfaction-survey.html (accessed 7 August 2017).

Imran, H., Arif, I., Cheema, S. & Azeem, M. (2014). 'Relationship between job satisfaction, job performance, attitude towards work, and organizational commitment', *Entrepreneurship and Innovation Management Journal*, Vol. 2, no. *2*, pp. 135–144.

Kotler, S. (2014). 'Flow states and creativity: Can you train people to be more creative?' *Psychology Today*. Available at https://www.psychologytoday.com/blog/the-playing-field/201402/flow-states-and-creativity (accessed 7 August 2017).

Lai, E. R. (2011). *Motivation: A literature review*, Pearson Research Report.

Maynard, D. C. & Parfyonova, N. M. (2013). 'Perceived overqualification and withdrawal behaviours: Examining the roles of job attitudes and work values', *Journal of Occupational and Organizational Psychology*, Vol. 86, no. 3, pp. 435–455.

McClelland, D. C. (1971). *Assessing Human Motivation*. Morristown, NJ: General Learning Press.

McGregor, D. (1960). 'The human side of enterprise', *New York*, Vol. 21, p. 166.

McLeod, S. (2014). 'Attitudes and behavior', *Simply Psychology*. Available at http://www.simplypsychology.org/attitudes.html (accessed 7 August 2017).

Menger, P. M. (2015). 'The market for creative labour', *The Oxford Handbook of Creative Industries*, p. 148.

Nakamura, J. & Csikszentmihalyi, M. (2014). 'The concept of flow'. In *Flow and the Foundations of Positive Psychology*. Springer, pp. 239–263.

Nelson, D. & Quick, J. (2015). *ORGB 4*. Stamford, CT: Cengage Learning.

Olson, M. A. & Fazio, R. H. (2001). 'Implicit attitude formation through classical conditioning', *Psychological Science*, Vol. 12, no. 5, pp. 413–417.

Pinder, C. C. (2014). *Work Motivation in Organizational Behavior*. New York: Psychology Press.

Rast, S. & Tourani, A. (2012). 'Evaluation of employees' job satisfaction and role of gender difference: An empirical study at airline industry in Iran', *International Journal of Business and Social Science*, Vol. 3, no. 7, pp. 91–100.

Reisel, W. D., Probst, T. M., Chia, S-L., Maloles, C. M. & König, C. J. (2010). 'The effects of job insecurity on job satisfaction, organizational citizenship behavior, deviant behavior, and negative emotions of employees', *International Studies of Management & Organization*, Vol. 40, no. 1, pp. 74–91.

Robbins, S. P. & Judge, T. A. (2022). *Organizational Behavior: Updated 18th Global Edition*. Essex: Pearson Educational Limited.

Rosenthal, T. L. & Zimmerman, B. J. (2014). *Social Learning and Cognition*. New York: Academic Press.

Rouse, K. A. G. (2004). 'Beyond Maslow's Hierarchy of Needs: What Do People Strive For?' *Performance Improvement*, Vol. 43, no. 10, p. 27.

Ryan, R. M. & Deci, E. L. (2000). 'Intrinsic and extrinsic motivations: Classic definitions and new directions', *Contemporary Educational Psychology*, Vol. 25, no. 1, pp. 54–67.

Saari, L. M. & Judge, T. A. (2004). 'Employee attitudes and job satisfaction', *Human Resource Management*, Vol. 43, no. 4, pp. 395–407.

Saintilan, P. (2019). *Managerial Orientations and Underlying Beliefs in Large Music Organisations*. PhD thesis. Melbourne: Deakin University.

Schwepker, C. H. (2001). 'Ethical climate's relationship to job satisfaction, organizational commitment, and turnover intention in the salesforce', *Journal of Business Research*, Vol. 54, no. 1, pp. 39–52.

Shostrom, D. E. (1968). 'Maslow and self-actualization'. Available at https://www.youtube.com/watch?v=x9ttmNTGZAM (accessed 7 March 2016).

Smith, J. (2010). 'Attitudes can be influenced', *Peoria Magazines*. Available at http://www.peoriamagazines.com/ibi/2010/mar/attitudes-can-be-influenced (accessed 7 August 2017).

Spector, P. E. (1986). 'Perceived control by employees: A meta-analysis of studies concerning autonomy and participation at work', *Human Relations*, Vol. 39, no. 11, pp. 1005–1016.

Spector, P. E. (1997). *Job Satisfaction: Application, Assessment, Causes, and Consequences*. Thousand Oaks, CA: Sage Publications.

Steers, R. M., Mowday, R. T. & Shapiro, D. L. (2004). 'Introduction to special topic forum: The future of work motivation theory', *The Academy of Management Review*, Vol. 29, no. 3, pp. 379–387.

Stohs, J. H. (1992). 'Intrinsic motivation and sustained art activity among male fine and applied artists', *Creativity Research Journal*, Vol. 5, no. 3, pp. 245–252.

Trofimov, A., Drobot, O., Kokarieva, A., Maksymova, N., Lovochkina, A. & Kozytska, I. (2019). 'The influence of management style and emotional intelligence on the formation of employees' commitment and loyalty', *Humanities & Social Sciences Reviews*, Vol. 7, no. 5, pp. 393–404.

Vogt, M. (2007). *Work and Employment in the Creative Industries*. Available at http://www.eurofound.europa.eu/observatories/eurwork/articles/labour-market-working-conditions-quality-of-life/work-and-employment-in-the-creative-industries (accessed 7 August 2017).

Vough, H. C. & Caza, B. B. (2017). 'Where do I go from here? Sensemaking and the construction of growth-based stories in the wake of denied promotions', *Academy of Management Review*, Vol. 42, no. 1, pp. 103–128.

Woolhandler, S., Ariely, D. & Himmelstein, D. U. (2012). 'Why pay for performance may be incompatible with quality improvement', *The BMJ*, Vol. 345, no. 7870, p. e5015.

Zimbardo, P. G. & Leippe, M. R. (1991). *The Psychology of Attitude Change and Social Influence*. New York: McGraw-Hill Book Company.

Conflict and negotiation in creative organizations

Chapter 5

HOW AN ARGUMENT OVER A MEAL TRIGGERED THE DESTRUCTION OF A TV SHOW WATCHED BY 350 MILLION PEOPLE

Creative workplaces can be volatile environments with highly committed, passionate people, pursuing their work with great intensity. Key players can have sizeable egos and egos can become inflated with years of star treatment. Large creative projects always carry a risk that a conflict can escalate to a point where the entire project is derailed. The case of Jeremy Clarkson's sacking from the British Broadcasting Corporation (BBC) shows how important managing conflict is in running successful entertainment organizations.

In 2015, Clarkson (Figure 5.1) was the star of the TV programme *Top Gear*, watched by a global audience of 350 million people. It was the world's most popular factually based TV programme and generated around £150 million in revenue per annum for the BBC. Clarkson was feted as one of the world's great TV stars and enjoyed a loyal following among a TV audience of male car enthusiasts who enjoyed his irreverent, politically incorrect style. This style had frequently brought

DOI: 10.4324/9781003262923-5

him into conflict with BBC management, the media and even the broadcasting regulator. Only the previous year he and his crew had been chased out of Argentina when filming a show. Clarkson was driving a Porsche whose number plate (H982 FKL) appeared to refer to the 1982 Falklands War, incensing the local community. Filming was abandoned as they came under attack from an angry mob who vandalized their cars. In other incidents Clarkson had jokingly suggested that public servants who were on strike should be 'executed in front of their families', and had also used racially offensive slang which had resulted in a warning from the regulator (Evans & Singh, 2015; Rayner & Furness, 2015).

Figure 5.1 UK TV presenter Jeremy Clarkson. Photo credit: Landmarkmedia / Shutterstock.com.

On the day it all went wrong, Clarkson and the film crew arrived back at a hotel in northern England at the end of an exhausting day's shooting. Expecting a nice hot meal, Clarkson discovered that rather than full catering, only cold food was available. Clarkson exploded, reportedly showering producer Oisin Tymon with a 20 minute tirade of verbal abuse, including an alleged physical assault. Some of this took place in front of shocked hotel guests. The attacked producer drove himself to hospital but did not call the police.

Clarkson was initially suspended, pending an internal BBC investigation. In a matter of days an online petition saw over one million fans urge his reinstatement. The view taken by the BBC was that given previous warnings, they needed to take a principled stand, and not condone conduct that should be unacceptable. When his sacking was confirmed, the director-general of the BBC received death threats.

In the aftermath all parties were criticized, and many organizations and individuals publicly waded into the debate. Clarkson was criticized for his behaviour, and the BBC was criticized for not being able to manage the conflict and Clarkson in a way that would have kept a much-loved programme on the air.

Non-profit organizations often take highly principled and ethical stands on organizational matters, as they may see their mission as involving more than simply making money. They can also attract idealistic, principled workers who care as much about the way business is conducted as they do about business outcomes. In this environment, principled stands by management to uphold values may be respected and appreciated by employees. When Joe Volpe, the managing director of the Metropolitan Opera House in New York, fired Kathleen Battle, a prima donna soprano who was insulting staff, he received a round of applause from the entire company (Volpe, 2007). But in commercial, for-profit environments, where financial results are vitally important, any manager who had presided over the destruction of a show bringing in £150 million of revenue would be asked: 'How could you let a disagreement over a meal, which should have been a small matter, destroy the entire show?!'

CHAPTER LEARNING OBJECTIVES

After studying this chapter, you should be able to:

- Define conflict;
- Provide examples of conflicts that can arise in creative organizations and propose a variety of ways to approach and resolve them;
- Analyse conflict situations using concepts such as task conflict, relationship conflict and process conflict, to better understand the situation and provide appropriate recommendations;
- Compare and contrast different strategies and approaches in dealing with organizational conflict and identify the most appropriate strategy for a given circumstance;
- Apply negotiation theories and techniques to achieve optimum outcomes in conflict situations.

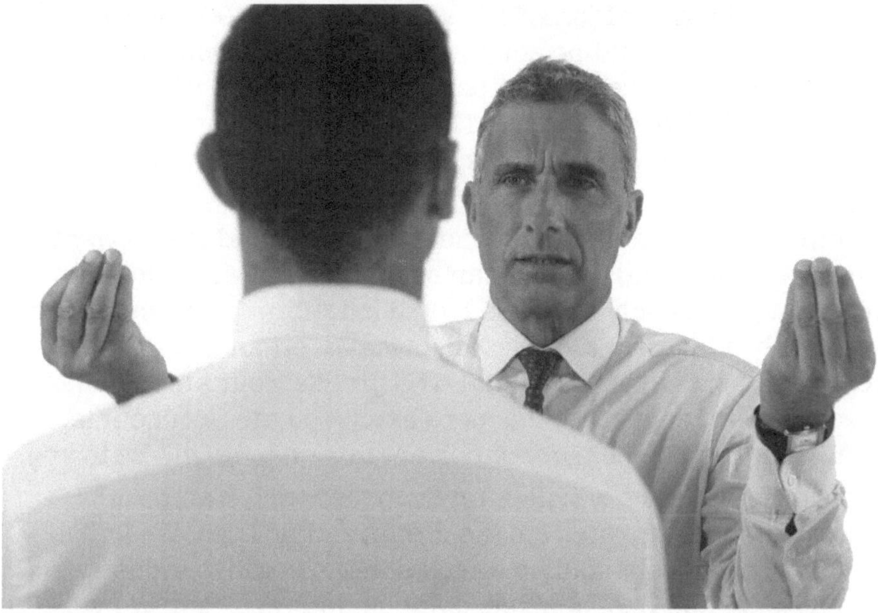

Figure 5.2 Dysfunctional conflict can be corrosive to employee morale. Photo credit: Phovoir / Shutterstock.com.

If we were transported 100 years into the workplace of the future, we would expect to see transformative change, particularly regarding the ways in which we use technology. However, for reasons that will be explored in this chapter, workplace conflict is likely to have changed little. This means that studying techniques and approaches for managing conflict has long-term value and won't become quickly outdated. Managing conflict is also a transferable skill, and while we will focus on conflicts that tend to arise most frequently in creative industries, the ability to manage conflict is important to managers in any environment.

Many organizations look from the outside like oases of tranquillity, yet those who work within them will admit to ongoing tensions and conflicts. For example, you would think that the entertainment giant behind Mickey Mouse, Snow White and Cinderella would be one big happy family, and that working there would be like a fairy tale. Yet the book *Disney War* highlights the tumultuous civil war that took place within 'The

Wonderful World of Disney' between 1984 and 2003 (Stewart, 2005). While it should be acknowledged that this was a specific era and doesn't necessarily bear any relevance to the present-day company (eg see Chapter 11), it still shows that there can be a gulf between how companies are perceived externally and the internal reality for employees who work there.

Conflict can be distressing and it is understandable to want to avoid it. Addressing conflict can seem like 'walking into pain'. Yet often pain is only increased, on a long-term basis, by failing to directly address it. Conflict is normal in organizations, and some conflict is even beneficial. The greater your ambitions in creative management, the more likely you are to encounter conflict, and thus the more important this chapter will be to you.

In this chapter we will illustrate concepts and frameworks using examples drawn from the creative industries. We will look at how conflict commonly manifests in the creative industries and how we can best analyse, manage and resolve it. We will also look at negotiation techniques, an important topic given the adage that you get in life not what you deserve, but what you negotiate.

ORGANIZATIONAL CONFLICT: DEFINITION AND EVOLVING THEORETICAL APPROACHES

We can define conflict as a process that commences when one party perceives that another party is negatively impacting its interests. Broadly speaking, theorists looking at organizational conflict first believed that conflict was always bad, then considered it a normal part of working life, and finally recognized that it could be both positive and negative depending on the circumstances.

Conflict can be viewed as 'functional' or 'dysfunctional'. *Functional conflict* is positive and constructive. *Dysfunctional conflict* is negative and destructive. (Note that we can use 'functional' in two different ways in organizational theory. As we will discover in the chapter on structure, we can also use the word 'function' to denote managerial functions like marketing or finance. So the expression 'interfunctional conflict' means conflict between different functions, such as a fight between the head of marketing and the head of finance over how large the marketing budget should be.)

TASK, RELATIONSHIP AND PROCESS CONFLICT

Theorists studying conflict have distinguished between 'task', 'relationship' and 'process' conflict (Jehn, 1995, 1997). Let us imagine that we are organizing an event to celebrate the launch of a new fashion label.

'Task conflict' in relation to this event would mean conflict that occurs between staff members about the content and goals of the project. Arguments may arise over the best way to structure the evening, the activities that should be run, or the outcomes the event should generate. Low to moderate levels of conflict are fine for this type of activity because disagreements can improve the quality of decisions. Ideally the culture should be one where 'the best idea wins': if someone comes up with a great event idea, even if it is an intern who has only been working at the company for five minutes, the idea should be accepted on its merits and the plan changed accordingly.

To turn to another example, imagine you are a marketing manager working on a big campaign for an entertainment company. You may resist presenting your campaign ideas and plan to staff as you may anticipate having to address internal criticism and unwanted feedback ('Why can't the main colour be cerulean not blue?'). Yet while some advice may be unhelpful, having experts from many departments look over one's plans is a healthy way to 'bullet proof' your campaign. Perhaps the price points and discounts have implications for people in the box office of which you were unaware, and need to be set up on their system. Perhaps there is something in the artist contracts that prevents you from doing something that was planned. The more you open yourself up to this sort of process, and therefore to potential conflict and criticism, the stronger your campaign and ideas will be. This process also allows other managers to become more invested in the campaign, because it will start to feel like *their* campaign, and not just yours.

'Relationship conflict' in this situation would refer to tensions that emerge in the team over the way colleagues behave, or their differences in personality, values or attitudes; this is almost always negative and dysfunctional. It may be that someone is overly authoritarian or rude in their style of communication. Relationship conflict can cause members of the team to become so offended that their commitment to the entire project is placed in jeopardy. Deeply entrenched personal hostility may lead to people changing their daily schedule to avoid one another, stopping communication with one another out of fear that it will trigger further conflict, taking extended sick leave or even searching for other jobs. No useful purpose is served by this conflict and senior people may need to intervene to create a more workable environment. Note that bullying, harassment and intimidation is covered in Chapter 8 on power and politics.

Finally, 'process conflict' pertains to tensions surrounding how a team should get things done. For the launch of a fashion label, who will handle budgeting and event management, develop a timeline, and allocate roles and responsibilities? Low levels of process conflict at this point may be useful, allowing assumptions to be questioned and challenged, which can then lead to superior solutions.

Groupthink is a phenomenon where apparently intelligent people do dumb things as a group because they suspend their own critical thinking and follow each other like sheep. In 'groupthink', group members give a higher priority to avoiding conflict than to solving the problem, improving the quality of the output, or achieving the objective. Positive conflict is the enemy of groupthink; when someone has the courage to put up their hand and say, 'I don't agree. I don't think that will work', this disrupts the atmosphere of instinctive conformity. The more experienced you become as a manager, the more you will reflect on times you had misgivings about an idea, didn't intervene, and then had to live with the subsequent negative consequences. After these experiences, you will be more likely to raise your hand in the face of groupthink, because you'll understand that by following the group and avoiding conflict, you won't avoid pain – you'll simply postpone it.

Research indicates the following relationship between work performance and organizational conflict seen in Figure 5.3 (De Dreu, 1997, p. 14).

In this figure, very low conflict in the workplace results in low performance, as there is no force to challenge and optimize outcomes, push for solutions or push to achieve deadlines. As conflict increases, all these positive benefits are realized. However, at a certain point the conflict becomes destructive and demotivating for staff, and work performance diminishes.

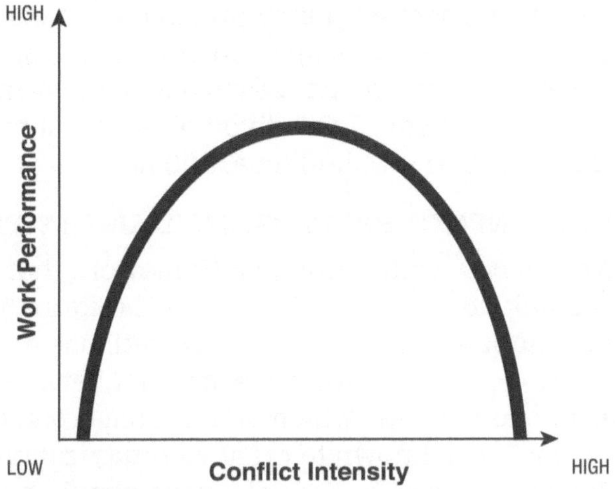

Figure 5.3 Relationship between conflict and performance. Reproduced with the permission of Carsten K W De Dreu and Sage publications.

YOUR PERSONAL RESPONSE TO CONFLICT

We can often find ourselves having an instinctive, aggressive reaction to conflict. Imagine that we receive an email from someone as we are about to leave the office, copied to everyone, criticizing us. White with rage at being humiliated in front of our colleagues we quickly ‘flame’ them, sending back an irate response. Overnight, going through the wording of the exchange in our mind, we may think of far better ways we could have responded. This is why anecdotal advice is often given in organizations to sleep on difficult situations and not respond until the morning (which is difficult to do, as you may theorize that some swift revenge will make you sleep better!). In emotional matters, email communication is hardly ever the answer anyway, and conflict between departments and managers is best resolved through face-to-face, mediated discussion. Executive maturity requires you to develop the ability to put reflective space between the events that happen to you and your reaction to those events. Immature managers react immediately and aggressively. Mature managers take a deep breath and look more deeply and strategically at their response. There are many practices that can be employed to develop this. For example, creating this 'gap' between emotional triggers and our responses is one of the principle objectives of the 2,500-year-old tradition of Buddhist meditative practice (Goleman & The-Dalai-Lama, 2004).

THE CONFLICT PROCESS: AN ILLUSTRATED EXAMPLE

We will now walk through a framework that can be used to break down the conflict process (Figure 5.4) (adapted from Robbins & Judge, 2022). We will use an example of 'interfunctional conflict' (i.e. conflict between two functions, as mentioned above), which arises from creative versus business tensions well known to creative organizations (and discussed in Chapter 1). Creative organizations simultaneously pursue artistic and commercial outcomes, which can sit uneasily together and create problems (Caves, 2000; Hesmondhalgh & Baker, 2011). For example, a magazine journalist may have a fantastic idea for an investigative story, but the sales manager opposes it because it could embarrass an important advertiser. An advertising agency creative team comes up with an imaginative idea they believe will 'cut through' and catch attention because of its audacity, but it is blocked by the clients and the 'suits' in the agency as being too high risk. An artistic director of an opera company proposes an ambitious new production that pushes the boundaries of the artform, but the general manager believes it would be financially perilous. An independent TV production company has an inspired idea for a documentary, but the commissioning agents they need for support have given their attention to another genre, like reality TV, and turn the idea down. A fashion designer creates designs they believe are distinctive, edgy and showcase their brilliance as designers, but the label head rejects them

Figure 5.4 The conflict process. Adapted from Robbins, S. P. & Judge, T. A., *Organizational Behavior*, 18th edition, ©2022. Reprinted by permission of Pearson Education, Inc.

for being 'off brand' and too far away from known consumer preferences. In all these examples, pure creative freedom is derailed by commercial considerations. The practical example that will be fleshed out below in detail will hopefully make the process clearer and more understandable, and demonstrate the opportunities for resolving conflict. It is set in a commercial for-profit context, and a non-profit case study examining the same issue is provided at the very end of the chapter.

*Conflict erupts in a meeting**

Sam Stossburg, the A&R Vice President at Galaxy Records sat opposite the label's Marketing Vice President Katie Jamieson in a meeting room. Tension had arisen over a new project for which Sam had great expectations, but which had disappeared from the charts without a trace.

SAM: 'Well, it was a hit when it left my desk. What did you guys do to it? There was no major marketing and promotional support as far as I could see. You guys f*#%ed it. You f*#%ed me. You f*#%ed the band. You guys are f*#%ed'.

KATIE: 'Yeah, well here's the thing Sam. Before you sign an artist, why don't you come to us for a reality check and talk to us about the commerciality of the project, the social metrics, the sort of budget we have to promote it, and where it's likely to land in the market? There was nothing to promote there. Hardly any audience to engage with. We should be in sync on these things. Single vision. And by the way, the quality of your analysis doesn't improve with the number of F-bombs you drop'.

SAM: 'It was a disgrace. And I'm the one who has to pick up the pieces with the band ... Now, turning to the Quantum release, we have a problem in terms of timing'.

KATIE: 'It's not slipping?'

* The authors would like to thank Simon Cahill for co-authoring this scenario and the case that appears at the conclusion of the chapter. Simon is the Senior Vice President of Commercial, Media and Audience of Warner Music Australia. Prior to Warner Music he has held positions at Sony Music in Artist and Repertoire (A&R), Marketing at BMG and Sales at Mushroom.

SAM: 'Yes, it's slipping. It's going to fall right out of Q3 and into the next financial year'.

KATIE: 'But it can't. We've just spent three months putting together the campaign. This is a big release. If it slips, the whole annual budget is blown. What's the problem?'

SAM: 'It's just not there. There's no point in putting out garbage'.

KATIE: 'Well, if we pull it, we've burned our bridges with some pretty key partners. I've spent an age doing the set-up, and a lot of the stuff we've organized is a one shot deal. Some of these influencers and media partners were doing us a favour, so it's not like that support is going to be there if we reschedule. This quarter is the best time to break new music, before you get into the end of year Christmas / Wrapped playlist car crash. If you push this release back you can take an axe to the projections. The other territories who are depending on this to make their numbers are also going to scream. You can take their zoom calls'.

SAM: 'What do you want me to do? If it isn't ready, it isn't ready. Do you think Beethoven had someone screaming at him saying 'If the Moonlight Sonata isn't ready by the full moon, you're not getting paid?'

KATIE: 'Some of it must be ready. Can't we just remix some of their last album, put out a cover, add a US MC, waterfall it as a bundle, and keep the release date*? Is it genuinely awful?'

SAM: 'I like where you're going with this Katie. Let's butcher the integrity of the whole project so in five years we can look back and be embarrassed'.

* To 'waterfall it as a bundle' is where a string of singles are released, each one building into an EP or album as they come out. The term emcee, MC or M.C., derived from 'master of ceremonies', is an alternative title for a rapper. So here Katie is advocating bringing in a MC from the United States. (It should also be noted that a differentiation by some in hip-hop culture has begun to appear between an 'MC' or 'emcee' and a 'rapper'. The MC/emcee is often associated with traditional aspects of hip-hop which connect to DJing, graffiti, and breakdancing, the other three root elements of the culture (Abe, 2013, p. 1).)

KATIE: 'If we continue blowing our numbers, none of us are going to be here in one year, let alone five'.

SAM: 'The artists are going to be here in five years, and they're the ones putting themselves out there, not us. Do you think the band or manager care if our annual budget is blown? There's no contractual breach. If they deliver it next year, there's nothing we can do'.

KATIE: 'Who writes these contracts? It's crazy'.

In this scenario, there is clear tension between the A&R vice president and the marketing vice president. Tensions between marketing and A&R departments are common and have been researched (Hesmondhalgh & Baker, 2011; Negus, 1992). The A&R vice president is upset that a project for which he had great expectations appears not to have been supported by his marketing colleagues, and the marketing vice president is upset because creative delays have negatively impacted marketing partnerships she has put in place. It is easy to attribute workplace conflicts to individuals (e.g. 'I hate that idiot down the corridor'), and in the case of relationship conflicts that may well be true, as individual behaviours may be the source of the problem. But often in organizational life the conflict is 'structural', in that it falls naturally out of different roles, responsibilities and objectives that people have in an organization, like those of the A&R and marketing vice presidents.

It is like we are characters in a play who are given different roles, scripts and objectives, which means our interactions are not going to be the same as if we were meeting socially. We may think someone is awful because they give us such a hard time and then be surprised to find when meeting them in a social situation that they're not quite as awful as we had imagined. We will explore this type of structural conflict as we go through this process framework.

Antecedent conditions setting up potential conflict and incompatibility

Let us look first at all the pre-existing or 'antecedent' conditions that provide the context and may have fuelled the conflict. The larger a record label or company becomes, the more sense it makes to have specific departments or groupings of managers who possess different specializations. As we will see in the chapter on structure, we may establish a finance department, a marketing department, an IT department, an A&R department, etc. If we select a group of people with similar specialized skills and place them in one department, they will mutually reinforce one another's specialist views. For example, if we create a department of A&R managers, they would excitedly share their thoughts on bands, music and genres that they love or see developing in exciting ways. Each manager may want to establish a professional reputation for being 'ahead of the curve', being a cultural 'frontier rider', tapping into the cultural zeitgeist and predicting new trends and emerging talents. Nothing confers greater kudos on such an executive than being pivotal in the rise of a great creative phenomenon. They want the creative work they're involved with to be seen by their peers as high quality as well as cutting edge. Many A&R managers have romantic ideas of standing by their artists through dark times – being attacked for believing in the quality of the creative work or weathering short-sighted marketing and finance people's attempts to terminate the artist's contract – only to see that artist rise to stratospheric success, thanks to the A&R manager's tenacity. A&R managers may have previously worked as professional musicians in their own right, or as audio engineers, or in any number of related musical careers. They may have grown up reading about great A&R managers such as Clive Davis and Ahmet Ertegün, who trusted their gut instinct when it came to creative decisions.

For a marketing manager, they may see themselves as being the bridge between art and commerce, easily moving between conversations with artists to conversations with the finance department and advertising creatives. They may see themselves as no less creative in what they do, developing creative marketing campaigns. They may see themselves as being both artistically savvy and business savvy. Success for a commercial marketing manager means connecting artists with audiences through creative means and leading the project to a point where it 'explodes', creating happy artists, happy audiences and lots of money. Marketing managers have increasingly undertaken marketing courses in business schools or colleges, learning marketing terminology and frameworks. They may have been taught to look for data to support their decisions, and may be more in control of the overall commerciality of the project and closer to retail intermediaries and marketing partners. They may see A&R executives as potentially too invested in their own enthusiasms and the friendships they have formed with artists, rather than in what might be in the best commercial interests of the company. They may see A&R as being more interested in long-term artist image building and unrealistic in terms of short-term sales expectations, while they themselves know marketing will be measured in the short-term. All of these differences create the potential for conflict.

Communication barriers between these two types of managers could further exacerbate the potential for conflict. We could situate A&R managers in one building or on one floor and marketing managers in another building or on another floor to further increase the potential for misunderstandings and conflict.

Processing: cognition and personalization

In terms of the above conflict, each manager understands the conflict in their own way, will define and frame it differently, and will link different events in different ways. Their emotional involvement and how they feel about the conflict may also be different. So, the A&R vice president will go back and think through all the times he had great expectations for an artist, but believed the company didn't spend enough money on them, which left the artist's potential unrealized. He will reflect on marketers not understanding the challenges under which A&R managers toil, making their position untenable with the artists they manage through failing to support important projects. The marketing vice president may reflect on her ongoing frustration with A&R managers failing to communicate with her, failing to 'bring her along on the journey' with an artist and being naïve with regard to the marketability of the project and the audience demand.

Conflict between these two functions can arise from many other factors: visual tools and materials that may be perceived by one group as being inappropriate; the choice of which single to promotionally prioritize; whether the primary target audience should be critics, bloggers and aficionado purchasers, the broader fanbase, or a larger market; whether certain aspects of the project may need to be compromised to make it more marketable; and finally, as in this case, potential slippage in the release schedule, which may cause conflict if delays will damage marketing campaigns and financial projections. All of these past experiences can be freshly drawn into new conflicts, and become the 'back story' to the most recent meeting.

'Attribution biases' may occur where the history between the parties leads us to suspiciously attribute false motives or intentions to the other party. For example, the A&R manager may believe the marketing manager is being deliberately unsupportive of him, when in fact the label president could have privately met with the marketing manager and expressed concern over the financial situation; thus, the A&R manager may attribute the decision to the marketing manager's prejudices when in fact she is simply 'following orders'. However, a good president who sees major conflict arising between two senior staff members will attempt to intervene. The steps that the president (or CEO in many organizations) can employ are suggested in the next section.

Intentions

At this point each team makes a commitment to act in a certain way to resolve the conflict. How strongly should each assert themselves? There are many options: digging in and attempting to win at all costs; trying to collaborate; sitting down and examining points on which they could compromise; simply giving in; or ignoring the conflict, avoiding one another and pretending that everything's fine.

This conflict is serious and immediate, and so avoiding the conflict will only exacerbate the situation. One circumstance where the strategy of avoidance might make sense would be if the organization were about to undergo major re-structuring, in which case the two managers may wind up not even working together. It should be admitted that in some instances like this, managers would be wiser to see how events unfold, as major organizational change may impact working relationships and priorities significantly.

The intention of the A&R managers may be to demand greater marketing support of key projects. The intention of the marketing managers may be to hold firm and defend their conduct with regard to the case in question.

The president or CEO to whom the two managers report may decide to intervene with some positive steps to reduce the gap between managers, such as:

- *Strong (CEO) mediation* – Strong intervention signals the importance that the whole company places on the two functions working constructively together (Gupta *et al.*, 1986). A skilled, experienced manager (the CEO) intervenes in order to win the trust and confidence of the managers, and to help explore new ways of working together. Good mediators lower the emotional temperature by being calm and measured. They start by listening, and then place the focus on the present and the future rather than the past. Because of the authority that a CEO brings, they're more than a mediator, and would be better characterized as an arbitrator with the authority to ultimately impose a solution. This distinction is covered further at the end of the chapter.
- *Superordinate goals* – The CEO could remind the managers of the overarching goals that are important for the whole company. Working together collaboratively is a fundamental assumption, and if a project fails, it damages both functions. Focusing on superordinate goals places attention on what unites managers rather than what divides them (Pinto *et al.*, 1993).
- *Providing greater formalization and clarity on ambiguous processes* – Perhaps ambiguities exist which could be better dealt with by clearly delineating lines of responsibility and clarifying processes. For example, the A&R vice president appeared to pursue the artist development project in

isolation, and according to the marketing vice president, failed to consult with her adequately. In future, the A&R vice president and marketing vice president could be co-signatories for the business case for new projects. They could jointly define and sign off each project, ensuring that both parties clearly understand the commitment that is being made, the plan that is being pursued, and are similarly invested in the project. It prevents one manager further down the line saying, 'I always thought this wouldn't work; it's got nothing to do with me'. This joint approach is now widely practised, and an academic case study on the process has been written featuring EMI Italy (Ordanini *et al.*, 2008). Clarifying who is responsible for what and how interactions should work in future may be a relief for all parties (Barclay, 1991; Maltz & Kohli, 2000; Pinto *et al.*, 1993).

- *Cross-functional training* – The CEO could attempt to break down the 'warring tribes' situation through 'job rotation', by giving marketing staff periods working in the A&R area, and vice versa, to give staff a greater appreciation of the role each function plays in the company (Maltz & Kohli, 2000).
- *Cross-functional teams* – Instead of the 'A&R area' pursuing a project in isolation and handing it over to the 'marketing area' like an assembly line, project teams could be assigned to each creative project. These project teams could be 'cross functional' so that they contain representatives from each function, including A&R and marketing, allowing everyone to work together and participate in decision-making (Maltz & Kohli, 2000; Ordanini *et al.*, 2008; Pinto *et al.*, 1993).
- *Cross-functional rewards* – Objectives are often reinforced with rewards and incentives, so when managers and departments come into conflict, thought should also be given to whether different rewards and incentives contribute to this, and whether they should be adapted to encourage greater shared commitment (Barclay, 1991; Griffin & Hauser, 1996). For example, instead of bonuses being paid to reward senior managers' individual contributions, the system could be changed to reward collaborative achievements involving both the marketing and A&R functions;

- *Removing barriers to communication* – Removing barriers to communication can reduce interfunctional conflict (Barclay, 1991; Crittenden *et al.*, 1993; Massey & Dawes, 2007; Ordanini *et al.*, 2008). Music organizations are using technology to enable staff to better share information on creative projects. One aspect of removing barriers to communication has been *physical proximity/co-location* where A&R and marketing are seated together in the same office area when they are on site, so they 'hang out' together, rather than being physically separated. They can overhear one another's conversations and get a clearer idea of what is happening on a day-to-day basis (Maltz & Kohli, 2000; Pinto *et al.*, 1993; Shaw & Shaw, 1998).
- *Social interaction* – The CEO may decide that more effort needs to be put into social events, parties and recreational activities designed to get managers to better understand one another as people, rather than company functionaries (Griffin & Hauser, 1996; Maltz & Kohli, 2000).

Behaviours

Models such as this conflict process framework generally separate 'intention' and 'behaviour'. This is because it is perfectly possible for an individual to make a commitment to act in a certain way, only to change their approach in the heat of a conflict. They may start out wanting to be accommodating and flexible, but become so offended by the hostile and aggressive approach of the other party that they become aggressive and hostile themselves. In this 'behaviour' phase, the A&R vice president, marketing vice president and CEO all get together and the consequences of their intentions play out.

Outcomes

The outcomes of this conflict and the way the parties seek to deal with it may be positive, and may result in improvements. Harnessing the expertise of both types of executive and having them work 'in sync' should have a very positive impact on organizational functioning and the new product development process. Bringing better projects to market faster should in turn have a positive financial impact. If there had been no attempt to broker and resolve the conflict, it could have resulted in a toxic environment, with little trust among staff and high turnover, with staff and artists leaving.

In very rare instances, escalating conflict rather than seeking careful mediation or arbitration may be a viable strategy. Operating under the idea that 'every great brand needs an enemy', Richard Branson, when launching Virgin Airways, publicly and ferociously attacked British Airways for unfair competitive tactics. Virgin began life as a music brand, but Branson skilfully extended it into a range of businesses and product categories. Branson's legitimate concerns with British Airways could have been dealt with quietly and legally, but he took out billboards because he saw it as an opportunity to position Virgin as a fresh, new, young operator being bullied by old competitors. He reasoned that a David-versus-Goliath battle would create sympathy for the underdog (Virgin) among air travellers.

NEGOTIATION

A negotiation is a debate over the correct exchange rate for a transaction or how to allocate scarce resources (Robbins & Judge, 2022). The term is used interchangeably with 'bargaining'. If, in the previous example, the company had a 'bonus pool' (a pool of money set aside to reward key staff for achieving performance targets over and above their salaries), and the A&R and marketing vice presidents were fighting against one another for a proportion of this pool, we would expect the solutions to be less obvious and less easy to reach, unless the pool was shared equally for joint projects. Bonus pools fall into the problem of being a 'zero sum' game, because every dollar secured by one executive as a bonus means one less dollar for everyone else. I can only gain an advantage at your expense; every positive for me is a negative for you. This is the world of the zero sum game, and it is a painful world. It is also known as 'distributive bargaining'.

I may wish to purchase an asset, such as a small production company. Every dollar I pay for this business is a dollar I am out of pocket and a dollar more the seller makes. In such a negotiation it is vitally important to know what one's 'walk away' price will be. At what point should I stand up and walk away because I believe I will be better off pursuing options outside this transaction? At what price would I commence the negotiation? Similarly, at what price should the other party walk away from the transaction? Do they have other buyers, or other uses for the equipment and facilities?

In contrast to the world of the zero sum game, 'integrative bargaining' was the approach fostered by the CEO in our conflict example above. Integrative bargaining involves coming at a transaction with a win/win attitude in an attempt to engineer an outcome that benefits both parties. Where the parties to the agreement need to work with one another on a long-term basis, win/win outcomes are far more important than in short-term transactions. If one party is damaged and walks away humiliated from a negotiation this will damage long-term co-operation, which is the last thing a business wants in relation to its own employees. There is a higher chance of disappointment and unethical behaviour in one-off deals because the parties do not need to do business with one another again and require no ongoing loyalty or constructive relationship. Building win/win outcomes requires flexibility, trust, respect, transparency and an ability to look at the other party's position as well as one's own (Brown, 2013).

THE NEGOTIATION PROCESS

Let us go through the stages of the negotiation process (Figure 5.5, adapted from Robbins & Judge, 2022) to see how we can best optimize the outcomes.

Preparation and planning

What are your goals? What are their goals? How do they perceive the negotiation and what will various outcomes mean

Figure 5.5 The negotiation process. Adapted from Robbins, S. P. & Judge, T. A., *Organizational Behavior*, 18th edition, ©2022. Reprinted by permission of Pearson Education, Inc.

to them? When should you walk away and when should they walk away from the negotiation? In this phase, it is important to obtain data to better understand the nature of the deal. If you are negotiating with an artist to appear at a festival, or an actor to appear in a movie, what sums of money have comparable artists been paid for this type of engagement? What other terms and riders are standard for an artist of that stature? What are the personal preferences of the artist, and their own tastes and enthusiasms, and how might I be able to create additional benefits for the artist with little cost to myself? Are there other artists involved in this project whom this artist respects and who might make the engagement more attractive to him/her? Is my event near some activity that is attractive to the artist, to which I could facilitate a visit? For example, if I am running the Montreux Jazz Festival, introducing the artist to other artists performing at the festival or arranging a beautiful Swiss excursion for them may make the engagement more attractive. The more I understand the party with whom I am negotiating, the better chance I have of creating an imaginative outcome that secures the artist at the lowest direct cost to me because of the other value I am creating for them.

Definitions and ground rules

In formal negotiations, such as union wage disputes, or the negotiation of broadcast rights for sports and entertainment franchises, there can be formal ground rules to the negotiation. Who will be invited to negotiate? Where will the negotiations take place? What is the timeline for various activities, and when will they start and end? What are the precise rights or conditions that are being negotiated, and so what is 'on the table' and 'off the table'? In the event of a failure to reach an agreement, are there processes such as mediation or arbitration that will follow (discussed below)? At this point initial proposals are lodged.

Clarification and justification

In this stage, proposals and assumptions are closely examined. Sometimes negotiation involves moving around 'mental furniture' so that new points of comparison are introduced which make people look at what is being asked in a new light.

For example, in an era when $30 CD prices were being criticized as being inflated and unreasonable, advocates would sometimes ask questions such as, 'How much would you pay for a dinner for yourself and your partner? If you're spending $100 for an hour or two of dinnertime enjoyment, $30 for hours of musical enjoyment looks like a bargain'. Great negotiators and advocates are masterful at thinking up lateral comparisons like this to soften people's preconceptions. We recommend Robert Cialdini's book *Influence* if you wish to look further into the psychology of persuasion (Cialdini, 1984).

Bargaining and problem solving

In this stage, there is give and take between the parties to attempt to forge a deal. For example, in negotiations to purchase a new series of the TV sitcom *Frasier*, last-minute concessions were made by the studio (Paramount) and the network (NBC) to sweeten the deal (Subramanian, 2002). This agreement was formed towards the end of the life of the series, and concerns existed over whether stars would depart the series, reducing its appeal in the marketplace. One set of concessions related to cancellation provisions. There were five 'principals' in the series: Kelsey Grammer (who played Frasier Crane), David Hyde Pierce (Niles Crane), Jane Leeves (Daphne Moon), John Mahoney (Martin Crane) and Peri Gilpin (Roz Doyle). It was agreed that in the event of Kelsey Grammer or David Hyde Pierce being unavailable, unfilmed episodes would be cancelled, and in the event of the others leaving, a reduction in the licence fee would be made, compensating NBC (Adalian, 2001). At its heart these concessions are designed to reduce the risk of the deal for both parties.

Closure and implementation

In this stage, the focus turns to formalizing, implementing and monitoring the agreement. Sometimes verbal agreements are sufficient; sometimes 'heads of agreement' are signed, which are summaries of the key deal points, and which are then followed by 'long form' contracts at a later date. It is common in some entertainment contexts for a project (such as a special charity concert) to take place long before all the legal agreements consenting to performance and recording are finally and fully signed off.

INTRODUCING THIRD PARTIES

Lawyers and attorneys

Introducing lawyers into a negotiation or conflict can bring both positives and negatives. It can elevate the perceived seriousness of a dispute for both parties. It signals that there is diminishing confidence the deal can be brokered in the current arrangement and that it looks like the parties are headed towards litigation. Lawyers bring specialist knowledge of contractual law, copyright law and other potentially relevant matters. They can also act as witnesses and provide personal support. However, lawyers can also exert a negative effect because they can escalate conflict, forcing the other party to secure legal representation, making interactions more formal and hostile and adding significantly to the costs for both parties. In some negotiations, if one party is significantly wealthier, they may introduce lawyers simply to intimidate the other party and financially drain them through expensive legal proceedings.

MEDIATORS

In mediation, a neutral third party is chosen, respected by those in the dispute, whose objective is to help the two parties facilitate a solution. Mediators control the process, but not the outcome. Instead of ordering a resolution, they hopefully bring a deep knowledge of this type of dispute to the table and a range of imaginative options that could be used by the parties to craft their own, hopefully, win/win solution. The meetings may involve a confidentiality agreement at the beginning of the process and an agreement at the end of the process, minuting agreed outcomes.

ARBITRATORS

In arbitration, which may become necessary under legislation or contractual undertakings, the warring parties come before an arbitrator who listens to both sides, and has the power to dictate a resolution, which is binding on the parties.

In negotiations, and in conflict generally, it is best to attempt to resolve conflict directly at the lowest and most immediate level prior to escalating it. For example, if I find the behaviour of a co-worker inappropriate, and feel strongly enough about the matter to want to lodge a complaint, ideally I should attempt to raise my concerns directly with the employee prior to lodging the complaint. I would naturally choose a moment that didn't humiliate the person, and would attempt to use wording that was not hostile ('You may not be aware of this, but it does upset me when you [do whatever is the source of the complaint] and I would be grateful if you wouldn't do it'). If the co-worker rebuffs this approach, and is even ruder, I can then legitimately take it to my manager, or the manager of my co-worker, and state that I had attempted to sort out the problem directly but had failed. Apart from allowing the co-worker an opportunity to respond and argue their reasons, it is also important preparatory work before lodging a complaint, because the first question that a supervisor will often ask is, 'Is the co-worker aware that you feel that way, and have you ever attempted to discuss it with them?' Some courts and legal arbitrators will not allow matters to be brought before them until an attempt has been made at self-resolution. Sometimes conflicts can be short-circuited quickly, without any escalation required. If an employee feels that a direct approach would objectively place themselves at a degree of personal risk, then they may have grounds to proceed without taking this step.

SUMMARY AND CONCLUSION

This chapter has examined conflict and negotiation processes in creative firms. Studying this chapter will help you in a number of ways as a practising manager, and increase your capacity to:

- *See where conflict is structural rather than personal:* When you encounter conflict in the workplace, you will be less likely to see it automatically as an aberration driven by someone you don't like and more likely to study the situation to see if structural issues are at play. You will be more sophisticated at analysing the nature of the conflict, which increases your chances of resolving it.

- *Be open to conflict being positive:* You have also seen through examples that not all conflict is bad; while interpersonal conflict is destructive, low levels of task and process conflict can open up positive advantages and allow people to make suggestions that will help strengthen processes.
- *Search for win/win outcomes:* By following the example of the CEO in the A&R versus marketing example, you can look more flexibly and creatively at conflicts to see how they can be crafted to create better outcomes for both parties and the organization. You also have in this example a variety of angles and options that can be employed to resolve organizational conflict.
- *Try to understand the other party's situation in a negotiation as intimately as your own:* The more you try to understand what is driving the other party, the more this will assist you in constructing the best possible outcomes for both parties.

This chapter has focused on organizational conflict. If you are experiencing conflict as an artist working with other artists, there are resources that specifically discuss this challenge (Arts & Ashdown, 2015; John-Steiner, 2000). There are also specialist conflict management resources for designers working in design project teams (Brown, 2013).

Discussion questions and class exercises

Research exercise

1. Identify an organizational conflict that has arisen between managers in a creative organization. This may come from a media article or your own investigation. What created and fuelled the conflict? What solutions could be employed in an attempt to resolve the conflict? (Perhaps one or more of the solutions the CEO attempted to bring to the A&R versus marketing dispute in this chapter is relevant?)

2. With reference to the Metallica movie *Some Kind of Monster*, categorise the conflicts that take place between

band members in terms of 'task conflict', 'process conflict' and 'relationship conflict'. (Note that Phil Towle, who features in the movie, has contributed to the Teams chapter of this textbook, reflecting on what he has learned about maximising the performance of creative teams from experiences such as working with Metallica).

3. Case Study 3.1: Crisis in the Opera House

Refer back to the case study at the end of Chapter 3 (Case Study 3.1). Answer the following questions in relation to that case:

1. Compare and contrast the conflicting positions around the table. Looking at the conflict between the managers participating in the meeting, would you describe the main source of the conflict as task conflict, relationship conflict or process conflict?
2. Where should we draw the line with prima donna behaviour (both in terms of this case and the Jeremy Clarkson case that opened the chapter)?
3. What should Impresario do, both in terms of the key decision and the way she communicates it?
4. What other policies, practices and processes should Impresario review?

CASE STUDY 5.1: ARTISTIC VERSUS MARKETING INTERFUNCTIONAL CONFLICT IN A NON-PROFIT CONTEXT

This case explores interfunctional conflict at the artistic/marketing interface in large non-profit music organizations (a commercial example is provided earlier in the chapter).

The Artistic Administrator Natalie Marnier sat opposite Steve Spring, the orchestra's new Marketing Director. She had met the previous day with the orchestra's Principal

Conductor and Musical Director, who had expressed grave concerns over the orchestra's marketing.

NATALIE: 'Maestro Cellini isn't happy with the draft season brochure'.

STEVE: 'OK'

NATALIE: 'There are some things he says you've "dumbed down". You edited down his opening page, removing a lot of information and credits'.

STEVE: 'Between you and me it was boring. No one cares. A lot of that stuff should be at the back of the brochure in micro type'.

NATALIE: 'But I agree with him that it damages morale among team members if they're not being acknowledged. A mention is a small thing in a brochure, but can mean a lot to the person being credited. And you deleted his comments on the music. Your short little summaries for each event are too glib and simplistic'.

STEVE: 'His writing is too musicological. Too technical. Too jargonistic. Too long. We should be writing more experientially about the music, about how it makes you feel. We need to give a richer context that is going to help shape the listener's experience, and help them relate to the program, even if they know nothing about classical music'.

NATALIE: 'But we're not after just anyone. We're after thinking, active listeners who are going to make an investment in the experience. We're not going after some mainstream pop audience with the attention span of sparrows. Our core audience are knowledgeable and will feel patronized by what you're writing'.

STEVE: 'If you want to keep the audience to a closed club of dying subscribers, then sure, we can do that, but you will be the last one left here to switch the lights off'.

She looked further down her list. 'And we took six months to get a photo of the Russian soprano, and you didn't even put it in'.

STEVE: 'It was *hideous*! She looked like her eyes were going to pop out of her head, hitting a high note. It gives me nightmares just thinking about it. Who does the photos for these artists?!'

NATALIE: 'And by the way, I would be really grateful if you didn't use the word "product". That language is quite offensive to some of us. Turning someone's most personal, spiritual, artistic quest into some plastic commodity, like a tube of toothpaste, it's just crass and awful'.

STEVE: 'Fine. I'll add that to "brand", "content", "NFT", "NPD", "CRM", and all the other terms I'm banned from using here'.

NATALIE: 'Also, Maestro complained that in the printed concert program last night you had minutes against each of the movements'.

STEVE: 'It helps orientate newcomers so they know roughly where they are in the program. Newbies need assistance to help them navigate the experience. This stops them clapping between movements, which I know really offends you, even though when I hear clapping between movements I am relieved, because it means we have some new people in the hall'.

NATALIE:	'The thing that offends Maestro is that he may want to take 13 minutes for a movement rather than the 10 minutes stated in the program. He is not a machine. He doesn't want to be artistically defined by your prescriptions and pronouncements'.
STEVE:	'He doesn't have to. They're just general indications'.
NATALIE:	'And your advertisements communicate at the most banal, superficial level. It's a missed opportunity because there's so much more we could be communicating, which I'm sure would be better marketing. Sometimes you don't put all the artists, or all the composers, or there isn't any information at all on some really important things'.
STEVE:	'Natalie, the media environment is so competitive and cluttered, you have to reduce things to one clear, simple proposition, or you make no impact. Artistic Administration always wants a hundred things put across in a 30 second TV spot, or a print ad in a magazine or a social media post. Less is more. We need to make one clear, compelling statement. I'm happy for you to help define that statement'.
NATALIE:	'But I'm the one who needs to manage disgruntled artists who see themselves increasingly ignored by you in the process. Or steamrolled by your arrogance. You may be following your marketing textbooks, but it is pretty naïve politically to do what you're doing. You're annoying some pretty important people'.
STEVE:	'I'm just fighting my corner, fighting it hard, and doing what a Marketing Director is supposed to do. Others like the Managing

	Director can arbitrate, and I'll live with their decisions'.
NATALIE:	'Well Maestro isn't happy, and he says he will be talking to the Managing Director'.

The authors would like to thank Simon Cahill for co-authoring the non-profit and commercial interfunctional conflict cases provided in this chapter. Simon is the Senior Vice President of Commercial, Media and Audience of Warner Music Australia. Prior to Warner Music he has held positions at Sony Music in A&R, Marketing at BMG and Sales at Mushroom.

Discussion questions and class exercises

1. Examine the points of conflict in the case. What are the underlying issues that are driving the tensions?
2. Which of the conflict resolution approaches mentioned in this chapter (in the discussion on the conflict process) would be appropriate in this situation?

   A video of managerial responses to this case study is available to instructors from the companion website: www.routledgetextbooks.com/textbooks/MMCCI

References

Abe, D. (2013). 'MC/Master of Ceremonies (Emcee)', *Blackpast.org*. Available at https://www.blackpast.org/african-american-history/mc-emcee-master-ceremonies/#:~:text=MC%2FMaster%20of%20Ceremonies%20 (accessed 16 July 2022).

Adalian, J. (2001). '"Frasier" couched at NBC for 3 years', *Variety*, Available at http://variety.com/2001/tv/news/frasier-couched-at-nbc-for-3-years-1117794806/ (accessed 13 September 2015).

Arts, H. & Ashdown, K. (2015). *Conflict Resolution for Musicians (and Other Cool People)*. Vancouver: Conflict Resolution for Creative Press.

Barclay, D. W. (1991). 'Interdepartmental conflict in organizational buying: the impact of the organizational context', *Journal of Marketing Research*, Vol. 28, no. 2, pp. 145–159.

Brown, D. M. (2013). *Designing Together: The Collaboration and Conflict Management Handbook for Creative Professionals*. San Francisco, CA: New Riders.

Caves, R. E. (2000). *Creative Industries: Contracts Between Art and Commerce*. Cambridge, MA and London, England: Harvard University Press.

Cialdini, R. B. (1984). *Influence: The Psychology of Persuasion*. New York: HarperCollins.

Crittenden, V. L., Gardiner, L. R. & Stam, A. (1993). 'Reducing conflict between marketing and manufacturing', *Industrial Marketing Management*, Vol. 22, no. 299–309.

De Dreu, C. K. W. (1997). 'Productive conflict: The importance of conflict management and conflict issue'. In C. K. W. De Dreu & E. V. D. De Vliert (eds.), *Using Conflict in Organizations*. London: SAGE Publications.

Evans, M. & Singh, A. (2015). 'Sacked Clarkson could now face assault charge', *The Weekly Telegraph*, April 1–7, p. 1.

Goleman, D. & The Dalai Lama. (2004). *Destructive Emotions: And How We Can Overcome Them*. London: Bloomsbury.

Griffin, A. & Hauser, J. R. (1996). 'Integrating R&D and marketing: A review and analysis of the literature', *Journal of Product Innovation Management*, Vol. 13, pp. 191–215.

Gupta, A. K., Raj, S. P. & Wilemon, D. (1986). 'A model for studying R&D – Marketing interface in the product innovation process', *Journal of Marketing*, Vol. 50, no. *2*, pp. 7–17.

Hesmondhalgh, D. & Baker, S. (2011). *Creative Labour: Media Work in Three Cultural Industries*. London: Routledge.

Jehn, K. A. (1995). 'A multimethod examination of the benefits and detriments of intragroup conflict', *Administrative Science Quarterly*, Vol. 40, no. 2, pp. 256–282.

Jehn, K. A. (1997). 'A qualitative analysis of conflict types and dimensions in organizational groups', *Administrative Science Quarterly*, Vol. 42, no. 3, pp. 530–557.

John-Steiner, V. (2000). *Creative Collaboration*. Oxford: Oxford University Press.

Maltz, E. & Kohli, A. K. (2000). 'Reducing marketing's conflict with other functions: The differential effects of integrating mechanisms', *Journal of the Academy of Marketing Science*, Vol. 28, no. 4, pp. 479–492.

Massey, G. R. & Dawes, P. L. (2007). 'The antecedents and consequence of functional and dysfunctional conflict between Marketing Managers and Sales Managers', *Industrial Marketing Management*, Vol. 36, no. 8, pp. 1118–1129.

Negus, K. (1992). *Producing Pop: Culture and Conflict in the Popular Music Industry*. London: Edward Arnold Publishers Ltd.

Ordanini, A., Rubera, G. & Sala, M. (2008). 'Integrating functional knowledge and embedding learning in new product launches: How project forms helped EMI Music', *Long Range Planning*, Vol. 41, pp. 17–32.

Pinto, M. B., Pinto, J. K. & Prescott, J. E. (1993). 'Antecedents and consequences of project team cross-functional cooperation', *Management Science*, Vol. 39, no. 10, pp. 1281–1297.

Rayner, G. & Furness, H. (2015). 'Clarkson may face sack over "fracas" with producer', *The Weekly Telegraph*, March 18–24, p. 1.

Robbins, S. P. & Judge, T. A. (2022). *Organizational Behavior*, 18th edition. Global Edition. Essex: Pearson Education Limited

Shaw, V. & Shaw, C. T. (1998). 'Conflict between engineers and marketers: The engineer's perspective', *Industrial Marketing Management*, Vol. *27*, pp. 279–291.

Stewart, J. B. (2005). *Disney War*. New York: Simon & Schuster.

Subramanian, G. (2002). 'Frasier Case Studies (A) and (B)', *Harvard Business School Case 801-447*, May 2001 (revised June 2002).

Volpe, J. (2007). *The Toughest Show on Earth: My Rise and Reign at The Metropolitan Opera*. New York: Vintage Books.

Stress, wellbeing and self-care in creative organizations

Chapter 6

CHAPTER LEARNING OBJECTIVES

After studying this chapter, you should be able to:

- Define and explain concepts such as 'bad work' in the creative industries, 'self-exploitation', 'commoditization', 'self-estrangement', and 'presenteeism';
- Identify workplace issues that increase the risks of negative mental health;
- Develop options and strategies for addressing these challenges and supporting creative industries workers, at both an organizational and individual level.

DOI: 10.4324/9781003262923-6

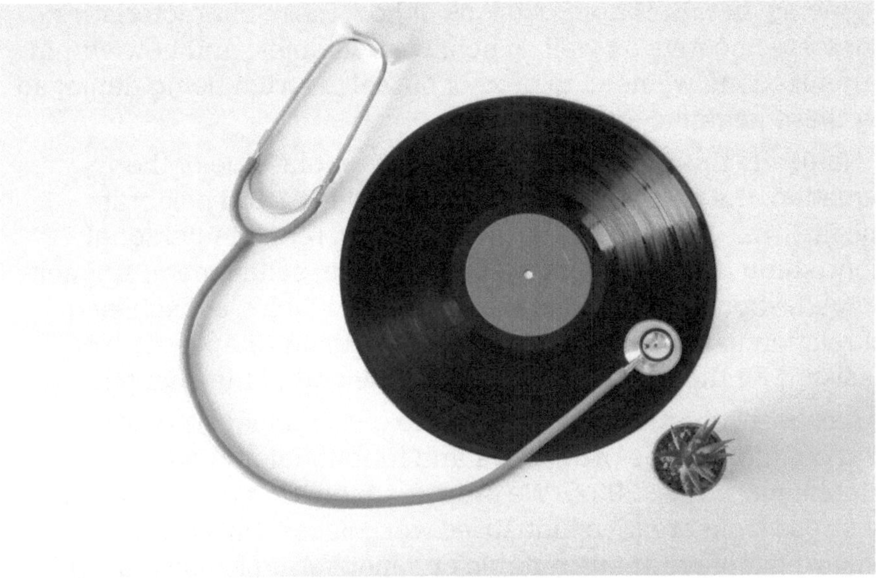

Figure 6.1 Wellbeing and self-care are seen as increasingly important for workers in the creative industries. Photo credit: Beautyimage / Shutterstock.com.

INTRODUCTION

Wellbeing and self-care in the workforce received increasing attention in the years leading up to the global Coronavirus pandemic. But the pandemic elevated it to an entirely new level. We know that within the creative industries workers historically have had to deal with high levels of occupational stress (Vaag *et al.*, 2014). In fact some researchers have claimed that the statistics reveal a mental health crisis (Everymind 2018; van den Eynde *et al.*, 2016). The additional stress placed on segments of the creative industries through the postponement of projects and events during the global pandemic only exacerbated stress during this period.

In Chapter 1, we looked at idiosyncrasies of the creative industries. These are either characteristics that are unique to these industries due to the nature of developing creative work, or characteristics that exist in other industries (such as financial insecurity) but research shows are heightened in the creative economy. In this chapter we look at how these characteristics generate negative as well as positive outcomes, and how within organizations we need to protect ourselves from being damaged by these negative aspects.

Naturally this chapter only focusses on one side of the equation, the negative side. We acknowledge and celebrate the fact that creative industries work can result in personal flourishing and fulfilment, self-affirmation, self-esteem, and self-actualization. Indeed all of these needs (which we discussed in relation to Maslow's Hierarchy of Needs in Chapter 4) are assisted by the solutions we offer at the end of the chapter.

As observed elsewhere in this book, certain levels of stress and conflict can be productive and functional in workplaces (Robbins & Judge, 2022). We are not advocating the elimination of stress from creative industries workplaces, but rather ensuring it stays at sustainable and motivating levels that will not impact the long-term health of employees. This is not the case currently in many workplaces. For example, the following statistics on the creative industries illustrate the problem and should concern us:

- A 2018 Australian creative industries study found that compared to the general population, 20% more creative industry workers showed mild to severe symptoms of depression, and 29% more showed symptoms of anxiety (Everymind, 2018);
- A 2016 Australian entertainment industry study found that 44% of workers exhibited moderate to severe anxiety (van den Eynde *et al.*, 2016). The same study found 15% of entertainment workers exhibited moderate to severe indicators of depression symptoms. Suicide ideation in the creative industries was six times greater than the general population, suicide planning is more than four times greater, and suicide attempts are more than double;
- A 2018 Irish creative industries study found that the likelihood of a mental health problem in the sector is three times that of the general population (Shorter *et al.*, 2018);
- A 2016 study of UK musicians found that 71% had experienced anxiety and panic attacks, and 68% experienced

incidences of depression, three times more likely than the general population (Gross & Musgrave, 2016). There have been calls from artists for psychological support from record labels (Smith, 2021);

- People in the fashion industry are 25% more likely to experience mental illness than in other industries, with a high comparative suicide rate (iCAAD, 2020). Models in the fashion industry are at risk of sexual harassment, low self-esteem through objectification, as well as health risks and body image issues through the pursuit of impossibly thin physiques. The tragic deaths of designers Kate Spade and Alexander McQueen shone a spotlight on mental health in fashion (iCAAD, 2020);
- Within architecture, concerns about mental health and work-related wellbeing have been identified which has resulted in burnout and departures from the profession (Stead & Gusheh, 2020);
- Novelists/authors were singled out in one study as being specifically associated with increased likelihood of schizophrenia, bipolar disorder, unipolar depression, anxiety disorders, substance abuse, and suicide (Kyaga *et al.*, 2013);
- Actors can experience poor mental health from a variety of factors including financial instability, rejection, lack of creative autonomy, a reaction to traumatic themes, and identity confusion as a result of a blurring of boundaries between actor and character (Arias, 2019);
- The potential for the global pandemic to have increased these numbers can be illustrated by the UK statistic that in 2021 nearly 80% of organizations (across all industries) reported stress-related absence in their organization over the previous year, which rises to 91% of organizations with more than 250 employees (CIPD, 2021).

Creative organizations usually have project teams that include permanent full-time employees and independent contractors who join for individual projects. To ensure that project teams function at the optimal level, and everyone is protected, we need to concern ourselves with all these workers. Let us look in greater detail at the challenges they face.

'BAD WORK' IN THE CREATIVE INDUSTRIES AND WORKPLACE PRESSURES

In looking at negatives within creative industries work that could contribute to the above statistics, David Hesmondhalgh and Sarah Baker's 2011 book *Creative Labour: Media work in three cultural industries* provides a good foundation for this discussion, because they look squarely at the creative industries and propose a model which contrasts 'good' and 'bad' work. They look at the work of three creative industries through this lens: music, magazine publishing and TV production.

In their study 'good work' provides the potential for the worker to flourish. As summarized in Figure 6.2, features of good work are: good wages, working hours, high levels of safety; autonomy; interest and involvement; sociality; self-esteem; self-realization; work-life balance; security; and the potential to create excellent products that contribute to the common good. This relates to the higher-order need fulfilment in Maslow's hierarchy and what motivates us at work, covered in Chapter 4.

In contrast, 'bad work' creates a negative experience and dysfunctional outcomes for the worker. Features of bad work are:

	Good work	**Bad work**
Process	Good wages, working hours, high levels of safety Autonomy Interest, involvement Sociality Self-esteem Self-realisation Work-life balance Security	Poor wages, working hours and levels of safety Powerlessness Boredom Isolation Low self-esteem and shame Frustrated development Overwork Risk
Product	Excellent products Products that contribute to the common good	Low-quality products Products that fail to contribute to the well-being of others

Figure 6.2 Good and bad work. From: *Creative Labour: Media Work in Three Cultural Industries*, 2011, David Hesmondhalgh & Sarah Baker, Routledge, p. 39. Copyright © 2011 David Hesmondhalgh & Sarah Baker. Reproduced with permission of Taylor & Francis Group through PLSclear.

poor wages, working hours and levels of safety; powerlessness; boredom; isolation; low self-esteem and shame; frustrated development; overwork; risk; and low quality products that fail to contribute to the wellbeing of others. The researchers document many examples of 'bad work' in the creative industries. It should be noted that sometimes one creative worker, such as a director or producer, seeking to prioritize their own self-realization and self-esteem, creates bad work for others, by micromanaging them and making their working life miserable. This can lead to workplace deviancy, as discussed in Chapter 4.

In the coming pages we will expand on the concept of 'bad work' to provide a detailed exploration of workplace, cultural and other pressures in the creative industries. By 'workplace pressures' we mean the sorts of issues unions concern themselves with, such as pay and workplace conditions. By 'cultural pressures' we mean the pressures created by industry stories, norms, shared assumptions and myths. We will walk through the summary presented in Figure 6.3, of factors which negatively influence wellbeing. But before we do this, let's step back and look at what macro-economic drivers may be contributing to the increase in stress in these industries.

MACRO DRIVERS OF PRESSURES: SUPPLY AND DEMAND IMBALANCES AND ITS ACCELERATION THROUGH DIGITIZED CONTENT

One of the key economic reasons for the often poor treatment of creative industries workers is the massive imbalance in the number of people wishing to supply their services, and the demand for these services (Hesmondhalgh & Baker, 2011). For example, Alan Krueger, in his 2019 book *Rockonomics: What the Music Industry Can Teach Us About Economics (and Our Future)* points out that in 2017 the top 0.1% of artists (i.e. one in a thousand) accounted for more than 50% of all album sales. 2017 Pollstar data indicated that the top 1% of artists account for 60% of concert ticket revenue. In the United States, only 1.1% of musicians achieve mainstream status, and 91% remain completely undiscovered (Resnikoff, 2019). Audiences are also increasingly overwhelmed by choice with (for example) 33.2 million different songs streamed in 2017, more than could be listened to in six lifetimes (Krueger, 2019). By 2021 these figures

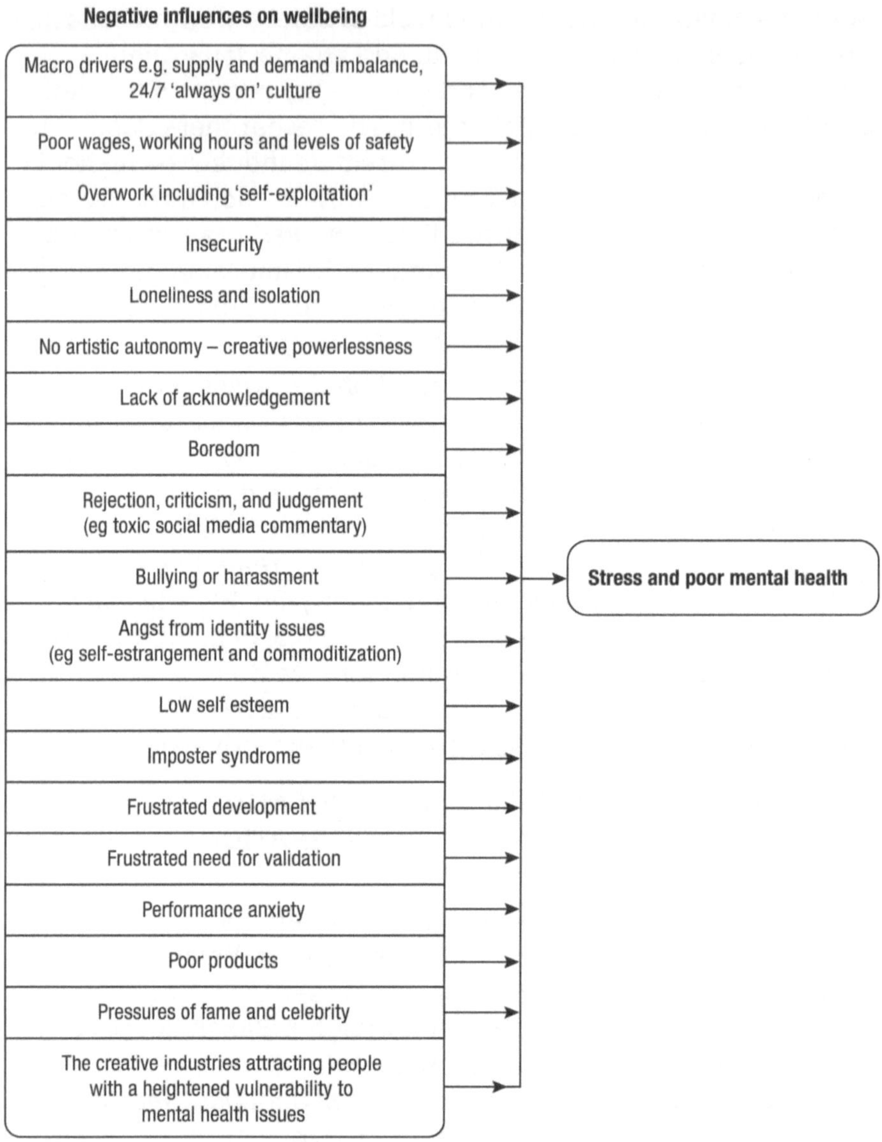

Figure 6.3 Summary of negative influences on wellbeing in the creative industries which lead to stress and poor mental health.

had more than doubled. Contemporary musicians are also more than ever competing with the past. Why experiment with new music, and take a risk that you may spoil some precious leisure time, when there is so much safe historical material to choose from? If 95% of pop musicians left the music industry it would have little impact on the businesses of streaming giants such as Spotify, major record labels, commercial radio stations, and other industry players due to their vast catalogues. This means that the leverage of musicians is low unless they can build a community around them that has commercial significance, but the competition makes this difficult.

This growing inequality is due to a number of factors: the scale afforded by digital distribution has allowed artists to conquer vaster and vaster swathes of geographical territory, which accelerates star building; our celebrity-obsessed culture channels more and more media attention onto a small group of artists; and online word of mouth can create bandwagon effects, snowballing small initial advantages. The power of luck is well acknowledged in creative industries, whether that be around collaborations, resonating with people in a subjective business, and media coverage.

This economic truth means there is a power imbalance in terms of those commissioning work and controlling enterprises, and those seeking paid creative work and employment in the creative industries. This imbalance can be exploited by those in organizations which can create misery and mental health issues for workers.

The digital distribution of content has also eroded the incomes of many in the creative industries. For example, the move from the sale of physical music product such as CDs to streaming has seen revenue from recordings decline for most musicians, as they generally pay a pittance (Gross & Musgrave, 2016, 2017). Music streaming revenues have been a salvation for large companies that control thousands (or even millions) of recordings such as major record labels, but not for musicians outside the top 1%.

Even before the rise of digitization, there was a 'work for free' culture within the creative industries, particularly when trying to break in. It is increasingly acknowledged that this prevents people from lower socio economic backgrounds participating (Dore, 2015). This has been exacerbated by digital distribution making it easier to illegally copy and distribute intellectual property, and lowering its perceived value.

There are other macro trends that are impacting work in all industries, such as the increased economic uncertainty and job insecurity (Robbins & Judge, 2022). There is also the transition to a 24/7 'always on' culture, but this will be dealt with in subsequent sections. Let us now look more closely at workplace pressures.

WORKPLACE PRESSURES (INDUSTRY-LEVEL WORKPLACE AND EMPLOYMENT CONDITIONS)

Research has identified a number of workplace pressures impacting the mental wellbeing of those in the creative industries, which we will examine in turn.

The insecure and precarious nature of employment

Hennekam and Bennett (2016) have described the insecure nature of work in the creative industries, which is very often project based, performed on short-term, freelance contracts as part of project teams. Creative workers are usually self-employed, and must make their own provisions for professional development, sick leave, insurance, and superannuation/pension. For example, as much as 90% of UK film and TV work is undertaken on a freelance basis. Because of the temporary, project nature of the employment, employers generally see little point in training schemes. Instead people learn by watching. Many creative industry workers comment that their formal education did not prepare for them for self-employed work, which requires entrepreneurial, management and business skills, as well as people skills, and the ability to handle criticism and rejection.

It is a well-documented fact that the nature of short-term employment for those in the creative industries can lead them to feeling insecure, vulnerable and dispensable (Hesmondhalgh & Baker, 2011). This in turn leads to feelings of anxiety and stress. Architecture for example has been described as 'desired and sustaining, yet precarious and unsustainable' (Stead & Gusheh, 2020). When the phone doesn't ring for freelance musicians, it can breed self-doubt and depression (Cooper & Wills, 1989). They can feel that their future is in doubt and that they may not be able to pay their bills. It can be hard to create a healthy, balanced life where there is no routine, no stability, too much work or not enough work (Gross & Musgrave, 2016, 2017). Managers working in the creative industries need to be mindful of these stresses.

Overwork and burnout

Workers in the creative industries report extremely long working hours (Hesmondhalgh & Baker, 2011). This can work against people who want to have a family, particularly women. A 'succeed at all costs' / 'make or break' ethos, and the intrinsic satisfaction and enjoyment people draw from creative work can mean that enormous numbers of hours are poured into one's work with little immediate success (Hesmondhalgh & Baker, 2011).

There can also be a blurring of work and leisure, as 'the thing you do for work is the thing you do for recreation' (Dore, 2015). So the risk of burnout is high. Creative industry workers can voluntarily assist in their own overwork, by pushing themselves to the limit to succeed, or taking on the full weight of under resourced projects, which has been termed as 'self-exploitation' (Hesmondhalgh & Baker, 2011). Workers can draw positive experiences from their work, but subsidize projects through free time gifted to the project, at the expense of other things in their life. This also adds to the risk of burnout. We can make a promise to give ourselves some mental health time when pressing deadlines have been met ('after fashion week is over', 'after the exhibition opens', etc.), but the relentless pressure of the creative industries means this can keep getting pushed back indefinitely (Idacavage, 2021).

In terms of unsocial working hours, many musicians and DJs are basically doing the night shift which is linked to a range of adverse health outcomes (Gardiner, 2019). Irregular hours create their own pressures, such as playing havoc with sleep patterns and relationships outside the workplace. These all increase workplace stress, which in turn can lead to self-medication with alcohol and drugs. This in turn can create the risk of developing dependency and addiction issues.

The 24/7 social media environment has only accelerated this historical problem. In the fashion industry, the social media world of a perpetual stream of content has seen the fashion calendar shift from two main seasons to an endless series of drops and capsule collections (Soar & Chen, 2019). In music, instead of artists releasing an album, touring it, and then taking a break, they are under pressure to release a relentless stream of content to keep themselves current. This in turn has increased workloads and stress. Case Study 6.1 at the conclusion of this chapter focuses on this problem. Artists may need additional support and may need to understand more deeply their audience segments, who they are communicating with on each platform, what audiences are saying and what is resonating.

Feelings of loneliness and isolation for remote workers

Even prior to the global Coronavirus pandemic, creative industry workers (such as freelancers working on magazines) reported high degrees of loneliness and isolation (Hesmondhalgh & Baker, 2011). For those working by themselves at home, in addition to loneliness there can be a blurring between work and home, so instead of compartmentalizing work for a particular part of the day, it bleeds into every hour (Dore, 2015). There can also be a sense of exclusion compared to those who work in the office, with the perception that freelancers who drop into the office get more work (Hesmondhalgh & Baker, 2011).

Powerlessness and devaluation

Many creative workers experience a sense of powerlessness; of being subjected to control and manipulation by others (Hesmondhalgh & Baker, 2011). For example, a UK study reported musicians' frustration with their inability to plan their time/ future which can be in the control of others or luck (Gross & Musgrave, 2017). Powerlessness can also be experienced where companies force artistic decisions on creative workers with which they are uncomfortable, such as changing artistic direction to maximize the commercial outcome. This destroys the autonomy that creative workers desire, so they can believe that what they are creating is authentic personal expression (Hesmondhalgh & Baker, 2011). People asking them to work for free or failing to get back to them can lead to a sense of devaluation. Failure to acknowledge and credit creative workers, particularly given the emotional and financial (e.g. training and equipment) investment many make in their work, can lead to them feeling devalued and ignored.

Other workplace problems

There are a number of other issues that creative industry workers have encountered, such as:

- Rejection, fear of judgement, constant criticism (which will be discussed in a subsequent section);
- Feelings of inadequacy when others succeed, such as constantly comparing yourself to other creative producers through chart positions, awards, scholarships, media recognition, and social media metrics;
- A lack of respect for the time, effort and expertise that is invested into creative activity, which can be demoralizing. 'A plumber doesn't work for "experience"; a doctor doesn't perform surgery for "exposure"' (Gross & Musgrave, 2017, p13);
- In the UK film and TV industry nearly 9 in 10 workers have experienced or witnessed bullying or harassment in the workplace, and it's one of the primary causes of poor mental health in the industry (The UK Film & TV Charity). The UK Musicians' Union reported that 48% of respondents to a membership survey have faced sexual harassment in the workplace, and some have left the industry because of it (Musicians' Union, 2019). Sexual harassment is covered in this book in Chapter 8;
- Fashion industry entry-level positions can see workers thrown in the deep end to see if they will sink or swim, with poor pay and a combative 'fight for your job' culture (Soar & Chen, 2019).

CULTURAL PRESSURES

The book and movie *The Devil Wears Prada* features an assistant to a powerful magazine editor in the fashion industry (Weisberger, 2003). Because it is a role that 'a million girls would die for' she is frequently reminded how privileged she is to have the role and how replaceable she is. The editor leverages the power imbalance to intimidate her; to accept the barrage of rudeness she throws at her. This leads to an abusive organizational culture where workers have no rights, no job security, and little dignity. While the fictional character has a 'love/hate' relationship with her job, this is a recipe for poor mental health, and she eventually leaves.

In the creative industries there are a range of culturally supported beliefs which encourage self-destructive behaviour from creative workers such as:

- That 'great art comes from pain', 'you need to suffer for your art', you need to be a 'tormented, tortured soul';
- That great art is a 'calling' like a religious pilgrimage or climbing Himalayan mountains and one should do it irrespective of payment or the expectations you would bring to a normal job;
- To write great lyrics or novels, you need to have a part of you that is broken and damaged, and you need deep demons, which drive your creativity;
- That it is romantic to 'live fast and die young', never having to grow old, captured forever in time as someone young and beautiful like Marilyn Monroe. Another angle on this is that some artists are too sensitive, too beautiful for this world;
- That 'you're only as good as your last gig' – which heaps further pressure on artists (Dobson, 2010);
- That the industry lives by the motto of 'Whatever it Takes' [to be successful] – this was the official war cry of Casablanca Records, which subsequently collapsed due to its excesses (Dannen, 1990);
- That 'The Show Must Go On', despite whatever personal sacrifice and suffering this may entail;
- That some artists give themselves up to be sacrificed, like psychedelic travellers that bring back magical objects from strange lands, but may not survive the trip, e.g. 'Messily sacrificed on the altar of opiates, the New York Dolls imploded before their spiritual progeny emerged to profit from their enduring legacy. But, like all good saviours, they've risen again' (Fortnam, 2006).

IDENTITY ISSUES

Creative industry workers can make their profession part of their identity, e.g. 'I am a dancer' (Hennekam & Bennett, 2016). This may be the case even if they only work a small proportion of their 'portfolio career' as a professional dancer, drawing most of their money from other work.

It is common for artists, especially those who achieve a high public profile, to experience angst from identity issues. These typically arise in two ways: a tension forms between their public persona and private self (Bryant Smalley & McIntosh, 2011); the artist wraps up their entire identity in being famous, and any shortfall is experienced as soul destroying. Let's examine each in turn. (We should also note that identity issues can arise when health risks such as drugs and alcohol become entwined in an artist's subcultural identity which it then pains them to reject – see Ward & Burns, 2000).

Public persona versus private self; self-estrangement and commoditization

In the film *Whitney: Can I Be Me* (and the title of the film itself is significant), Whitney Houston was initially positioned to appeal to a white audience, which led to huge commercial success. However, a consequence of this success was that she began to be seen by black audiences as having 'sold out'. This became clear when she was booed at the 1989 Soul Train Awards, an experience that she found emotionally devastating. It led to a deep discomfort with her public persona and she attempted to reposition herself. This type of experience is also related to the quest for 'artistic authenticity', the fact that artists will want to feel that they possess authenticity, integrity and credibility and fans will want to see this or will brand the artist a fake. Houston was complicit in the creation of this mainstream image (Davis, 2012), and benefitted from it financially, but it did not make the subsequent rejection and humiliation any less traumatic for her. When most people screw up in the office, it is usually their work that will be criticized – you didn't perform this task correctly. However for a performing artist this criticism will be seen, as with the Whitney Houston example, as a rejection of their whole identity, of themselves as an artist and human being.

Creating an image for a new artist can carry risks. Because if they are pushed into a persona that is uncomfortable for them, that they don't 'own' and feel they can get behind, even success can lead to a process of self-estrangement. They can feel used, manipulated and 'commoditized' (treated like a product rather than a human being). We saw this in Chapter 3 in relation to the 'Nashville' musician who suddenly found herself in LA being targeted to a completely different audience and performing completely different music. It can lead to comments from artists such as 'It makes me sick to think of being that person I knew wasn't really me' (Jepson, 2021). Janis Joplin suffered from a tension between her public and private personas, which was a contributory factor in her descent into addiction, ultimately dying from a heroin overdose at the age of 27 (Oksanen, 2013). Part of feeling commoditized is feeling surrounded by a web of 'fake' relationships that purport to be about friendship, but which are really about the potential utility value you may have to give someone work or create opportunities or make money for them (Hesmondhalgh & Baker, 2011).

Even for those who might manage or produce creative projects, this sort of problem can arise. Say for example I am on a production team putting together a reality TV program, and I supervise a 'villain edit' around one of the 'characters', portraying them in a bad or controversial light to increase the emotional intensity. Or I am a radio announcer and I play a trick on someone on air, phoning them up live on air and pretending to be someone I am not. Both of these examples could be seen as a normal practice to create compelling entertainment. Yet if the 'victim' in each instance committed suicide, because they were vulnerable and could not cope with the public nature of the humiliation, what would this do to our own self-perception as a creative industries worker? Would I experience self-estrangement from my actions? (Both these examples have in fact happened).

Identity is based on the assumption of stardom which then never materializes

One psychological problem that can arise, which can generate enormous psychological distress, is that an artist defines their whole sense of self-worth on the assumption of stardom, which then never materializes. Succeeding as an artist becomes part of their identity, and if they are not commercially successful they suffer enormous issues with self-esteem (Gross & Musgrave, 2016). Clearly the management of expectations is key to this problem, and what one understands as 'success'. To hope to make an impact in an artistic niche that one is passionate about should not be an unreasonable aspiration for an artist with talent and resilience. But to expect to be an international superstar, given the amount of chance that exists in the industry (Krueger, 2019) is no different to basing one's future happiness on a lottery win.

EMOTIONAL TURBULENCE, CRITICISM AND REJECTION

Creative workers generally care passionately about their work. Their personal investment in their work can be much greater than other industries, which heightens the emotional intensity (Caves, 2000; Dore, 2015). If we put down intimate thoughts and feelings in an artwork, and put it out into the world and have it criticized and trampled upon, how would this not be an emotional experience? As introduced in the section on identity, creative industry workers can hold uncompromising standards in terms of the meaning that they want to draw from their life's work. They want their life to be as personally meaningful as possible. Pursuing an artistic career can be seen as a struggle for self-actualization (Holm-Hadulla & Bertolino, 2014), and attempt to realize your ultimate potential and transcend the finite nature of your existence by leaving something behind. Once an artist decides to pursue their dreams, they will usually suffer criticism from others for doing so. As one musician commented to a researcher: 'I dislike people who think music isn't a real job' in spite of the fact that Elton John is probably bigger economically than British Steel (Cooper & Wills, 1989, p. 27). Or, as a London based Dubstep producer commented: 'They will ask "are you still doing your little music thing?" Well, yes. Are you still doing your little banking thing?' (Gross & Musgrave, 2017, p 21).

Workers in the creative industries may need to face rejection on a daily basis (Jepson, 2021). For example, architects can be exposed to public critiques that are harsh and capricious (Stead & Gusheh, 2020). Given the subjective nature of creative work, where it is hard to 'prove' which creative direction is best, criticism can lead to vulnerability and self-doubt. It can lead to negative self-talk such as 'You're not a musician/actor/writer. You're just pretending'. This can lead to 'Imposter Syndrome' where we feel like a fraud, in danger of being publicly exposed (Young, 2011). It is even an established practice in the creative industries to have your work criticized – official 'critics' exist to whom we send free product and tickets and await their verdict. One of the keys to resilience is developing strategies to manage the emotional toll of criticism. The rise of toxic social media commentary has been an even greater destroyer of emotional equilibrium. As one Sony Music executive told one of the authors about social media feedback for an artist:

> Looking at specific comments is a hiding to nowhere, and then doing things based on those comments, for every one person you please, 20 trolls pop up... and it's a very hurtful and painful process for an artist. I mean I see it, and it's horrible.
>
> (Saintilan, 2019, p. 228)

Kathryn Frazier, owner of PR agency Biz3 told *Billboard* 'I have seen huge artists who read the comments and spin out on a handful of negative seeds planted by five or 10 people' (Gardiner, 2019, p. 48). Guarding mental health can involve pulling the plug on this sort of commentary, and placing some boundaries around it.

A FRUSTRATED NEED FOR VALIDATION

Part of the anxiety of creative work can be the fear of its reception, and the anxiety you can carry until it is 'validated' by a positive audience and/or critical reaction (Hesmondhalgh & Baker, 2011). As discussed in the section on identity, if you decide that artistic popularity and success is the very meaning of your life, that it is the only thing that will validate your sense of self-worth, you have also placed yourself psychologically in a very vulnerable situation. You will begin to experience criticism and rejection in an intensely personal way, because you have invested so much of yourself into the work and so much is at stake.

To be mentally healthy we need to move away from our self-esteem and self-acceptance being entirely conditional on the success of the next project, but feeling that we possess intrinsic worth, meaning and value quite independently of the success of any project.

PERFORMANCE ANXIETY

Performance anxiety, where we feel anxiety in much the same way as people fear public speaking, is very common in the creative industries. For example, in a survey of 552 UK musicians conducted in 2014, 75% had experienced some form of performance anxiety in their careers (Help Musicians UK, 2014). Another study estimated that around half of all performing musicians suffer from performance anxiety. The objective is not to eliminate performance anxiety which can be positive at certain levels but to prevent it becoming unmanageable or creating dependency issues from self-medication.

Performance anxiety symptoms include: general tension, trembling of various parts of the body such as shaking hands, pounding chest, negative or catastrophizing thoughts, excessive sweating and clamminess, hot or cold flushes, adrenalin rushes, nausea, dry mouth and 'butterflies in the stomach'. Other symptoms are increased breathing rate, shortness of breath, severe apprehension, distracted thoughts, memory blanks, eye focussing problems, isolating behaviour and increased visits to the toilet (Lehmann, Sloboda & Woody, 2007; O'Dair, 2016; Roland, 1994). For singers, actors and comedians, anxiety can be over the fear that their voice will wobble, crack or break. Anxiety can be compounded by negative commentary and poor reviews.

In certain professional groups of classical musicians, approximately 20–30% use beta-blockers to control their anxiety (Lehmann, Sloboda & Woody, 2007). 'It is difficult to imagine another profession where up to 30% of workers believe that they require medication to do their job effectively' (Patston & Loughlan, 2014, p. 5). Beta-blockers arose in the late 1970s and address the fight or flight responses such as increased heart rate, sweating, nausea, and trembling. It lowers the heart rate, and can affect respiratory and cardiac function, so it is recommended that they are taken under medical supervision to monitor side effects (Patston & Loughlan, 2014).

Mental stress can be exacerbated by perfectionism, where we perform something 99% to our satisfaction but reject the entire performance over the 1% with which we are dissatisfied. Even in architectural projects creative perfectionism has been found to compound stress (Stead & Gusheh, 2020).

Deep down, all artists fear public embarrassment. In a 'normal' job, the worst that is likely to happen if we screw up is a reprimand from our supervisor. But in live entertainment, if an artist screws up there is a risk of public humiliation, which can breed fear and psychological stress. A meltdown will receive even greater coverage via media critics and social media commentary. Negative public reaction, critical comments in the media and social media commentary (trolls) can be distressing for artists. Amy Winehouse's infamous Belgrade concert, where she used drugs and alcohol to self-medicate performance anxiety (as had become habitual for her), resulted in audience boos and a 'train crash' performance, followed by vitriolic social media. A month later she was dead. We need to understand that 'putting yourself out there' can bring enormous dangers for artists.

THE CREATIVE INDUSTRIES ATTRACTING PEOPLE WHO HAVE HEIGHTENED VULNERABILITY TO MENTAL HEALTH ISSUES

There is evidence that the creative industries can attract people who are working through mental health issues, working through their demons and using creative work to process trauma (Saintilan, 2020). Many people approach their artistic life as a need to remake themselves (Jepson, 2021). This factor contributes to the worrying mental health statistics in the chapter's introduction. However, it is ambiguous in many studies as to what proportion of those who suffer from anxiety or depression is due to the industry attracting people with problems who use art as medicine, or what proportion develop problems due to the pressures of the industry.

PRESSURES OF FAME AND CELEBRITY

Fame and celebrity bring their own pressures (Spunt, 2014), as both Amy Winehouse and Whitney Houston observe in the films *Amy* and *Whitney: Can I Be Me*. Brian Wilson of The Beach

Boys spoke of the rise to fame being a scary process that mixed feeling excited with feeling sick (Wilson, 2016). Nerves and fear of failure creep in. People start swarming around you wanting a piece of you with their own agendas. It makes it difficult to find true, new friends. Eminem became irate that he couldn't go to the gas station or a 7–11 store (Bozza, 2009). Fame can lead to physical risks to security, and having your life threatened, which can happen to even the most loved bands such as The Beatles (Turner, 2016).

The achievement of fame means that the public begins to project onto an artist things that may have absolutely no relationship to them as a real person at all. The artist can become alienated, with fans loving a fantasy object often quite removed from the reality of the star's self-identity, which then makes any sort of real and meaningful communication between the artist and audience unlikely. Some artists also experience a strange ambivalence about fan appreciation, which on one hand can be fulfilling, affirming and adrenaline producing, but on another level, alone in a motel room at the end of the evening can be empty, as you don't really know them and they don't really know you (Lindvall, 2010).

Artists who are under siege from fans and the media need a protective bubble wrapped around them, which a good artist manager or record label will attempt to facilitate. But if you don't have a protective bubble, it is tempting to use drugs to create one (Knafo, 2008).

What also happens is that if and when an artist decides that they do need some professional help handling a mental health issue, instead of it being a confidential, private matter, as would be the case with most human beings, it is played out under the full glare of media attention. As the *Amy* documentary made clear, the media swarming around Amy Winehouse's rehab visits was disgraceful. Steven Tyler of Aerosmith picked up a guitar lying around in a treatment facility, and within seconds all the patients in the unit were taking photos as they had heard that tabloids were offering great money for photos of him, the more embarrassing the better (Tyler, 2012). Phil Jamieson of Grinspoon had a nurse at a detox centre tip off the tabloids (McMillen, 2014). Even journalists themselves are starting to call

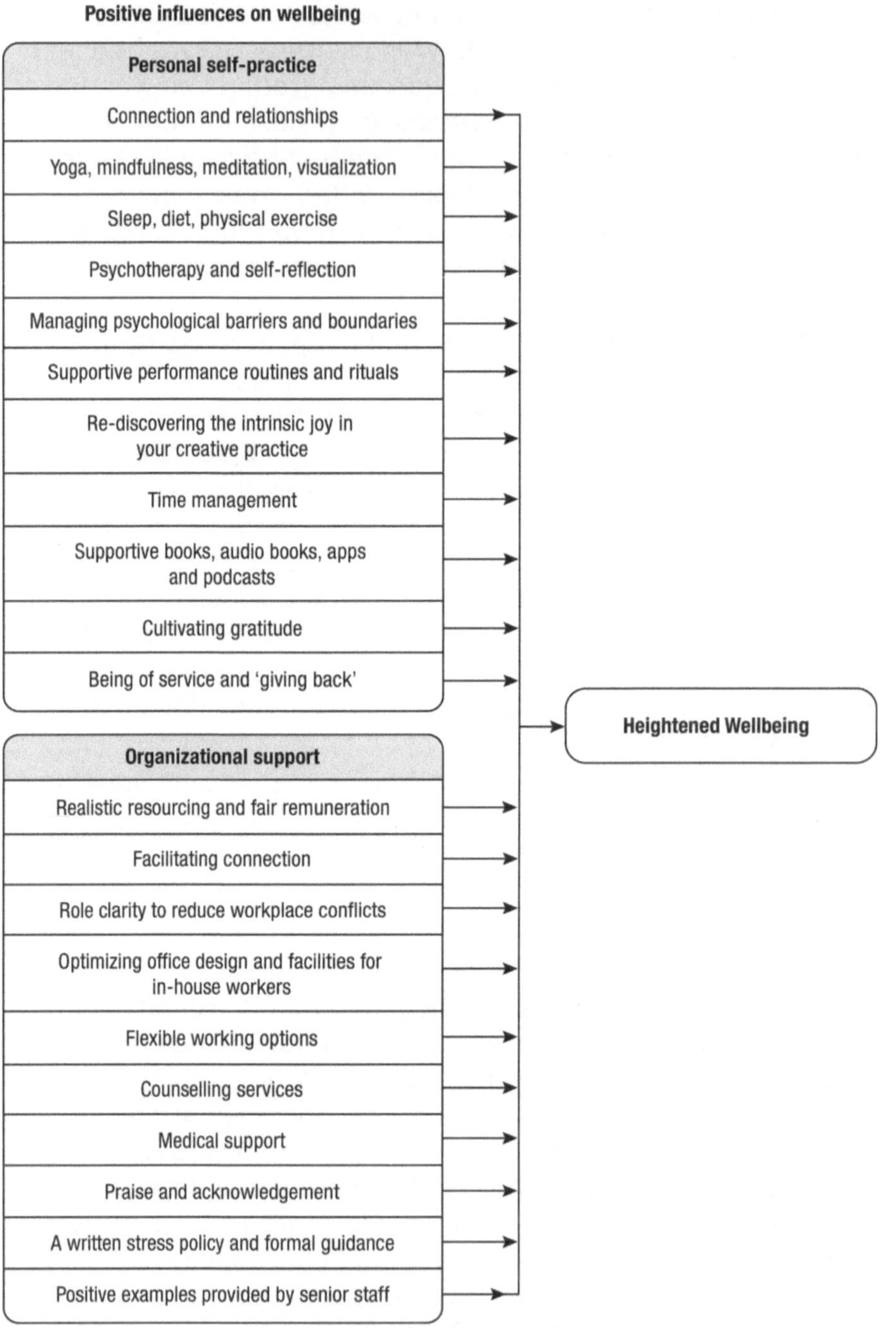

Figure 6.4 Summary of positive influences on wellbeing in the creative industries in terms of both personal self-practice and organizational support.

for higher standards in the way celebrity addiction is covered in the media: 'Currently, the way the press covers addicts is barbaric, like bear-baiting or throwing a witch in a pond to see if she will sink or swim' (Orr, 2011).

Celebrities who publicly stumble because of substance abuse problems can also suffer a backlash from audience members who interpret it as a publicity stunt. So the resulting media splashes from Amy Winehouse meltdowns elicited a level of cynicism among some audience members that it might be a ploy to generate self-publicity (Shaw, Whitehead & Giles, 2010).

Finally, there is the issue of coping with the loss of fame and celebrity, which happens eventually to almost every artist. The movie *Sunset Boulevard* captures the pain experienced by a once-famous silent-movie star who loses her fame with the advent of talking motion pictures. It is a poignant reminder that time passes, that life is transient, careers can be ephemeral, that once huge trends and developments give way to the next trend and development, often leaving artists fading from public awareness.

Now that we have scoped out many pressures of working in the creative industries, let us turn to steps that can be taken to combat these challenges. The remainder of the chapter will walk through Figure 6.4, which looks at all the things we can use to heighten wellbeing at both an organizational and individual level.

A TOOLKIT FOR ADDRESSING THESE CHALLENGES

Elite athletes are often surrounded by an army of nutritionists, sleep consultants, psychologists, visualization coaches and personal trainers to assist with their development and pursuit of success. Why should artists and creative industries workers deserve any less attention? The following section provides a smorgasbord of positive mental health initiatives, drawn from research studies, employer guides, and the personal accounts of creative industry workers. Employers might coordinate some initiatives while making other wellbeing supports available to individuals who need them.

The organization and the individual both need to contribute to positive mental health in the workforce. Employers need to take the issue seriously, build in initiatives, policies and procedures designed to support workers, and institute policies and ensure there are opportunities to check in on how people are tracking. The individual employee needs to take responsibility for their individual wellbeing and their own workplace experience, and push back when the demands become unsustainable. As they say about oxygen masks in aeroplanes, you need to make sure you have your own mask secured before helping others, or may find yourself unable to help anyone.

Health and wellbeing in the workforce is becoming an increasingly important and resourced issue (CIPD, 2021). Considerable effort is also being placed into understanding resilience, human flourishing and happiness. One model, Dr Seligman's PERMA model (Seligman, 2020) corresponds to the positive psychological benefits of undertaking 'Good Work', as outlined earlier in this chapter. The components of Figure 6.4 are designed to restore an authentic connection to creative work, which will then allow human flourishing to occur. Elements such as intrinsic joy, gratitude, connection and relationships, are seen as positive to mental health in a variety of models. Figure 6.4 also lists elements which have been found to be important to building resilience, such as time management skills, exercise, relaxation and increased social support (Robbins & Judge, 2022).

Depending on the size of the creative organization, the following employee benefits may be available, all of which have research evidence underpinning their efficacy (CIPD, 2021):

- Facilitating connection between workers to combat isolation. This may include team building, socialization activities, and mentors and buddies for new workers;
- Optimizing office design for workers such as having productive and calming spaces, natural light, breakout spaces, standing desks and ergonomically designed office furniture, comfortable temperature and acoustics;
- Counselling services and employee assistance programmes and the involvement of occupational health specialists;
- Regular on-site classes on topics such as mental health first aid, stress management, yoga, mindfulness and meditation, Pilates, time management, sleep and diet;

- Flexible working options for improved work–life balance (see Chapter 12 for further information on flexible working);
- Medical support such as free eye tests, flu vaccinations, health screening, advice on healthy eating/lifestyle etc.;
- In-house gym or subsidized gym membership or programs to encourage physical fitness (e.g. a Fitbit or other fitness trackers);
- Access to physiotherapy and complementary therapies (e.g. reflexology or massage);
- Stop smoking support;
- Insurance assistance;
- A written stress policy and formal guidance;
- Providing contact details of external bodies who can support workers, both generally and those specific to the industry, of which there are many;
- Positive examples provided by senior staff – It is no good putting up posters highlighting the importance of staff wellbeing initiatives if senior staff don't manifest these values in action and 'walk the talk'. This can be things like not feeling they need to clock up the maximum number of hours in the office;
- Praise and acknowledgement of great work such as credits on product where appropriate and public acknowledgement within the organization.

The *Architects' Mental Wellbeing Toolkit* (The Architects' Mental Wellbeing Forum, 2019) highlights a number of additional practical steps that can be taken within creative workplaces (in this case architectural practices) to make the best possible environment:

- Obtain the best possible role clarity to reduce workplace conflicts;
- Promote a culture which values outcomes and productive working during contracted hours rather than huge numbers of hours in the office and 'presenteeism' (the compulsion to always be at your desk to prove you work, even when feeling unwell) which can lead to burnout and tired work;

- Encourage the use of time management tools such as The Pomodoro Technique. Even simple techniques such as 'to do lists', or tackling priorities and hard tasks first can make situations more manageable (Robbins & Judge, 2022);
- Remember The Pareto Principle ('the 80/20 rule' – that 80% of outcomes can result from 20% of inputs or causes) when becoming overly perfectionist;
- Proactively discuss whether realistic resourcing exists for projects, and encourage people speak up if the necessary resources are not being made available;
- Give staff control over the office environment and allow for personalization.

Additional points for supporting artists and creatives working within organizations:

- ***Remunerate fairly*** and be careful of taking advantage of creative industries workers by demanding free services (in return for 'experience' for example);
- ***Psychotherapy and self-reflection for artists***: Many artists have a tortured relationship in their careers with the pursuit of fame, approval and validation and so it is worth probing these areas, through tools such as managed self-reflection and psychotherapy. For example: what does success or 'making it' mean for an artist? Is it being a superstar or making a living doing what you love? (Jepson, 2021); Questions to ask may include 'Do I need validation and from what sources?', 'How strong is my own self belief and esteem not to need external validation?', 'How much of my motivation is 'intrinsic' (i.e. the love of the work, the intrinsic pleasure of creative work) and extrinsic (fame, money, awards)? (as discussed in Chapter 4)', 'Do I have private and public personas and if so, how do I feel about the difference and reconciling the two?', 'Will I feel comfortable as a commercial artist 'monetizing' and commodifying' myself?', 'Am I using creative work to process past trauma or using it to redeem myself in some way, and if so, what pressures is this creating

for me?' (Saintilan, 2020)*. Within an organizational context, reflection may involve seeing how far a team has progressed towards goals, and how much has already been accomplished (Robbins & Judge, 2022);

- ***Establishing boundaries:*** Contemporary developments such as 'always on marketing' and social media abuse can be draining and undermine emotional equilibrium. For this reason it is important for creative industry workers to draw strong, protective barriers around themselves. It is increasingly common to hear of artists 'unplugging' from social media after becoming fatigued by trolls. Cristi Williams (Hayley Williams of Paramore's mother) lectures students at Belmont University in Nashville on staying healthy in the industry and argues it is important to set boundaries and unplug from social media at times (Williams, 2014). Artists may need support to negotiate the challenges of social media, both in terms of better understanding their audience, and help in the workload and technical challenges of updating content on multiple platforms;
- ***Performance routines and rituals:*** Performance routines and rituals can be very helpful for artists to strengthen focus. Pre-performance routines can involve things like exercise, mental rehearsal, visualizing what you are trying to achieve, remembering successful past performances, healthy eating, listening to a pre-prepared song playlist (etc.). Cues can be used during a performance to remind you to refocus if your attention has strayed. A guitar player for example might check the tuning of their guitar every couple of songs, and use that process as a reminder to take a deep breath and refocus their attention on the present. Post-performance rituals are needed to wind down, and come off the adrenaline high. Meditations have been specially developed for performing artists, dealing with pre-show performance energy, or post show wind-down;
- ***Re-discovering the intrinsic joy in one's creative practice:*** For many artists at the beginning of their careers, creative

* The authors would like to thank London-based musician and psychotherapist Adam Ficek for his valuable work in this area, which has influenced our recommendations.

work was their sanctuary, their special place, where they found joy and fulfilment. They had the personal space to make it their own, and it had a childlike innocence. As their career gathered momentum the dynamic changed from being a personal hobby to a professional vocation with other people attempting to shape their work and criticize their work, resulting in conflict and tensions. This changed the dynamic from 'play' to 'work'. When developing a self-care plan there is an opportunity for artists to hit the re-set button. They can try to rediscover the 'original joy' of their creative practice (Normandie, 2021, p. 10). They can put aside ideas of commercial success for a period and follow artists like Picasso in making music a childlike state of play. Moby speaks of rediscovering the magic and connection of music in his autobiography (Moby, 2019). Music itself can be part of our own therapy – many musicians believe it has an intrinsic power to heal (Saintilan, 2020);

- ***Supportive books, audio books, apps and podcasts:*** Many creative industries workers use books to draw inspiration, get tips, and reinforce changes in their life. Chrissie Hynde combatted her dependency problems by reading Allen Carr's 'Easy Way to Stop' books and the Bhagavad Gita (Hynde, 2015). There has been an explosion of apps which could be integrated into a self-care plan. For example: Calm, Delightful Journal, Happify, Headspace, iBreath, Mindshift, Reflectly, Shine, Smiling Mind, Ten Percent Happier and Tide. There are a number of podcasts which are also available on good mental health in the creative industries;
- ***Cultivating gratitude:*** Cultivating gratitude may sound rather 'hippy' but is in fact a powerful way to address a perceptual distortion we all face. Our mind naturally focusses on problems and negatives, as solving them is necessary for our own survival. But focussing constantly on problems and negatives is not a pathway to happiness. For example, newspapers may tell us that a plane crashed the previous day, killing all on board. But the newspaper will not run a story telling us that 100,000 flights landed safely the same day. Thus our perception is constantly skewed to the negative which colours our mood and outlook. A musician with a punishing attitude of perfectionism might perform at

an outstanding level for 99.9% of a concerto, but one small mistake can negate and invalidate any enjoyment they might have received from the performance. Gratitude practices are designed to lift our gaze away from the one problem, to the 100,000 good things that we routinely ignore, thus creating a more objective perspective. There are programs designed to cultivate gratitude such as Naikan in Japan (Krech, 2002). Even a community ritual such as Thanksgiving in North America is a gesture towards cultivating gratitude. A gratitude practice may simply be a moment of self-reflection where we raise into our awareness people who have helped us, or we could make a 'gratitude list' of things in our life or career for which we should be grateful but routinely ignore. Journaling is also a tool that can be used to explore gratitude (Normandie, 2021);

- ***Being of service and 'giving back':*** Research has shown that generosity, being of service to others and 'giving back' can have a positive impacts on our mental health (Layous *et al.*, 2014);
- ***The Alexander Technique*** – in addition to some of the mainstream complementary therapies listed above, The Alexander Technique is building a following in some areas of the creative industries. It is an approach for your body and mind that provides strategies to deal with the physical and mental impact of performance. See for example Judith Kleinman and Peter Buckoke's book *The Alexander Technique for Musicians*;
- ***Specialist support*** such as support in the music industry in relation to preventing hearing loss.

To be effective within organizations, mental health initiatives need to be hardwired into policies and processes. For example, the annual performance review discussion provides an opportunity to discuss stress levels, obstacles that might be creating stress, and potential supports such as flexible working. Other meetings and events can provide an opportunity for people to check in, to note changes in behaviour, to show they are available to listen and to make people aware of the support that is available.

A note on medical advice

It needs to be stressed that there are a number of situations people can find themselves in that require medical advice and support. This book is not a substitute for medical advice and your organization will not be equipped to offer medical advice itself. For example, people with underlying conditions like clinical depression and anxiety may require medication. We should encourage people to obtain medical advice appropriate to their own circumstances and to make informed choices on what is best for them. This may be their own doctor/general practitioner (GP), or a psychologist, occupational therapist, social worker, counsellor, mental health professional or psychiatrist.

Summary and key points

- 'Bad work' in the creative industries leads to negative experiences and dysfunctional outcomes for the worker. Features of bad work are: poor wages, working hours and levels of safety; powerlessness; boredom; isolation; low self-esteem and shame; frustrated development; overwork; risk; and low-quality products that fail to contribute to the wellbeing of others (Hesmondhalgh & Baker, 2011);
- The significant imbalance between supply and demand in the creative industries contributes to the conditions that lead to worker exploitation;
- Other challenging characteristics that can be observed in the creative industries are: the insecure and precarious nature of employment; feelings of loneliness and isolation for remote workers; feelings of devaluation; emotional turbulence, criticism and rejection; sexual harassment and focus on physical appearance; cultural pressures (e.g. 'great art comes from pain', 'you need to suffer for your art', 'The Show Must Go On' despite whatever personal sacrifice and suffering this may entail); identity issues among artists, such as a tension between their public persona and private self; a frustrated need for validation; performance anxiety; and the pressures of fame and celebrity;
- Organizations can address these problems through activities such as: facilitating greater connection between workers; creating flexible working options; optimizing office design;

creating support and awareness of resources around mental health first aid, stress management, yoga, mindfulness and meditation, Pilates, time management, and sleep and diet; instituting programs to encourage physical fitness; providing positive examples provided by senior staff; ensuring staff are aware of services and resources; acknowledging and praising workers for their contribution; valuing outcomes rather than huge numbers of hours in the office and 'presenteeism'; ensuring realistic resourcing exists for projects;

- Artists additionally have found the following helpful in strengthening their mental health: seeking remuneration they believe is fair rather than succumbing to pressure to offer services for free; psychotherapy and self-reflection; establishing boundaries; performance routines and rituals; re-discovering the intrinsic joy in creative practice; supportive books, audio books, apps and podcasts; cultivating gratitude; being of service and 'giving back'; specialist support as required.

Discussion questions and class exercises

- Prepare an employee wellbeing plan for a creative organization, drawing from the suggestions listed above and your own additional research.
- Prepare your own customized self-care plan, drawing from the suggestions listed above. Identify risks that might result from the nature of your work, and your own assessment of your strengths and areas for development.

CASE STUDY 6.1: THE 'ALWAYS-ON' ARTIST/ INFLUENCER – BLOWING UP OR BURNING OUT?

© 2023 Cindy James* & Paul Saintilan

The demands on artists working in the creative industries have changed with the rise of short-form video platforms. Fans and users want increased access and to see more of the artists' lives than ever before. For some artists who struggle with social media platforms at the best of times, this is an anxiety-driven battle that creates more pressure than writing that next hit song. They need to create art, but they also need to be influencers and keep the audience engaged. This case explores the 'behind the scenes' stresses that arise when the demands of increased access, content, and tech-savviness are placed on artists who just want to create music.

*Cindy James has worked for Sony Music in Sydney, London, and New York and now works for Virgin Music Label & Artist Services/Universal Music Group in Los Angeles.

Keywords: anxiety, attention-based economy, content, fan engagement, influencer, NFTs, short-form video platforms, web3

'So, you need me to create MORE content?' spluttered Dane.

'Yes, we need content to post on your page at least once a day. Or, every other day, if we want the algorithm to serve up your profile and keep fans engaged', said Corina, the label's Marketing Manager.

'Well, what kind of content do you need?'

'It can be you rehearsing music or 'a day in the life of', but we do see that when you're being funny, it cuts through with fans. I have some consumer insights and past advertising campaign reports we can walk you through, which will show you the types of content your demographic engages with the most'.

'Funny? But I'm not funny. I write sad songs about girls'.

'We just need you to be authentic', reassured Corina.

'So, in addition to this content, do you still need these acoustic and piano versions of each of my singles? And you also want me rehearsed so you can film it? Doesn't that stimulate the algorithm, too?'

'Yes, it does, but only on streaming platforms. We're in an attention-based economy now. We need regular content of you in your everyday life, showing fans what you're into'.

'So, you need me to be an influencer, not an artist?'

'We need more. Content is king, and a good song isn't going to cut it if there isn't an engaged audience to listen to it or create a dance'.

'But what about all this talk of "boundaries," and "unplugging," and "creating space" so I can be mentally healthy and creative? The country artist Eric Church says he doesn't even pay attention to social media'.

'That may be because his demographic is older and engages with him differently. We do want to create boundaries and protect you from toxic commentary and trolls, and we do want you to take time now and then to unplug, but creating content like this on an ongoing basis is necessary for success these days. And the bottom line here is that we want you to succeed'.

'It can take me hours to make one video, let alone create content daily', Dane explained. 'My best-performing videos often have nothing to do with my music. I don't use these short-form video platforms, so knowing what kind of video to create, to be on top of what is trending that week, and what hashtags to include, plus the most up-to-date way to engage with the ever-changing algorithm is overwhelming. I want to be an artist, to write and perform my songs, not be a social media influencer. Creating enough content to be posted every day will take me at least four hours a day. It's not just one platform you need this for, right? It's all of them. And the demographic of my fans across each of these platforms is different, so what works for one platform that caters to my younger fans doesn't necessarily resonate with my older, more casual fans. Then there's the anxiety that comes with how the content performs. If I start to lose followers, I spiral. If I don't get enough views, I agonize over why the algorithm isn't surfacing my content. I panic as to whether the label will release the advanced music that I tease if it doesn't go viral. This is exhausting. I'm going to burn out. What happened to the days when a label could just run a good old advertising campaign?'

With a look of exasperation, Dane apologized and left the video call while Anthony, Dane's manager, and Corina continued on.

Corina confided: 'Look, I know this is a lot for Dane, and I appreciate your efforts, too. I didn't want to overwhelm him further by moving to the next topic on our call, but we need to discuss and make sure you all understand Web3 and the metaverse and are thinking about some authentic offerings we can package as an NFT as we build into the album release'.

'Can you remind me about NFTs and how that all works?'

'Non-Fungible Tokens. A unique digital piece of content, access, or event that hasn't yet been commercialized that we can offer to your superfans. We are also exploring options for him to do a concert in the metaverse. Web3 will revolutionize the way artists engage with fans, and we need Dane at the forefront. This technology will provide a layer of entertainment and fan access we haven't seen before, but blockchain technology can also change the way transactions are processed and royalties paid. Web3 initiatives are experiencing ups and downs, but blockchain technology will ultimately revolutionize the industry and how we own our relationship with the fans'.

'OK, thanks, Corina. So let me get this straight. Not only do we need to have Dane create daily content for these short-form video platforms, but we need him to deliver on the other alternative versions of the each of the singles, AND finish the album, AND prepare for the upcoming tour, AND supervise a new merchandise line, AND now have him wrap his head around NFTs, the metaverse and blockchain technology? I can't even keep my head on straight, let alone have Dane deliver on what he needs to. How am I going to broach this with him?'

'We have presentations and documentation that can help!' assured Corina.

'But he's creative, he's an artist. His brain doesn't work that way. He doesn't need to be bored with PowerPoint presentations, he needs to make music! Isn't all this what we pay you, the label, to do?'

'Well', concluded Corina, with some finality, 'we can build the foundations, but we need the content and creativity to be authentic. And authenticity comes from the artist. We also need the artist to be in the content if we're to expand his brand identity'.

Anthony winced.

Discussion questions

1. What steps could be taken to reconcile the conflicts in this case?
2. What are the implications of this case for training and preparing artists for their careers?
3. What are some ways Anthony could broach the Web3 topic with Dane?

CASE STUDY 6.2: BURNOUT IN ARTS AND CULTURAL WORKERS

By Abe Watson & Guy Morrow, University of Melbourne

This case pulls apart the notion of 'burnout', allowing constituent elements to emerge and receive targeted interventions, at both an individual and organizational level.

Defining and diagnosing 'burnout'

The term 'burnout', relating to psychology and mental health, was first used in a journal article published by German-American Psychologist Freudenberger (1974). Freudenberger defined burnout as 'a state of mental and physical exhaustion caused by one's professional life', as well as naming a number of key symptoms: quickness to anger; closed thinking; sleeplessness; and headaches (Freudenberger, 1974). More recently, Leiter and Maslach

(2016) published their *Latent burnout profiles: A new approach to understanding the burnout experience*. They used in their research the Maslach Burnout Inventory (MBI), which has three dimensions: exhaustion; inefficacy (ineffectiveness); and cynicism (Maslach and Jackson, 1981). Five individual profiles emerged:

- Burnout (high on all three dimensions);
- Engagement (low on all three dimensions);
- Overextended (high on exhaustion only);
- Disengaged (high on cynicism only); and,
- Ineffective (high on inefficacy only). (Leiter and Maslach, 2016, p. 89).

Their research provided evidence that enabled them to argue against the use of exhaustion alone as a proxy for burnout, by demonstrating that, in fact, the Disengaged profile was more negative than the Overextended. It also has important implications for research and interventions. Solid understanding of this research allows for tailored measures to address the specific challenges for each profile, and may help to stop fully-fledged burnout, by early and targeted intervention.

Disengaged (high on cynicism)

> *'I hesitate to say it, but I think I hate the industry'*
>
> — Aaron, Designer & Production Manager.

A Disengaged profile scores higher on the cynicism dimension than on exhaustion or inefficacy. There is a loss of belief and a sense of scepticism that things can get better. Growing cynicism leaves people feeling 'helpless', and wanting to leave the industry because the strain becomes too much:

> *My burnout has had profound and life changing consequences. I have now withdrawn almost fully from*

a highly successful design practice which — after ten years of working hard — was on the brink of being balanced and sustainable. I don't know if I can go back to it; it's irreparably tainted for me.

— Aaron, Designer & Production Manager

Ineffective (high on inefficacy)

'It feels like a fog'

— Kerry, Artistic Associate.

An Ineffective profile scores higher on the inefficacy dimension than on exhaustion or cynicism. An early career performing arts professional offered this insight:

'I am unable to be clear and decisive in my work so my confidence takes a hit. Everything takes longer and is more arduous. I am afraid of getting it wrong and so don't take risks. In the end I make compromised choices. I cannot see the big picture. I don't have energy to push through difficulty after a certain point. I've also seen people avoid difficult tasks entirely because of burnout'

— Kerry, Artistic Associate.

Overextended (high on exhaustion)

'*I'm exhausted a lot of the time*' — Alison, Executive Producer.

An Overextended profile scores higher on the exhaustion dimension than on cynicism or inefficacy. This dimension has also been described as wearing out, depletion, dehabillitation, loss of energy and fatigue (Maslach and Leiter, 2016). This profile is more closely linked to workload than any of the other profiles.

Moving forward

'The employer is responsible for developing a workplace which encourages equity and wellbeing through

reasonable workloads and expectations, but an individual is responsible for highlighting the need for assistance when required to address mental health issues' — Peter, Director of People and Culture

Suggested changes

More skilled arts managers and stronger governance	Arts and cultural organizations need clearer organizational hierarchies, more robust governance, and more skilled arts managers.
Stable employment, higher wages, overtime caps	Increases in wage levels would reduce the pressure on arts workers to juggle multiple jobs to achieve sustainable remuneration. Further, the casualization of labour and 'gig economy' adds a considerable amount of stress to workers who are already under immense pressure.
Flexible working arrangements, beneficial rest	Given the passion that employees in the sector have for their work, combined with other factors (including under-resourcing of organizations), it is unsurprising that arts and cultural workers can feel guilty – or even fearful – of taking leave. It is important that workplace environments are established which support and encourage arts and cultural workers to take periods of meaningful rest.
Individual responsibilities	While workers in the arts and cultural sector can identify many external causes of burnout, they do have the power to take responsibility for their own experience, to actively take responsibility for their own mental health, and reduce the risk of burnout themselves.

Case References

Freudenberger, H. J. (1974). 'Staff Burn-Out', *Journal of Social Issues*, Vol. 30, pp. 159–165. https://doi.org/10.1111/j.1540-4560.1974.tb00706.x

Leiter, M. P. & Maslach, C. (2016). 'Latent burnout profiles: A new approach to understanding the burnout experience', *Burnout Research*, Vol. 3, pp. 89–100.

Maslach, C. & Jackson, S. E. (1981). 'The measurement of experienced burnout', *Journal of Organizational Behavior*, Vol. 2, no. 2, pp. 99–113. https://doi.org/10.1002/job.4030020205

References

Arias, G. L. (2019). 'In the wings: actors & mental health: a critical review of the literature', *Expressive Therapies Capstone Theses*. 109. Available at https://digitalcommons.lesley.edu/expressive_theses/109 (accessed 3 March 2022).

Bozza, A. (2009). 'Being Eminem', *The Guardian*, May 17, 2009.

Bryant Smalley, K. & McIntosh, W.D. (2011). 'The loss of fame: psychological implications', *The Journal of Popular Culture*, Vol. 44, no. 2, pp. 385–397.

Caves, R. E. (2000). *Creative Industries: Contracts Between Art and Commerce*. Cambridge, MA and London, England: Harvard University Press.

CIPD (2021). *Health and wellbeing at work survey 2021*. London: Chartered Institute of Personnel and Development.

Cooper, C. L. & Wills, G.I.D. (1989). 'Popular musicians under pressure', *Psychology of Music*, Vol. 17, pp. 22–36.

Dannen, F. (1990). *Hit Men: Power Brokers and Fast Money Inside the Music Business*. New York: Times Books, Random House.

Davis, C. (2012). 'Whitney', *The Soundtrack of My Life*, pp. 308–341. New York: Simon & Schuster.

Dobson, M. C. (2010). 'Insecurity, professional sociability, and alcohol: young freelance musicians' perspectives on work and life in the music profession', *Psychology of Music*, Vol. 39, no. 2, pp. 240–260.

Dore, M. (2015). 'Why we are burning out in the arts', *ArtsHub*, published 16 October, 2015, available at https://www.artshub.com.au/2015/10/16/why-we-are-burning-out-in-the-arts-249582/ (accessed 3 March, 2022).

Everymind (2018). *Never Not Creative: Mentally Healthy 2018 Survey*. Available at *https://nevernotcreative.org/mentally-healthy-2018* (accessed 3 March 2022).

Fortnam, I. (2006). 'New York Dolls: appetites for self-destruction', *Louder*, July 27, 2006.

Gardiner, R. (2019). 'Not enough has changed', *Billboard*, March 30, 2019, p. 48.

Goodwin, D. W. (1973). 'The muse and the martini', *Journal of the American Medical Association*, Vol. 224, no. 1, pp. 35–38.

Grant, S. (2019). 'Joe Walsh, Ringo Starr and the mission to end America's addiction crisis', *Rolling Stone*, March 16, 2019.

Gross, S. A. & Musgrave, G. (2016). *Can Music Make You Sick? Music and Depression: A Study into the Incidence of Musicians' Mental Health, Part 1: Pilot Survey Report*, London: University of Westminster/MusicTank/Help Musicians UK.

Gross, S. A. & Musgrave, G. (2017). *Can Music Make You Sick? A Study into the Incidence of Musicians' Mental Health, Part 2: Qualitative Study and Recommendations*, London: MusicTank Publishing, University of Westminster.

Help Musicians UK (2014). *Health and Wellbeing Survey*. London.

Hennekam, S. & Bennett, D. (2016). 'Self-management of work in the creative industries in the Netherlands', *International Journal of Arts Management*, Vol. 19, no. 1, Fall 2016, pp. 31–41.

Hesmondhalgh, D. & Baker, S. (2011). *Creative Labour: Media work in three cultural industries*. Abingdon & New York: Routledge.

Holm-Hadulla, R. M. & Bertolino, A. (2014). 'Creativity, alcohol and drug abuse: The pop icon Jim Morrison', *Psychopathology*, Vol. 47, pp. 167–173.

Hynde, C. (2015). *Reckless*. London: Ebury Press, Penguin Random House UK.

iCAAD (2020). 'Fashion X Mental Health'. Available at https://www.icaad.com/blog/fashion-x-mental-health (accessed 18 October 2021).

Idacavage, S. (2021). 'Introduction: Fashion & Mental Health', *The Fashion Studies Journal*. Available at: https://www.fashionstudiesjournal.org/notes/2021/7/3/introduction-to-our-fashion-amp-mental-health-issue (accessed 18 October 2021).

Jepson, R. (2021). *Mental Health in the Music Industry: A Guide*.

Kleinman, J. & Buckoke, P. (2013). *The Alexander Technique for Musicians*. London: Royal College of Music, Methuen Drama, Bloomsbury.

Knafo, D. (2008). 'The senses grow skilled in their craving: thoughts on creativity and addiction', *Psychoanalytic Review*, August 2008, Vol. 95, no. 4, pp. 571–595.

Krech, G. (2002). *Naikan: Gratitude, Grace, and the Japanese Art of Self-Reflection*. Berkeley: Stone Bridge Press.

Krueger, A. B. (2019). *Rockonomics: What the Music Industry Can Teach Us About Economics (and Our Future)*. London: John Murray Publishers.

Kyaga, S., Landén, M., Boman, M., Hultman, C. M., Långström, N., Lichtenstein, P. (2013). 'Mental illness, suicide and creativity: 40-Year prospective total population study', *Journal of Psychiatric Research*, Vol. 47, no.1, January 2013, pp. 83–90.

Layous, K., Chancellor, J. & Lyubomirsky, S. (2014). 'Positive activities as protective factors against mental health conditions', *Journal of Abnormal Psychology*, Vol. 123, no. 1, pp. 3–12.

Lehmann, A. C., Sloboda, J.A & Woody, R.H. (2007). 'Managing performance anxiety' in *Psychology for Musicians: Understanding and Acquiring the Skills*, Oxford University Press, pp. 145–162.

Lindvall, H. (2010). 'Behind the music: why are musicians more likely to suffer from depression?' *The Guardian*, December 18, 2010.

Lopes, P. (2005). 'Signifying deviance and transgression', *The American Behavioral Scientist*, Vol. 48, no.11, pp. 1468–81.

McMillen, A. (2014). *Talking Smack: Honest Conversations About Drugs*. Brisbane: University of Queensland Press.

Moby (2019). *Then It Fell Apart*. London: Faber & Faber Ltd.

Musicians' Union (UK) (2019). 'Sexual harassment widespread across the UK music industry', October 22, 2019. Available at https://musiciansunion.org.uk/news/sexual-harassment-widespread-across-the-uk-music-industry (accessed 3 March 2022).

Normandie, J. M. (2021). *The Mindful Musician: Finding a Healthy Balance*, Normandie Publishing

O'Dair, M. (2016). ''Pardon me, I'm very drunk': alcohol, creativity and performance anxiety in the case of Robert Wyatt', *Popular Music*, Vol. 35, no. 2, pp. 207–221.

Oksanen, A. (2013). 'Female rock stars and addiction in autobiographies', *Nordic Studies on Alcohol and Drugs*, Vol. 30, pp. 123–140.

Orr, D. (2011). 'Celebrity and self-consciousness: A recipe for addiction', *The Guardian*. Thursday July 28, 2011. Available at https://www.theguardian.com/commentisfree/2011/jul/27/amy-winehouse-celebrity-selfconsciousness-addiction (accessed 3 March 2022).

Patston, T. & Loughlan, T. (2014). 'Playing with performance: the use and abuse of beta-blockers in the performing arts', *Victorian Journal of Music Education*, Vol. 1, pp. 3–10.

Record Union (2019). *The 73 Percent Report: A report that looks at the state of independent music makers' mental health and wellbeing*. Available at: https://www.the73percent.com/ (accessed 3 March 2021).

Resnikoff, P. (2019). '91% of artists remain undiscovered – here's how Show4Me is planning to change that', *Digital Music News*, November 5, 2019.

Robbins, S. P. & Judge, T.A. (2022). *Organizational Behaviour*, 18th edition, Global Edition. Essex: Pearson Education Limited.

Roland, D. (1994). 'How professional performers manage performance anxiety', *Research Studies in Music Education*, no. 2, June 1994, pp. 25–35.

Saintilan, P. (2020). *Musicians & Addiction: Research and Recovery Stories*. Sydney: Music Australia.

Saintilan, P. (2019). *Managerial Orientations and Beliefs in Large Music Organisations*, PhD Thesis. Melbourne: Deakin University [section 5.2.1 on 'Nobody Knows' insecurity/uncertainty/ambiguity pp 152–158].

Seligman, M. (2020). 'PERMA – Interview with Dr. Martin Seligman', *Coursera*. Available at https://www.coursera.org/lecture/teaching-character/perma-interview-with-dr-martin-seligman-j0HF4 (accessed 3 March 2022).

Shaw, R. L., Whitehead, C. & Giles, D.C. (2010). ''Crack down on the celebrity junkies': Does media coverage of celebrity drug use pose a risk to young people?', *Health, Risk & Society*, Vol. 12, no. 6, pp. 575–89.

Shorter, G., O'Neill, S. & McElherron, L. (2018). *Changing Arts and Minds: A Survey of Health and Wellbeing in the Creative Sector*, Ulster University. Available at https://www.inspirewellbeing.org/media/9236/changing-arts-and-minds-creative-industries-report.pdf (accessed 19 October 2021).

Smith, R. (2021). 'Iggy Azalea urges music labels to hire psychologists for artists' mental health', *Newsweek*, published 17 August 2021.

Soar, S. & Chen, C. (2019). 'Inside fashion's enduring mental health epidemic', *Business of Fashion*, published August 2, 2019. Available at https://www.businessoffashion.com/articles/workplace-talent/inside-fashions-enduring-mental-health-epidemic (accessed 18 October 2021).

Spunt, B. (2014). *Heroin and Music in New York City*. New York: Palgrave Macmillan.

Stead, N. & Gusheh, M. (2020). 'Work-related mental wellbeing in architecture', *Architecture Australia*, March 2020 edition published online 28 May, 2020. Available at https://architectureau.com/articles/work-related-mental-wellbeing-in-architecture/ (accessed 18 October 2021).

The Architects' Mental Wellbeing Forum (2019). *Architects' Mental Wellbeing Toolkit*, June 2019. Available at: https://docs.wixstatic.com/ugd/fb91f8_33c556b0fe9b4855824da571826586d6.pdf (accessed 3 March 2022).

The Arts Wellbeing Collective (2019). *Tour Well for Tour Managers: Tips and Techniques for Designing Tours to Promote Positive Mental Health and Wellbeing*.

Tolson, G. H. & Cuyjet, M.J. (2007). 'Jazz and substance abuse: road to creative genius or pathway to premature death', *International Journal of Law and Psychiatry*, Vol. 30, pp. 530–538.

Turner, S. (2016). *Beatles '66: The Revolutionary Year*. New York: Ecco, HarperCollins Publishers.

Tyler, S. & Dalton, D. (2012). *Does the Noise in my Head Bother You?: A Rock 'N' Roll Memoir*. New York: Ecco, HarperCollins Publishers.

Vaag, J., Håkon Bjørngaard, J. & Bjerkeset, O. (2014). 'Symptoms of anxiety and depression among Norwegian musicians compared to the general workforce', *Psychology of Music*, Vol. 44, no. 2, pp. 234–248.

van den Eynde, J., Fisher, A. & Sonn, C. (2016). *Working in the Australian Entertainment Industry: Final Report*. Melbourne: Victoria University commissioned by Entertainment Assist.

van den Eynde, J., Fisher, A. & C. Sonn (2014). *Pride, Passion & Pitfalls: Working in the Australian Entertainment Industry.* Melbourne: Victoria University commissioned by Entertainment Assist.

Ward, G. & Burns, K. (2000). *Jazz: A History of America's Music.* New York: Alfred Knopf.

Weisberger, L. (2003). *The Devil Wears Prada.* New York: Broadway Books.

Williams, C. (2014). 'Cristi Williams (Hayley Williams of Paramore's Mom) on The Music Project Radio', *TheMusicProjectTV,* [video] posted February 10, 2014, on YouTube.

Wilson, B. & Greenman, B. (2016). *I Am Brian Wilson: A Memoir.* Boston: Da Capo Press.

Young, V. (2011). *The Secret Thoughts of Successful Women: Why Capable People Suffer from the Imposter Syndrome and How to Thrive in Spite of It.* New York: Crown Business, Random House Inc.

Movies and documentaries cited:

Amy (2015) Documentary on Amy Winehouse. Directed by Asif Kapadia and produced by James Gay-Rees, George Pank, and Paul Bell and co-produced by Krishwerkz Entertainment, On the Corner Films, Playmaker Films, and Universal Music, in association with Film4.

Sunset Boulevard (1950) Directed and co-written by Billy Wilder, produced and co-written by Charles Brackett. Stars William Holden and Gloria Swanson.

Whitney: Can I Be Me (2017) Documentary on Whitney Houston. Directed by Nick Broomfield and Rudi Dolezal. A Lafayette Films, Passion Pictures and Showtime Networks production.

Decision-making in creative organizations

Chapter 7

CHAPTER LEARNING OBJECTIVES

After studying this chapter, you should be able to:

- Explain and apply the decision-making process for programmed and non-programmed decisions;
- Explain the difference between the rational model of decision-making and 'bounded rationality';
- Describe key influences on decision-making;
- Evaluate the desire for status and recognition and explain how this can be a key driver in decision-making within the creative and cultural industries;
- Recognize the differences in how decisions are made in small and large organizations in the cultural sector;
- Critically evaluate the use of taste and professional judgement in making creative decisions;
- Critique the challenges in the use, and increasing role, of 'big data' in creative organizations.

DOI: 10.4324/9781003262923-7

Decisions: whether simple or complex, managers live and die by the implications of them every day. Decisions determine the outcome of a project, they influence the morale of a team and impact whether a company finds success in any given year. In the creative industries, the margin of error can be quite small. Seemingly, small decisions can often have significant implications for artists and complex decisions can ripple throughout a large corporation. To explore this further, we provide an example of an artist's decision as to whether he should release his music as an album or as an EP.

Figure 7.1 Decision-making is not only an individual process but also a team one as well. This chapter will explore all aspects of decision-making within the creative organization. Photo credit: G-Stock Studio/Shutterstock.com.

Even the smallest of decisions can be considered strategic in the creative industries: an artist's choice of album formats

Dean Fields, a singer-songwriter based in Richmond, Virginia, in the United States, is your typical 'do-it-yourself' (DIY) artist. He has leveraged the technological

Figure 7.2 Dean Fields, singer-songwriter and recording artist, 2022, Nashville, Tennessee, USA.

changes that have transformed the recording industry since the late 1990s. Legally, Dean is considered a sole proprietor who writes and records his own songs but also acts as his own manager, booking agent, publisher and record label. Even though he controls his intellectual property rights, including those in his songs and recordings, he has chosen not to recognize each of these operations as separate legal entities. Each operates under his personal name, Dean Fields. This is typical of any DIY artist, musician or entertainer that is pursuing a career in the creative and cultural sector.

The collapse of traditional physical distribution channels in the 2000s within the recording industry and the power of digital accessibility have enabled many artists to produce, distribute, market and promote their own music directly to audiences around the world. This virtual accessibility to the market has brought with it new opportunities and challenges for many musicians with far-reaching implications. Recently, Dean needed to determine whether to record an extended play album (an EP: 4–6 songs) or a traditional full-length album (10–12 songs) for his upcoming release. This type of decision, faced by almost all DIY artists, is considered by many as a 'tactical' decision but in Dean's case became more 'strategic' in nature.

Financial concerns – can he even afford to do a full-length album?

The financial costs were of the utmost concern for Dean. The economic resources he needed for recording the full-length album instead of the EP were more than double. For an artist like himself, who may gross $40,000 a year, the additional $6,000–$10,000 it would cost him weighed heavily on his mind. It didn't take much to determine that he didn't have enough money to make a full-length record. It would have required a lot of borrowing which wasn't desirable. He felt constrained by his lack of financial resources to do what he felt he needed to, to achieve what he wanted to achieve. Not having enough money was evident, but it was not the only factor he was considering. If the decision was simply a financial one, it would have been easier for him to make and he would not have viewed it as a major one. He felt there was more at stake as he considered his options – enough to think about taking on considerable debt. He was also worried about the extra time it would take to record and release the album. This would have implications for the time he would need to wait to see revenues flow in from the sale of the album. He felt that with the EP, he would spend half as much time recording, he could get it out quicker and spend half as much money doing so. He also considered whether he could improve his cash flow if he released the album when he started promoting it. He could sell an album for more than an EP, even though he spent more making it.

Concerns for reputation and fan perception

In addition to the affordability of the two formats, Dean's decision was also grounded in two other concerns. One, he wanted to be seen as credible by his fans and colleagues; and two, if he decided to release an album rather than an

EP, it might help differentiate himself from other artists competing in the same genre. In Dean's decision-making process, he struggled with how he and his 'artist brand' would be perceived. How a product is viewed in the creative industries helps to determine its ultimate success or failure. The importance of creating hype around the release of a cultural product cannot be underestimated. Dean felt that if he released the full-length album, business partners and fans would take him more seriously; he felt they would want to invest their time and money in his music and that the action would improve his likeability among fans. Fan engagement has the potential to increase loyalty, which can turn into both emotional and financial support for the artist. Therefore, he felt that making the full-length album would better position him and improve how he is seen in the industry, thereby better serving his long-term interests.

Furthermore, Dean felt that releasing an EP may jeopardize his 'standing' with his fans, creating a perception of a 'smaller' release. He felt this wouldn't align with his touring and recording activities at that time. It is important for the reputation of the artist to uphold a perception of being 'relevant' and 'on the cutting edge' of music. Fans, from the newest to the longest-standing, desire exclusivity – the need or desire to feel involved with the next 'great' thing or success before it reaches the masses. This makes *them* feel important, relevant and capable of identifying trends before their peers. Artists, by portraying themselves and their creative businesses in a fashion that reinforces this image, help to create a social network of people who want to be involved with them before success is achieved. The situation was no different for Dean as he struggled with his decision of how to record and distribute his new release. This decision, which is typical of decisions that need to be made in a creative context, will be used below as a straightforward example to illustrate the decision-making process.

Discussion questions

1 In Dean's circumstances, would you decide to release an EP or a full-length album? Why or why not?
2 Do you think going significantly into debt out of concern for his reputation is a viable decision for Dean or any musician? Why or why not?
3 What do you think this decision-making process may have looked like for him? Was it more calculated or emotional?
4 Is the evolving nature of social media changing the equation?

DECISION-MAKING PROCESS

Programmed and non-programmed decisions

We make decisions every day, from the simplest 'no-nonsense', 'don't even think about them', 'no brainer' decisions, to those that may be the result of months of tortured contemplation. Those that are determined quickly with little thought are considered '**programmed**' decisions and those that are more deliberate, purposeful and planned are called '**non-programmed decisions**' (Pettigrew, 2014). Programmed decisions often come easily because we make them in a habitual way, or because they are similar to situations we have experienced before, like going to lunch or picking up a ringing phone. Non-programmed decisions involve more risk, may be more complex or rely on creative solutions to a problem. If a music publishing company is seeking to expand its catalogue through a merger or acquisition, or if they desire to form a joint venture with a copyright administration firm, the owners are likely to use analysis and modelling to weigh the risks of these choices before deciding. This process requires time, creativity, thought and the tools to scope out the economic benefits.

THE DECISION-MAKING PROCESS

When we recognize that a solution to a problem is needed, we go through the decision-making process (Figure 7.3). As we

Figure 7.3 This seven-step decision-making process is but one outlined approach to illustrate the complexities of how an individual recognizes a problem, through to making a decision and following up on its outcome.

just discussed, this could be programmed or non-programmed; as a decision-maker we will go through a series of steps that will ultimately lead to making a decision. Depending on its complexity, we may go through the process quickly, even skipping some of the steps, or we may go through it systematically until we arrive at a decision.

During the first step of the process, the decision-maker will recognize, consciously or unconsciously, that a problem needs to be solved and a decision made. This may be as simple as replying to an email or sending out a royalty statement, or as complex as signing a film distribution deal, or in Dean's case, realizing that it's been quite some time since he's put out new music for his fans. It is important that the individual making the decision understands the true cause of the problem. A misdiagnosis can lead to addressing a perceived cause rather than the actual one.

After it has been determined that a decision needs to be made, the individual will identify the objective, or what she hopes to attain from the decision. Using Dean as an example again, this may be as simple as recording a quick demo and releasing it digitally or as complex as seeking a third party to record, distribute and promote his new album.

The third step in the process involves diagnosing the situation or gathering the information needed to best understand what the decision-maker is tackling. In Dean's example, he had determined that it was time to release a new record. Once he determined that this was the case, he naturally went into the fourth stage of the process and began thinking about and evaluating the different options available for releasing his album. He determined the two best and most viable options for him were the EP or a full-length album. As he continued for some time in this stage, he went back to information gathering to better inform himself. Once he felt that he had the best information possible to make an informed decision, he moved on to the fifth step and decided to release the EP. He proceeded to implement the decision and evaluated it on an ongoing basis.

Although we like to break down these processes step by step to make it seem like they are more formal, in reality, many decisions made in the creative industries like the one Dean struggled with are quite informal. He thought through options and naturally went back through different steps as he contemplated his options. Nothing formal was written down, there was no 'profit and loss statement' generated; the process was based on his current experience, past experiences and other short-cuts in order to reach a decision fairly quickly (Kahneman, 2011).

RATIONALITY AND BOUNDED RATIONALITY

The decision-making process just discussed is a 'linear', step-by-step illustration of how we go about making decisions. As we now know, some types of decision-making will follow this approach much more strictly while others are more iterative, depending on whether we're dealing with a programmed or non-programmed decision. The Rational Decision-Making Model is one approach suitable for making decisions, where we try to maximize outcomes by examining all available alternatives (Simon, 1979). However, the rational model assumes that people are *perfectly* rational. Although some of us make a strong attempt at being perfectly rational, the model presents challenges when applied to decision-making in a strict fashion. First, the model assumes there is a clear and definite problem that needs to be addressed and that we are able to know exactly what that is. In addition to this, it assumes that as we try to find alternatives to address the problem, every conceivable alternative will be available to solve it. Furthermore, as we evaluate those options, the money and time spent making the decision are assumed to be limitless, which is hardly ever the case. We are usually limited by our ability to take in information because of the constraints on our time, resources and our own knowledge. This is called 'bounded rationality'. Bounded rationality is a belief that we 'satisfice' our decision-making – meaning that we make decisions based on what we believe will generate the best possible outcome with the limited information we have available to make that decision, often based on the first acceptable outcome that is generated (Simon, 1979). We simply don't have the time, money and information to process all the available information, and so fast forward to an option that seems most likely to address the problem. We will often choose the best of two or three potential options rather quickly with limited information to support that choice. In a sense, we are saying this option will 'suffice' and 'satisfy' the issue so that we can move on to address the next problem.

ESCALATION OF COMMITMENT AND SUNK COSTS

For as many decisions that we make, we are still struck by the difficulty of walking away from a bad decision. There is a temptation to throw further resources at a problem to try to solve it or rescue any reputational damage that might arise from failure. This is considered an 'escalation of commitment'. When we look backwards at what we have invested, rather than forwards at what the future outcomes are likely to be, we call this a 'sunk-cost fallacy'. It is an 'irrational decision to invest more future resources in a situation after an investment has been made (costs are sunk) compared with the same situation without an investment' (Strough *et al.*, 2011, p. 61). For example, say that I invest one million dollars in a vinyl record pressing plant. I believe that vinyl records are making a comeback, and

I could become an exclusive provider. Despite my investment I find that the demand is far less than I anticipated, and the business is in danger of bankruptcy. The true decision that lies in front of me doesn't actually involve the one million dollars that I have already spent, which is a sunk cost. It involves calculating and comparing the projected future income and expenditure that flows from each of the future options available to me (one of which may be liquidation). To say 'if I have already spent one million dollars on it, I should be happy to spend another half a million dollars to make it work' is to fall victim to the sunk-cost fallacy. All that may happen is that you 'throw good money after bad' and squander another half a million dollars.

Some researchers have found a relationship between age and the tendency to move forward with a decision to escalate financial risk through sunk costs. In one study looking at adults 21 years and older and 20 years and younger, it was found that older adults are less likely to commit to the sunk-cost fallacy and are more likely to make decisions to correct it. In addition, a link was found between the demographic characteristics of an individual, like education, and the likelihood of falling victim to the sunk-cost fallacy. In one study looking at faculty and college seniors, they found that those with a lower income status had poorer economic judgement leading to a higher probability of financial escalation. In addition, they also found a positive relationship between 'intelligence' and those individuals who use microeconomic principles like cost-benefit rules that lead to more successful life outcomes (Larrick *et al.*, 1993). You will recall that in Case Study 3.1 at the conclusion of Chapter 3, the financial controller, Colin Cash, proposes a cost-benefit analysis as a fundamental first step in making the decision about whether to terminate the services of the singer. It is a suggestion to which the CEO readily agrees. It enables managers to fully understand the financial and other implications of the decision they are about to make.

Business strategies that rely on the capitalization of, and piggy backing off, past success, which is often the case in the creative and cultural industries, can be stifled by a lack of knowledge transfer or sharing. Knowledge transfer occurs when one department or division in an organization shares their knowledge and experience or when it is somehow acquired by another department (Argote & Ingram, 2000). For example, attempts to draw upon the experience of launching previous work to help launch new work can be frustrated by little sharing of what was successful and what wasn't. 'Most of what is known about how to create complementary linkages is based on accumulated industry know-how, on trial and error, rather than systematic analysis' (Lampel *et al.*, 2006, p. 74).

INFLUENCES ON THE DECISION-MAKING PROCESS

Heuristics

Heuristics help simplify the decision-making process in uncertain situations. In a sense they are short-cuts to the process. They find a receptive home in the creative industries due to the need for quick decisions based on little information. Creative industry decision-makers often need to act quickly based upon trends in the market place or judgements that are open to subjectivity and uncertainty. Often heuristics are used to come to satisfactory solutions with modest amounts of thinking or planning involved (Simon, 1990). They enable the decision-maker to streamline the process and use less information when making the decision.

Intuition

In addition to heuristics, intuition has been identified as a cognitive influence on decision-making. Intuition is linked to the thoughts, conclusions or choices that come to mind quickly, without much thought or reflection, often through subconscious thinking (Kahneman, 2002; Miller, 2008). It is a dynamic concept that is often seen as separate from judgement or logic (Miller, 2008). Although intuition has been limited in its study due to the challenges involved in direct observation (Agor, 1989), some researchers have found ways in which to quantify its qualities so that we can look at its role in decision-making (Behling & Eckel, 1991).

The subjective nature of creative and cultural products and services (Hirschman, 1983), and the rapidly changing style preferences of its consumers, encourage the use of intuition and heuristics in the decision-making process. Often referred to as 'gut-feelings' or 'hunches', decision-makers rely on their subconscious reactions to provide quick judgement on these products. This is especially true within creative or product acquisition departments or Artist & Repertoire divisions within these organizations. People in charge of finding new talent, the 'gate-keepers', who are responsible for developing and producing cultural products, must be in touch with the latest cultural trends resonating in the marketplace. Being tuned-in in this way is a delicate and often unpredictable task that encourages the use of their knowledge of trends as they attempt to foresee crowd or consumer reaction and potential profitability. They are often hired as potential cultural 'tastemakers', or because of their professional judgement in anticipating trends. This is hard to predict through forecasting, logical or analytical techniques (see Case Study 7.1). In the music industry, Seifert and Hadida (2009) identify intuition and its influence on talent selection decisions as having a positive impact. This demonstrates how the unconscious process of intuition lends itself to finding new songwriters or artists in the music industry.

Trust

Trust has also been shown to play an important role in decision-making for managers. In today's business environment, the reliance upon subordinates or other colleagues to aid in decision-making has become more prominent. Trust refers to an 'individual's willingness to be vulnerable to another based on the belief that another party is competent, honest, reliable and concerned about the individual's own interest' (Mishra & Spreitzer, 1998, p. 159). It enables a manager to rely on someone else's expertise in areas that may be less familiar to them. Managers are more likely to include employees in the decision-making process when trust between the two has been established (Mishra & Spreitzer, 1998). Trusting members of a decision-making team and relying upon them even when disagreements emerge can improve the quality of the decision outcome. Furthermore, relying on 'external advisors' in seeking information before making decisions is also quite common in organizations (Liberman-Yaconi *et al.*, 2010; Schreiber, 2014). Using 'external advisors' enables managers to seek out perspectives with which they are less familiar. An outreach in this manner on major decisions is indicative of a trust relationship between decision-makers and perceived professionals. This happens often in the creative industries, especially when an individual is also relying on their 'gut' or intuition in making those decisions. Because we tend to use less formal quantitative modelling when going through the decision-making process, managers will seek advice from colleagues or other gatekeepers to reassure or validate those intuitive feelings (Negus, 2011; Schreiber, 2014). When making talent selection decisions, choosing songs or licensing art for commercial product, these 'gatekeepers' will often only listen to, or consider potential signings from, others they trust in the industry. Attorneys, managers or other agents help to assist in these decisions through soliciting their own client's works. This process is only successful because the decision-makers trust each other's judgement and have come to learn they will not pursue them with artists that aren't worth considering.

Past experiences

An individual's previous experience can also influence their future decision-making. Often, people who have had positive prior experiences will likely make similar decisions in the future with the expectation of a similar outcome (Juliusson *et al.*, 2005). This holds true given a negative outcome as well – a negative past experience can lead to a belief that, given a similar situation, another negative outcome will occur. Past experiences have also been found to be critical in complex decision-making, especially in confusing situations (Li *et al.*, 2009). Learning from past reactions and situations helps the brain to re-shape how we comprehend that experience so that we can change how we respond to future events. The impact that past experience has on us physically as well as cognitively has been shown to influence how decision-makers perceive future scenarios and impact biases, heuristics and other evaluative practices.

Personal bias

Personal biases have also been shown to impact the effectiveness of the decisions we make. Cognitive biases are thinking patterns based on observations and generalizations that may lead to memory errors, inaccurate judgements and faulty logic (West *et al.*, 2008; Dube *et al.*, n.d.). There are many different types of biases that influence our decision-making, but some of the most common cognitive biases include: (1) belief bias – the over-dependence on prior knowledge in arriving at decisions; (2) hindsight bias – people tending readily to explain an event as inevitable, once it has happened; (3) omission bias – generally, people having a propensity to omit information perceived as risky; and (4) confirmation bias – people tending to perceive new information as confirmation of what they already believe (Blank *et al.*, 2008; West *et al.*, 2008).

While biases may lead us to making decisions that aren't always in our best interest, they do enable individuals to make efficient choices with the assistance of heuristics (Shah & Oppenheimer, 2008). Using short-cuts such as these may or may not result in the desired outcomes. Take for example, a situation where you find a new 'up-and-coming' artist who is enjoying local and regional success and who you believe is going to be the next emerging talent in R&B. With just the right amount of development and production, they could be on their way to being a top ten seller. You decide to back them significantly with your resources. However, they flop. The market never picked up on what you felt was the 'next big thing'. 'They were ahead of their time' said some critics, but either way, sales, streaming and social metrics never achieved the projections and you had to drop them from the label. In this scenario, your decision was affected by confirmation bias. With this, you interpreted information and your market research about the artist in a way that confirmed your preconceptions. Instead of seeing it objectively, you made a wrong decision as a result. This situation is much more common in the world of music or film than we'd like to admit. Often driven by this kind of bias, decisions related to determining audience taste and preference can be a particular challenge when driven by biases and heuristics, though they're often necessary.

REPUTATION AND DESIRE FOR RECOGNITION IN DECISION-MAKING

As we've discussed throughout this chapter, the decision-making process is influenced by a number of factors ranging from our own past experiences, intuition, trust and the industry in which we work. However, we can also be influenced by our own desire for success and the power that accompanies it. Our aspirations to be recognized for who we are and what we do, either individually or as a company, can be a powerful motivator in how and why we make certain decisions. The need to maintain credibility among our colleagues, our reliance upon those relationships to get things done and the reputation we develop in the process, is often at the forefront of our minds when making decisions. Achieving status is often seen as a driver of the decision-making process, especially in industries where much of the business is driven by status and recognition like the creative and cultural industries (Schreiber, 2014). If the decision-maker or the company has not acquired a certain level of recognition or status in the industry, they will often go to great lengths to create a perception that it has been acquired. This is often done through the use of 'aggrandizement' – to exaggerate one's power, influence, stature or reputation.

Aggrandizing provides a perception of legitimacy of the decision-maker and his or her company through creating an illusion of having greater accomplishments, networks and other resources than they actually possess. Because 'accumulated prestige and power' (Bourdieu & Thompson, 1991) can be a strong motivating factor, the decision-maker can feel compelled to inflate his or her position or company to the outside world. To them, it is seen as a way to project the image of being 'legit' and having done something important in the industry, without actually having done so. For example, if an entertainment company decides to create separate business entities for different functions like recording, publishing, management and booking as opposed to creating separate departments within the company, in order to be seen by others as having greater resources, this would be seen as aggrandizing. It is motivated by an intention to inflate other people's perceptions. Or, if the artist grossly over-exaggerates their accomplishments, partnerships or backers, this could also be considered aggrandizing.

Not only does a person's drive for status and recognition play a prominent role in the decision-making process, but also the mere notion of 'association' is believed to foster a 'quicker' path to legitimacy. Associating with more prominent artists and executives tells others that you 'have what it takes to get things done' and achieve what others are after. It may also be an attempt to indicate to people that you do have the knowledge and network needed to 'sit at that table' with other prominent, successful people in the industry. The earning of gold and platinum record certifications, a Grammy, Oscar, Tony or ceremonies of recognition like the Golden Globes or the American Music Awards, are industry-constructed vehicles that confer legitimacy. Associating oneself with those individuals or firms that have been 'recognized' also demonstrates that you have the knowledge and network to make things happen.

The drive to achieve status and recognition in the creative industries cannot be understated. Decision-makers will go to great lengths to create a perception of legitimacy for themselves among others, and this should be seen as a key driver in many decisions being made in the cultural sector.

DECISION-MAKING IN SMALL AND LARGE CREATIVE INDUSTRY FIRMS

As discussed previously, in the creative industries, small firms account for over 90% of all businesses in major Western economies, and within these industries specifically, micro-businesses dominate (Partnership, 2006; Pratt & Jeffcutt, 2009). There has been research conducted outlining the differences in decision-making between small and large companies. For example, one study found (Welbourne & Pardo-del-Val, 2009) that smaller firms place more value on the importance of 'relational capital' than larger organizations. This isn't to say that relationships aren't important for larger businesses, but the reliance upon them in smaller organizations is quintessential. Here, relational capital refers to the contacts and relationships that small business owners need to foster and develop in order to survive. They are so pivotal to their success that if the network no longer exists, it can lead to the company's failure. These relationships can influence decision-making by creating a sense of 'collaborative entrepreneurship', where firms work together to achieve a competitive advantage. This collaborative entrepreneurship is a cornerstone of the ways in which many small businesses in the creative industries conduct business. For example, an independent music producer will rely on his professional relationships to be recommended for future projects. From executives in a record label, to music publishers, engineers, studio musicians and prior recording artists he or she has worked with, her reputation and network will help provide her with the work she needs. If that close network disappears, so does her business.

We also know that some characteristics in decision-making are particular to small firms. Because smaller companies tend to be less formal in their planning and analysis, owners will tend to rely on their personal experience, personal limitations and biases (Bazerman, 2009; Simon & Houghton, 2002). In particular, McCarthy (2003) studied traits in entrepreneurs and found that the process of planning in these smaller companies is largely dependent on the owner's personality, which can cause this overreliance on personal experience and biases.

Furthermore, we have learned that fewer people tend to be involved in the decision-making of smaller companies, while larger firms tend to be more rational in their decision-making process. They search for information to make decisions, they prefer to have more detailed choice alternatives and potential outcomes outlined before making a decision, and the managers in larger companies are more willing to take on higher levels of risk (Gibcus *et al.*, 2004).

THE PREFERENCE OF 'TASTE' AND 'PROFESSIONAL JUDGEMENT' IN MAKING CREATIVE DECISIONS

Taste is an individual's aesthetic preference. In the creative industries 'conscious aesthetic preferences arise, in terms of what we personally "like" (Halpern *et al.*, 2008), as well as beauty judgements, tastes (Nieminen *et al.*, 2011) and affective responses such as feelings of pleasure or displeasure (Müller *et al.*, 2010)' (Saintilan, 2016, p 6). Taste is influenced by personal experiences, and social and cultural factors, and enables someone to make judgements on what they believe to be beautiful, good or of high quality. Your personal preferences will inevitably arise when making decisions in the creative industries. Since we know that much decision-making is cognitively based through our own past experiences, heuristics, biases and intuition, how then can we rise to the challenge of filtering out our own personal taste preferences and making 'objective' decisions? Professional judgement on the other hand differs from aesthetic preferences in seeking to be a more objective evaluation, such as assessing the commercial potential of a creative product. It may involve predicting whether a piece will resonate with an audience, niche or otherwise. To put it another way and provide an example:

> A manager may like a pop song and want to see it receive extra promotional support, demonstrating an aesthetic preference. This is not the same as a manager who draws upon years of commercial experience to predict the success of a popular music single (Davis, 2013). The latter draws on memory of a large volume of similar products and is seeking to make a predictive judgement based upon a comparative analysis.
>
> (Saintilan, 2016, p. 7)

This type of predictive analysis doesn't need to have any relationship to one's own taste. Thus, a creative manager is usually attempting to select music or artwork which he or she believes to have commercial potential, not necessarily music or art that he or she personally likes (though there may be an overlap). When should decisions that affect the selection, production and marketing promotion of cultural products for an organization be based on one's personal taste for the product, service or experience and when should they be a cold commercial judgement? An artistic director of an arts organization may argue that their taste is their own signature, their own 'imprimatur' and they are paid to introduce their personal taste as a tastemaker. Are these two aspirations mutually exclusive? These questions are explored in further detail at the end of this chapter (Case Study 7.1: Should artistic leaders drive decision-making from their own taste?) Here, you can explore different professional perspectives on this issue.

THE CREATIVE AND CULTURAL INDUSTRIES ENVIRONMENT

As we have reiterated in previous chapters, within the creative and cultural industries, the quantity of disparate products and the uncertainty of demand makes decision-making particularly challenging. Risk and uncertainty, coupled with subjectivity and a lack of reliable data, creates an environment in which we rely on quick decision-making, based on intuition and 'gut feeling'. Some research has found that businesses in these environments engage in open discussions and use more, not less, information when making decisions (Eisenhardt, 1989). Scanning the environment through data gathering, increasing alternative solutions and modelling different situations was found to occur more often in the creative and cultural industries, despite the pressures and time constraints inherent in a turbulent environment. These results challenge the traditional view that fast-paced environments will lead to less information being used (Eisenhardt, 1989). It has also been concluded that to be more effective, decision-makers in highly turbulent environments should encourage constructive conflict among its influencers (in this case the top executives) in order to foster better outcomes (Cosier & Schwenk, 1990; Cosier, 1982). As we saw in the chapter on conflict (Chapter 5), this 'devil's advocate' approach to decision-making in teams can counter the 'groupthink' that can occur. Groups affected by 'groupthink' may ignore viable alternatives and become biased towards internal opinions. This occurs because group members may be of similar background and are not open to outside opinion (Janis, 1982). Surrounding yourself with 'yes men or women' may not be as conducive to effective decision-making in the long term as having people around you who are not frightened to challenge poor assumptions and seek to improve decision-making. Good decision-making rules should be in place to avoid groupthink. We must exercise some caution to prevent being too aggressive when playing a 'devil's advocate', as some research has suggested that consensus can create more effective decisions in some circumstances, especially in diverse, privately held small firms (Cosier & Schwenk, 1990), which characterize the creative and cultural industries (Pratt & Jeffcutt, 2009).

'BIG DATA' IN THE CREATIVE AND CULTURAL ORGANIZATION

Even though the use of 'gut feelings', instinct and other heuristics have been long practiced in the creative economy, we have undoubtedly entered a new era of 'big data' and information to support these feelings, or in some cases, alter the decisions that would previously have been taken. One major development that has arisen from the growth in online commerce and the easy access to, and collection of personal information, is the use of 'big data' and analytics. Today, data science is being used as a tool to understand markets, trends, consumer behaviour and our culture in ways we haven't before. Specifically, predictive analytics is playing a crucial role in creating value by understanding audiences better or by helping to create new business models.

The value of market research has often been questioned in creative firms because managers believe that every product is different and so conclusions drawn from consumer feedback on other historical products are not necessarily predictive (Hesmondhalgh, 2013). It can also be dismissed by managers because they perceive it as only telling them what they already know and is thus backward looking and lacking in imagination (Negus, 2011).

However, the use of market data, particularly market analysis, is now redefining the relationship between cultural production and consumption. From creative or talent selection decisions, to marketing, promotion, tracking of royalty payments and developing new business models, the era of 'data' for the creative and cultural sector continues to grow and have impact as managers seek to mitigate the 'uncertainty' and risk inherent in the creative industries. More and more companies are emerging to provide information solutions for the music, film and video game industries. Tracking of sales, streams, social media activity, airplay broadcasts and recommendation engines are among the many insights being provided to help managers make more informed decisions beyond what they may see as a best course of action, because their 'gut' tells them so.

Big data in Music

For years, *the* Music Genome Project had been classifying music data with identifiers that reached almost 450 per song (Marr, 2016). These identifiers include timbre of voice, gender, genre, tempo and other genre classification data that can then be used to enhance the listener experience, as they engage with and discover new music. Providing richer and more insightful data for artists, managers, publishers and record labels makes it easier to make informed decisions. But these identifiers are just the tip of the proverbial iceberg in how far the industry has come in collecting and using data, not just on music, but in all creative industry sectors as well.

Today, we see a cascade of data collection beyond that of music identifiers and the Genome Project. Streaming services like Spotify, Apple Music and Deezer create playlists based on listening habits, current activities and certain moods. TikTok is being used to identify trends while record labels are using data to better target fans, determine release schedules and align global PR campaigns. The live entertainment industry is using data to engage live audiences with their talent while using blockchain technology to take better control of the secondary ticketing market (see further discussion below). As we learn more about how trends begin, and how user engagement leads to fandom, more informed decision-making can be done that saves organizations and artists time and resources, while making the user feel more relevant and less targeted. For example, listener data is often used to personalize and more closely target ad experiences. Targeting can be based on fan qualification which helps determine how often and what types of ads will be served. For example, the degree of engagement a listener has with an artist's back catalogue can alter the ads that are served to that listener promoting new releases (James, 2022).

Furthermore, data is also being used to identify off-platform trends for music listening experiences. By recognizing listener moods and activities, music services are able to target specific playlists and various passive listening experiences for consumers. In a sports or gym context this may be using blood pressure and heart rate levels to recommend high energy music to work out to. Knowing and responding to user mood and activities which can be captured through biometric data will continue to inform our user and decision-making experiences (James, 2022).

In other situations record labels are making data informed decisions with artists on release configurations, schedules and formats. 'Waterfalling' has become a more common practice where multiple singles are released over weeks or months, each building into the other to form an EP or album (Unlock Your Sound, 2022). Since more frequent releases are necessary in order to maintain audience engagement, this, along with 'coupling multiple versions of a song ensures listeners are consuming the artist's content and not being steered into DSP "radio algorithms" or "continuous listening", which happens automatically when a user finishes listening to the intended song' (James, 2022). With social media platforms like TikTok having greater influence on pop culture trends, this too is a hotbed of user activity that can be tracked and used to make pre-release decisions that will help drive listening and artist engagement. Music video, having been a staple since the early 1980s with the advent of MTV, continues to play an important role in generating engagement that can help labels and artists track user behaviour as well. Whether it be an official or lyric video, when one is played, it couples with the stream of the song thereby influencing familiarity and deeper engagement (James, 2022).

Big data in television & movies

Gone are the days where movie releases are solely driven by concept (Rangaiah, 2021). The evolution of big data has impacted television and movies in ways that impact what is produced, who is cast or what is recommended to us for viewing. Driven by consumer data generated by box office success and consumer engagement, streaming services such as Netflix, Hulu, Disney+, Apple TV and many others are at the forefront of using data science to determine the content they create and recommend to their viewers (Wallace, 2022). What shows to 'greenlight' and personal recommendations are all driven by consumer insight and the data being generated and used to make creative and business decisions. In 2018 it was revealed that 20th Century Fox used machine learning through artificial intelligence (AI) to analyse movie trailers to find out what audiences will like (Vincent, 2018) and the likelihood that viewers will go see the film in the theatres when released. Studios are able to track viewer engagement through comments, likes, shares and search engine activities which can lead to pivoting or reinforcing marketing efforts for the film. Making decisions based on data and information are now commonplace and gut feelings and other heuristics are being limited.

Prior casts, directors, genre, storylines and format data can all be mined to help studio executives make more informed decisions about the potential success of new productions. The explosive popularity of the Netflix Original series *Squid Games* could not have been entirely foreseen, but producers were able to quickly follow-up with a sequel as it became clear the series would vasty exceed their expectations.

Big data in video games

More recently, the video game industry and its use of big data has been at the forefront of employing user generated insights for game development and business model innovation. Monetization and optimization in online and social gaming is now being leveraged in an industry where graphics and storylines aren't enough to keep users engaged over the long-term. Companies like Zynga (creators of Farmville) or King (creators of Candy Crush Saga) and other online game developers 'monitor and record user behaviour to see how well their games are being played and use those insights to tweak and improve gameplay' (Rands, 2018). For example, the company can use behavioural data to update the game so that users may find it challenging, but not so much that they grow frustrated and stop playing (Rands, 2018). Using real time consumer data can help developers tweak parts of the game to keep people engaged and coming back for more.

In addition to game development, analytics plays a big role in the video game Freemium model, or 'free to play games', that has grown over the years. Almost all of us are likely familiar with how this works. Buying rare animals in Tap Zoo or having unlimited attempts at Wordle are charged at a premium, they are considered additional features over and above the free version that are optional to enhance the user's experience. Through this business model, developers may not make large amounts of revenue through subscriptions but rather through multiple micro-payments over months or years. 'Freemium' encourages immediate engagement and is designed to motivate the players to make in-game purchases. Since there is no initial cost, it allows developers to track behaviour of new customers and see where they are struggling (Rands, 2018)

Tracking user data in online gaming also allows for more personalization and targeted advertising. Many of us find it invasive and off-putting if we are engaged with online content only to be interrupted by some company's product or service that is irrelevant to our current activities or interests. We are all too familiar with these marketing strategies and online gaming is no different. Through big data, gaming companies can create meaningful marketing messages for users that range from in-game interstitials to relevant product placements and activities. Not all of this would be possible without the use of data and analytics.

Big data and the management of Intellectual Property (IP)

Not only do activity metrics, insight dashboards and other consumer analytics influence marketing or artist acquisition decisions, but also the era of information has proven to be critically important in managing intellectual property and ownership rights as well. The multiple rights involved in any given copyright and the ownership splits that may accompany it have created a market environment strangled by the complexities of current law. Often, users of these works diligently attempt to track who owns what but are road-blocked by the difficulties of clearing licences and making payments. Specifically, the music industry has been immersed in this issue for some time. Because of the global appeal and distribution of pop music, tracking and managing this data has proven to be one of the industry's greatest challenges. Not only does it contribute to delays in clearing rights, but it also limits its potential growth in the marketplace. If information is freely shared and managed properly, it can lead to more efficient royalty payment systems while fostering goodwill and transparency among rights holders. To alleviate some of these challenges, there are initiatives involving the use of blockchain technology that aim to create a global database. This could end up being a 'one stop shop' of ownership information that will provide any firm with the ability to clear rights and make payments faster and with more accuracy.

Blockchains, NFTs and ticketing in the creative industries

As Non-Fungible Tokens (NFTs) and the use of the blockchain become more prominent, the ticketing industry will see many advantages as well. Due to its efficiency of tracking information, event organizers can easily monitor the sales of tickets as they are sold and resold in the marketplace (Blockchain and NFT Ticketing, 2021). Transactions are entered into the blockchain while sales are securely linked to the purchaser. This precise accounting of each ticket 'limits or even eliminates the possibility of scalping, uncontrolled price gouging, and fraudulent transactions' (Blockchain and NFT Ticketing, 2021) while putting into place a system that allows for royalties or payments back to the issuer or artist on any reselling that may occur. By alleviating fake tickets or the bots that frequently buy up large blocks of tickets only to be resold at outrageous prices on ticket reselling sites, this technology helps to alleviate security concerns and consumer exploitation.

How ethical is all this?

Consumers of creative content spend more time engaging with online media platforms than ever before, all of which is being tracked, providing information and behavioural data to decision-makers. As a consumer of digital content on social media platforms, music, video streaming and gaming services, you freely provide invaluable data so that 'gut feelings' can be affirmed or challenged. But of course, with the ever-increasing access to personal information comes the challenges of using that data ethically. Users must be kept well-informed of the intended use of data. When businesses collect personal information about you and what you do, how they collect it and how they use it must also have its limitations so that it isn't mined for unintended purposes. A lengthier discussion about this concern is beyond the scope of this text, but the prominent role of big data in decision-making is here to stay and those who are willing to embrace, train up and have it be a part of their skill set will be valued in the workplace.

Why have the creative and cultural industries been so slow to adopt data analysis?

Many creative workers are ill prepared for jobs in data analysis. It is often misunderstood and perceived as 'mysterious' to work for a math or 'data' guru. This misunderstanding often leads to a lack of interest or confidence in working with or presenting information to colleagues. It takes time to develop the necessary skills to share, manage, store and analyse data in an effective and ethical way (Parkinson et al., 2020).

Moreover, it can be expensive. The costs associated with various software and syndicated data resources can be well beyond the means of many small to medium sized businesses that dominate the creative industries. The ability to access information or develop internal dashboards to help make better decisions shouldn't be beyond the scope of running your business effectively, but too often it can be.

Some academics and professionals (including the authors of this text) believe that it is highly beneficial for those working in the contemporary creative industries to possess some knowledge of statistics, programming and data analysis (Hadzic, 2021). Not only does it help to improve employability, but managers are quickly learning that there is an economic benefit that comes with the use of new flows of information (Morelli & Spagnoli 2017). They are expecting their employees to be better informed and engaged with data and information because it makes their job easier and will potentially improve decision-making.

SUMMARY AND KEY POINTS

- The decision-making process, which all decisions go through, consists of seven steps, though these steps are not necessarily undertaken in sequence, or in their entirety.
- Decision-making is often influenced by internal cognitive processes as well as external industry characteristics.
- Influences on decision-making include heuristics, personal biases, intuition, past experiences and trust.
- The desire to achieve status and recognition in the creative industries is a driving factor in how we perceive and make decisions.

- The differences in how decisions are made in large and small firms in the creative industries range from a more rational approach in large companies to a more intuitive approach in small businesses.
- Taste in decision-making refers to a personal value judgement of whether we like or dislike a product, service or experience.
- Professional judgement, in terms of the commercial potential of a creative product, refers to an estimate based on previous experience.

CASE STUDY 7.1: THE PROBLEM WITH TASTE – 'THE TASTE CASE'

Should the artistic leader of a music organization select artists and repertoire based on their own personal taste? Is it natural and inevitable or an unprofessional indulgence? A group of artistic directors and A&R heads argue over lunch…

Blake and Jade arrived at the restaurant slightly ahead of the others and took their seats at a table overlooking Sydney Harbour. It was a beautiful day, and a ferry glided through the sparkling water, making its way out of the Quay towards Manly. Blake was the artistic director of a large international orchestra and Jade the artistic director of a music festival. Within minutes they were joined by Cindy and Chris, who both worked as A&R heads for major record companies. All four had spent the morning as guests at a government funded seminar on 'business creativity'.

They ordered their meals and spent some time discussing the difference between artistic and managerial creativity, a topic that had surfaced during the seminar. But then the conversation lost momentum. As an aside, Blake commented: 'I thought it was really interesting what Ariel was saying at the coffee break about the relationship between 'taste' and one's own professional judgement in selecting artists, repertoire and projects. I've been reflecting on what my own views are. I think I do drive my orchestral programming decisions out of personal taste. I don't see how you can do otherwise. Your personal response to music, your passions, your enthusiasms, your musical addictions, how can you clinically disengage them from your professional judgement? And if I personally respond to something, it convinces me that it's an authentic choice, and if I like it others might like it, and then I can fight for it, and hope it connects with others in the same way it connects with me'.

Cindy reached across the table and grabbed a bread roll. 'Yeah, I'd like to be able to do that. But I don't have the luxury of my personal tastes in music. If I was running my own small indie label, then maybe I could, but we're a big company that needs to cater for a really diverse range of tastes. We're not creating music for ourselves, we're creating music for a whole spectrum of artists and audiences. So it needs to be a lot broader than just my taste'.

'Sure' Blake continued. But I think to some extent an artistic leader needs to stand for something and take a leadership position. Or why have them? You need to play to your strengths, not pretend that you know about a million genres when you don't. You know? If you want someone who knows their way around K-Pop or electronica, don't come to me. My musical tastes define me, it's part of who I am. As artistic leaders we need our own signature, our own imprimatur, our own brand. To some degree I was hired for my taste, I'm a 'tastemaker', so surely it's legitimate for me to exercise it?'

'That sounds great, don't get me wrong', countered Cindy, 'but in my situation, it's really important that I don't have any emotional skin in the game. 'Cause sometimes you need to pull the plug on projects, and that's hard to do if you're too passionate, or personally committed'.

'Sure. But don't you find that projects are always emotional? They're always an emotional brawl! I need to fight for my vision on a daily basis. You know there are always doubts and fears and uncertainties in music organizations, and it's our job to sell new projects and sell them hard. I think an audience can sense passion, and belief and conviction, and the more passionate I am, the more passionate I believe the audience will eventually be. I think we actually impose our taste on others down the line, and in your business people like Clive Davis have been doing that for years'.

Cindy smiled. 'My job is to make profit. Pure and simple. We're a publicly listed company. We need a return on investment. So I need to take myself out of the equation and maybe do things that other people will like, even if I don't. In fact, I need to work on projects that I personally loathe and detest if it connects with some audience we can make a buck out of. And if you can't do that, you're not a professional. You know, that's actually been the problem with some A&R guys, that they're wanting to be so cool and credible and edgy, that they hate the mainstream bands that actually pay their salary or refuse to sign them in the first place. You also need to understand that the era of 'gut feel' has largely ended in commercial music. Our decision-making is more and more driven by social metrics and consumer data'.

'Well...', concluded Blake, shaking his head, 'I bet that nine times out of ten when an A&R person signs a band, it's because they like them. And they will selectively choose the data to support their position. Seriously. What do you other two think?'

Chris put down a glass of wine. 'It's an interesting discussion. I think artistic leaders should be really transparent and upfront about acknowledging their tastes. I might think that my taste is really broad, but it probably isn't. Have you ever had the experience where you ask someone what they like, and they say "everything", but when you get down to it, and offer them tickets and stuff, it becomes apparent that there's a ton of things that they actually hate, things that other people might love. If I declare that I hate salsa or reggae or jazz, then the organization can put decisions relating to those genres out to other people, so it's worth the organization knowing. Otherwise I may be making decisions that aren't in the best interests of the business, simply because I don't have any empathy with a certain type of music'.

'I agree with that', responded Blake. 'I believe an artistic director needs to stand for something and be hired or fired on that basis. So I agree with you that honesty and accountability are important. If I hate hip hop, and the organization needs hip hop, then fire me and give the gig to someone who loves hip hop. What about you, Jade?'

'I believe that I have internalized the audience into my own personal responses. I think I have spent so much time seeing what my audience reacts to, what they love, what they hate, that when I look at new ideas it is impossible for me not to compute that into my thinking, even subconsciously'.

'Interesting... What about people who don't attend often – who aren't part of your current audience. Are you choosing for them too?'

A waiter interrupted the conversation, carrying out the first of the meals. They turned their attention back to the sparkling Harbour.

Discussion questions and class exercises

1. Which of the artistic leaders do you agree with and why?
2. Who do you disagree with and why?
3. Explore how the organizational context in which each executive works has influenced their views. For example, should not-for-profit entities like orchestras differ in how they make artistic decisions over 'for-profit' firms like commercial record companies?

* Rob Cannon is a coach, consultant and educator specializing in the arts and entertainment industry. He is an academic lecturer at the Australian Institute of Music and has previously held international record company roles.

The authors would like to thank Shae Constantine and Jeremy Youett for ideas that strengthened the case.

All characters in this work are fictitious. Any resemblance to real persons, living or dead, is entirely coincidental.

This topic is further explored in the article 'Aesthetic preferences and aesthetic 'agnosticism' among managers in music organisations: is liking projects important?' by Paul Saintilan. Published in the *International Journal of Music Business Research*, October 2016, vol. 5 no. 2, pp. 6–25. Available at https://musicbusinessresearch.files.wordpress.com/2016/10/volume-5-no-2-october-2016-saintilan.pdf

A video of managerial responses to this case study is available to instructors from the companion website: http://www.routledgetextbooks.com/textbooks/MMCCI

CASE STUDY 7.2: 'THE DATA CASE – DID YOU FIND THE VOICE OF GOD IN THE DATA?' HOW USEFUL IS CUSTOMER DATA FOR MUSIC NEW PRODUCT DEVELOPMENT?

Sheldon Cybertron, the newly appointed VP of Data Analytics at Galaxy Records, was on fire. He had already earned the respect of his colleagues for his valuable marketing insights. Yet he wanted more. He wanted to help guide the new creative work of the label's biggest stars. But the CEO was dismissive of his ideas. 'You know, Sheldon, every time the Romans were saying "Vox populi, vox Dei", "the voice of the people is the voice of God", that was when they didn't know what to do!'

Sheldon Cybertron had recently been appointed Vice President of Data Analytics and Customer Insight at Galaxy Records. From deep within his social and digital media Command & Control Centre, a nuclear bunker in the building's basement, his department crunched through enormous volumes of customer data. The sources of data had exploded in recent years, from social media, to e-commerce, streaming and licensing platforms, to new Web3 data coming from NFT sales and the label's involvement in 'play to earn' video games. His work also extended to building the label's market research capability, proactively testing customer needs, tastes and preferences.

Sheldon's department enjoyed analysing behaviours, intentions and affinities, identifying geographic 'hotspots' for artists and personalizing and improving the user experience for fans using their digital assets. Yet he felt – and probably persuaded himself – that he could add more value to the business and increase his influence, by contributing to discussions on new product development. His future was bright and the application of his work appeared limitless.

To move forward this potential expansion of his role, he found himself ushered into the office of David Kong, Galaxy's President. Kong, affectionately known as 'King Kong' reclined deeply in his chair.

'So you're the 'Data Man'? As a President/CEO, I guess I'm seen as a 'numbers man', so we have something in common. I don't mean 'Data Man' in a patronizing way, I assure you. I love data geeks, some of my best friends are data geeks, and you're making a great contribution to the marketing side of the business'.

'Thanks. We are supposed to be in The Data Era now – isn't everything data-driven these days?'

'In terms of new product development there's probably a bunch of things you could do in back catalogue exploitation. There might be some new themes you could identify. You know, *The Best Geek Album in the World Ever* (sorry). You could also look at our broader artist and repertoire portfolio and assess the balance of what we have versus what we should have'.

‘I’m already doing work in that area. I was thinking about helping some of the bigger acts with new creative work’.

‘There are some acts we manufacture from A to Z, ‘boy band’ type acts, you know, but this is actually a small proportion of the roster’.

‘I think every artist could benefit from the sort of analysis I provide’.

‘In creating new material?’

‘Yes’.

‘And how would that work?’

‘By better understanding tastes and preferences of audiences, they will be able to better respond to them’.

King Kong smiled. ‘How long have you been crunching numbers here?’

‘Six months’.

‘And over that time, what extraordinary creative breakthroughs have emerged from your analysis?’

‘I would need to do a bit more work, and I would be looking to better inform the process. We must be able to get more sophisticated at this, as other industries are, and proactively engineer creative work in our favour, so it’s not just a series of random casino bets’.

‘Even if I gave you a year, do you think you’re ever going to find God in the data? Do you think Monet’s *Water Lilies*, or Van Gogh’s *Starry Night* suddenly sprang out of an analysis of art consumers? Do you think the Beatles’ *Sgt. Pepper’s* album came out of some survey data? Or a focus group? Great art is magic. Great art is extraordinary. Great artists lead audiences, they don’t respond to them. They lead out of conviction and passion and inspiration, and remorselessly innovate, staying ahead of the audience. The Beatles could have stuck with their initial success, and been a guitar driven rock and roll band. But they evolved into a psychedelic band, a concept album band, they took listeners on a journey that they couldn’t have imagined. And what could they really learn from an audience? How is an audience going to envision and articulate an entirely new creative direction? So just reflect for a minute or two Sheldon on what this company and the music industry really needs today'.

'Well', replied Sheldon, 'if I found the Holy Grail, it would be how to make hits through a deep insight into consumer tastes. The second thing I guess is to do it again and again ...?'

'I like your enthusiasm and your ambition Sheldon, and so don't take this the wrong way, but your Holy Grail doesn't exist. Not so long ago a numbers man bought the great British record company EMI and promised his investors that like King Arthur he knew how to find the Holy Grail. But do you know what happened? He destroyed one of the world's oldest and most successful record companies, lost his shirt and his investors' money and EMI was broken up and sold to the other three big companies. You talk about technology. The ongoing viability of this industry is about building on the success of streaming, to increase the number of people paying for and accessing music to every corner of the earth. We also need to develop artists with real longevity to build the catalogue of tomorrow. How many stadium acts are we creating these days? Over the last 20 years long term artists have become short-term, one-hit wonders. Fans have become consumers. Songs have become sounds. Long-term investment has become short-term return. Belief in talent has submitted to belief in data'.

Sheldon was taken aback. 'But technology is opening up opportunities we haven't even discussed. Some artists these days are involving audiences in their creative processes, interacting with them. Technology and social engagement are actually part of their creativity, they use the world as an orchestra'.

'You know, Sheldon, if we go back to the time of the Romans or the Middle Ages, every time they were saying *Vox populi vox Dei* (the voice of the people is the voice of God) that was when they didn't know what to do! In music, the artist is the voice of God. This industry has been built on the work of people who were *not* normal, not the voice of the people'.

'But there is so much talk these days of a new model emerging, a participatory, co-creation model?'

'What you're giving me is an old model. A derivative, conservative, sales analysis model, not a cutting edge artistic leadership model. 'They liked Ed Sheeran. The engagement indices are high for Ed Sheeran. Let's try to find another Ed Sheeran.' Doh!'

Sheldon Cybertron looked out of the window dejectedly. It all seemed so much easier for his friends working at Procter & Gamble and Unilever. Their companies really appreciated customer insight.

Discussion questions

1. How should customer data and research inform new product development decisions in music organizations?
2. What data usage is appropriate and what is inappropriate in this context?
3. What type of decision-making process is Sheldon advocating here? Is this an appropriate practice for the creative industries?
4. To what extent do music fans know what music they want to discover?

*JF Cecillon is the former Chairman and CEO of EMI Music International.

All characters in this work are fictitious. Any resemblance to real persons, living or dead, is entirely coincidental.

A video of managerial responses to this case study is available to instructors from the companion website: http://www.routledgetextbooks.com/textbooks/MMCCI

References

Agor, W. H. (1989). 'How to use and develop your intuition in management', in W. H. Agor (ed.), *Intuition in Organizations*. Newbury Park, CA: Sage Publications, pp. 217–46.

Anon. (2022). Personal communication, April 25th, 2012.

Argote, L. & Ingram, P. (2000). 'Knowledge transfer: a basis for competitive advantage in firms', *Organizational Behavior and Human Decision Processes*, Vol. 82, no. 1, pp. 150–169.

Bazerman, M. H. (2002). *Judgment in Managerial Decision Making*. New York: Wiley.

Behling, O. (1991). 'Making sense out of intuition', *The Executive*, Vol. 5, no. 1, pp. 46–54.

Blank, H. Nestler, H., von Collani, G. & Fischer, V. (2008). 'How many hindsight biases are there?' *Cognition*, Vol. 106, no. 3, pp. 1408–1440. Available at http://www.sciencedirect.com/science/article/pii/S0010027707001990 (accessed 8 August 2017).

Bourdieu, T. & Thompson, J. B. (1991). *Language and Symbolic Power*. Cambridge, MA: Harvard University Press.

Cosier, R. A. (1982). 'Methods for improving the strategic decision: Dialectic versus the devil's advocate', *Strategic Management Journal*, Vol. 3, no. 4, pp. 373–374. Available at http://search.ebscohost.com/login.aspx?direct=true&db=bth&AN=12569946&site=ehost-live (accessed 8 August 2017).

Cosier, R. A. & Schwenk, C. R. (1990). 'Agreement and thinking alike: Ingredients for poor decisions', *Executive*, Vol. 4, no. 1, pp. 69–74. Available at http://search.ebscohost.com/login.aspx?direct=true&db=bth&AN=4274710&site=ehost-live (accessed 8 August 2017).

Davis, C. (2013). *The Soundtrack of My Life*. New York: Simon and Schuster.

DCMS (2006). *SME Music Businesses: Business Growth and Access to Finance*. London: DCMS.

Dube, C., Rotello, C. M. & Heit, E. (2010). 'Assessing the belief bias effect with ROCs: It's a response bias effect', *Psychological Review*, Vol. 117, no. 3, pp. 831–863.

Eisenhardt, K. M. (1989). 'Making fast strategic decisions in high-velocity environments', *Academy of Management Journal*, Vol. 32, no. 3, pp. 543–576. Available at http://search.ebscohost.com/login.aspx?direct=true&db=bsh&AN=4406007&site=ehost-live (accessed 8 August 2017).

EventMB (2021). *Blockchain and NFT Ticketing: The 2021 Guide*. [online] Available at https://www.eventmanagerblog.com/blockchain-ticketing (accessed 24 April 2022).

Gibcus, P., Vermeulen, P. A. M. & de Jong, J. P. J. (2004). *Strategic Decision-Making in Small Firms: Towards a Typology of Entrepreneurial Decision-Makers*. Available at http://ideas.repec.org/p/eim/papers/n200416.html (accessed 8 August 2017).

Hadzic, A. (2021). *The impact of data science in creative industries*. [online]. Available at: https://medium.datadriveninvestor.com/

the-impact-of-data-science-in-creative-industries-eb650f3590ec (accessed 23 April 2022).

Halpern, A. R., Ly, J., Elkin-Frankston, S. & O'Connor, M. G. (2008). '"I know what I like": Stability of aesthetic preference in Alzheimer's patients', *Brain and Cognition*, Vol. 66, no. 1, pp. 65–72.

Hesmondhalgh, D. (2013). *The Cultural Industries*. London: Sage.

Hirschman, E. C. (1983). 'Aesthetics, ideologies and the limits of the marketing concept', *The Journal of Marketing*, pp. 45–55.

James, C. (2022). *Personal correspondence*, May 18, 2022.

Janis, I. L. (1982). *Groupthink: Psychological Studies of Policy Decisions and Fiascoes*. Boston, MA: Houghton Mifflin.

Juliusson, E. Á., Karlsson, N. & Gärling, T. (2005). 'Weighing the past and the future in decision making', *European Journal of Cognitive Psychology*, Vol. 17, no. 4, pp. 561–575. Available at http://www.tandfonline.com/doi/abs/10.1080/09541440440000159 (accessed 8 August 2017).

Kahneman, D. (2002). *Maps of Bounded Rationality*. New York: Nobel Prize Committee.

Kahneman, D. (2011). *Thinking Fast and Slow*, 1st edition. New York: Farrar, Straus and Giroux.

Lampel, J., Shamsie, J. & Lant, T. K. (2006). *The Business of Culture: Strategic Perspectives on Entertainment and Media*. Mahwah, NJ: Psychology Press.

Larrick, R. P., Nisbett, R. E. & Morgan, J. N. (1993). 'Who uses the cost-benefit rules of choice? Implications for the normative status of microeconomic theory', *Organizational Behavior and Human Decision Processes*, Vol. 56, no. 3, pp. 331–347. Available at http://www.sciencedirect.com/science/article/pii/S0749597883710587 (accessed 8 August 2017).

Li, S., Mayhew, S. D. & Kourtzi, Z. (2009). 'Learning shapes: The representation of behavioral choice in the human brain', *Neuron*, Vol. 62, no. 3, pp. 441–452.

Liberman-Yaconi, L., Hooper, T. & Hutchings, K. (2010). 'Toward a model of understanding strategic decision-making in micro-firms: Exploring the Australian information technology sector', *Journal of Small Business Management*, Vol. 48, no. 1, pp. 70–95. Available at 10.1111/j.1540-627X.2009.00287.x (accessed 8 August 2017).

McCarthy, B. (2003). 'Strategy is personality-driven, strategy is crisis-driven: Insights from entrepreneurial firms', *Management Decision*, Vol. 41, no. 4, pp. 327–339.

Marr, B. (2016). 'How Big Data will change the music industry forever'. *LinkedIn*. Available at https://www.linkedin.com/pulse/how-big-data-change-music-industry-forever-bernard-marr (accessed 8 August 2017).

Miller, C. C. (2008). 'Decisional comprehensiveness and firm performance: Towards a more complete understanding', *Journal of Behavioral Decision Making*, Vol. 21, no. 5, pp. 598–620.

Mishra, A. K. & Spreitzer, G. M. (1998). 'Explaining how survivors respond to downsizing: The roles of trust, empowerment, justice, and work redesign', *Academy of Management Review*, Vol. 23, no. 3, pp. 567–588.

Morelli, G. & Spagnoli, Francesca. (2017). *Creative Industries and Big Data: A Business Model for Service Innovation*, pp. 144–158. 10.1007/978-3-319-56925-3_12.

Müller, M., Höfel, L., Brattico, E. & Jacobsen, T. (2010). 'Aesthetic judgments of music in experts and laypersons—An ERP study', *International Journal of Psychophysiology*, Vol. 76, no. 1, pp. 40–51.

Negus, K. (2011). 'Producing pop: Culture and conflict in the popular music industry'. Available at http://research.gold.ac.uk/5453/1/Producing_Pop.pdf (accessed 8 August 2017).

Nieminen, S., Istok, E., Brattico, E., Tervaniemi, M. & Huotilainen, M. (2011). 'The development of aesthetic responses to music and their underlying neural and psychological mechanisms', *Cortex*, Vol. 47, no. 9, pp. 1138–1146.

Parkinson, C., Speed, C., Terras, M. and Somerville, R. (2020). *Developing Data-Driven Innovation in Creative Industries: White Paper Data Driven Innovation Programme*, University of Edinburgh, http://dx.doi.org/10.7488/era/507

Pettigrew, A. M. (2014). *The Politics of Organizational Decision-Making*. London: Routledge.

Pratt, A. & Jeffcutt, P. (eds.). (2009). *Creativity, Innovation and the Cultural Economy*, 1st ed. New York: Routledge.

Rands, K. (2018). 'How big data is disrupting the gaming industry', [online] *CIO*. Available at https://www.cio.com/article/228327/how-big-data-is-disrupting-the-gaming-industry.html (accessed 24 April 2022).

Rangaiah, M. (2021). 'How is Data Science revolutionizing the film industry? | Data Science in Movie Industry' [online] *Analyticssteps.com*. Available at https://www.analyticssteps.com/blogs/how-data-science-revolutionizing-film-industry (accessed 24 April 2022).

Saintilan, P. (2016). 'Aesthetic preferences and aesthetic "agnosticism" among managers in music organizations: Is liking projects important?' *International Journal of Music Business Research*, Vol. 5, no. 2, pp. 6–25.

Schreiber, D. (2014). *An investigation of influences on strategic decision-making in popular recorded music industry micro-enterprises*, Doctoral dissertation, University of Westminster.

Seifert, M. & Hadida, A. L. (2009). 'Decision making, expertise and task ambiguity: predicting success in the music industry', *Academy of Management Proceedings*, pp. 1–6. Available at: http://search.ebscohost.com/login.aspx?direct=true&db=bsh&AN=44257974&site=ehost-live (accessed 8 August 2017).

Shah, A. K. & Oppenheimer, D. M. (2008). 'Heuristics made easy: An effort-reduction framework', *Psychological Bulletin*, Vol. 134, no. 2, pp. 207–222. Available at 10.1037/0033–2909.134.2.207 (accessed 8 August 2017).

Simon, H. A. (1979). 'Rational decision making in business organizations', *The American Economic Review*, Vol. 69, no. 4, pp. 493–513.

Simon, H. A. (1990). 'Invariants of human behavior', *Annual Review of Psychology*, Vol. 41, no. 1, p. 1. Available at http://teach.belmont.edu:2048/login?url=http://search.ebscohost.com/login.aspx?direct=true&db=pbh&AN=9102251390&site=ehost-live (accessed 8 August 2017).

Simon, M. & Houghton, S. M. (2002). 'The relationship among biases, misperceptions, and the introduction of pioneering products: Examining differences in venture decision contexts', *Entrepreneurship Theory and Practice*, Vol. 27, no. 2, pp. 105–124.

Strough, J., Schlosnagle, L. & DiDonato, L. (2011). 'Understanding decisions about sunk costs from older and younger adults' perspectives', *The Journals of Gerontology Series B: Psychological Sciences and Social Sciences*, Vol. 66B, no. 6, pp. 681–686. Available at http://psychsocgerontology.oxfordjournals.org/content/66B/6/681.abstract (accessed 8 August 2017).

Unlock Your Sound. (2022). 'What is a waterfall release and how is it done?' [online] Available at https://unlockyoursound.com/waterfall-release/#:~:text=A%20waterfall%20release%20is%20where, is%20an%20outcome%20of%20that (accessed 18 May 2022).

Vincent, J. (2018). '20th Century Fox is using AI to analyze movie trailers and find out what films audiences will like'. [online] *The Verge*. Available at: https://www.theverge.com/2018/11/2/18055514/fox-google-ai-analyze-movie-trailer-predict-success-logan (accessed 24 April 2022).

Wallace, F. (2022). 'How data science is used within the film industry', *KDnuggets*. [online] Available at: https://www.kdnuggets.com/2019/07/data-science-film-industry.html (accessed 24 April 2022).

Welbourne, T. & Pardo-del-Val, M. (2009). 'Relational capital: Strategic advantage for small and medium-size enterprises (SMEs) through negotiation and collaboration', *Group Decision & Negotiation*, Vol. 18, no. 5, pp. 483–497. Available at 10.1007/s10726-008-9138-6.

West, R. F., Toplak, M. E. & Stanovich, K. E. (2008). 'Heuristics and biases as measures of critical thinking: associations with cognitive ability and thinking dispositions', *Journal of Educational Psychology*, Vol. 100, no. 4, pp. 930–941.

Power and politics in creative organizations

Chapter 8

Figure 8.1 Money does NOT equal power! Photo credit: rvlsoft / Shutterstock.com.

DOI: 10.4324/9781003262923-8

CHAPTER LEARNING OBJECTIVES

After studying this chapter, you should be able to:

- Explain the concept of power and contrast this with authority;
- Identify the sources of power that individuals and organizational leaders can draw on to influence others;
- Define symbolic power and explain why its power base is critical to successful people and organizations in the creative and cultural industries;
- Discuss Kanter's symbols of power and their manifestation in the firm;
- Explain the idea of powerlessness and how it can be identified in organizations;
- Explain what political skill is and its positive and negative implications;
- Identify the various influence tactics used in organizations;
- Define the concept of strategic sexual performance (SSP) and examine its implications as an ingratiating tactic in the creative and cultural industry firm;
- Recognize when SSP leads to sexual harassment;
- Discuss best practices in recognizing sexual harassment and how to manage through the implications of this behaviour in the workplace;
- Discuss best practices when it comes to managing political behaviour.

INTRODUCTION

Start thinking ...

- How is power utilized in the creative industries?
- Where does power come from within the cultural sector?
- What political behaviours are more effective on creative personalities?

Stop reading for a moment and think about the people you surround yourself with – family, friends, artists, screenwriters, songwriters, actors, writers? How do these people influence you? Are you willing to do certain things for some, and not for others? What are you willing to do for them? Why are you willing to do these things? What is it that gives them that kind of influence over you?

It is the 'influence' that one person has over others that we will be discussing in this chapter. We call this 'power' – the ability to influence the behaviour of others or resist someone's influence upon you (Nelson & Quick, 2019). Perhaps you immediately think negatively about how one individual may have 'power' over someone else, leading to domination and the potential violation of their rights. However, power is often used to navigate relationships, negotiate for a position or get things done. It can be used to leverage change, and may be an arbiter of efficiency, or a generator of inefficiencies.

In some cases, people may never even know they are exercising power, but nonetheless have great influence over others and situations. As this definition infers, power is not a 'one-way' street. Often, the ability to resist or not be influenced by others is also a form of power. The old adage 'don't give in to peer pressure' is a classic example of a person using their own power to refuse to do what they are being pressured to do. In the workplace, giving a dissenting opinion or challenging the ethical implication of a leader's decision is an example of this resistance.

POWER VERSUS AUTHORITY

Before we discuss the concept of power in greater detail, it's important to distinguish the difference between power and authority. When you have the 'authority' to do something, it is the institutional *right* to tell others what to do within the scope of your job or employment. Management scholar and business executive Chestor Barnard (1938) wrote a pioneering book on authority which is considered one of the most profound contributions to the management and organizational sociology literature, despite being written in 1938. Barnard believed that employees are willing to accept direction from an authoritative figure, a type of formal power (to be discussed in greater detail below), as long as four conditions are met:

1 He or she understands what is being asked of them.
2 He or she, at the time of the decision, believes it is not in conflict with the organization.
3 He or she, at the time of the decision, believes it is not in conflict with their own goals, ambitions and interest.
4 He or she is mentally able to comply.

Barnard's thoughts were some of the most forward thinking of the time on authority (Barnard, 1938). Although managers and thought leaders since then have developed his ideas further, the premise is still the same. The authority that is granted to any individual through legitimate means can be used to direct others under them. If those being directed are willing, they must then meet these criteria. However, if there is tension, or questioning of the intent of someone's authority, any willingness to continue with what was asked of them is being done under the auspices of power, not authority. For example, if a lead singer's wife is asking the drummer in a band to do something, she may not have any authority to do so, but the drummer's action or compliance to get it done would be due to the 'power' she may have over him.

So how is it then that sometimes we are willing to do things for people that go beyond what would flow legitimately from someone's position? Expanding one's influence beyond that authority is considered the 'zone of indifference' (Barnard, 1938). This zone of indifference is a place where an employee believes that direction is acceptable, but not necessarily within the bounds of his or her 'authority' granted by their position within the organization. The employee is willing to take direction without consciously questioning that authority. For example, as a runner on set for a film production, you've been asked to pick up a birthday gift for the director's daughter. He has completely forgotten that she turned ten today and has no means of getting to a store before attending her birthday party later that day. Although not in the scope of your employment, you are compelled to help her out in any way that you can ... of course, as long as it's reasonable, right? This request goes beyond the director's authority and into this 'zone of indifference'. Your willingness to pick up a gift is only possible because she is influencing you through a power dynamic. The space between authority and power is where this zone lies.

In organizations, when employees influence the decision-making of leaders, we consider this 'upward power'. However, when managers exert an influence on employees or direct them to do something, we call this 'downward power' (Greiner & Schein, 1988). Managing 'upward' can, and is, often a delicate dance of political skill. In organizations, the best managers are able to exercise different types of power in order to persuade or influence their superiors. They may not have the 'authority' to get things done through their boss, but they can persuade them to consider different actions.

FORMS AND BASES OF POWER IN ORGANIZATIONS

In 1959, notable social psychologists John French and Bertram Raven developed a model where they discussed five separate and distinct forms of power (Figure 8.2). They described these bases of power as legitimate, coercive, reward, referent and expert. Later, in 1965, Raven revised the original model to include a sixth power base: informational power (French Jr & Raven, 1959; Raven, 2008). Let's discuss these in turn.

Coercive power is when a person has the ability to punish others in the organization. When a manager relies on this basis of power to influence someone, they may threaten the employee with termination, demotion or a loss of privileges and benefits if they don't do what is asked. This form of power is rooted in fear as a motivating factor. The targeted employee may comply, but the compliance is often temporary or feelings of resentment may result after the experience. It is generally perceived as a poor form of power, but can be effective in certain circumstances when used in an appropriate manner. For example, in the context of unions the AFM (American Federation of Musicians) or SAG/AFTRA (Screen Actors Guild/American Federation of Television and Radio Artists) may threaten members or signatory organizations with a 'blacklist' for taking on work that isn't paid to the agreed upon union scale contracts. This is a highly visible ‘shaming’ list that discourages anyone from taking on work that isn’t adhering to the agreed upon wages and conditions. It is a highly effective way to maintain the integrity of collective bargaining by discouraging ‘under the table’ or ‘off the record’ deals.

Reward power is the influence someone holds because they control resources or rewards the recipient of that power desires. The user of this power may be able to motivate individuals through the auspices of reward, such as raises, tickets to special events or award shows, performance reviews or promotions. However, as is the case with coercive power, its long-term effects are also limited. Once the target of this power has received such rewards, the manager may need to turn to other forms of influence.

Legitimate power is power based on position and mutual agreement. Similar to ‘authority’, the individual who holds or exercises legitimate power likely holds a position of authority in the organization. There is an acceptance that the manager can legitimately ask employees to perform tasks within the scope of their employment. This is the classic example of the manager asking a subordinate to perform a task.

Referent power is an elusive power that is based on interpersonal attraction. Power may be ‘granted’ to a manager because an individual finds the person similar or has an affinity towards them. The manager may not always be aware that they hold this kind of power, but the dynamic of influence and persuasion can be seen because of a respect or likeability factor. Those with strong charismatic traits will elicit a sense of loyalty and respect from their followers. Google’s Larry Page or Walt Disney’s Bob Iger have often been rated highly likeable CEOs by their employees (Dishman, 2015).

Expert power is the power that exists when an individual has specialized knowledge, skills or talent. When the recipient of this power perceives an individual as an expert, they are more likely to be influenced by their requests. However, in order for this power to be effective, they must first be perceived as an expert, and the recipient must trust that what the expert is saying is relevant and legitimate. David Geffen (film studio executive and producer) and Irving Azoff (an entertainment executive and artist manager) are both seen as 'experts' in their respective fields.

Informational power is the ability of a person to bring about change through the use of information (Steiner & Fishbein, 1965). Raven (2008) believed that information is a form of influence when someone possesses knowledge that another needs or wants. Leaders or managers are often privy to information not available to others in the organization. For example, leaders may be aware of financial limitations that surround a project, but those tasked with implementing it may not have access to that information. Knowing the reasons behind the decisions to be made in these circumstances may give these individuals leverage over those who do not know of the financial constraints.

Since French and Raven discussed their ideas on power in the late 1950s, considerable research has been conducted to see which of the five forms are most effective. 'Coercive' and 'reward' are effective bases of power, but are usually temporary and may not lead to a long-term level of commitment or respect. 'Legitimate' power is also effective, but may not lead to organizational effectiveness or employee satisfaction (Nelson & Quick, 2019), and 'referent' power has its criticisms because of the intense feelings that may be involved.

Of the five bases of power, expert power has been seen to be the most effective long-term for influencing people. Not only does expert power provide a level of respect towards the individual, but the holder exhibits a skill-set that is also likely desired. When an individual possesses significant expert power, they are able to influence not only the people directly reporting to them, but potentially the organization, its stakeholders and even an entire industry.

An example of one who has obtained expert power would be 'record man' Clive Davis or director and producer Steven Spielberg. Their profile and reputation create a power base that is of special importance in their respective industries. It is a power that is perceived as genuine, which helps to create a form of political power – the ability held by individuals or groups that allows them to create and enforce policies for a group or community (Schreiber, 2014). For Clive Davis and Steven

Guidelines for the Ethical Use of Power	
Reward Power	Verify compliance. Make feasible, reasonable requests. Make only ethical requests. Offer rewards desired by subordinates. Offer only credible rewards.
Coercive Power	Inform subordinates of rules and penalties. Warn before punishing. Administer punishment consistently and uniformly. Understand the situation before acting. Maintain credibility. Fit punishment to the infraction. Punish in private.
Legitimate Power	Be cordial and polite. Be confident. Be clear and follow up to verify understanding. Make sure request is appropriate. Explain reasons for request. Follow proper channels. Exercise power consistently. Enforce compliance. Be sensitive to sub-ordinates' concerns.
Referent Power	Treat subordinates fairly. Defend subordinates' interests. Be sensitive to subordinates' needs and feelings. Select employees similar to oneself. Engage in role modelling.
Expert Power	Maintain credibility. Act confident and decisive. Keep informed. Recognize employee concerns. Avoid threatening subordinate's self-esteem.

Figure 8.2 Each of the various types of personal power can be used ethically; above are just a few examples of how leaders can help shape others' behaviour.

Source: Nelson, D. & Quick, J. (2019). *ORGB 6*. Stamford, CT: Cengage Learning.

Spielberg, their level of expertise enables them to be seen as experts in their given field, which allows them to influence the politics of their respective projects or companies. They sit on boards, are active in politics and education and can influence major industry events. Expert power takes time to accumulate through years of experience and often manifests itself in a reputation through something called symbolic capital (see below). This includes the knowledge of how the rules of the industry are structured and how to play the game politically with others. They can use their power to change the rules or continue to reinforce them if they desire.

SYMBOLIC POWER

Symbolic capital, the resources available to an individual through honour, prestige and recognition (Bourdieu & Thompson, 1991) also contributes to a person's power base. This form of power, discussed extensively by French philosopher, sociologist and anthropologist Pierre Bourdieu (Bourdieu, 1977; Bourdieu & Nice, 1986) exhibits similar qualities to that of French and Raven's legitimate power base. However, symbolic capital and the power that naturally extends from it is worthy of discussion here in its own form due to the nature of the product produced in the creative and cultural industries. The symbolic meaning of cultural product and the power that is associated with its mass production, marketing and distribution extends beyond the 'expert' into the symbolism of honour and prestige that accompanies that power. According to Bourdieu, symbolic power contributes to a shared meaning of value and prestige within the industry. For example, in theatre, when someone has been nominated for a Tony Award, it is immediately understood that this is an honour bestowed on a select few. The symbolism and meaning that this award exhibits will enable the winner to influence many people and do many things. For example, an actor may be considered for roles that he or she wouldn't have been called back for before. Or, a playwright may have access to better writers and an executive producer may have an easier time seeking funding for a project. These new opportunities that have arisen through symbolic capital can lead to other forms of power that can be exercised, such as referent, reward or expert. Within the creative and cultural industries, the Billboard charts, the Grammys, Emmys, Oscars or Tony Awards have some of the highest levels of symbolic power associated with their attainment (Schreiber & Rieple, 2018, Schreiber, 2014).

As we just discussed, receiving these awards and accumulating symbolic capital allows the user to transform their value into other bases of power in a number of different ways: they influence quality perceptions of the creator or business who won it (Hadida, 2015; Weick, 1995); an actor or recording artist may command a larger signing bonus or back-end commission on a project; this newfound leverage in negotiations can be used as others recognize this honour and what it means (Keuschnigg, 2015; Kretschmer *et al.*, 1999; Rindova *et al.*, 2006).

It can also influence consumer and industry behaviour. Grammy and Oscar 'bumps' are often seen on projects that win album or picture of the year. Sales will go up as customers see that the music and movie projects have been deemed 'valuable' and 'worthy' of purchase and consumption. Maybe they hadn't heard of them before *or* were reluctant to spend hard-earned money because they weren't sure whether it was worth it; either way this recognition has now turned into sales. Organizations within their respective industries also want to be associated with feted and awarded actors, musicians and teams of managers and agents because, to them, these people seem to have figured out a formula that works. The symbolic capital and power that is embodied within the charts and award shows helps to provide consensus among people who work in the industry. This is not just consensus around who are the top creative talents, but the status relationships within the industry and all stakeholders involved.

KANTER'S SYMBOLS OF POWER

When managers are in positions of power, they can accomplish more and focus their efforts on motivating others. They typically have better access to resources and information and professional relationships which can facilitate their work. This 'outward' perspective with stakeholders, as well as their ability to influence employees within the company, enables managers to focus on the criteria that will reinforce and grow their positions of power. Managers who have power can get things done. In Kanter's (1979) work, she identified eight practical things that leaders are typically able to do if they have accumulated power and are in a position of influence. They are able to:

1. intercede favourably on behalf of someone in trouble in the organization;
2. get a desirable placement for a talented subordinate;
3. get approval for expenditures beyond the budget;
4. get above-average salary increases for subordinates;

5 get items on agendas at meetings;
6 get fast access to top decision-makers;
7 get regular, frequent access to top decision-makers;
8 get early information about decisions.

This may play out in a number of different situations in the creative industries. For example, in the music industry, a popular recording artist's new album release may go over budget because of a need to record more tracks than anticipated, or because the studio work has taken longer than originally forecast. Depending on the artist (and their level of commercial success or accumulated symbolic capital), a powerful music producer and artist and repertoire (A&R) director may have no problem getting these expenses approved beyond what was originally budgeted. Or, maybe an artist's manager wants to discuss a last minute co-branding situation with their label. If the manager is a powerful one, it will not be an issue to add this to the meeting agenda. These types of situations play out every day and are indicative of the accumulated power, in all its forms, that an individual may use that allows them to make decisions, execute them and get things done. As Kanter explained, if someone is able to do the things she describes, they have accumulated the necessary power and are able to influence in ways many others are not.

SYMBOLS OF POWERLESSNESS

Kanter also believes that the 'powerless' find themselves in situations often riddled with the challenges of accomplishing tasks due to a lack of resources available to them and an inability to influence others. In the creative and cultural industries, the sensitivity to proprietary information can often be 'over-the-top'. Rightly, senior executives, contending with piracy issues, celebrities and their fanatical fans and the consequences of their own success, need these extra data security protections from piracy. However, when such a watchful eye is put on employees within the organization, it can be seen by many employees as symptomatic of a lack of trust and a sign that management is overreaching or micro-managing their work. Furthermore, since the demand to work in these industries is

Symbols of Powerlessness	
Any Level Employees	Passivity, over-dependence, frustration, disruptiveness
First Line Supervisors	Close supervision, 'micro-managing', inflexible adherence to rules, lack of training for employees – manager's will do jobs themselves, resistant, under-producing subordinates
Staff Professionals	Resistance to change, turf protection, controlling of information
Top Executives	Budget cuts, punishing behaviors, 'dictatorial top-down communications', retreat to comfort of like-minded subordinates

Figure 8.3 Often, individuals in the workplace may feel as if they are not empowered to accomplish their task. If you feel you are experiencing some of the above circumstances, you are likely feeling a lack of empowerment.

Source: Kanter, R. M. (1979). 'Power failure in management circuits', *Classics of Organization Theory*, pp. 342–351.

quite high, many organizations don't feel as compelled to train employees or put into place adequate programmes to maintain morale and limit turnover. There is an underlying assumption that employees can be easily replaced if they are no longer satisfied working under the conditions in which they find themselves. Because of this, employees tend to feel 'powerless' in their positions. Kanter laid out some guidelines or 'symbols' that are indicative of a lack of employee power or influence (Figure 8.3).

Whether you are a 'first line' supervisor or a top executive in a company, there are tell-tale signs that indicate whether employees feel as if they have limited power to control or influence their situation. When you see managers overly sensitive to changes in their departments or unwilling to share information for fear of being 'outperformed', it may indicate that they are feeling a sense of powerlessness. Furthermore, an executive or label president may feel similarly if decisions from the 'ivory' tower or corporate headquarters are perceived as dictatorial or autocratic. For example, if Sony Corporation out of Japan decided to slash the budget of Sony Music Entertainment without consulting the company's US leadership, US leaders may rely more heavily on their own trusted executive team while feeling a reduction in their powerbase.

KORDA'S POWER SYMBOLS

Yet another view on power comes from Michael Korda (Korda, 1985) who defines power as follows: there are more people who inconvenience themselves on your behalf than there are people on whose behalf you would inconvenience yourself. While Kanter's symbols focus on the ability to help others, Korda's symbols focus on status – a person's relative standing in a group based on prestige and having other people defer to him or her. Depicted in Figure 8.4, Korda's power symbols include 'time', 'furnishings' and 'on stand-by'.

'Time' is represented when someone of power uses it to his or her advantage. Giving people their 'time' through meetings or showing up 'late' to an appointment leaves

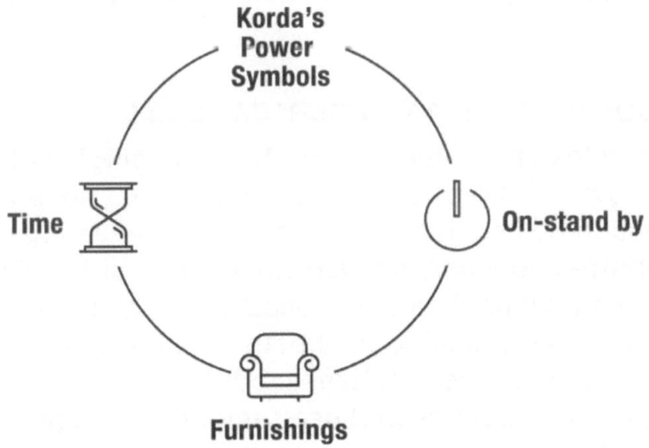

Figure 8.4 Korda's power symbols.

Source: Korda, M. (1985). *Power, How to Get It*. New York: Ballantine Books.

the impression that this person is busy and powerful. Full calendars and using the 'clock' or 'watch' to indicate power is a highly symbolic gesture according to Korda. 'Standing by' is represented by employees having continuous access to phones and email. This allows supervisors to be in contact with their team at any given moment, not during official office hours only. Easy access to work email through smart phones in the twenty-first century has given this increased sense of power to organizations and their leaders. The idea with 'standing by' is that the more you impose your schedule on others, the more power you have over them. Finally, 'furnishings' can indicate a sense of power as well. How elaborate an office one has, or the size of the desk, or how nice the cabinets or shelves are that occupy it can indicate the power one may have in an organization. Some executives hold little back in decorating their workspace with the most elaborate of cherry furniture, liquor cabinets or wine shelves – stocked with only the finest of each drink. Korda's symbols are worth mentioning, simply because this can be seen in organizations. Starting and ending recording sessions late, elaborate or larger than life corporate environments often illustrate the importance given to reputation and status in the creative and cultural industries, each of which can manifest themselves in the physical environment in which we work and in the time we give each other when we do business.

THE ROLE OF POLITICS AND POLITICAL SKILL

As people try to expand their power base, it usually calls for tactical behaviour and skills to accomplish it. Being 'political' doesn't need to be negative, as are many of the feelings and images conjured up when we hear the word 'politics'. On the contrary, being political can be a positive thing, and is one of those skills that is needed in effective organizations. Since we are writing about the creative and cultural industries in this text, the use of politics in these sectors is as important, if not more so, than in other industries. Of course, relationships play an important part in any business or industry. As 'people' we are political every day of our lives! From the clerk at the corner store, to our significant others, or the customer service representative we need to contend with when we want to complain about a bill, we call upon this skill to influence them in a way we find desirable for ourselves or the 'greater good'. However, the very characteristics that drive our industry, from risk factors, uncertainty of demand, the subjective nature of cultural product, to the use of 'A-listers' and 'B-listers' (Caves, 2000), mean it is especially important that your political skills are astute if you want to progress in your career, have access to the most powerful people in the industry or lead an effective project or organization. To increase your power base and ultimately your own influence, the more you know about how 'politics' works or the tactics that influence others in the organization, the more prepared you will be to expand the power base you need to manage and lead effectively.

By definition, 'political skill' is 'the ability to effectively understand others at work, and to use such knowledge to influence them to act in ways that enhance one's personal and/or organizational objectives' (Ahearn *et al.*, 2004). It comes down to your 'at work' social intelligence that enables you to adapt your own behaviour to situations as needed if it is genuine and sincere (Zellars *et al.*, 2008). We even know that there is a direct correlation between a person's level of emotional intelligence and political skill (Ferris *et al.*, 2005; Sunindijo, 2012). Researchers in the field of political skill understand that it has four dimensions: social astuteness; interpersonal influence; networking ability; and apparent sincerity. Being socially astute is indicative of the ability to assess social interactions and adjust your own behaviour as needed. Interpersonal influence is the ability to affect others in a subtle and convincing way. Networking ability is the capability of developing a diverse group of contacts that you can call on in order to maximize the organization's goals. Finally, apparent sincerity is the ability to show others that you are authentic, sincere and have integrity (Ferris *et al.*, 2005; Kimura, 2015).

The importance of political skill can't be underestimated. Not only does it enable you to further your power base, but having the political skills to negotiate relationships, resources and information also has a direct impact on other aspects in the workplace. For some time, we have known that having political skill is important to cope with stress in the workplace; it is critical to career success and has a profoundly positive impact on job performance, not only on actual performance, but a supervisor's impression of a subordinate's performance as well. Furthermore, being able to play the game of 'politics' in a positive way also impacts a manager's leadership effectiveness, how well the organization performs and the perception of leadership by workers (Kimura, 2015).

HOW POLITICALLY SKILLED ARE YOU? INFLUENCE TACTICS USED IN ORGANIZATIONS

Imagine this. One morning, as book editor for a prominent publisher, you arrive for work and get yourself settled. You notice an email from someone you don't know, but you quickly recognize that it is a proposal for a new book series that you have been contemplating for weeks. The idea seems a bit risky, but if your senior editors can be convinced that this is an untapped, potentially high-growth segment of the market, it could create a positive impression of you, them and the company. How you approach this delicate proposal with your superiors and other stakeholders, and whether it's ultimately accepted and green-lighted for production will depend greatly on your own political skill. What ways can you approach or influence others in your organization to convince them that though this is a costly endeavour, it is a potentially lucrative one, if the company is willing to pursue it?

In order to convince others of this, you must influence them in a positive way. There are eight basic influence tactics that we use in organizations in order to further our own aims or demonstrate our position of power (see Figure 8.5). These influence tactics are used to leave impressions of us on others. These impressions help people to form perceptions, opinions and ideas of each other and their capability in the workplace. Is this someone that I want to align myself with, or are his or her behaviours toxic?

Influence Tactics Used in Organisations	
Pressure	The person uses demands, threats or intimidation to convince you to comply with a request or to support a proposal.
Upward Appeal	The person seeks to persuade you that the request is approved by higher management and appeals to higher management for assistance in gaining your compliance with the request.
Exchange	The person makes an explicit or implicit promise that you will receive rewards or tangible benefits if you comply with a request or support a proposal, or reminds you of a prior favor to be reciprocated.
Coalition	The person seeks the aid of others to persuade you to do something or uses the support of others as an argument for you to agree also.
Ingratiation	The person seeks to get you in a good mood or to think favorably of him or her before asking you to do something.
Rational Persuasion	The person uses logical argument and factual evidence to persuade you that a proposal or request is viable and likely to result in attainment of task objective.
Inspirational Appeals	The person makes an emotional request or proposal that arouses enthusiasm by appealing to your values and ideals or by increasing your confidence that you can do it.
Consultation	The person seeks your participation in making a decision or planning how to implement a proposed policy, strategy or change.

Figure 8.5 Influence tactics used in organizations.

Source: Yukl, G. & Falbe, C.M., 1990. 'Influence tactics and objectives in upward, downward, and lateral influence attempts', *Journal of Applied Psychology*, Vol. 75, no. 2, p. 132.

In the editor's case, there are a few tactics listed above that are worth considering more than others. He could 'consult' fellow editors on how to best approach senior leaders on this idea. Furthermore, getting feedback on how to best make his case or 'persuade' his superiors could certainly be helpful. He may also approach senior leadership through an 'inspirational appeal' by making a connection between the project and their own or the organization's values. Of the above listed tactics, it would be safe to say that 'pressure' or creating an 'exchange' may not be the best of options in trying to persuade the editor's superiors to take on his project.

Inspirational appeals occur when someone makes a request that they know will engage others enthusiastically by appealing to what's important to them through values and attitudes. For those individuals who you know to be more logical in nature, it might be more appropriate to use factual evidence to persuade them. Personalities that prefer structure and rationality are more likely to be persuaded if your arguments are sound. Developing a coalition is yet another way. Having the support of a larger group of people may persuade your superiors to consider your proposal. Exchange occurs if there is something of value involved. It can be a reward or other benefits that are given if compliance happens. Furthermore, appealing upward, stating that 'upper management' has approved the request, can help in appealing to those you are trying to influence. A more negative approach would be to apply pressure, and threaten with a punishment if they don't comply. Lastly, ingratiation is when a person seeks to get you in a good mood or think favourably of them.

STRATEGIC SEXUAL PERFORMANCE (SSP) AS AN INGRATIATION TACTIC

Sexuality has been a part of certain sectors of the creative industries and organizational life since time immemorial. In today's 24/7 access to entertainment, social media and news reporting, it is a challenge to not be informed about the most recent attempt of a young male or female artist to use their sexuality to transform their image and brand themselves to garner a fanbase or sustain the longevity of their career. Artists such as Madonna, Miley Cyrus, Harry Styles or Doja Cat use sexuality for professional purposes to influence potential fans.

Cyrus in particular pushed this agenda with her controversial performance at the MTV Video Music Awards in 2013. There she overtly popularized 'twerking' (Hare, 2013), which was followed by the release of her not-too-subtle video swinging naked on a wrecking ball. Although these incidents capture the public attention with the likes of popular recording artists or other entertainment personalities, the use of an individual's sexuality (albeit more subtly) is often part of the everyday life encountered in firms (Baskerville Watkins *et al.*, 2013; Hearn & Parkin, 1995). This is despite management's attempt at controlling it to avoid potential sexual harassment lawsuits, and rationalizing or sterilizing its existence (Schultz, 2003).

The use of one's sexuality to influence others in the workplace has garnered some attention in the world of organizational behaviour (Baskerville Watkins *et al.*, 2013; Schultz, 2003). In particular, the use of sexuality and sexual appeal is quite prominent in the marketing and promotion of entertainment products in certain sectors of the creative industries (see Feature 8.1). The use of sex appeal can influence behaviours, as can the use of 'strategic sexual performances' in the workplace (Baskerville Watkins *et al.*, 2013). **Strategic sexual performances** (SSP) can involve a 'combination of verbal (e.g. speech), nonverbal (e.g. body position, tone of voice), and artefactual (e.g. dress, office décor) behaviours' (Gardner, 1992, p. 35). Sexual performances can be intentionally displayed as overtly intimate sexualized practices (e.g. kissing or sexual intercourse) or as less intimate and subtle behaviours directed towards acquaintances, colleagues, superiors, subordinates or customers/clients (e.g. winking, flirtatious touching, sexual banter). Each possesses qualities of sexual innuendo or meaning (Baskerville Watkins *et al.*, 2013). These performances do not necessarily require any actual sexual attraction between colleagues but may be used intentionally to get others to think favourably of them.

As we've learned, the ability to influence others is one of the most important determinants of managerial effectiveness and of a person's ability to achieve his or her goals (Barrick *et al.*, 2009). There have been numerous attempts to identify the various tactics people in organizations use to influence others (Yukl & Falbe, 1990), some of which we discussed above. Of these, the one that appears in prominent typologies used by management scholars, and that best characterizes the kind of sexual performances we are discussing, is ingratiating tactics. As defined above, ingratiating tactics are used as efforts by an employee to get you in a good mood or think favourably of him or her before asking you to do something (Yukl & Falbe, 1990). More generally, ingratiation is an attempt by someone to increase his or her attractiveness to others so he or she can influence others' behaviours. Ingratiatory behaviours can be directed towards any member of the organization, including superiors, co-workers and subordinates. They are essentially performed to persuade the target that the ingratiating person has positive or desirable qualities. Specifically, we see these behaviours practised not only in the workplace, but industry-wide in the entertainment industries as a way to sell product and increase consumer engagement. Using Harry Styles or Doja Cat as examples merely touches on the extent to which strategic sexual performances influence the entertainment experience. The particular portrayal of actresses, male country artists or even fashion lines exploits the nuances of sexuality to garner favourable impressions.

Feature 8.1 The use of sexuality in music – a recording artist's transformation.

Written by: Marissa Begin and David Schreiber

Taylor Andrews, Former Artist, Independent Label

After signing a record deal soon after graduating from college, Taylor Andrews experienced the rollercoaster ride of a career in music. As a singer-songwriter, she released two albums and toured the globe. However, the tale of these two releases couldn't have been more different. Through her story, we will explore the opportunities and challenges of life as a recording artist and touring musician in the commercial popular music industry. This journey, her journey, will help to enlighten us on how managers, agents, artists and others in music and entertainment use strategic sexual performances to influence potential audiences, other industry professionals and co-workers in an organization.

Taylor, a singer-songwriter, recording artist and touring musician, has had a lucrative six-year career in the spotlight. Her experience – the ups and downs, trials and tribulations – is an example of a career in entertainment and the artistic decisions managers, agents, marketers and even artists make in search of commercial 'success' and influence. Sexuality is at the cornerstone of what often sells music. It is ingrained in the culture of entertainment, both in the art itself and the branding of artists, actors and actresses. It also influences decision-making and can be linked to the struggles for power, influence and recognition in the entertainment industries. Taylor's story is an example of how these struggles can manifest themselves for artists in the music industry.

After growing up singing and dancing in Los Angeles, California, Taylor felt a calling to study and pursue music elsewhere. In her new home, she attended college and 'got her foot in the door' as a songwriter and recording artist. With one parent actively involved in music, Taylor was encouraged to develop her talents and a career in music. Having a keen understanding of the business, and the opportunities and challenges it can present, they instilled a sense of strong moral character in Taylor as a means of keeping her centred in a business with often transparent ethical boundaries.

After college, she signed her first recording contract with a local label. It was a pop genre deal that promoted the development of her songwriting, while fostering an outlet for creativity through performing on records and touring. This partnership would ultimately lead to the release of her self-titled debut album. The endeavour would also require trips to Los Angeles, and, on occasion, travel to Stockholm, Sweden in preparation for the recording and release of the album. In the following months, she toured and promoted the sound and image of what she believed to be a genuine portrayal of herself as both an artist and person. She loved to sing and dance barefoot, because that's 'who she was'. Her music said it, her image portrayed it. It felt natural.

Her initial release and subsequent promotions were largely an extension of what she was communicating as an artist – the image of a strong, fierce brunette with powerful vocals and heartfelt lyrics was at the core of her artistry. Her style was casual and laid back, including a wardrobe of ripped jeans and edgy shirts. She was influential in the direction her label would take in developing her brand, encompassing the message she communicated, the music she played and the transparent essence of her energetic and likeable personality.

After promoting and selling this release, Taylor's label felt an opportunity existed in leveraging her in an entirely different market – one populated with the likes of Ke$ha, Katy Perry and Lady Gaga. To capitalize on this highly sought-after niche of female pop artists, Taylor would require a complete rebranding and a strategy that would appeal to a broader audience – a strategy that would use sex and sexuality to influence and expand into a new and different fan base.

For the making of Taylor's second album, her label and management teams decided to take a different approach with her appearance, the songs she sang and the tours she went on. Taylor was given almost a year to write and develop her first album, while only having two weeks to write and record her second; time was of the essence. The controls were in high gear and there was no turning back this machine.

Now performing in this highly competitive female genre, Taylor was required to transform her image from an organic singer-songwriter to a highly sexualized pop artist, where the objectification of her body was at the core of how she was to influence her new fan base. Her dark hair was dyed blonde because she was 'screening' too old in her main demographic and her wardrobe changed drastically. 'I could only wear metallic, white, black, or army green'. This strict protocol was set to entice her new audience. She needed to be 'larger than life' and an object of a young man's fantasy or idealized for a young woman's self-image.

In the first video of this new release, she wore a bodysuit while dancing in 'bejewelled' heels, which drastically differed from her casual jeans and barefoot look just a year before. Taylor did explain that because she grew up as a dancer, wearing a skin-tight bodysuit wasn't uncomfortable. However, if she had to go any further, she would have definitely 'been out of [her] comfort zone'. As part of the filming she recalls 'being in a warehouse for about 10 hours that day, dancing in heels and a bathing suit and high socks, with all my girls behind me doing the same thing' – an exhausting endeavour, but often necessary to compete in a highly sought-after and lucrative segment of the female pop market.

As part of this transformation, Taylor recollects her limited involvement in the many changes being made to her appearance, her dancing or her sound. However, she didn't think too much about it at the time. She didn't want to let anyone down, and wanted to do everything possible to make her career a success.

As touring with her new image wore on, the demanding schedule and exhaustion started catching up to her. One week in particular stood out as a turning point in her thinking ... it was a 'reality check'.

'I was sick when I was on tour, I was losing my voice and I had a really bad schedule coming up, meaning, I had to yell over a dance class in Compton. I had just done "Extra" with Mario Lopez at the Grove and I was going to do a dance class at a charity center. I had to get a spray tan before getting on a flight – the red eye to Sacramento for a show the next day. Then, the next night I was going to be on another red eye to New York for the rest of the tour for another month or two. So, I'm losing my voice completely, I can't even speak much and for the biggest arena shows I had coming up, I was going to have no recovery time. So, this woman came up to me and she said "You know how you feel right now?" And I'm like "Yes!!!" I mean I felt that I had the weight of the world on me and luckily, I'm smart enough to know not to do something stupid just to survive. But she said "This is when people start doing drugs" and I was like "I get it"'.

If you ask Taylor today about her time in the industry, she responds more positively than anything else. However, it can wear on even the strongest and most grounded of people. The use of sexual innuendo and other strategic sexual performances, demanding schedules and a commitment to the craft, have become rooted in the industry's culture and the 'ways of doing things'.

Questions for review

1. In what ways is Taylor's sexuality being used as an ingratiation tactic? How common is this use of power in the creative industries? Specifically, entertainment?
2. Who is being targeted with her sexuality to garner a favourable impression of Taylor?
3. How do these marketing norms in entertainment influence workplace culture and how may strategic sexual performances be used or perceived?
4. How might organizational leaders deal with what can often be perceived as questionable sexual harassment issues, but may simply be someone using strategic sexual performances to garner favourable influence over others?
5. Since the use of strategic sexual performances appear to be rooted in the culture of commercial popular music, to what extent does this prominent use influence the culture of an organization and therefore its accepted and casual use?

WHEN DOES IT BECOME SEXUAL HARASSMENT?

Now that we know how sexuality can be used as an ingratiation tactic that someone may use in order to garner favourable opinions from others, what happens when it is unwanted or unwelcome or simply goes too far? Or creates an environment where others become uncomfortable? It may very well be considered sexual misconduct, sexual harassment or sexual coercion. Nearly everyone knows that sexual harassment in the workplace is illegal while stories of misconduct have littered the entertainment world where gender inequalities and impressionable young talent converge in environments that can foster inappropriate behaviour (Mathew & George, 2022).

We've come a long way in understanding and recognizing when these lines are being crossed, especially in light of the #MeToo movement, but even today, not everyone knows exactly what may constitute sexual harassment, and what employers can do to prevent it.

First and foremost, sexual harassment is an abuse of personal power. It is defined in the United States by the Equal Employment Opportunity Commission (EEOC) as 'unwelcome sexual advances, requests for sexual favours, and other verbal or physical harassment of a sexual nature' (Sexual Harassment, 2022). The United Kingdom defines it as 'unwanted verbal, non-verbal or physical conduct of a sexual nature which has the purpose or effect of violating the recipient's dignity, or of creating an intimidating, hostile, degrading, humiliating or offensive environment for the recipient' (Mathew & George, 2022, p. 1). By and through these definitions it is clear that sexual harassment is a legal term created with the intent of ending harassment and discrimination against individuals in the workplace. Even as we compare two different countries' definition of what it constitutes, it is constantly being redefined and extended in legislation and court decisions in the United States and around the world. However, not all sexual behaviour in the workplace is harassment, and the laws against sexual harassment do not extend to situations outside the workplace or school (Mathew & George, 2022).

To further our understanding, a guide to Human Resources (US EEOC, 2022) informs us that:

- The victim as well as the harasser may be a woman or a man. The victim does not have to be of the opposite sex;
- The harasser can be the victim's supervisor, a contractor for the employer, a supervisor in another area, a co-worker, or non-employee;
- The victim does not have to be the person harassed but could be anyone affected by the offensive conduct;

- Unlawful sexual harassment may occur without economic injury to the victim;
- The harasser's conduct must be unwelcome.

DEFINITION OF SEXUAL HARASSMENT

From a legal standpoint, there are two different categories of sexual harassment:

> **Quid pro quo** – This category of sexual harassment means 'this for that'. If you do something for me, I will in-turn reward you for doing so. It involves demands for expressed or implied sexual favours. Quid pro quo happens often in the entertainment industries because of the inherent power imbalance that can occur between agent, manager, director or executive and actors, dancers, musicians and artists. The former may take advantage of their positions by offering young career minded individuals job prospects in exchange for sexual favours.
>
> **Hostile work environment** – This type of sexual harassment can occur between any employees. It refers to the situation where an employee is offended or made to feel harassed by other employees. It is often the result of gender bias and could come in the form of touching, offensive jokes, inappropriate images, or other intimidating or unwelcome behaviour.

In the creative and cultural industries, women in particular are often stereotyped as being sex objects while young graduates with dreams of stardom and success are entering a competitive workforce where older experienced individuals may take advantage of this inequality. How an industry or company organizes its work, the culture it perpetuates and the various working arrangements and conditions may influence its capacity to address sexual harassment (ILO, 2020). Research has found that sexual harassment is more likely to occur in an environment of generalized disrespect and that a perceived tolerance and lack of sanctions is the strongest predictor of sexual harassment (Hulin *et al.*, 1996).

Much of this is occurring while we learn that sexual microaggressions are on the rise in the entertainment industry as are non-consensual or coerced sexual touching (Nelson, 2019). Auditions and large projects on-set, on-stage or in the studio continue to be spaces in which sexual harassment can occur (Mathew & George, 2022). However, as we've also learned, bystander intervention can help. Everyone on the project or in the workplace has a responsibility to hold others accountable and report incidences if they see them occur. And in order for people to feel comfortable doing so, it requires companies to have clear, safe and effective policies and reporting structures in place to mitigate this behaviour.

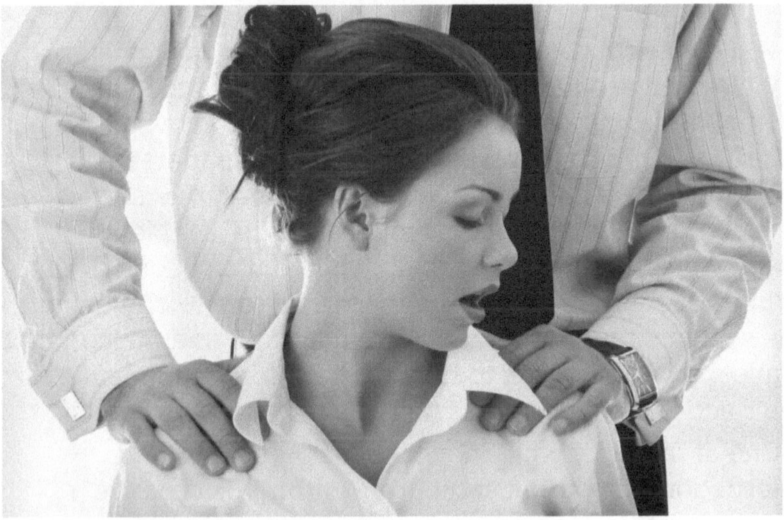

Figure 8.6. *#MeToo: You are not alone*
Photo credit: B.D.S Piotr Marcinski / Shutterstock.com.

#MeToo: You are not alone

In 2006, Tarana Burke founded #MeToo, a social movement against sexual abuse and sexual harassment that advocates for public awareness for those who have become victims of sex crimes and those who perpetrate them. Since its founding, #MeToo has provided resources and support for victims of sexual assault, where and when it is needed (me too, 2022). The movement includes a 'League of Disruptors' who join and support the cause while providing a 'Survivors Sanctuary', a self-guided digital support platform that includes modules ranging from deep breathing exercises to 'compassionate' self-touch. In 2017, with a bit of help from actress Alyssa Milano tweeting:

> Suggested by a friend: If all the women who have been sexually harassed or assaulted wrote "Me too" as a status, we might give people a sense of the magnitude of the problem.
>
> (Respers France, 2017)

The movement woke-up the world to sexual violence as people from around the globe found an outlet to share their own experience with sexual violence. Many, now aware of #MeToo, found a network of survivors to support them. The movement is stronger than ever before with the mission of helping 'young people, queer, trans, the disabled, Black women and girls, and all communities of colour' by bringing together a broad base of survivors to challenge the systems that perpetuate sexual assault and misconduct while expanding ways to hold perpetrators responsible for their actions (me too Movement, 2022).

One of the most well-known cases that generated international attention came from within the creative industries: that of movie producer and executive Harvey Weinstein (Miramax Films and The Weinstein Company). Although his case was one of many (including R. Kelly, Matt Lauer, Kevin Spacey, Bill Cosby and many others eg. see Reel, & Crouch, 2019), the Weinstein scandal showed in graphic detail an entertainment producer cynically leveraging his star-making ability to coerce sexual favours. As the scandal unfolded his reputation unravelled spectacularly. He lost his job, his wife left him and he was stripped of his membership in the Academy of Motion Picture Arts and Sciences. It led to over 80 accusations (Williams, 2017) of such acts, at least six were criminally prosecuted and he was eventually found guilty of rape, criminal sexual acts and sentenced to 23 years in prison (Arkin *et al.*, 2020). It showed that even the most entrenched industry power brokers can be brought down by the weight of collective action.

Once Weinstein and his predatory practices and sexual assaults were exposed, other stories started to emerge, including similar behaviours from leading US journalists such as Matt Lauer and Mark Halperin. In particular, Mark Halperin, an ABC TV commentator and news journalist was accused of unwanted touching, sexual comments, and physical assault by nine women (Darcy, 2017). For those who participated, better assignments were given and for those who didn't, they were overlooked for the high profile assignments.

The stories of the perpetrators have similar themes, whether it's rumours of Weinstein's 'casting couch' or Halperin's retaliation for not accepting his propositions. It comes down to an abuse of power by those in-charge taking advantage of their positions to victimize others for their personal gratification. So what has happened in the world of entertainment since this new found awakening in 2017? Has there actually been any changes to the industry and workplace cultures that perpetuate this behaviour? What progress has actually been made and how do people feel about it? Have company policies implemented better reporting systems and safe spaces for those who have been assaulted? Are perpetrators being held accountable for their actions? In 2019, the Hollywood Commission, which was founded after the Harvey Weinstein allegations surfaced, launched the largest, 'first-of-its kind climate survey about discrimination, harassment, and bullying in the entertainment industry'. Through this research, the commission sought to establish a baseline for accountability, identify vulnerable populations and recognize on-going gaps in harassment and discrimination prevention in the entertainment industry. They surveyed 9,630 entertainment workers in television and film, commercials, live theatre, music, broadcast news, talent representation, public relations, and corporate settings with the following key findings (The Hollywood Commission, 2020a, 2020b, 2020c, 2020d):

- Sixty-five percent of respondents don't believe that a powerful individual, such as a producer or director, would be held accountable for harassing someone with less power;
- Forty-five percent of men believed that a person would be held accountable, only 28% of women felt this way and 23% of biracial women;
- Forty-eight percent saw progress in addressing power abuse since the #MeToo movement;
- Twenty-three percent of workers said they had reported harassing behaviour to a supervisor, and only 9% to human resources departments and 4% to legal departments;
- Forty-one percent of respondents saying they'd experienced retaliatory behaviour for reporting harassment or other misconduct.

By no means do these statistics comprise the entirety of sentiments felt by those working in Hollywood. It does indicate some progress but clearly more needs to be done. The key takeaway from the Chair of the commission, Anita Hill, was that 'Things have improved, but not nearly enough'. People don't trust the system that has been designed to report harassment, they still believe that nothing will happen to the perpetrators and that any sense of 'anonymity in it, doesn't really exist', therefore they live in fear of retaliation (Noveck, 2020). Sexual misconduct still disproportionately effects women and those of colour (The Hollywood Commission, 2020) and only 48% feel progress in addressing abuse of power has been made.

TIPS TO PREVENT SEXUAL HARASSMENT IN THE WORKPLACE

Employers have an obligation to prevent sexual harassment from occurring in the workplace. If it can be shown that the employer knew or should have known that the harassment was occurring and they did not take all reasonable actions to stop it, then the employer can be held liable for an individual's actions. The following are tips recommended by Bridget Miller (2015) for employers to prevent sexual harassment in the workplace:

- **Create and communicate a clear antiharassment policy,** including anti-retaliation components. Get legal advice on this policy to ensure it is complete and that it complies with all federal, state, and local laws. Once complete, ensure that your policy is in the employee handbook and that every employee has a copy.
- **Conduct sexual harassment training and retraining** for everyone, especially all supervisors and managers, on at least an annual basis. Everyone in the organization should understand what sexual harassment is and what to do if it occurs. (Note: in some US states this training is mandatory.)
- **Ensure managers and supervisors understand their obligation to maintain zero tolerance** for harassment in the workplace.
- **Monitor emails and other electronic communications to scan for harassing content.** Monitor behaviour too. It is important as an employer to be on the lookout for inappropriate behaviour and stop it right away.
- **Ensure employees know their options if they find themselves in such a situation.** Employees should know that they have the right to request the behaviour to stop (and they should do so if possible). But employees should also know what to do next if they don't feel safe asking the person or people involved to stop, or if doing so does not stop the unwanted behaviour.
- **Clearly define the process to submit a complaint,** including a process for situations where the direct supervisor can be bypassed if necessary.

- **Define clear consequences for such behaviour** and consistently apply these when harassing behaviour is discovered.
- **Cultivate a culture where sexual harassment is not welcome or tolerated.** This might include many things. For example:
    - Ensure that work-sponsored activities after hours are professional in nature.
    - Ensure that supervisors and managers know where to draw the line with employees in terms of tolerating off-colour jokes and other offensive material. The workplace is not a place for crude jokes.
    - If a complaint comes in, treat it with complete care and always investigate. Treat every complaint seriously.
    - If harassment is discovered, take immediate and appropriate action to ensure it doesn't happen again, including disciplining or even terminating the employee(s) responsible.
    - Do not tolerate retaliatory behaviour against someone who has filed a complaint.
- **Have a clear process for investigating any complaint of harassment.** If a complaint comes in, look into it immediately and, if necessary, take steps to ensure the behaviour stops while the investigation is ongoing. Take every complaint seriously.

Obviously, we need to work together to prevent sexual harassment in the creative industries workplace. Not only is it a legal obligation, but it's also smart business. After all, a hostile work environment is unlikely to maximize productivity.

SUMMARY AND KEY POINTS

Studying this chapter will help you in a number of ways as a practising manager:

- *Understanding how people use power to help get things done quickly:* When you encounter challenging people or dilemmas that must be solved in the course of producing and marketing creative product, you can use these sources to pursue a positive resolution.

- *Perceiving political behaviour as a positive skill and understanding that it is normal behaviour:* Understanding the concept of politics and that people calling on a set of skills that influence others should be seen as a positive behaviour. Although being political can be negative when used for personal gain, it is often needed to achieve the organization's goals. Learning to defuse political behaviour through open communication or having a participative management style can help to mitigate any negative implications of its use.
- *Recognizing the role of sexuality in the organization:* Understanding that this type of ingratiation tactic is not uncommon in the entertainment industry, can help you differentiate between acceptable and unacceptable behaviours that may cross the line into sexual harassment, putting the organization and others at risk.
- *Recognizing sexual misconduct and how to respond appropriately:* Knowing when and how to respond to sexual misconduct is critical in fostering a safe and productive workplace for everyone. Knowing the best ways to prevent such behaviour and being prepared to react professionally and appropriately when it occurs is key to being an effective manager.

This chapter has focused on the concept of power and the political skill needed to effectively use it. As a manager or artist you will inevitably encounter powerful people and be caught in power plays. However, learning how to employ political skill or navigate through the consequences of power will better prepare you for a bright and productive career.

References

Ahearn, K. K., Ferris, G. R., Hochwarter, W. A., Douglas, C. & Ammeter, A. P. (2004). 'Leader political skill and team performance', *Journal of Management*, Vol. 30, no. 3, pp. 309–327.

Arkin, D., Reiss, A., Byfield, E. & Silva, D. (2020). 'Harvey Weinstein sentenced to 23 years in prison in landmark #MeToo case'. *NBC News*. Available at https://www.nbcnews.com/news/us-news/

harvey-weinstein-sentenced-23-years-prison-landmark-metoo-case-n11541669 (accessed 14 July 2022).

Barnard, C. I. (1938). 'The theory of authority', in C. I. Barnard (ed.), *The Functions of the Executive*. Cambridge, MA: Harvard University Press, pp. 161–184.

Barrick, M. R., Shaffer, J. A. & DeGrassi, S. W. (2009). 'What you see may not be what you get: Relationships among self-presentation tactics and ratings of interview and job performance', *Journal of Applied Psychology*, Vol. 94, no. 6, p. 1394.

Baskerville Watkins, M., Smith, A. N. & Aquino, K. (2013). 'The use and consequences of strategic sexual performances', *Academy of Management Perspectives*, Vol. 27, no. 3, pp. 173–186. Available at: 10.5465/amp.2010.0109.

Bourdieu, P. (1977). 'Outline of a theory of practice/Uniform Title: Esquisse pour une auto-analyse'. *Cambridge Studies in Social Anthropology*. Available at http://catdir.loc.gov/catdir/description/cam022/76011073.html (accessed 8 August 2017).

Bourdieu, P. & Nice, R. (1986). 'The forms of capital'. In J. Richardson (ed.), *Handbook of Theory and Research for the Sociology of Education*. New York: Greenwood, pp. 241–258.

Bourdieu, P. & Thompson, J. B. (1991). *Language and Symbolic Power*. Cambridge, MA: Polity Press.

Caves, R. E. (2000). *Creative Industries: Contracts Between Art and Commerce*. Cambridge, MA: Harvard University Press.

Darcy, O. (2017). 'Five women accuse journalist and 'Game Change' co-author Mark Halperin of sexual harassment' [online] *CNNMoney*. Available at https://money.cnn.com/2017/10/25/media/mark-halperin-sexual-harassment-allegations/index.html (accessed 2 May 2022).

Dishman, L. (2015). *'The 50 most well-liked CEOs in the U.S.'*, *Fast Company*. Available at https://www.fastcompany.com/3047217/the-50-most-well-liked-ceos-in-the-us (accessed 8 August 2017).

Ferris, G. R., Treadway, D. C., Kolodinsky, R. W., Hochwarter, W. A., Kacmar, C. J., Douglas, C. & Frink, D. D. (2005). 'Development and validation of the political skill inventory', *Journal of Management*, Vol. 31, no. 1, pp. 126–152.

Fishbein, M. & Steiner, I. D. (1965). 'Society for the psychological study of social issues', in I. D. Steiner & M. Fishbein (eds.) *Current Studies in Social Psychology*. New York: Holt, Rinehart & Winston, pp. xii. 532.

French Jr, J. R. P. & Raven, B. (1959). 'The bases of social power'. Available at http://www.communicationcache.com/uploads/1/0/8/8/10887248/the_bases_of_social_power_-_chapter_20_-_1959.pdf (accessed 8 August 2017).

Gardner, W. L. (1992). 'Lessons in organizational dramaturgy: The art of impression management', *Organizational Dynamics*, Vol. 21, no. 1, pp. 33–46.

Greiner, L. E. & Schein, V. E. (1988). *Power and Organization Development: Mobilizing Power to Implement Change.* Boston, MA: Addison-Wesley.

Hadida, A. L. (2015). 'Performance in the creative industries', *The Oxford Handbook of Creative Industries*, p. 219. Oxford: Oxford University Press.

Hare, B. (2013). *'Miley Cyrus twerks, stuns VMAs crowd', CNN.* Available at http://www.cnn.com/2013/08/26/showbiz/music/miley-cyrus-mtv-vmas-gaga/ (accessed 8 August 2017).

Hearn, J. & Parkin, W. (1995). *Sex at Work: The Power and Paradox of Organization Sexuality.* Brighton: Wheatsheaf Books.

Hr-guide.com. (2022). *Sexual Harassment: Legal Definitions of Sexual Harassment.* [online] Available at https://hr-guide.com/SexualHarassment/Legal_Definitions_of_Sexual_Harassment.htm (accessed 27 April 2022).

Hulin, C. L., Fitzgerald, L. F. and Drasgow, F. (1996). *Organizational influences on sexual harassment.* Thousand Oaks, CA: Sage Publications, Inc.

Kanter, R. M. (1979). 'Power failure in management circuits', *Classics of Organization Theory*, pp. 342–351.

Keuschnigg, M. (2015). 'Product success in cultural markets: The mediating role of familiarity, peers, and experts', *Poetics*, Vol 51, pp. 17–36.

Kimura, T. (2015). 'A review of political skill: Current research trend and directions for future research', *International Journal of Management Reviews*, Vol. 17, no. 3, pp. 312–332.

Korda, M. (1985). *Power, How to Get It.* New York: Ballantine Books.

Kretschmer, M., Klimis, G. M. & Choi, C. J. (1999). 'Increasing returns and social contagion in cultural industries', *British Journal of Management*, Vol. 10, no. s1, pp. 61–72.

Mathew & George (2022). *How Prevalent is Sexual Harassment in the Entertainment Industry?* [online] Available at https://www.caemployeelawyer.com/workplace-sexual-harassment-in-the-entertainment-industry/#:~:text=Quid%20pro%20quo%2C%20or%20%E2%80%9Cthis, in%20return%20for%20sexual%20favors (accessed 27 April 2022).

me too. Movement. 2022. *me too. Movement.* [online] Available at https://metoomvmt.org (accessed 1 May 2022).

Miller, B. (2015). 'Tips to Prevent Sexual Harassment in the Workplace', *HR Daily Advisor.* Available at http://hrdailyadvisor.blr.com/2015/08/28/tips-to-prevent-sexual-harassment-in-the-workplace/ (accessed 1 May 2022).

Nelson, D.& Quick, J. (2019). *ORGB 6.* Stamford, CT: Cengage Learning.

Nelson, J. (2019). *Sexually Objectifying Microaggressions in Film: Using Entertainment for Clinical and Educational Purposes* (Doctoral dissertation, Antioch University).

Noveck, J. (2020). 'Survey: In Hollywood, few believe harassers will be punished' [online] *AP NEWS.* Available at https://apnews.com/article/

us-supreme-court-harvey-weinstein-anita-hill-archive-65022861b845f8c64c15630e979a76a5 (accessed 1 May 2022).

Raven, B. H. (2008). 'The bases of power and the power/interaction model of interpersonal influence', *Analyses of Social Issues and Public Policy*, Vol. 8, no. 1, pp. 1–22.

Reel, J. J. & Crouch, E. (2019). # MeToo: Uncovering sexual harassment and assault in sport. *Journal of Clinical Sport Psychology*, Vol 13, no. 2, pp. 177–179.

Respers France, L. (2017). *#MeToo: Social media flooded with personal stories of assault*. [online] CNN. Available at https://edition.cnn.com/2017/10/15/entertainment/me-too-twitter-alyssa-milano/index.html (accessed 2 May 2022).

Rindova, V. P., Pollock, T. G. & Hayward, M. L. A. (2006). 'Celebrity firms: The social construction of market popularity', *Academy of Management Review*, Vol. 31, no. 1, pp. 50–71.

Schreiber, D. and Rieple, A. (2018). 'Uncovering the influences on decision making in the popular music industry; intuition, networks and the desire for symbolic capital', *Creative Industries Journal*, Vol. 11, no. 3, pp. 245–262.

Schreiber, D. (2014). *An Investigation of Influences on Strategic Decision-Making in Popular Recorded Music Industry Micro-Enterprises*, PhD thesis, University of Westminster.

Sexual Harassment: Summary Report. (2022). [online] UK Government, p. 1. Available at https://assets.publishing.service.gov.uk/government/uploads/system/uploads/attachment_data/file/446225/ADR005000-Sexual_Harassment_Summary_Report.pdf (accessed 27 April 2022).

Schultz, V. (2003). 'The sanitized workplace', *The Yale Law Journal*, Vol. 112, no. 8, pp. 2061–2193. Available at http://www.jstor.org/stable/3657474 (accessed 8 August 2017).

Sunindijo, R. Y. (2012). 'Integrating emotional intelligence, political skill, and transformational leadership in construction', *Civil Engineering Dimension*, Vol. 14, no. 3, pp. 182–189.

The Hollywood Commission (2020a). *The Hollywood Survey Report #1: Accountability*. [online] Commission for Eliminating Sexual Harassment and Advancing Equality in the Workplace, pp. 1–15. Available at https://static1.squarespace.com/static/6099a7247693533fc5285016/t/60a83ddb3e998f0fd92e4f15/1621638620073/The-Hollywood-Survey-Accountability.pdf (accessed 1 May 2022).

The Hollywood Commission (2020b). *The Hollywood Survey Report #2: Bias*. [online] Commission for Eliminating Sexual Harassment and Advancing Equality in the Workplace, pp. 1–15. Available at https://static1.squarespace.com/static/6099a7247693533fc5285016/t/60a83ddb3e998f0fd92e4f15/1621638620073/The-Hollywood-Survey-Accountability.pdf (accessed 1 May 2022).

The Hollywood Commission (2020c). *The Hollywood Survey Report #3: Abusive Conduct*. [online] Commission for Eliminating

Sexual Harassment and Advancing Equality in the Workplace, pp. 1–14. Available at https://static1.squarespace.com/static/6099a7247693533fc5285016/t/60a83ddb3e998f0fd92e4f15/1621638620073/The-Hollywood-Survey-Accountability.pdf (accessed 1 May 2022).

The Hollywood Commission (2020d). *The Hollywood Survey Report #4: Sexual Harassment and Assault.* [online] Commission for Eliminating Sexual Harassment and Advancing Equality in the Workplace, pp. 1–17. Available at https://static1.squarespace.com/static/6099a7247693533fc5285016/t/60a83ddb3e998f0fd92e4f15/1621638620073/The-Hollywood-Survey-Accountability.pdf (accessed 1 May 2022).

US EEOC (2022). *Sexual Harassment.* [online] Available at https://www.eeoc.gov/sexual-harassment (accessed 27 April 2022).

Weick, K. E. (1995). *'Sensemaking in organizations', Foundations for Organizational Science.* Available at http://www.loc.gov/catdir/enhancements/fy0655/95008203-d.html (accessed 8 August 2017).

Williams, J. (2017). *More than 80 women have now accused Harvey Weinstein of sexual assault or harassment.* [online] Newsweek. Available at https://www.newsweek.com/harvey-weinstein-accusers-sexual-assault-harassment-696485 (accessed 14 July 2022).

Yukl, G. & Falbe, C. M. (1990). 'Influence tactics and objectives in upward, downward, and lateral influence attempts', *Journal of Applied Psychology*, Vol. 75, no. 2, p. 132.

Zellars, K. L., Perrewé, P. L., Rossi, A. M., Tepper, B. T. & Ferris, G. R. (2008). 'Moderating effects of political skill, perceived control, and job-related self-efficacy on the relationship between negative affectivity and physiological strain', *Journal of Organizational Behavior*, Vol. 29, no. 5, pp. 549–571.

Leadership in creative organizations

Chapter 9

CHAPTER LEARNING OBJECTIVES

At the conclusion of this chapter you will be able to:

- Define leadership concepts and theories and critically apply them to a creative and cultural industries context. This includes trait and behavioural leadership theories, task versus relationship focus, contingency and situational leadership models, transformational leadership, and authentic leadership; and
- Analyse specific leadership challenges in the creative industries such as leading creative teams, tastemaking and dual leadership models that combine business and artistic leadership.

While running a seminar on arts leadership, one of the authors posed the students a question: who did they admire among current arts leaders, and why? One student admitted that she didn't have strong views on creative leaders, but within her own life, her father had been her true leader. She concluded that 'everyone is a leader for someone'. This final comment made an impression on those in the seminar, because she had succeeded

DOI: 10.4324/9781003262923-9

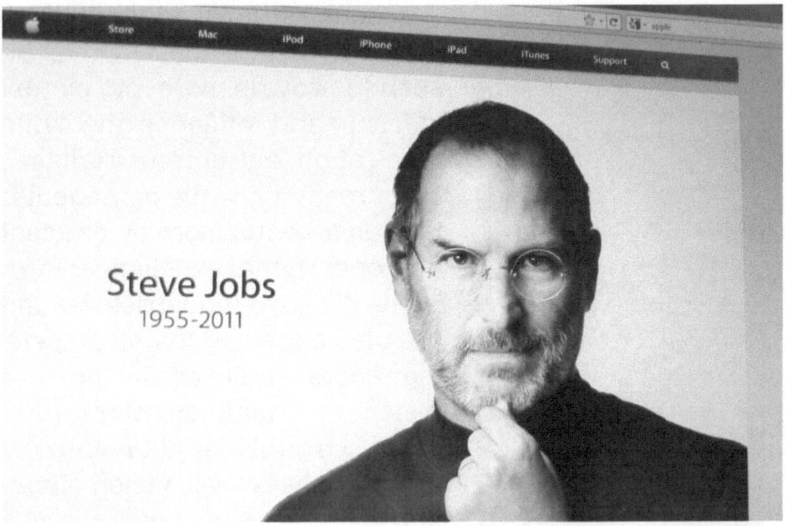

Figure 9.1 Steve Jobs, former leader of Apple Inc. Photo credit: Annette Shaff/ Shutterstock.com.

in taking something that seemed distant and unattainable (e.g. being Steve Jobs [Figure 9.1] or Sir Lucian Grainge [Figure 9.2]) and turning it into something that was real, personal and attainable – that was, in fact, almost inevitable. The topic of leadership can make people uncomfortable because they may interpret a desire to lead as an attempt to set oneself above others, with a view to bossing people around. But sometimes we provide leadership for others quite naturally, without even being aware of it, through our confidence, skills, experience and enthusiasm. This leadership is appreciated, not resented. Because we are looking at how we can intentionally lead others, leadership in this chapter is understood as intentionally inspiring and influencing others to achieve outcomes (de Voogt, 2006).

When you first become a leader in a professional context, you will most likely be running a small project team. Research suggests that team leaders get the most out of project teams by keeping them focused on the final goal, setting priorities, being clear about processes, keeping a collaborative spirit, and supporting and building confidence among team members (Abfalter, 2013). This is covered further in Chapter 10 on Teams.

Figure 9.2 Sir Lucian Grainge, Chairman and CEO of Universal Music Group. Photo credit: Kathy Hutchins / Shutterstock.com

In contrasting 'leadership' with 'management', leadership has been seen to provide more 'big picture' steering and influence, involving inspiration, entrepreneurialism and creativity, while management is seen to focus more on efficiency and operational excellence. But in the creative industries, leaders are also expected to be competent managers, and even the most visionary artistic director can get into trouble for not being able to deliver their vision (Caust, 2004).

Historically, arts leaders have also performed other roles, such as 'impresario' and 'custodian' (Rentschler, 2002). Famous impresarios such as Sergei Diaghilev were larger than life characters who were passionate advocates for artistic endeavour, loved networking with creative people and loved bringing stakeholders together around creative projects (Buckle, 1984). Diaghilev's circle of friends included visual artists such as Picasso, dancers such as Nijinsky and composers such as Stravinsky. Impresarios can be energizing and creative, but have also been portrayed as risky, financially naïve and dilettantish (Rentschler, 2002).

The 'custodian' role is where the arts leader seeks to protect the assets of cultural organizations such as galleries and museums. Custodians grow collections and educate people to appreciate their value. However, they have often been inward looking rather than outward looking, more focused on the collection than the people who use it. They can be naïve in terms of economic considerations such as return on investment or cost benefit analysis, and naïve in terms of marketing requirements such as audience development and optimizing the user experience.

Within the arts there has been a growing 'corporatization' of senior management. Decades ago the leader of a Ballet company might have been termed the 'Administrator'. Such a title implied that the leader was a humble servant of the artists, simply attending to administrative matters. In recent years, American influence has seen an explosion of President and Vice President roles, even within non-profits. These titles imply that beyond mere 'administration', these leadership roles make a valuable business contribution to the organization.

We will now examine some of the most influential leadership theories and explore their relevance for leading creative organizations.

TRAIT AND BEHAVIOURAL LEADERSHIP THEORIES

The 'trait' theory of leadership attempts to break down leadership into enduring personal qualities that can differentiate leaders from non-leaders. Traits are things such as personality attributes, cognitive abilities and values (Zaccaro, 2007). For example, emotional intelligence (abbreviated as 'EI' or 'EQ') has been seen to provide a natural advantage in leadership (Goleman, 1996). By 'emotional intelligence' we mean competencies such as self-awareness, empathy and social skills. Emotional intelligence has been identified as an important aspect of arts leadership (Suchy, 1999). The most fundamental mistake you can make in leading a creative team is to just 'boss people around', because good staff, particularly good creative staff, want to be able to invest their own ideas in their work; they want to be trusted, have autonomy and have their views heard. People with high EI are better at reading where employees sit emotionally in relation to their work and the way they are being managed. This assists them in pitching advice in a way that will be perceived positively rather than negatively.

The 'behavioural' approach to leadership is quite different from the trait approach, in that it attempts to ascertain what behaviours lead to effective leadership. By breaking down leadership into specific behaviours, people can acquire and hone these behaviours. Studies at the Ohio State University in the 1940s identified two factors that appeared to lead to effective leadership: 'consideration', which is concern, appreciation and respect for staff; and 'initiating structure', which is the organization the leader brings to roles, goal setting and communication (Judge *et al.*, 2004).

The behavioural approach is more optimistic about human potential than the trait theory approach, as it assumes leadership can be learned. For example, confident public speaking would be seen by most as an asset for leadership. But many confident public speakers were very poor when they first started and became more and more impressive over time as they developed confidence and expertise. So, if we break things down into skills, and attempt to learn these skills, we can improve our leadership abilities.

Consideration and initiating structure, however, do not fully describe the leadership style that creates big-picture motivation and direction-setting through symbols, stories and theatre. This approach became associated with 'transformational' leadership (Bass, 1991). 'Transformational' leadership involves charisma, inspiration, creativity and connecting with individuals in the organization at a personal level. Great transformational leaders deploy culture-building tools we will discuss in the culture chapter (Chapter 13), such as symbols and stories, to connect what they are trying to accomplish with the lives of employees in a meaningful way. By contrast, 'transactional' leadership is seen as more incremental and managerial, intervening when standards aren't met, rather than inspiring and painting a vivid picture of the goal that is being sought (Bass, 1991).

TASK AND RELATIONSHIP FOCUS

One of the most discussed and researched aspects of leadership style is whether a leader has a 'task' or 'relationship' focus (Bons & Fiedler, 1976). A task focus is prioritizing the successful completion of a task over any relationship fallout that may be required to achieve the result. Managers with this orientation will be more concerned if a project under-performs than if they alienate a team member. They may consider time spent on the social niceties of team interaction to be time wasted, or they may bring a quasi-military approach to the achievement of objectives.

A relationship focus prioritizes the happy functioning of the team and the preservation of good team relations over the achievement of goals. Managers with this orientation are sensitive to personal ramifications that result from decisions and outcomes, and take care to monitor body language and behaviour. They believe that time spent managing the social dimension of team interactions is time well spent. They will be more concerned if they hurt someone's feelings than if the project under-delivers.

Fiedler's Contingency Model of Leadership is based on the understanding that there is no one best way to manage, and either of the approaches described above could work best, depending on the situation (it is called a 'contingency' model because the best approach is 'contingent' on the situation – which is not like 'contingency planning', which means planning for unforeseen events). Fiedler developed a least-preferred co-worker (LPC) questionnaire and score (Bons & Fiedler, 1976), whereby a manager with a high LPC is relationship motivated, and a low LPC is task motivated. One of Fiedler's key focuses was matching the best approach to a given set of circumstances, which he saw as dependent upon things such as the power and relations of the leader to the team and the task structure. However, a key assumption in Fiedler's approach is that leadership style is fixed for a given person, and that different managers would need to be selected for different situations. Another 'situational leadership' model arose based on the behavioural assumption that one manager can learn to progress through different behaviours and styles.

SITUATIONAL LEADERSHIP

We can make some generalizations about leading creative organizations – for example, that skilled creative workers expect greater autonomy, trust and space to invest themselves in their projects. Thus they are likely to become upset with micro-management and highly directive, bossy supervision. It is generally more effective to paint a picture of the outcome that is being sought and to let managers define their own process, and to provide 'covert leadership' (Mintzberg, 1998). Instead of overt displays of power and blunt orders, creative workers generally appreciate being guided through gentle nudges and inflections. A good default position to hold when working with talented staff who expect autonomy is to project humility, humour and empathy for people's insecurities, and be keen to acknowledge and reassure, to celebrate the achievements of others and to help them succeed. However, would we really adopt an identical leadership style for an inexperienced worker who had no idea how to accomplish tasks and a celebrated veteran with enormous industry experience? No, we wouldn't, and so attention has been given by theorists to 'situational leadership' models, that recognize an employee's competence level. Highly directive supervision is appropriate for inexperienced staff, and less intrusive monitoring supervision is appropriate for experienced staff. There may be other situations apart from inexperienced staff that might warrant a more directive style. Someone coming in to turn around a failing organization would need to be far more authoritative, as the speed of intervention required may make the gentle pursuit of consensus largely impossible.

As we saw in Chapter 4, managers with a Theory X management style will tend to be more forceful and prescriptive around expectations and processes, while Theory Y managers will be more trusting and allow staff to invest more of themselves in their tasks. These approaches will be more or less successful depending on the context and the personnel involved. Theory X may be appropriate for very junior staff who are still very much in the learning phase, or for staff who have shown themselves to be unreliable when handed discretion, but in many cases it will be ineffective, such as in the case of wanting to get the best performance out of top people.

AUTHENTICITY IN LEADERSHIP

Leadership authenticity is an important aspect of leading creative teams (Abfalter, 2013). By 'authenticity' we primarily mean being yourself, enacting the values that you purport to stand for and 'walking the talk'. Definitions of 'authentic leadership' have many facets, such as bringing integrity and conviction to leadership, bringing elements of emotional intelligence and positive psychology such as self-awareness to leadership, and avoiding inauthentic behaviours such as being 'overly compliant with stereotypes' (Avolio & Gardner, 2005, p. 321). For example, if a leader trots out the latest management buzzwords and jargon but it all seems scripted, empty and disengaged from his or her life and the life of the employees, it is likely to be perceived as inauthentic. From another angle, the more a leader attempts to embody and follow the advice they are providing to staff, the more authentic they will appear and the more moral authority they will earn to be able to ask the same of others. The rising interest in mindfulness and meditation, which is also concerned with self-awareness, has led to authentic management being extended into 'mindful leadership' (Bunting, 2016).

LEADING CREATIVE PEOPLE AND MAXIMIZING CREATIVITY

Considerable research has been undertaken into creativity and methods for maximizing organizational creativity. Idea generation works on the principle that 'quantity drives quality' and the more ideas that are generated, the greater the chance an extremely good creative idea will emerge. This can be achieved in organizations by the leader eliciting and championing other people's ideas, not just their own (Amabile & Khaire, 2008). Junior employees at the 'coalface' of customer relations sometimes see possibilities and ideas that are missed by managers sitting in office suites. The more diverse the employees, the more angles and perspectives will be brought to bear on the problem, and the greater the chance of reaching a creative solution.

For example, the American animation film studio Pixar has achieved extraordinary success as a creative organization. It prides itself on its approach to creative leadership, which includes empowering and creating space for creative people, opening up creative processes and communication by inviting feedback and ideas, and undertaking constructive post-mortems identifying what should be retained or dropped for future projects (Catmull, 2008, 2014).

Companies seeking to encourage staff to be creative need to make it 'safe to fail', as experimenting and trying crazy things are necessary to achieve creative solutions. A safe environment for creatives also means one where their ideas won't be ridiculed, and where they will be appreciated and recognized when they do have a creative breakthrough. Organizations focusing on creativity also need to draw the line between the 'blue sky', brainstorming, divergent thinking phase at the start of a project, and the need in later stages to focus thinking in a more convergent way on execution and commercialization (Amabile & Khaire, 2008).

FOLLOWERSHIP

From one perspective, focusing on leaders only looks at half the equation, because to have leaders, we need followers. The readier someone is to follow a leader, the easier the leader's task will be. In organizations we can also fixate too much on the leader as the person who achieves everything, when the reality is much more complex. This myth of individual leadership (Koivunen & Wennes, 2011) prevents us from seeing organizational achievements as a collective achievement to which many have contributed. Many of the models in this chapter have evolved to accommodate the understanding that the characteristics of the staff we manage will impact the best approach. Leaders should also explore how they can share and decentralize power and leadership to maximize the sense of collaboration and group achievement.

DUAL LEADERSHIP (CREATIVE AND BUSINESS LEADERSHIP)

Generally, management theory favours one clear leader, due to the 'unity of command' principle that will be discussed in the following chapter on structure (the principle basically posits that having two bosses can lead to uncertainty, ambiguity and conflict). However, creative organizations often have two effective leaders: a business leader and a creative/artistic leader (de Voogt, 2006). The business leader looks after the administration and financial affairs and protects the ongoing financial viability of the organization. The creative leader supervises the artistic and creative dimension. In commercial organizations this creative dimension is often about driving innovative, exciting, creative output that will resonate with audiences. In non-profit organizations, it is often about protecting the artistic quality and integrity of the organization and maximizing the organization's potential with regard to its mission.

Dual leadership requires clearly delineated lines of responsibility to stop these two worlds colliding. Let's provide an example of a problem that could arise (briefly alluded to in the chapter on conflict). The artistic director of an opera company has ambitious plans for a new season, involving new commissions and bold productions which will be expensive to mount, given the quality that the artistic director is seeking, and risky in terms of their experimental nature. Most artistic directors of non-profit organizations see innovative, bold, risk-taking productions as being encouraged by their organizational mission. This approach is also likely to garner kudos from the artistic director's peers. But it may happen that the general manager looks at the new season plans and believes that the proposed programme is not financially viable, because the costs can't be justified against the projected revenue and failure could risk the solvency of the entire organization. If the artistic director sees it as a unilateral situation where he or she is the boss and others need to make his/her vision work, then such a view from the general manager will be considered unhelpful. 'Raise more money through sponsorship to realize my vision' may be the artistic director's response. If, however, the artistic director understands that it is a partnership, and that he or she needs to work collaboratively with the business head and gain their support in order to finalize the programme, then this will make for a more constructive situation. Ideally, the time for discussions about the limits and parameters of each role and its respective authority is when the individuals are being contracted at the beginning, not when the problem arises.

TASTEMAKING

Within the creative and cultural industries, leadership also works in relation to 'tastemaking' and fashion. The creative industries are driven by trends and fashions that require relentless innovation. The media industry and creative industries feed on one another, and the media industry is driven by change and

Figure 9.3 Iris Apfel (left hand side with glasses) is a New York tastemaker and fashion leader, celebrated in the 2015 movie *Iris*. Photo credit: lev radin / Shutterstock.com.

news, not stability and status quo. To some extent great artists lead audiences, because they are better equipped than the audience to envision future possibilities and drive this constant stream of change and innovation. Music artists have also become fashion leaders, and now have well known relationships with fashion designers. Adele, for example, has had a fashion partnership with Burberry (Friedman, 2016). Within the commercial music industry, Clive Davis and Ahmet Ertegun are two celebrated exponents of tastemaking leadership. Within the non-profit sector, managers believe that encouraging audiences to explore new aesthetics and worldviews can be personally and socially beneficial (Hirschman, 1983; Lord, 2012; Sorjonen, 2011). To some degree, creative leadership requires balancing the familiar with the unfamiliar. We want to 'push the envelope', but don't want to leave the audience completely behind.

FRAMING EXPERIENCES

In the chapter on conflict (Chapter 5) we discussed the negotiation technique of changing the frame of reference and points of comparison to soften people's assumptions regarding the negotiation. Creative leaders can also re-frame problems and situations (McFadzean, 2000). The creative industries generally deal in subjective products, where considerable disagreement may exist about the merits of a project. Leaders have an opportunity to contribute to meaning-building and contextualization of organizational events and products. The stories around why projects are being pursued and why they are important often need to be reinforced to stakeholders and revisited.

For example, say I am the leader of an arts organization that experiences a disastrous opening night's performance, and I head off to the gala dinner to celebrate the opening night, dreading the speech I need to give. I could pretend that the evening had been a triumph, but that will resonate poorly because it misrepresents the experience and pretends something took place which didn't. I could be honest about the shortfalls and criticize people who had contributed to the problem, but this would only demotivate the staff involved at the outset of the production and make me look as though I am unprofessionally blaming others rather than taking responsibility. It would be more effective to frame what had taken place in a positive way. So I could praise aspects of the production that had gone well, candidly acknowledge the problems that had arisen, and speak optimistically, positively and truthfully about the hazardous nature of theatrical undertakings. I could mention that theatrical productions are dynamic processes that improve over time. I could even attempt to spin it positively, saying that the more ambitious, challenging and risk-taking the vision, the more likely problems are to arise. Leaders in the creative industries need to develop skills in helping to frame and manage the experiences of people, but in a way that doesn't falsify the facts of the situation, which would destroy their credibility.

COMMUNICATING WITH ARTISTS BY PROXY

Sometimes arts leaders communicate with artists in an oblique way, designed to be gentle and not confrontational, while still eliciting relevant information. For example:

- An A&R manager could ask a newly emerging band 'if you could open for any act, who would it be?' The primary purpose of the question isn't to find out artists for whom they could open the bill. Rather it enables the A&R manager to obtain a clearer idea of who the band thinks their audience is, the way they think about their genre and who they most admire.

- The artistic director of a classical music organization could ask a composer what classical pieces might go well with the new work they have commissioned from the composer. Major classical concerts are programmed several years in advance to lock in prestigious soloists, often prior to commissions being completed, and so it is a reasonable question. But the artistic director may also be trying to gauge the character and flavour of the new work, which may be revealed through the conversation. If the artistic director was to ask this directly, the composer might consider it to be too intrusive into the 'artistic autonomy' he or she believes should be granted.
- A marketing manager could ask an artist what books, movies and other music they're into. Understanding what the artist connects with and identifies with will help the marketer get a fix on the tastes and values of the artist, which can then inform the marketing work.

Creative industries leaders need to communicate with a variety of different stakeholders, and it would be a mistake to use the same language for every stakeholder. Each audience needs to be addressed on its own terms in its own language. The language you would use talking to the financial controller or marketing head of an organization is likely to be different from the language you would use with an artist. Some artists are open to discussions about 'segmentation', 'products' and 'brands'. Others are far less comfortable. One needs to tread carefully.

One additional communications recommendation which is made in Chapter 10, is cultivating a 'collaborative voice' when providing guidance and feedback (Cohen, 2011). At the conclusion of this chapter a former artistic director discusses sacking opera singers and breaking bad news to them, the most difficult feedback that can be given. The example shows a thoughtful leader, prepared to learn and try new things. He arrived at his own approach not by following conventional wisdom (that bad news must always be broken to the person face to face or it lacks courage and respect) but by looking at what works. His higher objective was his duty of care to artists, and protecting them as much as he could. Given the fears and insecurities experienced by artists and creative industries workers, which we explored in Chapter 6, leaders who understand this vulnerability and seek to protect the artists will be appreciated by their employees.

CONCLUSION

This chapter first examined the leadership of creative and cultural organizations, and the way leadership theories can inform the way we approach leadership of these organizations. We concluded by examining idiosyncrasies of creative leadership such as dual leadership and tastemaking.

A challenge of creative leadership: Breaking bad news to artists

Sometimes we need to have confronting conversations with work colleagues, where we are bringing them bad news about their performance. These conversations can be difficult. Moffatt Oxenbould, the former artistic director of Opera Australia, discusses his approach to breaking bad news to artists and how it changed over the course of his career. It shows a thoughtful manager, capable of reflecting on how

Figure 9.4 Moffatt Oxenbould, former Artistic Director of Opera Australia. Photo credit: Michael Chetham.

he operates and changing his behaviour to optimize the way he works:

The first time I had to break bad news to an artist – telling a principal tenor that his contract would not be renewed at the end of the current season – I was a relatively junior administrator on tour with an opera company. I was assured that the artist in question was expecting this news and that confirmation was just a necessary formality. I was simply 'the messenger' relaying a decision made by others. Unwisely, I asked the artist to come to meet me before his evening performance. He was genuinely flabbergasted to receive such news, became distressed and angry, and considered not singing that night! Fortunately, I was able to persuade him to do the show, and he graciously didn't appear to bear any grudge when the dust had settled. But I have never forgotten the look in his eyes when he realized what I was telling him.

Subsequently, as my responsibilities grew and I became artistic director of the opera company, I had to make decisions about the future of artists and believed that in such circumstances I should meet the individual 'face to face'. Conventional wisdom holds that unless you do this for people you employ, you lack personal courage and respect for them. Such conversations are never pleasant, and I knew from that initial experience years earlier that I should never assume an artist was prepared for bad news. Whenever possible I endeavoured to find diplomatic ways of allowing the artist to participate in the process of deciding the appropriate time to leave the stage, particularly for senior artists who had a long association with the company. Often this proved to be a harmonious, mutually agreed celebration of a long and honourable career. Sometimes it was possible to suggest a different sort of ongoing relationship with the artist – from full-time salaried to occasional guest employment, for instance. Especially if another artistic administration colleague was present in the room, the worst outcome of a 'face to face' encounter was when a surprised artist became so distressed that he or she was unable to grasp everything that was being proposed, and began to say things that could never be 'unsaid'. This could involve accusing colleagues of ill-intentioned conspiracy or becoming personally abusive about staff, management or artists, thus making any ongoing 'solution' virtually impossible.

Over time I re-thought 'face to face meetings' and arrived at what I thought was a more humane approach. I would write a personal letter to the artist setting out very clearly the decision and intentions of management. I explained that I was writing because I knew from experience that such conversations, if taken by surprise, can place artists in a very difficult situation, because reacting emotionally is a perfectly reasonable and predictable response (never underestimate the meaning and sense of self-worth and identity artists derive from their careers). I further explained I respected them too much to 'blindside' them, and thought they should be allowed time for consideration, and the opportunity to consult with others close to them. I also made it clear that I did want to meet 'face to face' as a matter of priority and gave my contact numbers for the next 48 hours, saying I would make myself available at whatever time was most convenient for the artist. This allowed them space to reflect and take on board advice from people like partners, agents and managers and perhaps to arrange to be accompanied to the meeting. I made sure that the letter was personally delivered to the artist's home address, so that there was no chance it could be picked up in a mail tray in the theatre and opened before a rehearsal or performance, or in front of colleagues.

Several artists appeared to appreciate this method of breaking bad news, expressing the view that it showed both personal and professional respect, enabling them to be dignified and civil when confronting an inevitably difficult situation. Where appropriate, I commend this approach to you, and encourage you to be as compassionate as possible when having 'difficult' conversations with artists. What might be a potentially difficult ten o'clock appointment in your calendar can be a life defining moment for a vulnerable artist.

Discussion questions and class exercises

1. Which creative industries leader has most impressed you? Why? What traits and approaches did they bring to the leadership of their creative organization?
2. The Steve Jobs dilemma – Steve Jobs, the celebrated leader of Apple Inc., positioned Apple as being at the heart of the creative industries. His company was the computing partner of choice for the creative industries, through strengths such as its graphics software and iTunes platform. However, his management style could be abrasive and confrontational, with celebrated examples of him theatrically berating staff (Isaacson, 2011). Critique the strengths and weaknesses of his leadership style drawing on concepts tabled in this chapter.
3. The dual leadership challenge – Identify a creative organization that has a dual leadership model where one leader looks after the creative output and creative direction and one leader looks after the overall financial and business management. What issues arose and how did they resolve them?

References

Abfalter, D. (2013). 'Authenticity and respect: Leading creative teams in the performing arts', *Creativity and Innovation Management*, Vol. 22, no. 3, pp. 295–306.

Amabile, T. M. & Khaire, M. (2008). 'Creativity and the role of the leader', *Harvard Business Review*, Oct 2008, Reprint R0810G, pp. 1–11.

Avolio, B. J. & Gardner, W. L. (2005). 'Authentic leadership development: Getting to the root of positive forms of leadership', *The Leadership Quarterly*, Vol. 16, pp. 315–338.

Bass, B. M. (1991). 'From transactional to transformational leadership: Learning to share the vision', *Organizational Dynamics*, Vol. 18, no. 3, pp. 19–31.

Bons, P. M. & Fiedler, F. E. (1976). 'Changes in organizational leadership and the behavior of relationship and task motivated leaders', *Administrative Science Quarterly*, Vol. 21, no. 3, pp. 453–473.

Buckle, R. (1984). *Diaghilev*. London: Hamish Hamilton.

Bunting, M. (2016). *The Mindful Leader: 7 Practices for Transforming Your Leadership, Your Organisation and Your Life*. Queensland, Australia: John Wiley & Sons.

Catmull, E. (2008). 'How Pixar fosters collective creativity', *Harvard Business Review*, September 2008.

Catmull, E. (2014). *Creativity, Inc.: Overcoming the Unseen Forces that Stand in the Way of True Inspiration*. New York: Random House.

Caust, J. (2004). 'A festival in disarray: The 2002 Adelaide Festival: A debacle or another model of arts organization and leadership?' *Journal of Arts Management, Law, and Society*, Vol. 34, no. 2, pp. 103–117.

Cohen, Robert. (2011). *Working Together in Theatre*. New York: Palgrave Macmillan.

Friedman, V. (2016). 'Lady Gaga defines a new role: Fashion enabler', *The New York Times*, March 30, 2016. Available at http://www.nytimes.com/2016/03/31/fashion/lady-gaga-defines-a-new-role-fashion-enabler.html?_r=0 (accessed 25 April 2016).

Goleman, D. (1996). *Emotional Intelligence*. London: Bloomsbury.

Hirschman, E. C. (1983). 'Aesthetics, ideologies and the limits of the marketing concept', *Journal of Marketing*, Vol. 47, no. 3, pp. 45–55.

Isaacson, W. (2011). *Steve Jobs*. New York: Simon & Schuster.

Judge, T. A., Piccolo, R. F. & Ilies, R. (2004). 'The forgotten ones? The validity of consideration and initiating structure in leadership research', *Journal of Applied Psychology*, Vol. 89, no. 1, pp. 36–51.

Koivunen, N. & Wennes, G. (2011). 'Show us the sound! Aesthetic leadership of symphony orchestra conductors', *Leadership*, Vol. 7, no. 1, pp. 51–71.

Lord, C. (2012). *Counting New Beans: Intrinsic Impact and the Value of Art*. San Francisco, CA: Theatre Bay Area.

McFadzean, E. (2000). 'What can we learn from creative people? The story of Brian Eno', *Management Decision*, Vol. 38, no. 1/2, pp. 51–56.

Mintzberg, H. (1998). 'Covert leadership: Notes on managing professionals', *Harvard Business Review*, November-December, pp. 140–147.

Rentschler, R. (2002). *The Entrepreneurial Arts Leader*. Queensland, Australia: University of Queensland Press.

Sorjonen, H. (2011). 'The manifestation of market orientation and its antecedents in the program planning of arts organizations', *International Journal of Arts Management*, Vol. 14, no. 1, pp. 4–18.

Suchy, S. (1999). 'Emotional intelligence, passion and museum leadership', *Museum Management and Curatorship*, Vol. 18, no. 1, pp. 57–71.

de Voogt, A. (2006). 'Dual leadership as a problem-solving tool in arts organisations', *International Journal of Arts Management*, Vol. 9, no. 1, pp. 17–22.

Zaccaro, S. J. (2007). 'Trait-based perspectives of leadership', *American Psychologist*, Vol. 62, no. 1, pp. 6–16.

Teams in creative organizations

Chapter 10

CHAPTER LEARNING OBJECTIVES

After studying this chapter, you should be able to:

- Define the difference between a 'group', 'work-group' and 'team';
- Explain the benefits and disadvantages of using teams in creative work environments, both for the organization and individual;
- Describe the five stages of team development;
- Recognize the various team roles;
- Articulate and apply best practices to building and maintaining strong and effective teams;
- Explain the advantages and disadvantages of remote and hybrid work models.

BUILDING AND LEADING TEAMS

When people first enter leadership roles in the workforce, they are usually leading a project team. So what makes teams function and how can we best lead them?

Skilled, professional teams who are 'on point' can accomplish amazing things. A Formula One motor racing pit crew can

DOI: 10.4324/9781003262923-10

Figure 10.1 The ability to work in diverse, multicultural teams is critical to success in the creative industries.

Photo credit: Rawpixel.com / Shutterstock.com.

change all tyres on a car in under two seconds. Experienced technical crews working for superstar artists will bring the same focus and dedication to mounting stadium concerts. Each team member needs to be 'drilled' to make the spectacular something that can be delivered predictably on a nightly basis.

The economist Richard Caves observed that in the creative industries we work on creative projects with people possessing diverse and specialized skills, many of whom will have aesthetic views on what is being created (Caves, 2000). As previously observed in this book, he termed this the 'Motley Crew' (Caves, 2000, p. 6) because of the teams' ad hoc nature, driven by the specific needs of the project and the fact that these workers can come with strong opinions. So, we may have more challenges integrating our diverse teams than the pit crew of a Formula One team. Managing these challenges and the diversity of skills that may be needed for creative projects requires an understanding of how teams work, what drives individual behaviour within them and the reason organizations use them in the first place. Let's take a closer look at some of these dynamics as we explore the opportunities and challenges that come with working in teams in today's creative economy.

WHAT IS A TEAM?

Before we discuss the benefits and challenges of working in teams, let us first define the differences between 'groups' and 'teams'. Groups are considered to be two or more people with common interests, objectives and continuing interaction. Often a classroom full of students taking a course on Intellectual Property (IP) rights is considered a group. There may be 30 of your peers that share the common interest of working in the creative industries gathered together twice a week to learn more about the legalities of copyright, trademark and other forms of IP. Or when fans of a popular artist come together for a concert on a Saturday evening, those fans, too are considered a group. A 'team' (sometimes referred to as a 'work group') on the other hand is two or more people with '*complementary skills who are committed to a common mission, performance goals and approach for which they hold themselves mutually accountable*' (Katzenbach & Smith, 1993, p. 1). To this end, it is important to emphasize the 'complementary skills' and the 'mutually accountable' elements of this definition. These point to the essence of a team and how it differentiates itself from a group. In large scale film production, the reliance upon thousands of different complementary skill sets is critical for the film's success. From the 'above-the-line' creative and producing talent to the 'below-the-line' technical expertise like camera operators and sound engineers, each function is necessary to deliver the final project. Furthermore, the quality of work being done by each specialist is accountable to all the others within the project. The quality of the final film is only as good as the skills of those who were hired to create it.

Which sounds the most energized: an administrative committee or a sports team? For many people, a great sports team is energized, outcomes-focused, summons the best from those within the group and supports one another with positive comments and camaraderie. When we talk about a 'team' in this textbook, we use the term flexibly. It could apply to people tasked with progressing a creative project, but it could also mean an organizational department, a small music or fashion label, a theatre cast, a board of directors, a rock band, a *corps de ballet*, a technical crew, a performing ensemble or a finance committee. Each will have its own dynamics, but each of the above examples can involve the application of great technical knowledge and collaboration among diverse but gifted people, and all can contribute to the creative outcomes and objectives of an organization. Great teams also relax hierarchy and formality, and cultivate a 'we're all in this together' ethos, which can be motivating for all participants. Teams are great for work that can be complicated, complex, interrelated and/or bigger than one person can handle. They often are able to overcome individual limitations while providing a sense of intimacy and camaraderie among those involved.

Some teams will be defined by the formal organizational structure, such as 'the senior management team'. 'Cross functional' teams are where a project team has a representative from each organizational function, such as marketing, artistic, finance and IT. Such a team might be formed to progress a new creative project, or tackle a task such as lowering the organization's carbon footprint or celebrating the organization's centenary. By being cross functional, a team draws on the resources and expertise of all departments and ensures each has a voice in the project.

THE 'ROMANCE OF TEAMS' – BENEFITS AND DISADVANTAGES IN CREATIVE ORGANIZATIONS

Are teams as effective, ideal and essential as we often make them out to be in the work place? Some would argue that we've 'romanticised' (Allen & Hecht, 2004) the idea of a work-team as an essential part of organizations and getting things done efficiently. They have allowed organizations to champion collaboration with others while minimizing self-reliance and internal competition. While many managers, employees and the general population believe in the efficiency and effectiveness of team-based work, they can bring about some disadvantages beyond the efficiency that can come with individual decision-making. Let's explore each of these perspectives in turn.

BENEFITS OF TEAMS FOR ORGANIZATIONS

Promotes problem solving and boosts creativity

When diverse teams are formed, a wide array of perspectives, lived experiences, cultural backgrounds and skill sets can come together. The ideals of a team are to achieve a sum greater than its parts. When this happens, the potential for creative thinking that leads to innovation and problem solving increases exponentially. Much of this would not be possible without the coming together of these varied skill sets. When 'group cohesion' is high, members work together comfortably without fear of being ridiculed for their ideas while understanding their role and contribution to the team overall.

Increases productivity

When workload is distributed among multiple individuals, it allows for a more efficient use of time and resources. In cases where distribution of work becomes unbalanced and a member is overwhelmed, another can assist in alleviating the workload, freeing up 'bottlenecks' and therefore increasing productivity. Furthermore, when more than one person is working on a project, the likelihood of completing the project goes up due to each member being accountable to the other and the aims of the task. The sharing of ideas that can occur on a team and more efficient problem solving can also lead to increased productivity, whilst improving cross training, so as members leave or get reassigned others can more quickly and easily slide into their role (Schilder, 1992; Sloan, 2018).

Builds trust

A culture of trust where team members rely on each other for the success of the whole can only be achieved through open dialogue, honesty, respect and valuing opinions. Needing to rely on a skill set you do not have and clearly defining your strengths and weaknesses calls for vulnerability. An environment of trust and mutual respect builds team cohesion (Mattson, 2015).

DISADVANTAGES OF TEAMS FOR ORGANIZATIONS

Rose Johnson's (2018) article on the disadvantages of teams in organizations raises important issues to consider when deciding whether formulating a team is the right answer for tackling a project or developing new ideas. Working closely with others in creative environments can be challenging when egos get in the way of creative ideas and deciding whether it is appropriate for specific circumstances is something to carefully consider.

Interpersonal conflict

Hostility can occur when team members don't agree with each other's ideas or ways to approach problems. As we discussed in Chapter 5, not all conflict needs to be considered negative, but if a team member feels disrespected, this can undermine trust amongst members which can lead to resentment. This in turn can hinder productivity, creativity and can lead to poor decision-making. For example, A&R representatives within the same record company or music publisher can find themselves competing with each other when seeking and signing new talent. Although they may be part of the same work group, frustration, resentment and conflict can occur if one person erodes the trust or crosses an ethical line when attempting to sign new talent.

Incompatibility

Not all people work well on teams, even though their skill set could be a critical part of the project's success. If someone is not interested in working on a team or their personality is not compatible with others, they may detach themselves from the group, resulting in communication issues which hinders progress.

Free riding

Whether it's a school or work project, some members may take advantage of others and the team's efforts by not fairly participating in, or contributing to the work. Entitled members may feel it unnecessary to put forward work, while others may step in to pick up the slack, which can lead to resentment. This behaviour must be dealt with immediately, either through team members holding one another to account, or the team leader stepping in to set performance measures.

BENEFITS OF TEAMS FOR INDIVIDUALS

Provides an identity beyond self

Working on a team in which your skill set is valued provides an opportunity to identify with something bigger than yourself. You are involved in an achievement that is greater than you could accomplish by your own hands. You might be contributing to an academy award winning movie franchise or designing the latest tech product. It is rewarding to know that your efforts will be seen, respected and recognized.

Social intimacy

Teamwork provides opportunities to be social and to build trust and relationships with team members. As successes and failures build, so does one's desire to be vulnerable and develop relationships with peers at work, but this can also carry over into friendships and camaraderie outside the workplace. When socializing outside of work time, you are able to continue building social bonds and interpersonal relationships that help to promote better mental health and wellbeing. When this happens, you are more likely to enjoy your work and commit yourself to the organization's aims.

GROUP BEHAVIOUR

When we first join an established team, we will see that there are certain expectations and unwritten rules by which the team functions (termed here as 'group norms'). Performance norms will set expectations around work hours, the work quality that is acceptable and the intensity with which people work. Other norms may be established that govern things such as dress code and timeliness expectations. Leaders can help shape and reinforce these norms.

The chapter on conflict discussed the problems that can arise from too much or too little cohesion within the team, where people no longer challenge one another, or challenge one another so aggressively that the team falls apart. We also saw that 'groupthink' can paralyze teams, with individuals failing to challenge poor decisions because they don't want to get into an argument. On the other hand 'Group Cohesion', the interpersonal relationships that hold the team together, can lead to a better performing team. Leaders in creative organizations need to strike a balance between the two, where a cohesive team is still willing to challenge each other's thinking and assumptions. They can do so by being open, encouraging diverse viewpoints and allowing 'the best idea to win' no matter who comes up with it (Catmull, 2014).

FIVE STAGES OF TEAM DEVELOPMENT

One model of team development (Tuckman, 1965) in which a work group progresses through a series of five stages has long been studied to better understand how teams develop (Figure 10.2). The subtle nuances of members' assimilation into a team can be described through these stages.

Forming

When groups first form, members may have quite a few questions on how to proceed. There may be uncertainty over what is to be achieved and differing motivations. Socialization occurs and formal designation or informally manoeuvring may occur to determine who takes the lead. Guidance and direction is often needed by leaders in order to help facilitate clarity and direction.

Storming

As the team transitions from the 'forming' stage, they enter into a more conflict orientated state as it seeks clarity of purpose. Some members may become less engaged while others compete for specific roles. Emotions can run high as the members move toward group norms.

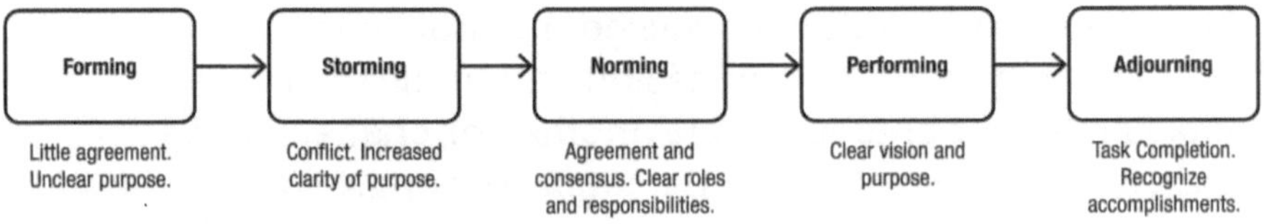

Figure 10.2 The five stages of team development – based on the 'Group Development Model' by Bruce Tuckman

Source: Tuckman, B.W. & Jensen, M.A.C. (1977) 'Stages of small-group development revisited', *Group & Organization Studies*, Vol. 2, no. 4, pp. 419–427.

Norming

In this stage of the model, team members come to agreements on how the work will be conducted while role responsibilities become clearer. Due to lower tensions, members may feel less anxiety and some relief as they become more engaged and mutually supportive. Group cohesion begins to form.

Performing

Now that the team has settled into their function, clear vision helps move the members towards accomplishing their goals. Shared participation, decision-making and problem solving often accompany this stage.

Adjourning

The final stage of team development is adjourning. Here participants celebrate the achievements and may recognize those accomplishments with each other. It may be more celebratory in nature now their task has been completed.

All teams go through phases of development and even though Figure 10.2 depicts a linear process, this isn't usually the case. Teams may go from one stage and back again as new initiatives are presented or new team members are introduced and others leave. For example, if a new alternative rock band is formed by a few college students, their initial conversations will be exciting as the potential for a new creative outlet is explored. The idea of becoming a band, creating new music, spending time with new friends, working on performances and recordings, will be topics of conversation. These initial conversations can be big on mutual enthusiasm and low on detail. As the band moves through the 'storming' phase, decisions will need to be made on the primary songwriter, songwriting splits, creative direction and influences, vocals and instruments, voting rights of band members and other major or less crucial decisions. One or two members may become more dominant while others appear happier to be in the 'background'. Tempers may get heated as egos are challenged and creative conflict sets in. As the band moves on to the norming stage, band agreements will be finalized, a consensus will be reached, regular rehearsals will have commenced, and a clear commitment from everyone is apparent. Members get along well and cohesion is achieved as everyone is clear on their roles and where the band is headed. As the band transitions to 'Performing', the next stage, goals are accomplished, deals are made and the band moves forward down its intended path. The final stage of 'Adjourning' may happen quickly if goals no longer seem realistic or if a member decides to move on, or it may happen 30–40 years after a successful career together. But at any point, changes in band membership, management, or record label may result in the band reverting back to the storming phase as new norms and roles need to be re-established.

WHAT YOU DON'T WANT IN A TEAM

As we have discussed, teams can be productive, efficient and even fun when working on projects. They serve an individual's needs for workplace socialization and intimacy and are a great way to boost creativity, efficiency and productivity. And on occasions the camaraderie that is built, the challenges you overcome and the truly innovative products that are created can stay with you for a lifetime. But not all teams are ideal or work effectively. There are specific behaviours that you want to avoid and can be indicative of ineffective teams (Collins & Collins, 2009; Nelson & Quick, 2016):

1. People shield those in power from unpleasant facts.
2. People assert strong facts without data.
3. Team members don't unify to make a decision.
4. Team members try to take as much credit as possible.
5. Team members blame others for failures.

When things go wrong and a team breaks down, you will often see a lack of personal accountability or a 'blame game' start to occur. The artist never showed up on time, the schedule was too much, or the actor came in 'high' or 'intoxicated'. Or, if things are going well, someone on the team takes all the credit. When you ignore the efforts of others or take undue credit for their work, team trust and unity breaks down, causing further interpersonal challenges. Making unsubstantiated claims, not speaking truth to leadership or shielding them from information that may be negative can throw a project off course.

TEAM ROLES

Going beyond the complementary skills team members may possess, Merideth Belbin (2010) in her research on why teams succeed or fail, emphasizes the importance of team member roles and interaction among members. Below is a list of roles that she has developed. Those of us who have worked on a team, can either recognize a member taking on this role or may recognize it in ourselves.

Belbin's nine team roles

- Plant (creates ideas)
- Resource Investigator (explores opportunities and contacts)
- Co-ordinator (clarifies goals, promotes decision making)
- Shaper (drives the team forward)
- Teamworker (provides support and encourages cooperation)
- Monitor Evaluator (discerning judgment)
- Implementer (turns ideas into action)
- Completer (attention to detail)
- Specialist (technical knowledge and skills)

Belbin, R. M. (2010). *Management Teams: Why They Succeed or Fail*, 3rd edition. London: Routledge. https://doi.org/10.4324/9780080963594

She goes on to argue that strong teams should have a complementary mix and leaders should be deliberate in choosing members that can play to these roles. Although this kind of selection is ideal, the realities of team formation may not always fit this perfectly. These roles can be fluid. Team members can move in and out of them depending on the task at hand or the circumstances of the moment. Team cohesion and established norms can also enable members to grow into these roles as needed.

GROUP COHESION AND EFFECTIVE TEAM BUILDING

Developing strong and effective teams is not an easy task and it takes a strong leader to continue to develop good working and interpersonal relationships among team members. The following are important considerations to reflect upon when developing teams in the workplace:

Know your leadership style

If you are leading a team, understanding your leadership style is a great place to start. As we discussed in Chapter 9, knowing how to lead is important to your success, but knowing how you work and correcting course when things aren't going well is also important. Being aware of your own style, techniques and their effectiveness can make a big difference in how the team will perceive you as a member and leader. Being honest with yourself, knowing what you do and don't do well will benefit everyone involved. But more most importantly, be flexible, not everyone on the team may appreciate how you work and being mindful of individual differences will help you to be a more effective leader for everyone.

Get to know your team

'Team building' may sound like the biggest cliché of the twenty-first century, but its importance can't be underestimated (Keane, 2012). Taking time to develop camaraderie and trust amongst everyone helps to develop a bond that increases individual commitment to each other and the project at hand. Great teams embrace differences, care for each other, understand each other's significance (Llopis, 2012) and know what each member contributes to the team. They learn each other's strengths and capabilities and rely on them to complete the task at hand. They help to mitigate weaknesses and aren't afraid to seek further input when capabilities have been reached. They encourage a sense of belonging and community, consistently seek open communication and challenge each other accordingly.

Set clear roles and responsibilities

Once you have a better idea of who is on your team and what they bring to it, it will be easier to define the roles and responsibilities of everyone. Making sure that each person is playing to their strengths can only happen if you can evaluate each person effectively. Each team member's expectations should be complementary and dependent upon one another. This is not unlike a concert band where specific instruments take on specific roles in the performance of the music. The low brass section that includes tubas, baritones, or trombones will provide rhythm, bass and harmony and a full-bodied sound. Flutes or clarinets provide the melodies and higher range while the percussion section helps to provide colour, nuance, reinforced melodic accents or set the rhythm and beat. Without each instrument the band can't play the music to its potential. Setting clear expectations helps the team know what is expected of each other and whether those expectations meet or exceed the skills they bring. Someone may be a better facilitator, while another will be great at organizing.

Provide consistent and regular feedback

Providing feedback is key to maintaining team dynamics, improving and staying on task. It should be proactive, consistent and regular so members know how they are progressing or if correction is needed. As a rule, it is best not to wait until problems occur to provide feedback on how things are progressing. Good communication is both formal and informal and becomes a regular part of the team's functioning. Understanding that every team is unique and that some may require more direction while others less is an important part of the leader's role when assessing the experience and expertise of the group. Working within the established norms of what has been established will help to maintain expectations and team cohesiveness (Llopis, 2012).

Acknowledge and reward

Most people need acknowledgement and recognition for doing things right. It's imperative a team leader publicly acknowledges success when it is deserved. Giving proper accolades when earned can go a long way to building team morale and motivation.

Celebrate success

This we do quite well in the creative industries!!! When an occasion calls for celebration, whether a top 10 hit or #1 song in the charts, an Emmy nomination or winning an Oscar for best picture, organizations in the creative and cultural industries usually bring considerable resources to celebrate these achievements. And they should! Not only do parties allow for acknowledgement and recognition of collective achievement, they enable the team to stop and reflect on what has been accomplished and what it took to get there. These events also make the organization a more attractive place to work.

GROUP COHESION AND MAINTAINING EFFECTIVE TEAMS IN REMOTE ENVIRONMENTS

While creative industries work has not necessarily been Monday to Fridays, 9–5 employment, the global pandemic forced a closer examination of flexible and remote working. 'Flexible working', which is about giving workers flexibility with regards to when and where they work (Dale, 2021), does not just mean the ability to work remotely, but also applies to other things like nine day fortnights, self-rostering and job sharing.

As we learn about how employees spend their time while working at home, we know that they are 13% more productive, take fewer and shorter breaks and are 50% less likely to quit (Barrero *et al.* 2021a; Grant, 2022). Of course, some employers are sceptical that the requisite creativity and innovation can be achieved when work is remote or hybrid in nature (Grant, 2022), but the research is telling us otherwise. When Barrero, Bloom and Davis (2021b) started researching people who worked from home two days a week, they found that they performed just as well and are just as likely to be promoted – in essence, there was no real difference in performance, but quit rates were down 35%!! Measures of job satisfaction, burnout, work-life balance were also significantly improved.

How much should you allow people to work from home? What is the right amount? Well, we know that 50% of the working population cannot physically work from home such as those in manufacturing jobs, emergency services and many service and ephemeral experience providers like concert presenters. For the remaining 50%, remote work conditions will depend on the work that needs to be performed. Call centre employees, many technology support gigs and accountants can more easily work remotely and companies should consider those positions first. Jobs like research and design or creative jobs where 'excellence depends on passing the project back and forth to other members of the team' will need more time together (Grant, 2022).

As books such as *Flexible Working* (Dale, 2021) outline in detail, remote working has both advantages and disadvantages:

ADVANTAGES OF FLEXIBLE WORKING

- *Empowerment and inclusivity:* Granting employees the discretion to work remotely increases employee empowerment, trust and autonomy, which we know from Chapters 1 and 3 are important to workers in the creative industries. It can also lower work/life balance stresses for staff and help retain staff who value flexibility. Flexibility increases workforce inclusivity, by allowing workers to more easily juggle family and other needs and responsibilities;
- *Potential increases in productivity and creativity:* Although this varies, some employers and employees have reported productivity increases through working undistracted at home. Some employees who had been granted increased flexibility 'highlighted how they feel that outside of the traditional workplace and its distractions it is easier for them to concentrate, think and be more creative' (Dale 2021, p. 43);
- *Low cost and lowering costs:* For staff who value flexibility, granting flexibility creates a valuable employment benefit for them that generates little if any additional cost to the organization. It can also reduce organizational costs through lower absenteeism and lower office space costs. It can reduce employee costs through things like lower transport and child care costs. Avoiding rush hours and shortening commuting time generates benefits for employees, the community and the environment;
- *Complying with evolving laws:* Some countries, such as the United Kingdom, legally require companies to grant flexible work opportunities, as long as they are reasonable given the nature of the work and the costs that would be borne by the employer.

DISADVANTAGES OF FLEXIBLE WORKING

- *Impossible to deliver the service:* Staff delivering events for example need to be physically present on site for much of the employment engagement to actually deliver the event;

- *Poorer communication:* It has been widely observed that platforms like Zoom or Skype or Microsoft Teams (at least in their 2022 state), are poorer than face to face communication in terms of allowing participants to read body language, and pick up on emotional nuances around disagreement and disengagement. Practical issues like poor internet connections can also create problems;
- *Disconnection:* Staff who come into the office access informal information through chance 'water cooler' or coffee break conversations and overhearing conversations while working in the office. This gives them access to information of which they had been unaware, and which remote employees do not receive. Not being privy to informal information-sharing results in remote employees becoming disconnected and feeling like an 'outsider'. Remote workers can also be judged by those who work from the office as not having the same level of commitment;
- *Thwarted serendipity:* 'Serendipity' means discovering something valuable by chance, and it has been observed in the organizational creativity literature that sometimes 'water cooler conversations' spark ideas amongst employees, which will not happen with staff working remotely;
- *Reduced team 'flow':* In Chapter 4 we examined the concept of 'flow', and it has been observed that

> remote work often breaks the mechanisms that allow a team to work together creatively. Studies have found that the best creative work occurs when a team is in a state of flow, or focuses its collective attention on a single problem together, known as 'team flow'. But remote work makes it harder to keep everyone engaged in solving that problem.
>
> (Nguyen, 2021)

- *Reduced 'esprit du corps':* Face to face social interaction can be important to building staff morale and understanding, creating high quality shared experiences, and keeping alive 'the spirit of the human hive' (Mintzberg, 2013, p. 51);
- *Increased stress through loneliness and blurred boundaries:* If an employee is working in the space that they normally use

to relax, it can result in them having difficulty switching off. Remote working can also be painful for extroverts who get energy from being around other people;
- *IT security issues:* Many companies possess IT security systems that becomes less effective when the workforce is geographically distributed, increasing the risk of hacking and compromised data.

Given these advantages and disadvantages, many organizations are coming to the conclusion that they need a 'structured hybrid model' (Nguyen, 2021) where in the post pandemic world the company designates certain times where office attendance is mandatory, and allows flexible working outside those times.

CHARACTERISTICS THAT MAKE REMOTE WORKING SUITABLE

- The degree to which onsite attendance is demanded by the nature of the project;
- The degree and complexity of collaboration that is required;
- The closeness of the supervision that is required;
- The degree to which collaboration is synchronous (done at the same time) versus asynchronous (can be done at different times).

As the creative and cultural industries evolve within this new model of hybrid and remote work, it is more important than ever to emphasize the importance of maintaining good communication, effective team building and group cohesion. Each of these is not dependent upon being physically present, but will take extra time and effort for remote teams.

TEAM MEETINGS

The character of team meetings will depend on the nature of the team and the function of the meeting. We would expect a meeting of the board of directors to be conducted more formally than a quick catch-up by members of a project team. However, to get the most out of meetings, useful protocols can be put in place, such as circulating agendas and documentation that needs to be reviewed well in advance of the meeting and minuting action points at the end.

Team leaders need to encourage everyone to contribute, bringing introverts out of their shell and gently but firmly stopping passionate extroverts from dominating the meeting. Great team leaders are adept at driving through the tasks that need to be accomplished as well as deftly managing the interpersonal dimension by complimenting, reassuring and making people feel good about being part of the team. Great team managers are experienced at setting up agenda items in a way that will invite broad comments and allow people to raise points, and then drawing the discussion together to synthesize and integrate contributions. Poor managers cling resolutely to their own views, ignore or dismiss other people's views, or pull rank and demand that staff follow their directives by virtue of their seniority. While staff may comply, they will do so grudgingly. Staff will respond far more positively to leaders who try to explain dilemmas, talk through the pros and cons of options, integrate input and explain the reason why one option is favoured or has been chosen. Leaders who attempt to persuade through winning arguments will command greater respect than those who simply order staff to 'do as you're told'.

TEAM COMMUNICATION AND THE 'COLLABORATIVE VOICE'

Team leaders in the creative industries are wise to develop a 'collaborative voice' (Cohen, 2011). For example, which is the more collaborative of these two formulations:

> 'Dear Sally, It is a complete DISGRACE that no one from my team was copied on these emails or invited to the meeting. How are we supposed to do our jobs when vital matters are kept from us?!!!! Regards, John'
>
> Or,
>
> 'Dear Sally, We would be grateful if we could be invited to future meetings and copied on these emails to give support to what you're doing, and ensure that the work of our two areas is properly integrated. Thanks so much, John.'

The first response dwells on the executive's emotional reaction to the situation. The second response, in a more factual way, simply provides the problem and solution. The first is likely to elicit a defensive or retaliatory response; the second is more likely to receive a conciliatory and helpful response.

Email as a communication medium can be highly effective for some types of communication, and highly ineffective for others. It can be excellent at conveying and minuting details of projects quickly to a large number of people. However, it is a very poor medium for resolving disagreements or handling matters that possess emotional sensitivity. If one division of an organization uses email to accuse another division of letting down a project, particularly if this email is copied to many people, the organization runs the risk of an email war erupting. Participants can feel publicly humiliated and honour-bound to defend themselves in front of their colleagues. Email missiles can fire from one department to another leading to warfare, which can go on until the leader of the organization sends an email such as 'Would everyone please stop sending these emails, get together, and sort this out'. Email wars tend to become less about genuinely resolving problems than about defending our egos, and so major warfare between teams will usually require senior management intervention to resolve. Leaders who intervene will seek to focus on what unites the departments rather than what divides them and help each team gain an appreciation of the needs and perspective of the other side (as we discussed in Chapter 5).

Figure 10.3 Take care with email communication.

Photo credit: Alessandro Tumminello / Shutterstock.com.

While the focus of this chapter is on examining the application of theory to teams, we will permit ourselves some 'professional practice' suggestions for people seeking to enter the creative industries. Sometimes new employees find themselves in disorganized creative workplaces with overly busy managers, asked to pursue tasks with ambiguous approval processes. The employee can sometimes feel that they risk either being blamed for not having achieved the task (if they delay until the situation becomes clearer), or getting into trouble for doing the wrong thing (if they charge ahead). One technique that can address this problem is to send out an email to all who may have a stake in the initiative, summarizing the task/problem and your proposed solution and plan. Keep it succinct and sign off your email with a conclusion such as: 'I am very happy to receive additional input/corrections here, but if I don't hear by [time/day] I will take action accordingly'. This will often trigger much needed feedback, because managers have a clear proposal to which they can respond. If no feedback is received, the young manager can move forward protected, because the intentions were clearly stated well in advance to everyone. Note that when canvassing plans in this way, you should allow a few days, as it is a professional courtesy to assume that everyone is very busy, and reacting to shorter timeframes (e.g. within one day) may not be possible due to travel and other commitments.

Finally, in terms of organizational communication, there is an aphorism that has been attributed to many people (such as Pascal): 'If I had more time I would have written you a shorter letter'. Sometimes the hardest thing is to communicate simply and succinctly. In a busy workplace, managers experience information overload due to being bombarded through multiple platforms. It is a fair assumption that very few people in an organization, except the most committed, are going to have time to skim more than a couple of pages of anything you send them. So try to summarize everything in two pages or less. Even if you have a lengthy report, create a two-page executive summary. Structure it into sections and conclude with a more action-focused section around 'Next Steps' or 'Proposed Action Points'.

Creative Teams: Insights from Phil Towle – a performance enhancement coach who has worked with elite sports teams and the heavy metal band Metallica

Phil Towle, M.A., is a former psychotherapist and performance enhancement coach for business, sports and entertainment, who became employed by Metallica, arguably the world's most successful heavy metal band having sold over 125 million albums. Phil was featured in the 2004 documentary Metallica: Some Kind of Monster, which chronicled a crisis and turning point for the band. In the subsequent video Metallica: This Monster Lives (Metallica, 2018), lead vocalist James Hetfield re-affirmed that Phil 'did take us to the place that we were afraid to go to, he did walk us into the fire, and walked us onto the other side'. Drummer Lars Ulrich concluded 'I believe he saved the band'. We have invited Phil to reflect on the challenges of maximizing the potential of creative teams.

The impact of society and the media

'In many ways, highlighting the value and importance of a great team ethos works against the global currents we see in media and society, which increasingly reveres individual stars and celebrities. The media, and its public, are interested in the star, the celebrity, the most valued player, the hero, the icon. This encourages and rewards egocentricity, which has a number of logical, negative consequences. It obscures the truth that cohesive, mutually supportive teams are far more effective than a fragmented collection of self-serving individuals. If we support one another we amplify each other to our mutual benefit. When a disproportionate amount of attention falls onto one member it can create envy and drive discord and separation. For example a promoted superstar becomes addicted to the external adoration they receive, which fuels their ego, and as their economic value and celebrity rise, they feel more important than their teammates.

Pre-conditions for good team functioning

For a team to function well, all members need to feel they are valued commensurate to their contribution. They also need to find a role for themselves which rewards their self-esteem. If they don't find either of these things, they will leave, literally or figuratively… or use their frustration to sabotage the whole. To bring a team together as a good leader is 'Ted Lasso' stuff: being authentic, legitimately praising your mates, holding yourself accountable for mistakes, checking your own ego at the door, role modelling a team-centric priority…empowering others, with truth affirming positivity and generosity… ultimately living the principles you wish your players, bandmates to own…

Conflict

Conflict is very misunderstood… because its real purpose is to bring people together, to remove things which prevent us getting closer to one another. Conflict erupts when relationships are stuck and stale and not working. The conflict between James and Lars in the Metallica film was absolutely necessary for them to re-forge their own healthier relationship. This in turn strengthened the platform on which the band's ongoing success would be built. What a coach often needs to do is to provide a safe space for conflict to accomplish its intended mission…co-building a foundation of appreciation and respect within which naturally evolving disagreements can be processed without winners and losers…We want conflicts to grow us closer rather than turn us away from one another…. And, when we all prioritize our collective mission more than ourselves, we are in the best position to grow individually and collectively from our temporary discord.

Family

The first place we learn about being in a team is inside our birth family. The more the family demonstrates shared celebration and shared responsibility, the better team-centric values will be internalized, so that later on in life, when asked to self-sacrifice for a greater whole, we can accommodate as if second nature… Those of us from dysfunctional families, where living is more about individual survival, are likely hungrier for individual acknowledgment (often as redemption for missed childhood attention). In truth all of us are at least unconsciously using our present adult lives to reset or heal wounded or simply unfinished stuff from our past.

The need for compassion

We create artists and we destroy them. When we're tired of them we just replace them. As fans we idolize for our needs… without acknowledging them as fellow humans… Like a one-sided breakup, our heroes are recycled to our timing, not necessarily theirs…and, many celebs aren't ready to leave us…especially on our terms… So, do we have some responsibility, here? And, I would encourage those who manage inside the creative industries to pay more direct attention to the overwhelming pressures upon public entertainers, preparing as best you can for their often short cycle of fame…'

Case references

Metallica: This Monster Lives (2018). Video posted to YouTube on Jan 30, 2018 available at https://www.youtube.com/watch?v=D9QPXNdAd08. Directed by Joe Berlinger, published by RadicalMedia. Accessed 8/11/2021.

Metallica: Some Kind of Monster (2004). Documentary directed and produced by Joe Berlinger and Bruce Sinofsky. Distributed by IFC Films.

SUMMARY AND KEY POINTS

This chapter first examined the differences between groups and teams before taking a closer look at the advantages and disadvantages of using them in the creative work environment. Organizations often benefit from the creative synergies that can develop when leveraging different skill sets and when new ideas come together. It not only helps to improve problem solving that can lead to innovation, but many employees also enjoy the intimacy and friendships that can develop when co-workers share a common goal and accomplish a shared task.

In order to develop strong teams, managers must know how you lead, adapt and leverage the strengths and needs of those within them. Getting to know your team while setting clear goals and expectations helps generate cohesiveness and productivity. As we learned in this chapter, all teams go through various stages throughout their existence. And although the foundations for strong teams haven't changed drastically, the need to work remotely in recent years has changed the way we need to formulate and lead teams.

In a post Covid work environment, leveraging old and new technologies to accommodate worker expectations and lead remote teams is more important than ever. Being adaptable and managing people within a flexible work environment will be key to successful team building and maintaining effectiveness over long distances. Keep in mind, remote work and coordinating employees in this fashion will not be constructive for all departments or functions. Some creative jobs will have less flexibility when attempting to work remotely, but departments that are administrative will have more. It will be necessary for leaders to find what works for their organizations and adapt to employee needs in order to be effective in this environment.

Discussion questions and class exercises

1 What are the differences between groups and teams?
2 What are some of the more effective ways to maintain cohesive teams in a creative environment?

3 Explain the various 'roles' that people play within a team. Can you provide a specific example of how you have taken on one of these roles when working in a team? Was this a personal preference or did it just result from the way work unfolded?
4 How effective are remote work and hybrid work environments in the creative industries? What departments or business functions would be more conducive to hybrid, in-person or remote work in a video game development firm or a record company?

References

Allen, N. J. & Hecht, T. D. (2004). 'The 'romance of teams': Toward an understanding of its psychological underpinnings and implications'. *Journal of Occupational and Organizational Psychology*, Vol. 77, no. 4, pp. 439–461.

Barrero, J. M., Bloom, N. & Davis, S. J. (2021a). *Why Working from Home Will Stick* (No. w28731). National Bureau of Economic Research.

Barrero, J. M., Bloom, N. & Davis, S. J. (2021b). *Let Me Work from Home, or I Will Find Another Job*. LSE COVID-19 Blog.

Belbin, R. M. (2010). *Management Teams: Why They Succeed or Fail* (3rd ed.). London: Routledge. https://doi.org/10.4324/9780080963594

Catmull, E. (2014). *Creativity, Inc.: Overcoming the Unseen Forces that Stand in the Way of True Inspiration*. New York: Random House.

Caves, R. E. (2000). *Creative Industries: Contracts between Art and Commerce*. Cambridge, MA: Harvard University Press.

Cohen, R. (2011). *Working Together in Theatre: Collaboration & Leadership*. New York: Palgrave Macmillan.

Collins, J. C. & Collins, J. (2009). *How the Mighty Fall: And Why Some Companies Never Give In*. New York: Random House.

Dale, G. (2021). *Flexible Working: How to Implement Flexibility in the Workplace to Improve Employee and Business Performance*. London: Kogan Page Ltd.

Grant, A. (2022). *WorkLife with Adam Grant*. [online] Link.chtbl.com. Available at https://link.chtbl.com/9omV9kHy (accessed 14 June 2022).

Johnson, R. (2018). *Benefits and Challenges of Teamwork*. [online] Bizfluent. Available at https://bizfluent.com/info-8210884-benefits-challenges-teamwork.html (accessed 17 May 2022).

Katzenbach, J. & Smith, D. (1993). *The Discipline of Teams*. [online] Harvard Business Review. Available at https://hbr.org/1993/03/

the-discipline-of-teams-2#:~:text=A%20team%20is%20a%20small, a%20 team%20is%20common%20commitment. (accessed 16 July 2022).

Keane, T. (2012). 'Leading with technology: 21st century skills= 3Rs+ 4Cs', *Australian Educational Leader*, Vol. 34, no. 2, p. 44.

Llopis, G. (2012). *6 Ways Successful Teams Are Built To Last.* [online] Forbes. Available at https://www.forbes.com/sites/glennllopis/2012/10/01/6-ways-successful-teams-are-built-to-last/?sh=18c6b45c2b55 (accessed 31 May 2022).

Mattson, D. (2015). *6 Ways Teamwork Teaches Trust | Sandler Training.* [online] Sandler Training. Available at (https://www.sandler.com/blog/6-ways-teamwork-teaches-trust/ (accessed 13 June 2022).

Mintzberg, H. (2013). *Simply Managing.* San Francisco, CA: Berrett-Koehler Publishers, Inc.

Nelson, D. L. & Quick, J. C. (2016). *Orgb.* Boston, MA: Cengage Learning.

Nguyen, M. (2021). 'Research shows working from home doesn't work. Here's how employers should tackle the problem', *Time Magazine.* Available at https://time.com/6088110/remote-work-structured-hybrid-research/ (accessed 20 September 2021).

Schilder, J. (1992). 'Work teams boost productivity', *Personnel Journal*, Vol. 71, no.2, pp. 67–71.

Sloan, K. (2018). *5 Ways Teamwork Increases Work Productivity.* [online] Calendar. Available at https://www.calendar.com/blog/5-ways-teamwork-increases-work-productivity/ (accessed 30 May 2022).

Tuckman, B. W. & Jensen, M. A. C. (1977). 'Stages of small-group development revisited', *Group & Organization Studies*, Vol. 2, no. 4, pp. 419–427.

Tuckman, B. W. (1965). 'Development sequence in small groups', *Psychological Bulletin*, Vol. 63, no. 6, 384–399.

Diversity, equity and inclusion in creative organizations

Edited by: Jennifer Duck and Sara Wigal

Chapter 11

CHAPTER LEARNING OBJECTIVES

After studying this chapter, you should be able to:

- Define and explain the concepts of diversity, equity and inclusion;
- Summarize the meanings of microaggressions, marginalization, discrimination, and the laws that have been implemented to protect certain populations;
- Explain and contrast how specific underrepresented groups are being impacted in the creative industries;

DOI: 10.4324/9781003262923-11

- Articulate ways in which creative organizations can develop inclusive strategies that positively impact all personnel;
- Explain how good DEI practices can strengthen the creative and cultural industries and its workers.

Walt Disney Company: How cultural awareness influences creativity and economic success

Written by: *Nadine Waran-Perrero*

The Walt Disney Company relishes its reputation for being a world-class and prestigious enterprise. Its contributions to the entertainment industries have led to numerous accolades and awards: Art Directors Guild Awards, the Critics' Choice Awards, BAFTA Awards, Golden Globes Awards, over 20 Oscars, and the International Association

Figure 11.1 One of the world's most successful entertainment companies educating through cultural awareness. Photo credit: chrisdorney / Shutterstock.com.

Awards to mention a few. Recognized for its ability to create magic and fantasy through creative storytelling and animation, Disney plays a critical role in the formative years of our global youth. Young media consumers develop a desire to connect themselves to the characters and their environments taking place on screen. While in the same accord, if what IS seen is superficial or stereotypical—such as their physical appearances and the fabric of their environments, it can have a detrimental effect on viewers' self-confidence (Stover, 2013). With Disney's global influence and marketplace, it is important that creative content producers and distributors are educated about and exposed to the foreign cultures which they aim to incorporate.

Although Disney caters to a wide variety of age groups, the majority of the company's media distribution heavily relies on its young audience members, between the ages 2 and 17. This age group constitutes 43% of the overall U.S. consumer value (Stoll, 2022). Worldwide, Disney+ was reported to have had 137.7 million subscribers in the second quarter of the year 2022 (Stoll, 2022). In 2014, *Forbes* released an article that announced that The Walt Disney Company held the No.1 spot as the world's most reputable company among an evaluation of 130 companies (Adams, 2014).

Like most globally renowned entertainment platforms, Disney has faced scrutiny over the years which includes cultural representation or the lack thereof. For instance, Disney princesses of diverse backgrounds have previously been voiced over by white artists, in lieu of using voice actors consistent with the characters' racial profiles. Accusations of whitewashing, inauthenticity, and cultural discrepancies have proliferated. More recently the company has taken leaps in telling stories of other cultures and countries by actively immersing the creators of these Disney films into foreign environments.

For example, when John Muske and Ron Clement (two American animation directors) offered up the idea of creating a Polynesian character for the Disney animated movie, *Moana,* their Chief Animator John Lesseter responded with two words, 'Go Research' (Robinson, 2016). This meant that before the production could be greenlighted, the creators had to undertake extensive exploration of the foreign culture. It required them to travel to Polynesia and to learn from anthropologists, cultural practitioners, historians, and linguists, to ensure the greatest accuracy in terms of the cultural representation (Robinson, 2016).

Encanto, another foreign-based Disney movie released in November 2021, had similar research support. The Directors Jared Bush and Byron Howard travelled to South America in the spring of 2018 to immerse themselves in the environment of the story whilst conducting their research. The creativity that we see in the animation of *Encanto* reflects the inspirations that the directors had gathered from their visit to the cities of Bogotá and Cartagena; the colours were influenced by the small villages and the people, the integration of their food discoveries such as the fat-bottomed ants came from physically witnessing the insects and understanding that these were among the country's delicacies. The fabric textures, architecture, soundscapes, local languages, local voices and pronunciations could then all be represented in the final production (Aranoff, 2021). Most crucially, this film included a fully representative cast of Columbians.

One of the most impactful examples of DEI at an international level is the production of Disney's *Soul,* which created significant social media buzz and applause. The movie's research and pre-production process was initiated prior to the revival and amplification of the *Black Lives Matter* movement in 2019, which arose through the public outcry over George Floyd, Breonna Taylor, Elijah McClain, Ahmaud Arbery, among many others. Disney's *Soul,* broadcast on Disney+ in June 2020 brought forth much needed conversations about racial disparity in the United

States and was mainly cast and led by an animation team of Black Americans (Rainbow, 2020).

Moving forward, Disney's example suggests a promising future for diversity, equity and inclusion practices as the organization aims to take responsibility and continue their mission to amplify underrepresented voices. The 'Reimagine Tomorrow' initiative published on the Disney website for example, depicts stories and perspectives of individuals from all over the globe (Reimagine Tomorrow Together, 2021). Additionally, Disney's 2020 Corporate Social Responsibility Report shows an increase in the number of employees who identify as people of colour, comprising 46%, compared to the 44% the previous year (The Walt Disney Company, 2020).

In essence, the vision for inclusivity and positive educational values can effectively impact the youth of today to aspire them to become the storytellers of tomorrow.

Questions for discussion

1. What further approaches could The Walt Disney Company consider to help make its representation of other cultures as authentic as possible?
2. Do you agree with the steps taken by the Walt Disney Company to explore and educate its content creators on foreign culture? If so, why? If not, why not?

Case references

Adams, S. (2014). The World's Most Reputable Companies. [Online] *Forbes*. Available at https://www.forbes.com/sites/susanadams/2014/04/08/the-worlds-most-reputable-companies/?sh=b9447a14024d (accessed 7 July, 2022).

Aranoff, J. (2021). 'How the Directors of Disney's 'Encanto' Brought the Magic of Colombia to the Big Screen', *Travel and Leisure News*, [Online]. Available at https://www.travelandleisure.com/travel-news/encanto-is-enchanting (accessed 24 June, 2022).

Rainbow, S. (2020). 'Soul: how Pixar's first Black-led film, on Disney+, is leading a change in animation', *www.standard.co.uk*, [Online]. Available at https://www.standard.co.uk/culture/film/

pixar-soul-disney-black-animation-diversity-b74917.html (accessed 24 June, 2022).

Reimagine Tomorrow Together (2021). Available at https://reimaginetomorrow.disney.com/reimagine-tomorrow-together (accessed 7 July, 2022).

Robinson, J. (2016). 'How Pacific Islanders Helped Disney's *Moana* Find Its Way', *Vanity Fair*, [Online]. Available at https://www.vanityfair.com/hollywood/2016/11/moana-oceanic-trust-disney-controversy-pacific-islanders-polynesia (accessed 24 June, 2022).

Stoll, J. (2022). Disney+ user distribution in the U.S. 2021, by age. [Online] *Statista*. Available at https://www.statista.com/statistics/1279494/disney-plus-users-us-age/ (accessed 7 July, 2022).

Stoll, J. (2022). Disney+ subscriber numbers worldwide 2020–2022. [Online] *Statista*. Available at https://www.statista.com/statistics/1095372/disney-plus-number-of-subscribers-us/#:~:text=The%20Walt%20Disney%20Company%20reported,the%20fiscal%20year%20of%202020 (accessed 7 July, 2022).

The Walt Disney Company 2020 Corporate Social Responsibility Report. (2020). The Walt Disney Company [Online]. Available at https://impact.disney.com/app/uploads/2022/01/2020-CSR-Report.pdf (accessed 24 June, 2022)

WHAT IS DIVERSITY, EQUITY AND INCLUSION, AND WHY IS IT IMPORTANT TO THE CREATIVE AND CULTURAL INDUSTRIES?

Arguably, nearly every industry sector in the broader economy would assert the importance of equitable hiring practices. These include the need to diversify our workforces, which is especially important to the creative industries. Why? With a broadening social awareness of the importance and value of encouraging and promoting diversity, the creative industries find themselves at the heart of cultural representation and change. The creative industries are the commercial representation of human essence and creativity, and if they fail to represent the full diversity of humanity, these industries will fail to reach their potential—creatively, ethically and commercially.

Being purposeful in setting clear, inclusive policies that welcome diversity of input not only promotes creative thinking and problem-solving but also helps to mitigate short-comings in decision-making (Frost & Alidina, 2019). However, in order for these policies to be effective, companies must not simply

Figure 11.2 Gender and racial discrimination remain issues, though they are improving in some areas. Photo credit: absolutimages / Shutterstock.com.

latch onto the latest trending issue, but they must also introduce purposeful actions and initiatives to make inclusive policies a permanent part of business culture and strategy. As leaders in the creative economy, we must continuously ask ourselves what we are doing and what we can do better.

With plenty of discussion in recent years about equitable representation in the creative industries, ranging from racial representation in leading roles in films, to a lack of women engineers in recording studios, it's important to clearly define what it is that we mean when we talk about diversity, equity and inclusion practices, or 'DEI' for short. In order for employees to feel safe, it's important that we get to a place where age, religious beliefs, skin colour, sexuality and/or disability doesn't influence professional opportunities. So let's start there: what exactly is meant by these terms and what might we be missing in our thinking?

DIVERSITY

In previous chapters we have argued for the creative benefit of diversity: diverse perspectives can assist in finding creative solutions. Some scholars and practitioners are encouraging organizations to think more intentionally about what we mean by 'diversity'. For example, Pumphrey and Williams (2019) describe diversity as being *'about bringing more people to the table',* whereas some argue that leaders would be better off thinking more about decolonization, which is about *'changing the way we think'* about race, diversity and inclusion practices (McLaughlin, 2020).

History teaches us that decolonization is about the emancipation of a state from colony status – for example, the American colonies which eventually became the United States of America, or, India, which has renounced membership as part of the global 'territories' of the United Kingdom. Taxation and legislation that is more favourable to the United Kingdom than the colony no longer shapes economic policy for the independent countries. In modern thinking and discourse, its meaning is broader; theoretically, decolonization is about how western society has been made possible by colonization, recognizing that this history has had detrimental impacts on many people while simultaneously influencing who we are as a culture and people. We also work to recognize and readdress that. Some companies are already at the forefront of this thinking. For example, *Decolonising Design*, a global editorial platform and research group, is setting a new standard, challenging the *'canon of typically white, male creatives [who] set the bar for what is considered good or bad'.* It won't be too long before we see other creative organizations implementing practices and ways of thinking that challenge race and diversity within the workforce. By extension, it is important to understand that diversity

> *refers to the wide array of differences among people and their perspectives on the world. 'Diversity' is an important organizational goal in its own right, but it may or may not be linked to the issue of equity. A diverse workplace is not necessarily an equitable workplace. Nor does the presence of people who are diverse necessarily produce decision-making that optimizes results for the groups their diversity reflects*
>
> (Race Matters Institute, 2022).

Educating and reframing how we think about under-represented groups (i.e. in terms of criteria such as gender, race, sexual identity, economic background and disability) while recognizing the value that all people bring to the creative process should be at the core of what we strive for in the creative and cultural industries. As our definition has already alluded to, this now brings us to the concept of 'equity'.

EQUITY

Equity as a term has been co-opted by organizations, board rooms, mission statements and committees, so we know it is important, but do we really know what it means? It's especially important to understand given that strong DEI initiatives allow for the creative and cultural industries to truly thrive. A dictionary definition of equity may include terms such as *'fair', 'impartial'* or *'justice according to natural law'* (Merriam-Webster, 2022). But this definition poses its own challenges. What is fairness and justice? These concepts are certainly not absolute in their own definitions, since so often they are relative to one's own biases and lived experiences. It is also important to understand that 'equity' is NOT 'equality' in which '*each individual or group of people is given the same resources or opportunities*'. Therefore, we must think more deeply. Equity recognizes that '*each person has different circumstances and allocates the exact resources and opportunities needed to reach an equal outcome*'. Furthermore, *'the route to achieving equity will not be accomplished through treating everyone equally. It will be achieved by treating everyone equitably, or justly according to their circumstances* (Race Matters Institute, 2014)'.

To illustrate this in practice, we could apply these definitions to benefits being offered by a book publisher to its employees. In this scenario, the president and human resource department have decided to offer a new stipend to their employees to write books related to sustainability practices in the creative industries – equality would be offering the same amount to all who are interested in writing on behalf of the company. Equity would be more akin to the president first understanding who may actually need more of a stipend than others based on past writing projects, seniority and other support measures. When trying to be more 'equitable' in resource allocation, organizations can help close the gaps by offering different stipends to employees as well as extending these opportunities to employees who don't typically apply due to lack of paid time off, funding, support, etc.

INCLUSION

Defining the word inclusion can take on a myriad of meanings but can often fall short when too narrowly outlined as having 'equal access' to engage in activities or simply the act of instituting a policy or practice that provides opportunity for those involved. Inclusion is both of those concepts, but to create a culture of belonging we must think of it more broadly and comprehensively. Similar to 'diversity' and 'equity', previously defined, the Race Matters Institute (2022) has captured a working definition that adopts the idea that should be considered in all creative organizations and their DEI initiatives. Inclusion should be '*reflected in the ability of diverse peoples to raise their perspectives authentically, and for those voices to matter and impact decisions*'. A culture that fosters an atmosphere and feeling of being valued IS inclusive. And when organizations institute inclusive practices, they offer their employees a more democratic process to decision-making which leads to a broader more comprehensive view of the world. However, it's not simply the ability to be heard, the key is in the '*impact*'; being truly inclusive is enabling these perspectives to be heard, valued, AND acted upon.

Being an inclusive organization involves a purposeful strategy that enables empowered employee participation among everyone within the organization. It is action-focused rather than simply stating platitudes. It strives to achieve a true sense of belonging for all stakeholders involved, whether it be employees in a company, or independent contractors hired for a project. We know that when employees feel supported and are treated fairly, they are happier, more engaged and more productive (Frost & Alidina, 2019).

MARGINALIZATION, MICROAGGRESSIONS AND DISCRIMINATION

As we've begun to argue for the benefits that come from diversifying workforces and fostering an equitable and inclusive culture, we must also consider the moral and ethical implications that come from strong DEI initiatives as well. When we fail at creating inclusive workplace scenarios, it's possible that we marginalize a specific person or particular group of people. And when we do, we are keeping them in a powerless position by not giving them an active voice, identity or place within it. This can manifest in subtle or overt actions, such as using derogatory language, assuming someone's accomplishments are not based on merit, and expecting individuals to act a certain way based on stereotypes. It is clear what an overt marginalizing behavior might be—using racial slurs or not promoting a woman for a position she is qualified for over someone, simply because she is a woman. However, everyday slights that marginalized people experience can be harder to discern on the surface level. 'Microaggressions' are put-downs or actions by a power-wielding member of the majority perpetrated on a member of an underrepresented group. They're often linked to implicit biases that occur outside of our consciousness, and may be unintentional on the part of the perpetrator because implicit biases often stand in conflict with our conscious thoughts and ideas about equality in a variety of forms. Microaggressions may occur verbally (like telling someone who speaks English as a second language 'you speak good English') or nonverbally (clutching one's purse more tightly when passing someone on the street) and can make victims of microaggressions feel ashamed and dehumanized (LGBTQIA Resource Center Glossary, 2022). Our implicit biases are often formed at a young age, through our cultural and social experiences or even through active teaching from parents and other role models.

The philosophical arguments against marginalizing and discriminating are many and varied. *'Utilitarian arguments'* focus on negative outcomes such as not optimally matching the best people for the best opportunities, and damage to society caused by the effects of racism, sexism and genderism. '*Kantian ethics'* argue individuals should not be deprived of the right to be treated with dignity and respect. Irrespective of the social outcomes, stereotyping is morally repugnant because it strips people of their individuality (Boatright, Smith & Patra 2018).

Even in lieu of the ethical and moral imperative to discourage discriminatory practices, it's important to note that most Western cultures follow anti-discriminatory principles and have scripted them into law. In the United States, the 1964 Civil Rights Act prohibits employers from using race, colour, religion, sex or national origin as a basis for discrimination in employment related matters, and this was later extended to include older people, the handicapped and pregnant women (Boatright, Smith & Patra 2018). This is only one example – most countries have enacted legislation to combat workplace discrimination. Despite the introduction of these laws human biases can still permeate organizations.

WOMEN IN THE CREATIVE AND CULTURAL INDUSTRIES

The gender inequality that exists in the creative industries continues to be well-documented. Research shows that women earn less in royalties (Strong & Cannizzo 2017), their music is played less on radio (McCormack 2016), they are de-emphasized in Spotify playlists (Pelly 2018) and are less likely to be crew members and have acting roles in film (Nesta, 2019). Furthermore, for every 3.6 male artists in popular music, there is one female. For producers of popular music, the number is significantly worse, with only one female for every 37 male producers (Smith, S.L., Choueiti, M. and Pieper, K., 2018). While the participation of women on boards appears to be making strides in Australia and the United States, demonstrating an increase in involvement with top decision-making bodies in the creative sector (McCormack, 2019), the progress towards gender parity is an ongoing one.

Furthermore, the recent impact of Covid-19 has re-emphasized the challenges women face in the creative workforce. A recent 'gender and creativity' report published by the United Nations Educational and Scientific and Cultural Organization (UNESCO) highlighted that gender stereotypes, sexual harassment, access to the labour market, resources, the pay gap and access to leadership positions continues to challenge women in the creative industries. As we learned in Chapter 1, the flexible, project-based and freelance nature of creative work further frustrates women's ability to access necessary resources. The

UNESCO report also asserted that women are confronted with barriers that limit their self-promotion in the creative economy and are hampered by the frequent travel that is often needed (Conner, 2021). With 'at-home' familial responsibilities often falling to women, they are likely to be hindered by these responsibilities. This is often due to differing attitudes about relationship roles and expectations within partners. Often, even when two straight parents work, women take on the majority of emotional and household labour despite working similar occupational hours.

With ongoing challenges such as access to resources, the labour market and the pay gap, it is pretty clear that there is plenty to do in regard to improving gender equality. Country music in particular has had an issue with this for years. For example, not playing women to the same degree as men on radio while telling them there is only room for one woman on record label rosters or playlists (Watson, 2020). When international artist Lady Gaga received Billboard magazine's 'Woman of the Year' award at the Women in Music 2015 event, she attacked gender discrimination in her acceptance speech, describing the music industry as 'a f***ing boys club' (Hendicott, 2015). Although these comments may not have had any direct effect, the message was clear and the music industry was put on notice about the need to equally represent the accomplishments of women. And since then, as seen from the data below, it appears that some progress is being made, at least with regard to Grammy nominations, but men still received more than 70% of all nominations in 2021 (Tables 11.1 and 11.2).

It's not just Grammy nominations in the music industry that pose continued challenges. A study of the Australian music industry revealed gender inequality in record companies and particularly in A&R work, though artist management was more evenly balanced (McCormack, 2016). In another realm, the visual arts are showing positive trends in terms of the representation of women artists, though the higher proportion of women entering the visual arts meant that professional success was still disproportionately skewed male (Richardson, 2016). In the screen and audio-visual industry, there is a gender imbalance in many creative roles such as film direction. To address this, Screen Australia (the Australian Federal Government's funding body for the screen production industry), launched 'Gender

Table 11.1 Grammy nominations by gender and year

	2013	*2014*	*2015*	*2016*	*2017*	*2018*	*2019*	*2020*	*2021*	*Grand Total*
Men	92.1% (n=105)	91.8% (n=156)	85.9% (n=134)	88.5% (n=138)	93.6% (n=190)	92% (n=92)	83.6% (n=138)	79.5% (n=124)	71.9% (n=100)	86.6% (n=1177)
Women	7.9% (n=9)	8.2% (n=14)	14.1% (n=22)	11.5% (n=18)	6.4% (n=13)	8% (n=8)	16.4% (n=27)	20.5% (n=32)	28.1% (n=39)	13.4% (n=182)

Source: Smith, S. L., Choueiti, M. & Pieper, K. (2018). *Inclusion in the recording studio? Gender and race/ethnicity of artists, songwriters & producers across 600 popular songs from 2012 to 2017.* Annenberg Inclusion Initiative.

Table 11.2 Female Grammy® nominations by category over time

	2013	*2014*	*2015*	*2016*	*2017*	*2018*	*2019*	*2020*
Record of the Year	11.8%	2.8%	18.8%	6.7%	7.5%	0	9.1%	8.5%
Album of the Year	2%	6.5%	8.2%	8.1%	4.4%	6.1%	13.3%	17.3%
Song of the Year	15.4%	31.2%	27.3%	33.3%	14.3%	12%	18.9%	44.4%
Best New Artist	16.7%	16.7%	50%	60%	33.3%	60%	58.3%	46.2%
Producer of the Year	0	0	0	0	0	0	20%	0

Source: Smith, S. L., Choueiti, M. & Pieper, K. (2018). *Inclusion in the recording studio? Gender and race/ethnicity of artists, songwriters & producers across 600 popular songs from 2012 to 2017.* Annenberg Inclusion Initiative.

Matters', comprising a number of initiatives to address gender imbalance within the Australian screen industry (see http://www.screenaustralia.gov.au/new-directions/gender-matters). The celebrated actors Emma Thompson and Helen Mirren have both publicly criticized the availability of acting roles for women and believe the situation isn't improving (Nesta, 2019, Plunkett, 2015). However, actor Meryl Streep believes that younger male executives working in Hollywood studios are more receptive to women's stories and engaging women film directors than their older counterparts (Vlessing, 2016), which creates the potential for change.

In a study of women working in the traditionally male domain of orchestra membership, it was found that while the momentum is towards gender equality, as the proportion of women increased, conflict within the orchestra also increased until a more balanced gender quorum was reached and organizational harmony was restored (Allmendinger & Hackman, 1995). At low levels of female participation (less than 10%), women just attempted to fit in, and the status quo was unaffected. In a transitory phase (between 10 and 40%) conflict was heightened. Above 40%, stability was achieved again as both gender groups felt fully legitimized. This shows that sometimes organizational pain and dysfunction are experienced before a gender balance is achieved, and stability returns.

PEOPLE OF COLOUR IN THE CREATIVE AND CULTURAL INDUSTRIES

When it comes to inclusionary practices, people of colour face their own set of challenges regarding inclusivity and equity. Attention to racial discrimination within the motion pictures industry flared at the 2016 Oscars when film director Spike Lee posted on Instagram, 'how is it possible for the 2nd consecutive year all 20 contenders under the actor category are white? And let's not even get into the other branches. 40 white actors in two years and no flava at all. We can't act?! WTF!!' (Child, 2016) This was widely acknowledged to have scarred the perceived integrity of the event, though it led to an increase in the representation of women and minorities in the voting pool (Cieply, 2016).

Some of the most prolific research currently being done in the creative industries is happening through the University of Southern California Annenberg Inclusion Initiative. Through comprehensive insight and analysis, they are able to provide context into some of the most under-researched areas affecting the creative and cultural industries. Their studies look into Asian Pacific Islanders in film (Yuen *et al.*, 2021), Hispanic/Latino representation in film (Case, Mercado, & Hernandez, 2021), race and ethnicity in film (USC Annenberg Inclusion Initiative, 2020), race and ethnicity in music (Smith *et al.*, 2021) and diversity portrayal on multiple digital and streaming platforms (Smith *et al.*, 2021; Smith, Choueiti & Pieper, 2016) and even ethnicity across the film critic population (Choueiti, Smith, & Pieper, 2018).

Given how comprehensive the institute's research is, the underlying data tells an alarming story. Of particular interest is the representation of people of colour in the executive suites (CEO/Chair/President) at some of the top music companies. Of the 70 major and independent companies studied, 86.1% of top executives were men and 86.1% were white. 10 non-white top executives ran independent companies and only 2 were women of colour. In total, just 3 top executives were Black (Smith *et al.*,

2021). In film *'there has been no meaningful increase in Black, Hispanic/Latino, or Asian characters in 2019 from 2018 or 2007',* despite Spike Lee's outcry in 2016. Furthermore, as Annenburg's study also points out, of the 112 directors across the movies released in 2019, 80.4% were White and only 19.6% (22) were from underrepresented racial/ethnic groups (Smith *et al.*, 2020) (Tables 11.3 and 11.4).

The numbers paint a picture worthy of ongoing discussion and action. How can future leaders and decision-makers of the creative industries, like those reading this text, do better when communicating the importance of equitable representation? The aim is not to be perfect but to make clear and steady progress in racial equality.

Table 11.3 Prevalence of character race/ethnicity on screen by year: 2007–2019

Year	*White*	*Black*	*Latino*	*Asian*	*Other*
2007	77.6%	13.0%	3.3%	3.4%	2.5%
2008	71.2%	13.2%	4.9%	7.1%	3.5%
2009	76.2%	14.7%	2.8%	4.7%	1.5%
2010	77.6%	10.3%	3.9%	5.0%	3.3%
2011	77.1%	9.1%	5.9%	4.1%	3.8%
2012	76.3%	10.8%	4.2%	5.0%	3.6%
2013	74.1%	14.1%	4.9%	4.4%	2.5%
2014	73.1%	12.5%	4.9%	5.3%	4.2%
2015	73.7%	12.2%	5.3%	3.9%	4.9%
2016	70.8%	13.5%	3.1%	5.6%	6.9%
2017	70.7%	12.1%	6.2%	4.8%	6.3%
2018	63.7%	16.9%	5.3%	8.2%	5.9%
2019	65.7%	15.7%	4.9%	7.2%	6.6%

Note: Characters coded as Middle Eastern/North African, American Indian/Alaskan Native, Native Hawaiian/Pacific Islander, and multiracial/multiethnic were included in the 'other' column. Percentages sum to 100% in each row, with deviation due to rounding.

Source: Smith, S. L., Choueiti, M. & Pieper, K. (2020). Inequality in 1,300 Popular Films: Examining Portrayals of Gender, Race/Ethnicity, LGBTQ & Disability from 2007 to 2019. USC Annenberg Inclusion Initiative. Available at https://assets.uscannenberg.org/docs/aii-inequality_1300_popular_films_09-08-2020.pdf.

Table 11.4 Artist underrepresented status by year

Measure	*2012*	*2013*	*2014*	*2015*	*2016*	*2017*	*2018*	*2019*	*2020*	*Total*
White	61.6% (n=122)	68.8% (n=148)	64% (n=144)	51.3% (n=100)	51.6% (n=99)	48.1% (n=103)	44.4% (n=96)	43.9% (n=75)	41% (n=71)	53.3% (n=958)
UR	38.4% (n=76)	31.2% (n=67)	36% (n=81)	48.7% (n=95)	48.4% (n=93)	51.9% (n=111)	55.6% (n=120)	56.1% (n=96)	59% (n=102)	46.7% (n=841)
Ratio	1.6 to 1	2.2 to 1	1.8 to 1	1.1 to 1	1.1 to 1	.93 to 1	.8 to 1	.78 to 1	.7 to 1	1.1 to 1

Source: Smith, S. L., Choueiti, M. & Pieper, K. (2018). Inclusion in the recording studio? Gender and race/ethnicity of artists, songwriters & producers across 600 popular songs from 2012-2017. Annenberg Inclusion Initiative.

LGBTQIA+

Gender identity is complex. Recently it's been attracting wider media commentary, but that doesn't necessarily translate to opportunities, support and understanding for non-binary people. Despite being one of the more progressive industry sectors, even the creative world has been slow in fostering a fully inclusive working environment (Table 11.5). As of this writing, women and gender-diverse artists and creative professionals continue to be the targets of harassment, bullying, abuse and misrepresentation (Conor, 2021). Holland (2020) recently studied lesbian representation in music videos. She found that the portrayals of lesbian women were found to be overwhelmingly white, thin, and highly feminized by traditional gender normed standards. This suggests that, while queer women may be represented in music videos, they are presented in ways that '*... exploit [their] sexuality...*' Despite this, however, some musicians are finding opportunity in a post-Covid environment to increase awareness and create a safer more authentically inclusive music scene for women, trans, and gender queer people (Howell, 2021).

Striving to become truly inclusive of queer and non-binary people begins by creating a positive working environment for everyone. Organizations must go beyond playing on the stereotypes, and as a creative community, we must be authentic and portray the actual lives and experiences of those within this identity group. One example of putting this type of change into action would be for those in the creative community that work in

Table 11.5 Prevalence of LGBTQ speaking characters across 600 top grossing films: 2014–2019

Measure	*2014*	*2015*	*2016*	*2017*	*2018*	*2019*	*Total*	*%*
Lesbian	4	7	9	9	17	10	5	<.3%
Gay	12	19	36	16	33	45	161	<1%
Bisexual	5	5	6	6	8	3	33	<.2%
Transgender	0	1	0	0	0	3	4	<.01%
Total	21	32	51	31	58	61	254	1%

Source: Smith, S. L., Choueiti, M. & Pieper, K. (2020). *Inequality in 1,300 Popular Films: Examining Portrayals of Gender, Race/Ethnicity, LGBTQ & Disability from 2007 to 2019.* USC Annenberg Inclusion Initiative. Available at http://assets.uscannenberg.org/docs/aii-inequality_1300_popular_films_09-08- 2020.pdf.

marketing, advertising or other cycle driven creative material, to be continuously showcasing inclusive content, and not simply running annual 'rainbow campaigns' (Fulleylove, R., 2020). In 2021, Meg Stalter, from the HBO Original Series *Hacks*, went viral with her 'Hi Gay' video about this very issue. Through comic parody, she highlighted corporations that take advantage of Pride month cynically for marketing purposes, when they don't attempt to interact with those communities in any meaningful way on a regular basis.

AFFIRMATIVE ACTION

'Affirmative action' is a temporary measure to socially engineer a better long-term outcome by forcing representatives of minority groups into professional positions, even if they may not be the best qualified applicants. The United Kingdom refers to a similar practice as 'positive discrimination', where favouring individuals belonging to groups known to have been discriminated against previously are hired into positions when equally qualified individuals are applying. For example, a company may decide that at least 20% of people on their corporate board should be women, setting a quota. This may result in allegations of 'reverse discrimination', where people who believe they were better qualified to do a job are passed over because they are not a woman or a member of a disadvantaged group. However, this approach provides a way of addressing deeper structural injustices in the workforce on a long-term basis.

BEST PRACTICES FOR IMPACTFUL DIVERSITY, EQUITY AND INCLUSION STRATEGIES

As we have seen, some sectors of the creative workforce do not reflect the diversity of society or the culture in which it operates. And too often, the leadership within these organizations is even less diverse (Wreyford *et al.*, 2021). Like any initiative worth pursuing, DEI practices take strong leadership and dedication to implement, and DEI initiatives almost always begin in the 'C-Suite', which as we learned is often the least diverse area in organizations.

Many of these initiatives, often designed by those with power and privilege, may counterproductively reinforce the structure to benefit the majority of those that are white, male or both (Ferry, 2020). Do those that are not marginalized and in power know what's best for those who are? *'At best, this top-down approach further decenters the voices of those who should be centered and at worst, it reinforces a patronizing cultural deficit approach that undermines the very crux of the work itself' (Ferry, 2020, p. 1).* Researchers and practitioners contend that companies that give more attention to DEI are able to improve employee engagement, creativity, innovation and profitability (Chamorro-Premuzic, 2017).

First and foremost, DEI should be an integral part of an organization's business strategy, not only an affirmative action policy or point of discussion to 'tick a box'. Furthermore, it should not simply be about hiring diverse employees. If an organization only sees DEI as an onboarding issue, it can lead to tokenism, or the perception that the effort is merely symbolic. Serran (2021) has identified some ways of placing DEI front and centre in organizational activities that include:

- Ensuring that there's diversity and representation across all employee levels;
- Keeping high level employees accountable – include DEI goals in performance reviews;
- Mitigating instances of implicit bias in workplace policies and processes - consider a neutral party to keep managers and leaders more accountable;
- Acknowledging and honouring different cultural and religious practices – such as holidays, dietary restrictions;
- Embracing the philosophy of 'culture add' instead of 'culture fit' – embrace employees from all demographics and backgrounds;
- Measuring DEI efforts and communicating goals –start collecting data; monitor and set clear targets to improve;
- Providing all-gender bathrooms;
- Providing a nursing lounge or appropriate space for working moms;
- Using gender neutral pronouns such as 'they' in official documents and policies.

Inclusive creative firms embrace a culture that makes ALL people feel as if they belong and have the opportunity to contribute to the success of the organization's strategy. Employee differences should be encouraged when providing ideas and perspectives which feed into agendas and initiatives. Whether it be a small firm or a large one like Universal Music Group, initiatives such as seminars, nursing rooms for mothers, sponsoring Pride events or seeking regular feedback from team members on ways to improve workplace inclusivity, can all go a long way towards achieving this aim. Other initiatives that have been embraced by organizations include extending maternity leave.

Lastly, organizations can move toward a more inclusive culture through the building and maintaining of networks. Encouraging internal and external networks for communities within your organization can provide a space to advocate for needs, access opportunities and undertake leadership development. These efforts can go a long way towards creating a more approachable mechanism for upward communication while making people feel they are an appreciated and contributing member of the team.

It's also important to keep in mind that people often respond to compulsory training with resistance while many participants report animosity toward those who are requiring it. However, voluntary training can evoke a more welcome response which can lead to more positive results and less resentment (Ferry, 2020). Providing multiple touch points and opportunities for ongoing training can help to ensure that when ready, people will be able to take advantage of those training opportunities.

Overall, it's important to create a culture that works for your organization whether it be a micro-enterprise with three employees or a larger corporation with over 500. Creating a purposeful strategy and developing an inclusive culture should involve asking your employees what THEY need. Gather feedback, informally and formally through conversations, surveys or workplace chatbots. Keep listening and learn how your company can support the people you value.

Earlier in the chapter we mentioned that the creative industries are the commercial representation of human essence and creativity, and if they fail to represent the full diversity of humanity, these industries will fail to reach their potential—creatively, ethically and commercially. But we never explained why this is important. The creative industries are fundamentally built on human creativity. This cluster of industries has found ways to make money from that creativity – a lot of it! But when we impose cultural, political, moral and ethical limitations on who may be invited to the conversation, we are limiting the potential for new ideas, improvements on existing products, or transformative innovations that may change an industry as we know it. When someone with a different lived experience is no longer marginalized but can be embraced in the working groups that make these things happen, new products and marketing abound. Embracing this diversity should be at the core of what the creative industries represent, for being 'creative' is to be unique and different while transforming the mundane into something new and entertaining.

With all this being said, let's keep in mind that there is growing evidence that we are on the path towards greater diversity, equity and inclusion in the creative industries workforce:

> …for the first time in more than a decade, film is on par with television with regard to the quantity of stories about girls and women. The percentage of leads/co leads from underrepresented racial/ethnic groups also increased slightly in 2019. Moreover, 16 underrepresented female leads/co leads worked across the top 100 films last year. The continued progress toward greater inclusion is important to celebrate, even as we urge ongoing change—particularly for women age 45 and over, and for individuals (especially women) from racial/ ethnic groups who are routinely erased in popular film.
>
> (Smith *et al.*, 2020, p. 3)

CONCLUSION

Whether you are a large commercial corporation, a not-for-profit arts organization, a small production firm or a freelance musician, it should be apparent that Diversity, Equity and Inclusion strategies should be an important aspect of your organization's business strategy and culture. What you expect from those with whom you work, what you embrace and what you ignore, will have an influence on DEI, whether you are on your own or a contributor to a corporation. There is a lot of work to do when it comes to reaching parity for those from underrepresented populations, but that shouldn't undermine the importance of this aspiration of fully realizing the potential of the creative economy in terms of its creativity, the utilization of its workforce, and the enjoyment of its audiences.

Discussion questions and class exercises

1. Define DEI and each of its components.
2. What are the benefits and challenges of implementing 'positive discrimination' and 'affirmative action' in the workplace?
3. Describe how one marginalized group has been impacted in the creative industries.
4. What are some ways we can improve diversity, equity and inclusion in the creative industries?
5. What are some of the barriers limiting the progress to achieving an inclusive organization?

What major award ceremonies are accomplishing in the climate of under-representation in the entertainment industry

Written by: Nadine Waran-Perrero

Industry award shows play a pivotal role in recognizing the accomplishments of its members, by and for each other, whether it be the annual Grammy Awards, the ARIA Music Awards in Australia, the Golden Globes, the Oscars out of Hollywood or the Filmfare Awards in India. The symbolic significance of these ceremonies reinforces reputations and promotes the artistic quality and technical excellence of these industries. Not only do they help to signify the 'who's who' or the 'best of', but they also provide a glimpse into the values of the establishment hosting them. Despite the glamour of these ceremonies, the trade groups hosting

Figure 11.3 Award shows demonstrate that change is possible as they begin to address DEI issues. Photo credit: Vitaliy Hrabar / Shutterstock.com.

them certainly haven't been immune to the challenges of fairly representing the works of its best and most prominent creators. The evidence is increasing that these trade groups and the creators they represent have been listening to calls to do better and are moving in the right direction.

Grammy Awards

The Grammys haven't been without controversy over the years, and some have put into question the decision-making behind the determination of award categories and even going as far as to allege racism (Fitzgerald, 2022) and sexism ('The Grammys finally faces up to its diversity problem', 2019). The infamous comment in 2018 by then Recording Academy President Neil Portnoy, in response to criticism about the lack of female representation, demonstrated a clear challenge in the organization's thinking:

> *I think it has to begin with women who have the creativity in their hearts and their souls who want to be musicians, who want to be engineers, who want to be producers, who want to be part of the industry on an executive level, to step up.*

As we've discussed throughout this chapter, effective DEI practices start with strong leadership and sound business strategy. With changes in recent years and since this comment, it has become apparent that the Recording Academy is indeed doing better. A change in leadership and responding to the public and industry criticism that surrounded their DEI practices, the Academy has since made strides to improving best practices.

For example, in 2021 the Recording Academy became the first major award show to issue an inclusion rider addendum to support diversity recruitment for the 2022 Grammy Awards. Part of the clause stated that more underrepresented communities such as '*Black, Indigenous, Asian American & Pacific Islander, and other Non-Black people of colour, those of Hispanic or Latino/a/x descent, women of all backgrounds and identities, people with disabilities, people over the age of 40, people from certain religious minorities, and Lesbian, Gay, Bisexual, Transgender, or Queer ("LGBTQ+") people*' – will play a role in supporting the broadcasting; be they on or off the stage (Nazareno, 2021). They have also done a better job of balancing the make-up of committee members, where gender, age and people of colour (now 48%) are better balanced. They have also started partnering with women's organizations like Women in the Mix. And in response to criticisms about not appreciating Black artistry, the Academy has taken a close look at who is creating music and making sure it is being represented accordingly. To help in these efforts they started the Black Music Collective and have partnered with Colour of Change (Carlos, 2021).

Academy Awards

By the same token, the Oscars, organized by the Academy of Motion Picture Arts and Sciences, has committed to improvements in DEI practices. Despite recent efforts to improve equitable opportunities, the 94th Oscars ceremony saw women nominees represented in only 27% of the overall non-acting categories (Statista, 2022). This was the lowest rate in the past three years (Buchholz, 2022) and alarmingly so since the Academy announced new representation and inclusion standards for films – especially the highly coveted 'Best Picture' category. Although meeting these criteria are not required until the 96th Oscars in year 2024, the Academy Inclusion Standards is still required for all subsequent award ceremonies, which is an efficient way for the Oscars to prepare the industry in upholding its commitment on the topic of DEI, moving forward (Academy Establishes Representation and Inclusion Standards for Oscars ® Eligibility, 2020).

Golden Globes

Another champion of the arts that is enacting change to outdated practices in the case of representation is the Golden Globes. As a part of the Awards, the Hollywood Foreign Press Association (HFPA) is reinforcing the subject of diversity, equity, and inclusion by building partnerships with diverse leaders such as the Leadership Lab International (LLI) to actively challenge the future of diversity in the industry. Within three weeks of pledging a reformation to their diversity standards, this major award organization began putting in the work on internal reformation through DEI development initiatives, training for employees, and hiring advisors that are well educated in the field (HFPA, 2021).

There are grounds for hope that the next generation will build on these endeavours to further increase diversity within the creative industries.

Questions for discussion

1 Do you believe the steps being made by the Recording Academy, the Academy of Motion Picture Arts and Sciences and the Hollywood Foreign Press Association

to improve the recognition of underrepresented populations is adequate? Why or why not?

2 Knowing that progress is being made by some of the world's most recognized award shows, where do you feel more work needs to be done to more accurately reflect the work of its membership equitably?

Case references

Academy Establishes Representation and Inclusion Standards for Oscars ® Eligibility, (2021). Oscars.org. [Online]. Available at https://www.oscars.org/news/academy-establishes-representation-and-inclusion-standards-oscarsr-eligibility *(accessed 24 June, 2022).*

Buchholz, K. (2022). 'Where Women Lack Representation at the Oscars', *Statista.com*, [Online]. Available at https://www.statista.com/chart/27121/female-representation-oscars-non-acting-categories/ (accessed 24 June, 2022).

Carlos, I. (2021). How a music industry veteran is shaping DEI efforts for the Grammys. [online] *Bizjournals.com*. Available at https://www.bizjournals.com/bizjournals/news/2021/08/06/recording-academy-ceo-harvey-mason-jr-on-dei.html (accessed 1 July, 2022).

Fitzgerald, A. (2022). The Racist History of the Grammy Awards - BANG. [online] *BANG*. Available at https://bcgavel.com/2022/02/21/the-racist-history-of-the-grammy-awards/ (accessed 1 July, 2022).

Nazareno, M. (2021). 'Grammys 2022 to Be First Major Awards Show to Use Inclusion Rider', *Billboard.com*, [Online]. Available at https://www.billboard.com/music/awards/2022-grammys-inclusion-rider-9647024/ (accessed 24 June, 2022).

Stoll, J. (2022). 'Number of Academy Awards TV viewers 2000–2022', *Statista.com*, [Online]. Available at https://www.statista.com/statistics/253743/academy-awards--number-of-viewers/ (accessed 24 June, 2022).

The Future HFPA (2021). Golden Globe Awards, [Online]. Available at: https://www.goldenglobes.com/articles/hfpa-hires-dei-advisors (accessed 24 June, 2022).

'The Grammys finally faces up to its diversity problem', (2019). *Independent* [London, England], 12 Feb, 50, available at https://link.gale.com/apps/doc/A573658133/ITOF?u=tel_a_belmont&sid=bookmark-ITOF&xid=aa53bf99 (accessed 1 July, 2022).

Jennifer Duck is an Emmy award-winning producer and Assistant Professor in the Department of Cinema, Television, and Media at Belmont University. Prior to her work in academia, Jen was a producer with Anderson Cooper, Katie Couric, Oprah Winfrey Network (OWN) and ABC News.

Sara Wigal is an Assistant Professor and Chair of the Media Studies Department at Belmont University. She previously worked in literary public relations before entering academia. She is the Editor of Belmont Story Review and publishes in both literary and commercial publications, directs programming at WriterFest Nashville, and volunteers in a variety of literary-related organizations including the Nashville Public Library Foundation.

References

Allmendinger, J. & Hackman, J. R. (1995). 'The more, the better? A four nation study of the inclusion of women in symphony orchestras', *Social Forces*, Vol. 74, no. 2, pp. 423–460.

Boatright, J. R., Smith, J. D. & Patra, B. P. (2018). *Ethics and the Conduct of Business*, 8th Edition. Chennai, India: Pearson India Education Services Pvt. Ltd.

Brook, O., O'Brien, D. & Taylor, M. (2021). 'Inequality talk: How discourses by senior men reinforce exclusions from creative occupations', *European Journal of Cultural Studies*, Vol. 24, no. 2, pp. 498–513.

Broyles, S. J. & Grow, J. M. (2008). 'Creative women in advertising agencies: Why so few "babes in boyland"?', *Journal of Consumer Marketing*, Vol. 25, no. 1, pp. 4–6.

Case, A., Mercado, Z. & Hernandez, K. (2021). *Hispanic and Latino Representation in Film: Erasure on Screen & Behind the Camera Across 1,300 Popular Movies*, USC Annenberg Inclusion Initiative. Available at https://assets.uscannenberg.org/docs/aii-hispanic-latino-rep-2021-09-13.pdf (accessed 29 June 2022).

Chamorro-Premuzic, T. (2017). 'Does diversity actually increase creativity?' [online] *Harvard Business Review*. Available at https://hbr.org/2017/06/does-diversity-actually-increase-creativity (accessed 29 June 2022).

Child, B. (2016). 'Spike Lee to boycott the 2016 Oscars over lack of nominee diversity', *The Guardian*, January 18, 2016. Available at http://www.theguardian.com/film/2016/jan/18/spike-lee-boycott-2016-oscars-nominations-academy-awards-lack-of-diversity (accessed 6 March 2016).

Choueiti, M., Smith, S. L. & Pieper, K. (2018). *Gender and Race/Ethnicity of Film Reviewers Across 300 Top Films from 2015–2017*. USC Annenberg Inclusion Initiative. Available at https://assets.uscannenberg.org/docs/critics-choice-2.pdf (accessed 29 June 2022).

Cieply, M. (2016). 'Film Academy broadens voting pool after Oscars criticism', *The New York Times*, June 29, 2016. Available at http://www.nytimes.com/2016/06/30/business/media/film-academy-broadens-voting-pool-after-oscars-criticism.html?_r=0 (accessed 12 October 2016).

Conor, B. (2021). *Gender & creativity: Progress on the precipice*. UNESCO Publishing.

Dayan, M., Ozer, M. & Almazrouei, H. (2017). 'The role of functional and demographic diversity on new product creativity and the moderating impact of project uncertainty', *Industrial Marketing Management*, Vol. 61, pp. 144–154.

Ferry, S. (2020). *Decolonizing Diversity, Equity, and Inclusion Work: Centering Equity Through Equity-Centered Design*. [online] The Inclusion Solution. Available at http://www.theinclusionsolution.me/decolonizing-diversity-equity-and-inclusion-work-centering-equity-through-equity-centered-design/ (accessed 29 June 2022).

Frost, S. & Alidina, R. K. (2019). *Building an Inclusive Organization: Leveraging the Power of a Diverse Workforce*. London: Kogan Page Limited.

Fulleylove, R. (2020). *How to be an ally to your non-binary colleagues*. [online] www.creativereview.co.uk. Available at https://www.creativereview.co.uk/supporting-non-binary-colleagues-advice/ (accessed 27 March 2022).

Harvey, S. (2013). 'A different perspective: the multiple effects of deep level diversity on group creativity', *Journal of Experimental Social Psychology*, Vol. 49, no. 5, pp. 822–832. Available at https://doi.org/10.1016/j.jesp.2013.04.004 (accessed 27 March 2022).

Hendicott, J. (2015). 'Lady Gaga on the music industry: "It's a fucking boy's club"', *NME* magazine online, December 12, 2015. Available at http://www.nme.com/news/lady-gaga/90304 (accessed 7 March 2016).

Higdon, J., Topaz, C., Siau, E., Kerkhoff, H., Young, E., Mendiratta, S. & Smith, G. (2022). *Life Unseen Study: Diversity in the Creative Industries*. [online] Williamstown: Institute for the Quantitative Study of Inclusion, Diversity, and Equity (QSIDE Institute), pp. 1–38. Available at https://lifeunseen.lifewtr.com/docs/default-source/lifeunseen/lifeunseen-study-diversity-in-the-creative-industries-210409.pdf?sfvrsn=c3fcc242_2 (accessed 5 July 2022).

Holland, S. A. (2020). *Examining Diversity in YouTube Music Videos with Queer Women Couples from 2006–2019* (Doctoral dissertation, Syracuse University).

Howell, C. (2021). 'Creating the conditions to create: an anti-oppressive lens on the post-pandemic music scene', *Critical Studies in Improvisation/Études critiques en improvisation*, Vol. 14, no. 1, pp. 1–4.

LGBTQIA Resource Center (2022). *LGBTQIA Resource Center Glossary*. [online] Available at https://lgbtqia.ucdavis.edu/educated/glossary (accessed 8 July 2022).

McCormack, A. (2016). *Girls to the front – by the numbers: Women in the music industry*, Australian Broadcasting Corporation, March 8, 2016. Available at http://www.abc.net.au/triplej/programs/hack/girls-to-the-front/7223798 (accessed 29 May 2016).

McCormack, A. (2019). *By the numbers 2019: The gender gap in Australian music revealed.* [online] triple j. Available at https://www.abc.net.au/triplej/programs/hack/by-the-numbers-2019-the-gender-gap-in-australian-music revealed/10879066#:~:text=Men%20continue%20to%20hold%20the, per%20cent%20the%20previous%20year) (accessed 3 July 2022).

McGregor, J. (2016). 'Saatchi executive says gender issue 'is over': Days later his career is', *The Washington Post*, August 3, 2016. Available at https://www.washingtonpost.com/news/on-leadership/wp/2016/08/03/with-a (accessed 12 October 2016).

McLaughlin, A. (2020). 'Why it's time to decolonize the creative industries', [online] *Creative Review.* Available at https://www.creativereview.co.uk/decolonise-creative-industries/ (accessed 7 July 2022).

Merriam-Webster, Incorporated (2022). [online] Available at https://www.merriam-webster.com/dictionary/equity (accessed 10 July 2022).

Nesta, C. (2019). *Big data analysis reveals staggering extent of gender inequality in creative industries.* [online] Theconversation.com. Available at https://theconversation.com/amp/big-data-analysis-reveals-staggering-extent-of-gender-inequality-in-creative-industries-121482 (accessed 4 July 2022).

Noriega, V. (2020). *The Lack of Asian American Representation in American Pop Music.* Available at: https://digitalcommons.pace.edu/cgi/viewcontent.cgi?article=1313&context=honorscollege_theses (accessed 4 July 2022).

Plunkett, J. (2015). 'Emma Thompson: sexism in acting industry is worse than ever', *The Guardian*, 21 July. Available at http://www.theguardian.com/film/2015/jul/21/emma-thompson-sexism-in-acting-industry-is-worse-than-ever (accessed 6 March 2016).

Pumphrey, A. & Williams, E. (2019). *Inclusivity and Diversity: Inviting More People To Your Table.* [podcast] Strategy Hour. Available at https://bossproject.com/podcast/draft-inclusivity-and-diversity-inviting-more-people-to-your-table (accessed 29 June 2022).

Race Matters Institute (2014). *Racial Equality or Racial Equity? The Difference it Makes.* Available at https://viablefuturescenter.org/racemattersinstitute/2014/04/02/racial-equality-or-racial-equity-the-difference-it-makes/ (accessed June 29 2022).

Race Matters Institute (2022). 'Advancing racial equity', *ABOUT US – Advancing Racial Equity* [online] Available at https://viablefuturescenter.org/racemattersinstitute/about-us-2/ (accessed 29 June 2022).

Reed, S. (2019). 'Corporate boards are diversifying. The C-suite isn't: How companies use women and minorities as window dressing' [online] *The Washington Post.* Available at https://www.washingtonpost.com/

outlook/corporate-boards-are-diversifying-the-c-suite-isnt/2019/01/04/c45c3328-0f02-11e9-8938-5898adc28fa2_story.html (accessed 29 June 2022).

Rees, W. (2020). *'I Will Not Be Conquered': Popular Music and Indigenous Identities in North America*. Master's Thesis, University of Exeter. Available at https://ore.exeter.ac.uk/repository/bitstream/handle/10871/40948/ReesW.pdf?sequence=2&isAllowed=y (accessed 16 July 2022).

Richardson, E. (2016). *The Countess Report*. Available at http://www.thecountessreport.com.au/ (accessed 29 May 2016).

Rodney, P. E. (2021). 'Prison and the law in modern American and British popular music', *International Journal for the Semiotics of Law-Revue internationale de Sémiotique juridique*, Vol. 34, no. 1, pp. 211–223.

Serrano, P. (2021). *7 Strategies to Improve Diversity and Inclusion in the Workplace*. Accessible at https://www.hcamag.com/us/news/general/7-strategies-to-improve-diversity-and-inclusion-in-the-workplace/256545 (accessed 27 March 2022).

Smith, S. L., Choueiti, M. & Pieper, K. (2016). *Inclusion or Invisibility? Comprehensive Annenberg Report on Diversity (CARD)*, USC Annenberg Inclusion Initiative. Available at https://annenberg.usc.edu/sites/default/files/2017/04/07/MDSCI_CARD_Report_FINAL_Exec_Summary.pdf (accessed 27 March 2022).

Smith, S. L., Choueiti, M. & Pieper, K. (2020). *Inequality in 1,300 Popular Films: Examining Portrayals of Gender, Race/Ethnicity, LGBTQ & Disability from 2007 to 2019*, USC Annenberg Inclusion Initiative. Available at http://assets.uscannenberg.org/docs/aii-inequality_1300_popular_films_09-08-2020.pdf (accessed 27 March 2022).

Smith, S. L., Choueiti, M. & Pieper, K. (2021). *Inclusion in the recording studio? Gender and race/ethnicity of artists, songwriters & producers across 600 popular songs from 2012–2017*. Annenberg Inclusion Initiative. Available at https://assets.uscannenberg.org/docs/aii-Zinclusion-recording-studio2021.pdf (accessed 27 March 2022).

Smith S.L., Lee, C., Choueiti, M., Pieper, K., Moore, Z., Dinh, D. & Tofan, A., (2021). *Inclusion in the Music Business: Gender & Race/Ethnicity Across Executives, Artists & Talent Teams*. USC Annenberg Inclusion Initiative. Available at https://assets.uscannenberg.org/docs/aii-inclusion-music-industry-2021-06-14.pdf (accessed 27 March 2022).

Smith S.L., Pieper, K., Choueiti, M., Yao, K., Case, A., Hernandez, K. & Moore, Z. (2021). *Inclusion in Netflix Series & Film*. USC Annenberg Inclusion Initiative. Available at https://assets.uscannenberg.org/docs/aii-inclusion-netflix-executive-summary.pdf (accessed 27 March 2022).

Stover, C. (2013). 'Damsels and Heroines: The Conundrum of the Post-Feminist Disney Princess', *LUX: A Journal of Transdisciplinary Writing and Research from Claremont Graduate University*. Vol. 2, no. 1, Article 29. Available at: https://scholarship.claremont.edu/lux/vol2/iss1/29 (accessed 27 March 2022).

Strong, C. & Cannizzo, F. (2017). Australian Women Screen Composers: Career Barriers and Pathways, RMIT, Melbourne. Available at https://assets.apraamcos.com.au/images/PDFs/About/2017_Australian_Women_Screen_Composers-Career_Barriers_and_Pathways.pdf (accessed 27 March 2022).

Vlessing, E. (2016). 'Meryl Streep on director gender gap: 'We need 40- to 50-year old white males to be interested', *Hollywood Reporter*, 14 February. Available at http://www.hollywoodreporter.com/news/berlin-meryl-streep-director-gender-865121 (accessed 6 March 2016).

USC Annenberg Inclusion Initiative (2020). *Inequality in 1,300 Popular Films: Examining Portrayals of Gender, Race/Ethnicity, LGBTQ & Disability from 2007 to 2019*. USC Annenberg Inclusion Initiative. Available at https://assets.uscannenberg.org/docs/aii-inequality_1300_popular_films_09-08-2020.pdf (accessed 27 March 2022).

Watson, J. (2020). Opinion | Country music has a women problem. And we have the data to prove it. *NBC News*. Available at https://www.nbcnews.com/think/opinion/country-music-radio-has-ignored-female-artists-years-we-have-ncna1137571 (accessed 22 July 2022).

Wreyford, N., O'Brien, D. & Dent, T. (2021). *Creative Majority*: An APPG for Creative Diversity report on 'What Works' to support, encourage and improve diversity, equity and inclusion in the creative sector. A report for the All Party Parliamentary Group for Creative Diversity. Accessed here: http://www.kcl.ac.uk/cultural/projects/creative-majority (accessed 27 March 2022).

Yuen, N. W., Smith S. L., Pieper, K., Choueiti, M., Yao, K. & Dinh, D. (2021). *The Prevalence and Portrayal of Asian and Pacific Islanders across 1,300 Popular Films*. USC Annenberg Inclusion Initiative. Available at https://assets.uscannenberg.org/docs/aii_aapi-representation-across-films-2021-05-18.pdf (accessed 27 March 2022).

Structure of creative organizations

Chapter 12

A CONTEMPORARY CONTROVERSY: TAKING CHAINSAWS TO ORGANIZATIONS

Employees can be expensive. Sometimes managers seeking to lower costs or improve the financial position of their companies take a proverbial chainsaw to their company's structure, chopping off pieces of it and sacking large numbers of employees in the process (e.g. Twitter). Layers of management can be eliminated, divisions closed, services outsourced or automated and operations moved offshore. The digital transformation of industries such as music, movies and newspapers has seen an enormous number of employees lose their jobs at major organizations. Much thought is placed in organizational structuring on reducing 'overheads' and fixed costs, which are seen as inflexible burdens on the organization, and which can be under-utilized when demand falls or skills need to be

Figure 12.1 Organizations are complex: take care when restructuring with chainsaws. Photo credit: Anterovium / Shutterstock.com.

DOI: 10.4324/9781003262923-12

updated. This industry turbulence was discussed in Chapter 2 on organizational change. Sometimes such downsizing actions are vital to bring costs into alignment with falling revenues, which if left unaddressed would result in bankruptcy. Sometimes organizations decide that instead of doing everything in-house, they need to identify an area of expertise to focus on, and then outsource the rest to organizations that can perform those functions better or more cheaply. At other times enormous damage has been done to complex organizations through brutal, naïve vandalism. A (humorous) phenomenon has been identified called *anorexia industrialosa.* This affliction affects industry rather than individuals and is 'an excessive desire to be leaner and fitter, leading to emaciation and, eventually, death' (McDonald & Wilson, 2002, p. 26). Constant restructuring is more likely to plague publicly listed companies (i.e. large entertainment organizations traded on the stock market) than privately owned or non-profit organizations. This is because for companies traded on the stock market, short-term profitability is highly scrutinized and drives both the valuation of the company and the bonuses and survival of senior executives. When a company announces disappointing profits, the market expects costs will be lowered or sales increased to restore profitability. One quick way organizations can choose to lower costs and/or send a signal that they are seeking to lower costs is to announce a programme of organizational re-structuring. The problem is that organizations may become too focused on the short-term and do damage to the organization in the long-term. An upside for employment is that even when jobs are outsourced, the jobs often aren't destroyed; they are just taken over by outside contractors, which the company (and others) employ on an as-needed basis. One negative social consequence of outsourcing though is that outsourced employees can see an erosion of their employment rights and entitlements, versus being employed 'in house'.

In this chapter we will first look at key concepts used in organizational structure that can help us determine the optimal structure for a given organization. Next, we will look at examples of structures and the way we depict them in organizational charts (or diagrams, sometimes called 'organograms' by academics – see Figure 12.2). We will then look at where

CHAPTER LEARNING OBJECTIVES

At the conclusion of this chapter you will be able to:

- Identify, define and explain structural concepts, such as chain of command, span of control, centralization, decentralization, formalization, organic structures and mechanistic structures;
- Describe, draw models of and apply generic organizational structures such as the simple structure, departmentalized functional structures, matrix structures and bureaucracy;
- Describe trends in the structuring of creative organizations to more efficiently manage processes and better support creative work;
- Explain concepts which have the potential to influence structure such as 'co-creation', 'agile project management', 'lean start-up', and 'design thinking'.

Figure 12.2 Organizational charts (or 'organograms') depict graphically the structural relationship between individuals or departments. Photo credit: winui / Shutterstock.com.

structure is heading in the creative industries and how we can use structure to support creative work.

KEY CONCEPTS IN ORGANIZATIONAL STRUCTURE

Imagine that you've walked into a large organization that has no structure at all. You would have lots of people all staring at one another, with no consensus as to who should focus on what, how information should flow or how collaboration will work. When we talk about organizational 'structure', we mean the way people organize themselves into working groups, divide their responsibilities, and coordinate and interact with one another. How do we arrive at the optimal structure for an organization? We can use the following eight considerations to break down and answer this question:

- objectives and strategy
- specialization
- departmentalization
- chain of command
- span of control
- centralization and decentralization
- formalization
- organic and mechanistic structures

Let's discuss each in turn.

Objectives and strategy

Structure is only a means to an end. We create a structure to support achieving something. We first need to set the objectives that we wish to achieve. We then decide on a strategy we hope will achieve the objective, and then we choose a structure that best supports the strategy. For example, if a US-based organization sees an immediate commercial opportunity in Italy and Germany and the strategy requires them to have a presence in both countries, they may need to establish offices in the two countries, and hire and allocate responsibilities to personnel in those offices. So strategy (exploiting international opportunities) translates into structure (opening two European offices who report to the US office).

Specialization

Manufacturing processes have historically relied on giving staff very precise, specialized jobs, which when combined in an assembly process create highly sophisticated products such as cars and aeroplanes. Henry Ford's name is often associated with this quest because he pioneered the mass production of cars. Specialization can provide efficiency because workers become highly proficient in the specific task they are required to perform. The process ensures each worker's contribution can be far less complex than the overall project being attempted. The key question here is, to what degree might it be better to take a 'job', break it down into components and employ specialists to handle each component? For example, we could ask certain marketing staff to coordinate a variety of activities such as social media, public relations, photography, graphic design, video production, publishing, and data analysis. This gives variety to their work, but they will not be expert in every aspect. Small organizations with limited resources may require staff to stretch themselves across all these activities. But if the size of the company, the volume of work and the available resources make it possible, the company could employ specialists who possess expertise in certain areas. So the photographer and photographic commissioner would be specialists, and the person undertaking data analysis would be a specialist data analyst. This reduces work variety for those employed on these tasks, but increases specialization and potentially the quality of the output. When we break down roles into smaller and smaller components, we need to ensure that the scope of each job still possesses some variety; otherwise employees can become bored or fatigued. Specialization can also cause loss of creativity, where imaginative connections and overall solutions become less easy to make (Martins & Terblanche, 2003). Where we have lots of specialized employees, we also then need to bring them together to create one harmonious, integrated team. This can be difficult due to the subcultural differences between functions that we explored in the chapter on conflict (Chapter 5).

Departmentalization

Once we have defined the specialist contributions we need (i.e. webmaster, videographer, accountant), we then need to examine whether people should be grouped together in a department to help them work together as a team. A large arts venue may establish a number of departments that specialize in various aspects of the business such as artistic planning and artist liaison, operations, building and facilities maintenance, marketing and visitor services, box office and ticketing services, fundraising, finance, IT and legal. A company could also organize itself by product, service or brand. We can organize by geography, so that we create branches in a number of different countries. We can organize by process, so that in the process of making a fashion garment, for example, we design in Paris, manufacture in Asia, and market and sell internationally. We can also create departments structured around target audiences, so that we could conceivably create a department that makes products for 'aficionado' (expert) purchasers and another for consumers new to the product category who need more assistance (e.g. for classical music, wine or cigars). We could create a department focused on a target audience of business-to-business users (e.g. 'synchronization' departments in music companies, which license music for use in ads and films to businesses such as advertising agencies and TV production companies). We could create a department that focuses on a specialist demographic, such as female purchasers. The way we structure a company is simply at the service of the broader objectives that the organization is trying to pursue.

Chain of command

In a military context, an army General issues a command, which must then find its way to the soldier in the field who executes it. For this to work, there needs to be clear agreement as to who reports to whom and the lines of responsibility down which authority flows. This is called the 'chain of command'. Certain managerial positions carry certain levels of authority. We understand that the president of a company will possess more authority than a vice president, who will possess more authority than a manager, who will possess more authority than an intern. If CEOs have an issue with the work of the marketing department, following the chain of command principle, they would take their concern to the marketing vice president responsible for the team, who would then flow the advice down to the team. Otherwise marketing vice presidents may feel insufficiently consulted in the running of their own departments (it's likely that they would feel that if they are to be held responsible for the outcomes of a department, they should have a say in the way their department is run). The 'unity of command' principle is the rule that each person should only have one supervisor to whom they directly report. If this principle is broken, managers may receive different directives from different people resulting in confusion and conflict.

Span of control

'Span of control' is the number of people a manager can directly supervise. For a single manager, six people directly reporting to him or her may be the optimal number. If the manager tries to manage ten people, he or she may have insufficient time, leading to undesirable outcomes such as poorer employee performance. If the manager has three direct reports, he or she may be under-utilized, or start to micro-manage employees in a way that annoys them and is counter-productive. The larger the span of control, the less supervision is being provided; this means that fewer levels may be needed in the organizational hierarchy (because fewer supervisors are required), and the total overhead costs will be lower. This is depicted in Table 12.1.

In Organization A, the span of control is four, and for Organization B it is eight. The advantages for Organization A are that the supervision will be closer, as the manager has more time

Table 12.1 Savings from higher spans of control

Organizational level	*Organization A* *Employees at each level* *(based on span of control of 4)*	*Organization B* *Employees at each level* *(based on span of control of 8)*
1 (highest)	1 (CEO)	1 (CEO)
2	4	8
3	16	64
4 (lowest)	64	
Total employees	**85**	**73**

for each direct report. This may increase support and reduce stress. However, Organization B has a number of advantages, which explains the popularity of wider spans of control. First, it is cheaper, employing 12 fewer people (73 versus 85). If each employee costs the organization $100,000 on average in terms of salary, expenses and other costs, this would result in an annual saving of $1.2 million. These savings significantly multiply the more additional levels an organization requires due to its size. Second, Organization B has only three levels rather than four, which makes it easier for information to flow to senior managers. Third, the looser supervision in Organization B provides greater autonomy for employees, and employees in creative industries value autonomy. The financial benefits of larger spans of control have led to calls for 'flatter' organizations. Organization B is a flatter organization than Organization A. Researchers have seen evidence that flat structures are more conducive to organizational creativity (Martins & Terblanche, 2003).

As was discussed in the chapter on leadership, large groups of people can be managed if you are working with experienced specialists who expect some degree of autonomy. This is because they need less supervision time due to their experience. Conversely, inexperienced staff require more attention, meaning the optimal span of control will be reduced.

Centralization and decentralization

Highly centralized organizations concentrate decision-making in the hands of a small number of people at the centre of the organization (for example, 'head office'). In decentralized organizations, decisions are made at lower levels in the organizational hierarchy, by people who are often closer to the 'action' and closer to the end consumers. Organizations that want to ensure quality control and consistency across the entire operation will usually centralize decision-making. Decentralization allows organizations to respond more quickly to local opportunities and better motivates managers at lower levels in the organization. Researchers have found evidence that decentralization is generally more conducive to creativity than centralization (Martins & Terblanche, 2003).

For example, large record companies were traditionally highly decentralized, allowing managers for specific countries a considerable degree of autonomy and decision-making control. This enabled them to identify local artists (e.g. artists in places like Italy, not just in London and New York) and appeal to the needs of local audiences. Because of the tight relationship between the entertainment and media industries and the short response times needed to make the most of media opportunities, decentralized companies were better equipped to capitalize on these opportunities. Each country was a 'profit centre', meaning it had its own autonomous budget and was expected to make money and operate independently. There was centralized financial control and accountability, and the company's head office still insisted on support for international priority projects.

However, in recent years the internet has undermined these partitioned, divided geographic markets, opening up the whole world for everyone. In the globalized music market, where you are on the planet matters little. This worldwide instant availability is driving greater centralized coordination of release schedules and international marketing campaigns. Major artists want to sign to companies who can help them achieve international success, not just local success in one region. The International Meeting case study at the conclusion of this chapter explores the tensions between centralization and decentralization.

Formalization

Formalization refers to how tightly defined and standardized jobs are within the organization. Highly formalized jobs have detailed job descriptions, standard operating policies and procedures, and allow little room for individual discretion. Creative and cultural organizations for the most part have less formalization, and create space for autonomy and discretion. In fact, centralization and formalization have been seen to lead to destructive conflict in creative organizations such as advertising agencies (De Gregorio *et al.*, 2012). When we develop creative and cultural products, we want them to be exceptional and unique, not standardized and predictable. However, while the creative process may need high levels of flexibility and discretion to arrive at creative solutions (Amabile, 1998), and while formalization may work against creativity (Martins &

Terblanche, 2003), at the end of this process the project may need to be plugged into a larger marketing and distribution machine which follows more formalized rules and procedures. This is discussed further in the next section, in relation to organic and mechanistic structures.

Organic and mechanistic structures

There is a clear contrast between 'mechanistic' structures, which are highly formalized, structured, hierarchical and transmit information vertically, and 'organic' structures, which are more fluid, less formalized, and have a more horizontal communication flow (Burns & Stalker, 1961). Organic structures have been found to be more conducive to cultivating organizational creativity (McLean, 2005). It should be acknowledged that in large organizations there is room for both mechanistic and organic structures as different activities require different approaches. For example, book publication has a commissioning process that must be flexible and responsive to the needs of authors and projects. It will need to be organic. But once there is a commitment to deliver a book by a certain date, the process will become more machine-like and mechanistic because a large volume of book titles need to be printed and distributed in a reliable, predictable way. The difference between a record 'label' and a record 'company' is that the label is the organic, creative hub that works with creative talent in a responsive way. We may find at some point in the creative process that the project has naturally grown in ways that could not have been anticipated at the start, which needs different skills and staffing to support the project. However, the broader company possesses mechanistic processes that are still vital for the company, such as payroll, royalty accounting and tax accounting. A mechanistic structure is best suited to a stable, predictable environment, and an organic structure is best suited to an unstable, unpredictable environment.

FUNDAMENTAL ORGANIZATIONAL STRUCTURES

Now that we have developed a vocabulary of the concepts that we can employ to arrive at the best structure for a given organization, we will look at four archetypal organizational structures which can be adapted for real organizations: the simple structure, the departmentalized structure, matrix structures and bureaucracy.

The simple structure

If you establish your own business, the chances are that you would employ a simple structure, designed for sole proprietorship. You may decide that you need web and social media support, to continuously update online content. You may need accounting support to keep control of your finances and manage invoicing, receipting and taxation. You may also need some general administrative support. The structure that this creates is depicted in Figure 12.3. Structural charts such as this depict each position and map the reporting relationships, so the three positions depicted in the lower boxes report to the owner/CEO in the higher box. Simple structures are 'flat' structures, because they don't have multiple levels of managers. They also have low levels of formalization and centralize key decision-making in one person. In terms of 'span of control' in this example the CEO's is three.

Many small arts organizations or start-up digital companies commence as simple structures. As they grow they may experience problems because the volume of work and decisions start to overwhelm the leader. At a certain point the organization needs to move to a more departmentalized structure.

A functional, departmentalized structure

In this organizational chart (Figure 12.4), the number of jobs in a small arts organization has expanded and the number of levels has increased by one. It is structured by managerial 'function' (i.e. production/operations, marketing and finance). This structure has the potential to accommodate significant

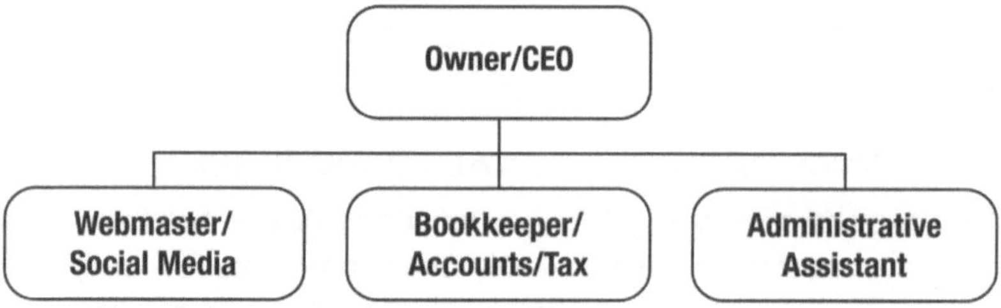

Figure 12.3 A simple structure

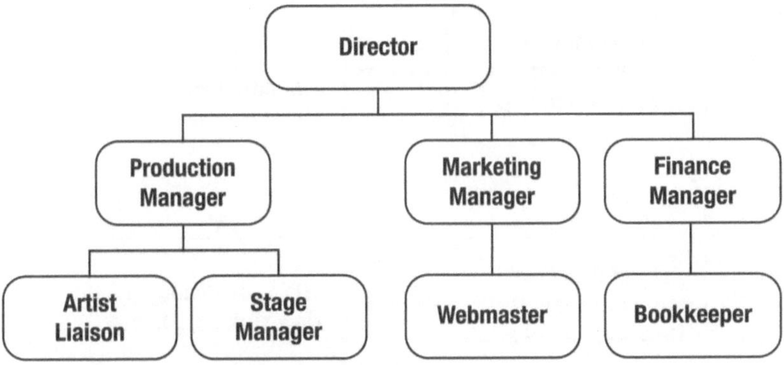

Figure 12.4 A functional, departmentalized structure.

growth in the number of specialist positions without changing its fundamental structure.

Matrix organizations

Matrix organizations partly break the 'unity of command' principle discussed earlier because an employee can effectively report to two people, though they are usually accountable to the supervisors in different ways. Matrix structures are used in a number of creative industries, such as advertising agencies and multinational record companies. To provide a fictitious example, I may be responsible for representing a New York Jazz (recorded music) catalogue in the United Kingdom. The New York Jazz label may be headquartered in Manhattan but may be owned by a large multinational record company with offices around the world. As the UK manager of The New York Jazz label I may need to report to two people: the worldwide president of the New York Jazz label, and also the UK CEO for the multinational company (e.g. Universal, Sony or Warner – whoever owns this label). This is depicted in Figure 12.5. The lines in the figure depict where authority flows, from the more senior manager to the less senior manager.

To explain in greater detail, the CEO of the multinational company in the United Kingdom is responsible for developing, marketing and distributing the group's artists and catalogue in that geographical territory (of which the New York Jazz label would be one of its many labels). The president of the New York Jazz Label in New York focuses on internationally advancing the interests of that specialist jazz label and its artists.

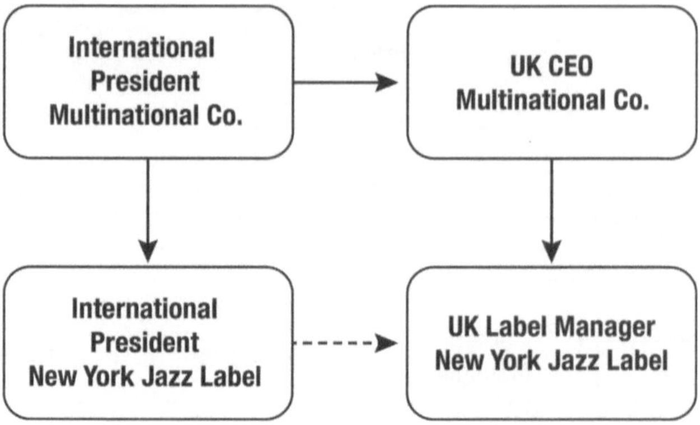

Figure 12.5 Matrix structure: the (fictitious) New York Jazz Label.

Usually, in this type of arrangement, of the two reporting relationships, the one that is the strongest (marked with an unbroken line) is the relationship between the UK CEO and the UK label manager. The UK CEO formally employs and pays the salary of the UK manager. The UK CEO is primarily after financial accountability and the achievement of sales and budget targets, as well as ensuring the manager follows UK policies and procedures. The president of the jazz label in New York shares with the UK CEO the desire to increase sales but also has the objective of advancing the broader profile of the label and its artists in the United Kingdom versus other labels. The relationship between the New York president and the UK label manager is represented by a dotted line, because while the label manager is accountable to the label president, the territory CEO (United Kingdom in this instance) would usually possess greater authority over the employee.

Conflict can result in matrix structures if the label manager is given different and contradictory instructions by these two supervisors. For example, say that the UK CEO's primary objective is short-term sales. The CEO will want to direct the UK company's marketing resources into the projects that are likely to generate the greatest short-term return on investment. The label president, on the other hand, may have just signed a great artist development priority in New York, a young jazz artist who has yet to establish an audience in the United Kingdom.

The label president may ask the UK label manager to prepare a campaign to promote this artist in the United Kingdom to coincide with a tour. But the UK CEO may undermine the instruction by reducing the available budget, as the financial return on this initiative is likely to be long term, not short term. In the event of major conflicts, a situation will be escalated to regional managers, and ultimately the worldwide president for resolution.

To look at another creative industry, if I was employed as a senior manager in a South American country within a fashion empire such as Louis Vuitton or Gucci, I would simultaneously have an accountability and reporting relationship to the fashion house in Paris or Milan (wherever it is headquartered) and the local regional management in South America which supervises the management and growth of the fashion house in the region. To the extent that these two forces act on me, I am working in a matrix structure.

Bureaucracy

Bureaucracies are often found in very large organizations that need to process high volumes of information and handle repetitive processes. Bureaucracies thrive on standardization, dislike exceptions to rules and can be inflexible. You can be sure you are dealing with a bureaucracy if you go to the reception counter requesting a service and you're told: 'But you haven't completed Form 41A!' This type of interaction is the hallmark of a bureaucracy.

In the culture of creative industries, 'bureaucracy' is often considered the enemy, standing for inflexibility, slowness, 'red tape', inefficiency and things of this nature. If an archive, for example, requires so much paperwork to access its treasures that no one can be bothered to access them, then clearly it is overly bureaucratic, as its cumbersome processes are undermining the very purpose of the archive. It should be acknowledged, though, that very large, complex organizations do need a certain amount of bureaucracy, as some degree of standardization is required to process and manage a high volume of complex transactions.

STRUCTURAL TRENDS IN THE CREATIVE INDUSTRIES

In this section we will examine evolving organizational structures in the creative industries.

Organizational structure in the movie industry

One metaphor that has been used in relation to industrial processes has been the stream. A stream begins high in the mountains and then flows down into the ocean. Processes that are 'upstream' are those that lie at the start of the process, such as writing a song in the music industry, or writing a book manuscript. Processes that are 'downstream' are closer to the end consumer, and usually involve more people and greater marketing and distribution infrastructure. This picture is a vertical one, where the beginning of the process is at the top and the end of the process is at the bottom. This will help in understanding the concept of 'vertical integration' discussed below.

Until the late 1940s, Hollywood studios made movies, distributed movies and exhibited movies in cinemas (Gil & Spiller, 2007). They aspired to have 'everything under one roof', which would enable them to capture the profits from the whole process of making and retailing movies. This is known as 'vertical integration' because the whole process, from top to bottom (as in the stream metaphor), is integrated within one organization. This is depicted in Figure 12.6.

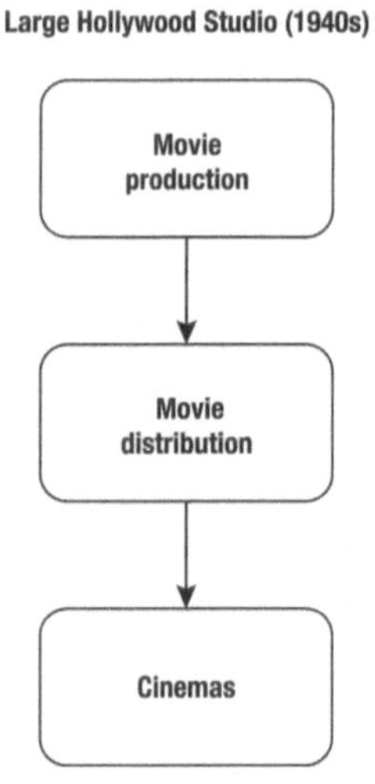

Figure 12.6 Vertically integrated Hollywood studio structure.

Over time, the large movie studios moved from this type of structure to divesting themselves of certain activities, and being 'hub' organizations drawing on a network of suppliers (Lampel & Shamsie, 2003). This process began when US government 'anti-trust' (anti-competitive) intervention prevented the studios from exclusively distributing and exhibiting their own products. This behaviour was considered restrictive and monopolistic compared to allowing a variety of retailers to compete openly in the marketplace. Regulators seek to intervene when they believe companies are attempting to stifle competition, as it may result in audiences paying higher prices. Competition from the rise of the TV industry in the late 1940s also shook up the movie industry at that time.

More recently, changes to the competitive landscape led to regulatory changes (Pakula, 2021). This has led to a rise in Hollywood studios pursuing downstream vertical integration (such as Paramount and Disney creating their own streaming services) and upstream vertical integration (in the case of streaming services such as Amazon Prime becoming a Studio). This is depicted in Figure 12.7.

In Figure 12.7, upstream vertical integration is where a streaming platform such as Amazon Prime Video decided to create its own content, establishing a Studio to make its own movies. By developing its own exclusive content, unavailable elsewhere, it creates additional incentives for audiences to subscribe. Downstream vertical integration is where a traditional Hollywood Studio such as Paramount creates its own streaming platform (Disney is a similar example). This allows Studios to strengthen distribution, take a retailer and distributor margin, and obtain consumer data which can be used for marketing purposes.

One trend which has grown over time, and looks set to continue irrespective of vertical integration, is the growing

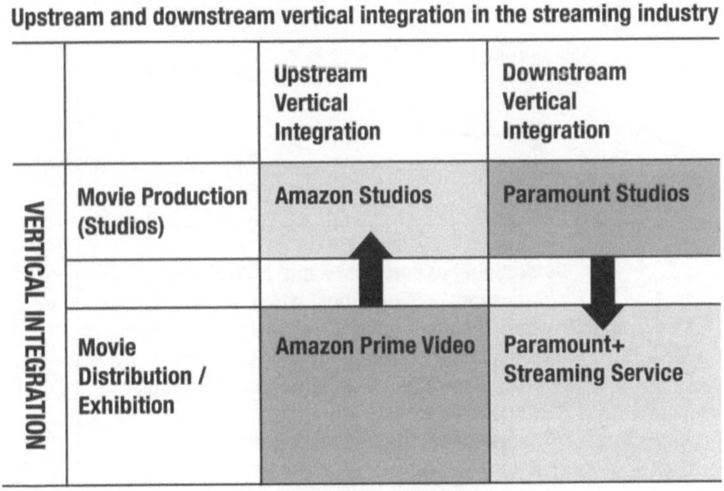

Figure 12.7 Vertical integration in streaming businesses.

use of outsourcing to produce movies. The growing cost, risk and complexity of making movies has led to an increase in co-productions (partnerships between companies to share costs, risks and skills), and outsourcing work to specialist companies. A major movie project will require specialist skills and expertise that may be necessary for one project but inappropriate for others. Just as a director may be chosen who is renowned for a certain type of style or aesthetic, a company may be employed which has a reputation for a certain type of contribution (eg special effects). It wouldn't make sense for these individuals or organizations to be permanent employees, as their skills would be underutilized, wasting the company's money and squandering the employee's talents. It is smarter to engage them on a contractual basis for relevant projects. Entertainment and media companies can still have an element of vertical integration, but increasingly an entire constellation of companies will assemble around a major project to deliver the necessary expertise and support. Usually a separate legal structure will be created for the movie to ensure intellectual property, sales and cost allocations are clearly tracked and understood. The commissioning studio will own or fund this company. This is depicted in a simplified way in Figure 12.8, where a variety of vital roles are brought in, not as employees of the company, but as independent contractors employed on a project (short-term contract) basis.

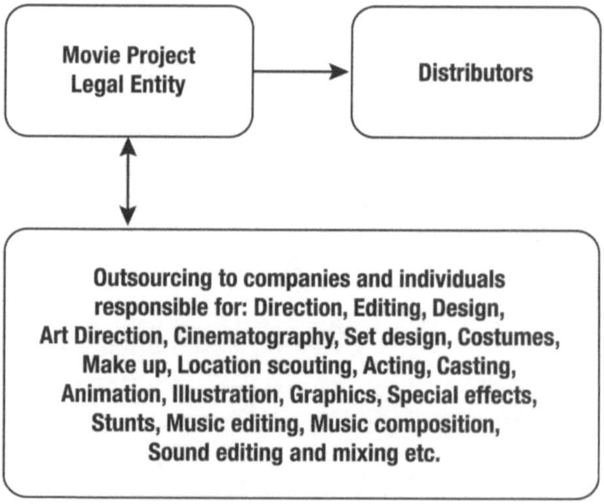

Figure 12.8 Outsourced components for a movie project, coordinated by contract.

This way of working is true of a variety of creative projects, such as computer games, TV productions, music albums or events. Resources are assembled around a project and then break off and head in separate directions once the project has been completed. Creative freelancers are engaged on a contractual basis, project by project, and form their own informal communities. Freelancers actively network to keep up to date with trends and fashions, and to be kept in mind for future work, whether that is in London's advertising industry (Mould, Vorley & Liu, 2014) or the Norwegian animation industry (Johnsen, 2011).

This is part of a general rise within the creative industries of 'temporary forms' (Bakker, 2010; Bechky; 2006), or 'latent organizations' (Ebbers & Wijnberg, 2009). These structures are responsive to the fluid, changing demands of projects (Bakker, 2010; Bechky; 2006). In 'temporary organizations', the participants, although freelancers, bring shared assumptions about the roles people will play, which means they can quickly combine and work effectively with one another (Bechky, 2006). In movie production, the foundations of these understandings and roles were defined in early negotiations between unions and the Hollywood studios. The concept of 'latent organizations' was introduced to make the point that in industries such as TV and film production, while individual projects may start and end, the companies may re-employ the same people on similar projects. Thus creative workers, while involved on a project basis rather than full-time basis, form an ongoing relationship with the company, and quickly re-integrate back into the team when a new project commences (Ebbers & Wijnberg, 2009). To provide an example, a TV production company may be commissioned by a broadcaster to develop a comedy, home improvement or lifestyle series. They then assemble a project team, which is disbanded once the series is complete. However, a similar project or a new series may be commissioned where members of the previous team are re-engaged (Starkey *et al.*, 2000). There is actually a likelihood that this will happen for talented staff, as trust and expertise have been built up which makes it more efficient and less risky for an organization to work with them compared to an unknown freelancer.

Structural trends in large music organizations

The music industry has followed a similar evolution. At one point the major companies were vertically integrated. Thus EMI Music in the United Kingdom in the 1990s, prior to being broken up and sold off, had every element of the process of releasing a sound recording under its roof, from sound recording (Abbey Road Studios) to marketing and distribution (EMI Records UK at Manchester Square) and retail (HMV stores throughout the United Kingdom). This is depicted in Figure 12.9. Large companies now need to work out what resources are unique, strategically valuable and vital to hold internally, and what is cheaper and more efficient to outsource. There have been exceptions to this trend, such as the three large Korean entertainment houses that were behind the success of K-Pop. All three were vertically integrated studios, but they succeeded through targeting a very tight niche (Shin & Kim, 2013).

In the music industry, project teams are formed around creative projects, defined by contracts rather than membership of an organization (Lorenzen & Frederiksen, 2005). Even within large music organizations, 'cross-functional teams' form around creative projects, where representatives from a variety of functions (e.g. A&R, marketing, finance) participate in project decision-making (Ordanini *et al.*, 2008). This type of interaction is valued in large organizations to avoid 'silos' and 'silo'd thinking', terms which are employed negatively in organizations to denote someone locked in their own specialization, who can't see the bigger picture or refuses to communicate or collaborate with people working in other departments.

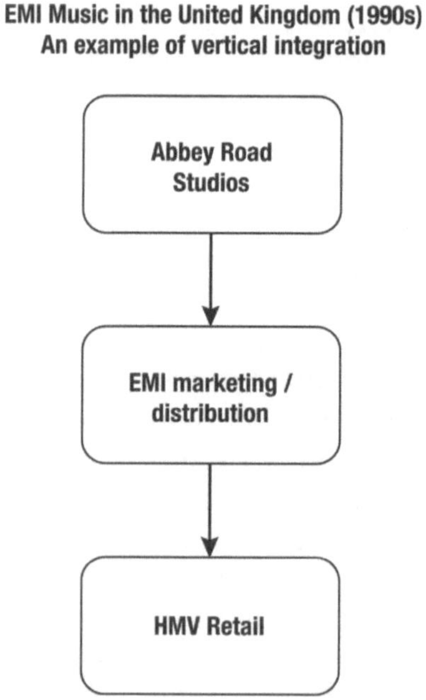

Figure 12.9 Vertical integration in the music industry.

New concepts and terms have entered into organizational

behaviour and management thinking, such as 'co-creation', 'agile project management', 'lean start up' and 'design thinking'. There are commonalities between these concepts which we will explore. They have the potential to influence organizational structure in ways that will be explained.

Consumers have historically played a role in the delivery of service products, from filling cars at petrol stations to taking over transactions previously undertaken by bank tellers. The idea of 'co-creation' is that consumers and audience members have a role to play in the development, production, marketing or distribution of products (Hartley *et al.*, 2013). Increasing power is being granted to audiences to allow them to customize their own experiences (Ramaswamy & Ozcan, 2014; Ramaswamy & Ozcan, 2016; Shirky, 2008). Audiences increasingly create and share content online via social media platforms, where user-generated content has driven the economic value of these platforms (Hartley *et al.*, 2013). If audiences start to be involved in the marketing and promotion of creative products, and even participate in the creation of products, this has implications for organizational structure because it further externalizes production (Shirky, 2008).

One of the authors of this book interviewed a major label executive about co-creation within their organization who used the example of Imogen Heap:

> One of our most wonderful examples within the family of artists that we represent is a woman called Imogen Heap, and she is someone who has essentially co-opted her fans in everything that she does – she tweets, she uses social media, she actually uses them as a creative network, they've helped her with her artwork, they've helped her with ideas, she's actually hired one of them to build her website… to the point where she's actually partnered with YouGov, which is a research agency, to do research into herself, using proper research methods… technology and social engagement is actually part of their creativity…setlists, album covers, and what should I do next, creating a mosaic of sound samples that people send in to… that they're then tessellated into it…. she's out there in terms of using the world as an orchestra, as part of the band, and it's very compelling to her audiences.
>
> (Saintilan, 2019, pp. 226–227)

More recently Imogen Heap has been experimenting with the use of the blockchain and smart contracts to acknowledge and pay members of her creative team (Ehrlich, 2019). The blockchain has the power to restructure industries, but the internal impact it has on organizational structure (the focus of this book) will depend on the specific organization. So a database business for example, would see its resources and focus shift from an internal 'silo'd' database, to the external blockchain (Owen & O'Dair, 2020).

Thus co-creation is an interesting concept which has implications for musical composition (potentially opening it up to contributions from the audience), marketing and promotions (by inviting the audience into the process), and even structure, because activities once purely undertaken within the organization start to involve participants and stakeholders outside the organization, such as the audience. Writers are now extending 'co-creation' to mean the collaboration of businesses with suppliers and the collaboration between disparate divisions of the same company (Pijl *et al.*, 2016).

The concept of 'lean start up' arose from Toyota which sought to incorporate insights from workers in the manufacturing process. It aspired to 'just in time' manufacturing where components were only delivered as required (thus reducing expensive inventory), and which sought to continually optimize processes, making them leaner, faster and more efficient (Ries, 2011). As many industries are undergoing transformative change, which involves considerable uncertainty, the approach of spending vast amounts of money building products in a bunker, and then unveiling them at the end of the process, is proving to be increasingly risky. Changes to technology, competition and consumer behaviour can take place so quickly that by the time the great new product is brought to market it can be redundant. In technology markets, streamlined products are brought to market as soon as possible, to test, to assess and then to 'pivot' if necessary (Ries, 2011), which may involve changing things such as the software, platform or target consumer segment. In this way, the organization is better able to adapt and flexibly synthesize its overall business objective with the real and validated needs of the marketplace. To give a practical example, someone looking to develop an App would find it better to release prototypes and see what the target audience reacts to and engages with, and then modify and adapt accordingly. Sitting in a bunker spending the entire development budget before any feedback has been received is a much higher risk approach. It is true this approach in physical products has seen problems created by low inventory levels, which then makes the producer vulnerable to supply chain shortages.

'Agile project management' is being applied to areas such as software development, and has integrated customer collaboration as one of its principles. It focuses on continual improvement of products and processes by testing consumer reactions in the marketplace, to validate ideas (Layton, 2012). It 'focuses on early delivery of business value' and 'scope flexibility, team input, and delivering well-tested products that reflect customer needs' (Layton, 2012, p. 2). Like the lean start-up approach, the instinct is to jump into the marketplace early to test, and iterate, rather than assume that one can create the perfect product in isolation from market feedback. The approach also brings products to market faster.

'Design thinking' draws on many of these concepts. It involves designing business and products in an iterative way, building, testing and learning in a continuous cycle (Pijl, 2016). Small tests are conducted which are validated, and then scaled up.

One common thread linking these concepts is designing from the standpoint of the customer, and trying to integrate the customer into the development process where possible. This has structural implications. For example, Netflix in 2011 decided to structurally separate its DVD and video streaming businesses (Pijl, 2016). Each of these businesses had separate operational and marketing needs, so the move seemed to make sense to company employees. The only problem was that no one asked the customer before making the change. It turned out that having two different businesses with two different websites was highly confusing for customers. The company had to finally respond to the customer feedback by reverting to the original one business and one website (Pijl, 2016).

The iterative development processes described above even have a conceptual similarity to changes that have occurred in release cycles of commercial music. In previous eras, musicians could spend a year in a bunker making an album, and then unveil it and take it on tour. However, the contemporary reality is completely different. As we saw in Chapter 6, social media has created an 'always on' marketing environment, where we need to respond 'in the moment' to unfolding events. To disappear for a year is no longer an option for an artist. Instead there is pressure for a continual stream of product and news. While this can be exhausting for an artist, it does give artists an opportunity to test ideas in the marketplace and quickly 'pivot' if there is a particular creative direction that resonates with audiences.

Remote and flexible working is another big discussion point in creative organizations, particularly since the pandemic, but this has been previously covered in Chapter 10.

SUMMARY

This chapter commenced with defining and explaining some key structural concepts such as departmentalization, chain of command, span of control, centralization and decentralization, and formalization. It then examined generic structural types such as the simple structure, the departmentalized structure, matrix structures and bureaucracy. The chapter then examined other concepts which have the potential to influence structure: 'vertical integration', 'co-creation', 'agile project management', 'lean start-ups' and 'design thinking'.

CASE STUDY 12.1: THE INTERNATIONAL MEETING

© 2013, 2023 Paul Saintilan, Michael Smellie & Cindy James

This case explores issues such as the organizational tension that occurs between centralization and decentralization, and tensions that arise between head offices and branches in large international creative organizations (Figure 12.10).

Michael Smellie is the former chief operating officer of Sony BMG worldwide. Cindy James has worked for Sony Music in Sydney, London and New York, and now works for Virgin Music Label & Artist Services/Universal Music Group.

'Impossible! This won't work in my market. Just because something explodes in Norway doesn't mean it will translate to France'. Executives working at an international record company argue about the freedom to pursue local priorities and the impact of increasing centralization.

Figure 12.10 The creative industries are truly global, creating opportunities and challenges. Photo credit: Digital Genetics / Shutterstock.com.

Tom Black glanced around the boardroom overlooking Hyde Park, London, which was abuzz with around 20 international delegates who had flown in the previous evening. All were senior managers of Galaxy Music, an international record company and concert promoter. Big changes were underway at Galaxy, as Black, the newly appointed worldwide president, was pushing hard for greater centralization of the organization. Traditionally they had operated a decentralized, 'federated' structure, with geographic territories such as the United States, United Kingdom and Germany run as separate companies with enormous freedom. Each had the power to make their own business decisions in terms of who to record or tour, and which artists to support that had already been developed by other operating companies. In this internal market, if Galaxy UK developed and broke an artist in the United Kingdom, Galaxy Germany could choose to promote the artist in Germany, receiving the revenue from German sales and paying the UK company a royalty.

The worldwide president had recently imposed far greater centralized control, a step that had angered some staff. This meeting had been convened to both reinforce that control and address the growing hostility.

Black sensed a lull in the conversation and decided to open the meeting.

> OK, let's begin. Welcome everyone. I know you're all flat out and these meetings are tough to make time for, but it's vital that we're all aligned and all our planning is synchronized. This is also your opportunity to help define the future of the company. Your collective judgements and sales projections provide us with a mandate to pursue future projects and move into new areas. It is also an opportunity for us to spend a bit of social time together, and I know the UK company has put together a great evening programme for us. So that's something to look forward to.' Noticing a few still playing with their phones, he added, 'And it would be great if you could power down your devices so you're really present in the room for the discussions, rather than mentally thousands of miles away.
>
> One theme I would like to pursue today is more unified support for those projects which are designated international priorities. For us to be able to make commitments to major artists and major projects we need you to back us. If we can't count on that, it compromises our ability to pitch for major projects, it reduces our international competitiveness and it means we can't fully maximize the potential of our artists. In an increasingly global music market we need to break artists and projects internationally, and build international catalogue for the future. An online world also makes old geographic silos meaningless. We need increasingly centralized management and the coordinated marketing of international projects.

Alain Legrand, the veteran managing director of the French company, quickly interjected before the president went further.

'Thank you so much, and may I say how good it is to be here with my old international colleagues in London this morning. I would just like to ask whether in this new world, we as local companies will still be able to make our own business decisions, to respond quickly and flexibly to local opportunities, local tastes and local talent. One thing I have always loved about working in this company is that I felt like I was running my own business within the bigger business. I felt like I had the space and freedom to do my own thing. I feel more recently the dead hand of centralization, formalization, standardization, rigidity, all of these things which we know are hostile to creativity. And for me it is a great sadness, because we work in a creative business. How can you reassure us that these new steps will not damage the company?'

> Thanks Alain. Look, like you, we want a company of entrepreneurs, not a company of nine to five employees. We want you to feel a sense of ownership in your local company and your decisions. We want you to be handsomely rewarded for your successes, and held accountable for your failures, and this is only fair when you are living and dying by your own decisions. I'm not talking here about your day to day business of identifying local projects which are evolving organically through social media which you might take to the next level. You don't need any directives from me to pursue these. I'm talking about superstar acts we need to see the full company behind, those projects where we see so much evidence of potential we seek to maximize it internationally. Where we believe it makes international sense to become market makers and drivers in some territories, rather than being purely reactive. We need to keep an eye on the bigger picture. We want you to think global and act local. We're after a balanced win/win.

But I don't think we are in balance, or maybe what is "balance" for you, is not "balance" for me' replied Legrand. 'Our market has idiosyncrasies which need to be respected, and which change the risk profile and return on investment. Furthermore, every day we receive some new directive of things that now need to be done differently, things which now need to be centrally authorized, policies and strategic plans that have to be developed for everything. Increasingly we have all these new people from head office (most of whom don't appear to have worked in the music industry I might add) strangling my staff with bureaucracy and red tape. They tell us the new organization will still be "organic", "fluid" and "responsive", but then overwhelm us with requests for reports on a million things. Instead of my people spending time on things which would drive the business forward and help deliver our numbers, they're compiling piles of statistics for some new intern. And when my staff complain, they are ignored. Maybe we should not create and sell music anymore, because it is getting in the way of all the very important form filling work we should all be doing.

Black smiled.

We have taken on some new staff. They're all keen to show how much they can contribute to the business, and so we might not be dealing with you in the most coordinated way, and they might not be aware of the opportunity cost of these tasks. So, let me go away and review what we're doing and see if we can do it better. And thank you for raising it, Alain, because I know you are very respected in the organization, and I want you all to feel comfortable raising problems, so we can try to resolve them. Now let's turn to the Bangkok Project. I'm interested in twelve-month projections for the next calendar year in terms of Track Equivalent Albums. You've previously been sent the material. Katie?

Katie Jamieson, the US marketing manager, looked up from her iPad.

> Well, we're pretty comfortable with this one, because, as you know, the artists will be based in New York for three months, they all speak English, and they're all committed to promotion. In fact, the hardest part is getting them not to promote it themselves, but to hold back until everything is in place. It's all pretty strong, the visual identity, video material, the social metrics, the back stories and narratives being woven around it, the whole package. So, we don't see any reason to change the initial projections that are in the spreadsheet, and we believe it's a viable investment.

'Great, thanks, Katie. What about the French market, what sort of numbers?'

Philippe Collard, the marketing director for Galaxy France, who sat next to Legrand, paused and shook his head.

Black sensed a problem. 'Let me guess, this project is an affront to the entire French nation, and you would be run out of Paris if you backed it?'

> What can I say? You ask me to be honest. It's impossible. There is no respect in France for this type of project. There is no real social footprint in France that could serve as a platform for this project. There is limited availability from the artists, not to mention language barriers. Just because something explodes in Norway or Shanghai or Albuquerque doesn't mean it's going to work in France. We must pass. Throwing money at this project would be throwing good money down the drain. It also means with the tight new budgets that have been imposed, that we have less to spend on artists who we know will be successful in France. This seems like a lose/lose, not a win/win.

Black responded:

> The problem is that if I give you a free pass to opt out, we set a precedent for others as well. We're then not doing the hard yards around international artist development. We're not setting ourselves up for the future. I'm the one who needs to look an artist in the eye and say "the entire organization is behind you on this one", and "we are the best company to be the home for this project". And then they come to Paris, and they see nothing, and they're on the phone screaming at me. Sure, there are going to be times when we can get music away in some territory that won't break in another, but all I'm asking you to do is try. No one has perfect knowledge of their market. There is always something that surprises us. But if you're not pushing the envelope and experimenting, you leave yourself a hostage to fortune. If you don't support something that is highly successful elsewhere, and you're not trying to be a team player, it just makes your territory look poor in comparison, and before long people are whispering "what's the problem with France?", which is never healthy for the executives involved. We respect a company's right to make their own decisions about local artists and repertoire, but for the small category of releases designated international priorities, the situation is quite different. I am not politely suggesting that you release it. We mandatorily require its promotion in all territories, and everyone in this room will be sending us a serious marketing plan for the project with sales projections.

Black reached across and poured himself an Evian. He knew that with those words the tone of the meeting had changed, and caught a raised eyebrow or two. But how was he to pull together a company that had for so long been run like a group of sovereign states or fiefdoms?

Discussion questions

1 List the strengths and weaknesses of centralization versus decentralization at Galaxy.

2 What could Galaxy do to ease the tension between the international head office and the operating companies (i.e. geographic branches like France)?

A video of managerial responses to this case study is available to instructors from the Routledge website.

References

Amabile, T. M. (1998). 'How to kill creativity', *Harvard Business Review*, September–October, pp. 77–87.

Bakker, R. M. (2010). 'Taking stock of temporary organizational forms: A systematic review and research agenda', *International Journal of Management Reviews*, Vol. 12, pp. 466–486.

Bechky, B. A. (2006). 'Gaffers, gofers, and grips: Role-based co-ordination in temporary organizations', *Organization Science*, Vol. 17, no. 1, pp. 3–21.

Burns, T. E. & Stalker, G. M. (1961). *The Management of Innovation*. London: Tavistock.

Dale, G. (2021). *Flexible Working: How to implement flexibility in the workplace to improve employee and business performance*. London: Kogan Page Ltd

De Gregorio, F., Cheong, Y. & Kim, K. (2012). 'Intraorganizational conflict within advertising agencies: Antecedents and outcomes', *Journal of Advertising*, Vol. 41, no. 3, pp. 19–34.

Ebbers, J. J. & Wijnberg, N. M. (2009). 'Latent organizations in the film industry: Contracts, rewards and resources', *Human Relations*, Vol. 62, no. 7, pp. 987–1,009.

Ehrlich, B. (2019). 'Imogen Heap and the blockchain revolution: Creative Passport is on the way', *Tidal*, Published May 1, 2019. Available at https://tidal.com/magazine/article/imogen-heap-and-the-blockchain-revolution/1-55072 (accessed 7 February 2022).

Forde, E. (2019). *The Final Days of EMI: Selling the Pig*. London: Omnibus Press.

Gil, R. & Spiller, P. T. (2007). 'The organizational dimensions of creativity: Motion picture production', *California Management Review*, Vol. 50, no. 1, pp. 243–260.

Goldberg, E. (2021). 'The worst of both worlds: zooming from the office', *New York Times*, published November 16, 2021. Available at https://www.nytimes.com/2021/11/16/business/return-to-office-hybrid-work.html (accessed 17 November 2021).

Hartley, J., Potts, J., Cunningham, S., Flew, T., Keane, M. & Banks, J. (2013). 'Co-creation (user-generated content)', *Key Concepts in Creative Industries*. London: Sage, pp. 21–24.

Johnsen, I. H. G. (2011). 'Formal project organization and informal social networks: Regional advantages in the emergent animation industry in Oslo, Norway', *European Planning Studies*, Vol. 19, no. 7, pp. 1165–1181.

Lampel, J. & Shamsie, J. (2003). 'Capabilities in motion: New organizational forms and the reshaping of the Hollywood movie industry', *Journal of Management Studies*, Vol. 40, no. 8, pp. 2189–2210.

Layton, M. C. (2012). *Agile Project Management for Dummies*. Hoboken, NJ: Wiley.

Lorenzen, M. & Frederiksen, L. (2005). 'The management of projects and product experimentation: Examples from the music industry', *European Management Review*, Vol. 2, pp. 198–211.

McDonald, M. & Wilson, H. (2002). *The New Marketing: Transforming the Corporate Future*. Oxford: Butterworth Heinemann.

McLean, L. D. (2005). 'Organizational culture's influence on creativity and innovation: A review of the literature and implications for human resource development', *Advances in Developing Human Resources*, Vol. 7, no. 2, May, pp. 226–246.

Martins, E. C. & Terblanche, F. (2003). 'Building organizational culture that stimulates creativity and innovation', *European Journal of Innovation Management*, Vol. 6, no. 1, pp. 64–74.

Millar, C., Choi, C. J. & Chen, S. (2005). 'Globalization rediscovered: The case of uniqueness and "creative industries"', *Management International Review*, Vol. 45, pp. 121–128.

Mintzberg, H. (2013). *Simply Managing*. San Francisco: Berrett-Koehler Publishers, Inc.

Mould, O., Vorley, T. & Liu, K. (2014). 'Invisible creativity? Highlighting the hidden impact of freelancing in London's creative industries', *European Planning Studies*, Vol. 22, no. 12, pp. 2436–2455.

Nguyen, M. (2021). 'Research shows working from home doesn't work. Here's how employers should tackle the problem', *Time Magazine*. Available at https://time.com/6088110/remote-work-structured-hybrid-research/ (accessed 20 September 2021).

Ordanini, A., Rubera, G. & Sala, M. (2008). 'Integrating functional knowledge and embedding learning in new product launches: How project forms helped EMI Music', *Long Range Planning*, Vol. 41, pp. 17–32.

Owen, R. & O'Dair, M. (2020). 'How blockchain technology can monetize new music ventures: an examination of new business models', *Journal of Risk Finance*, Vol. 21, no. 4, pp. 333–353.

Pakula, O. (2021). 'The Streaming Wars+: an analysis of anticompetitive business practices in streaming business', *UCLA Entertainment Law Review*, Vol. 28, no. 1.

Ramaswamy, V. & Ozcan, K. (2014). *The Co-creation Paradigm*. Stanford: Stanford University Press.

Ramaswamy, V. & Ozcan, K. (2016). 'Brand value co-creation in a digitalized world: An integrative framework and research implications', *International Journal of Research in Marketing*, Vol. 33, pp. 93–106.

Ries, E. (2011). *The Lean Startup: How Constant Innovation Creates Radically Successful Businesses*. London: Portfolio Penguin.

Rishi, S., Breslau, B. & Miscovich, P. (2022). *The Workplace You Need Now: Shaping Spaces for the Future of Work*. Hoboken, NJ: John Wiley & Sons, Inc.

Saintilan, P. (2019). *Managerial Orientations and Beliefs in Large Music Organisations*, PhD Thesis, Department of Management, Deakin University.

Shin, S. I. & Kim, L. (2013). 'Organizing K-Pop: Emergence and market making of large Korean entertainment houses, 1980–2010', *East Asia*, Vol. 30, pp. 255–272.

Shirky, C. (2008). *Here Comes Everybody: The Power of Organizing Without Organizations*. London: Penguin Books.

Starkey, K., Barnatt, C. & Tempest, S. (2000). 'Beyond networks and hierarchies: Latent organizations in the U.K. television industry', *Organization Science*, Vol. 11, no. 3, pp. 299–305.

van der Pijl, P., Lokitz J. & Solomon, L. K. (2016). *Design a Better Business: New Tools, Skills, and Mindset for Strategy and Innovation*. Hoboken, NJ: Wiley.

Organizational culture in creative organizations

Chapter 13

APPLE INC.

Apple Inc. is a technological giant with strong links to the creative industries. It has been the technology company of choice for generations of designers and creative professionals and drove

Figure 13.1 Apple Inc. Photo credit: TungCheung/Shutterstock.com.

DOI: 10.4324/9781003262923-13

the digital transformation of the music industry through the iTunes platform and iPod. It is also a company that is widely seen to possess a strong corporate culture (Isaacson, 2011). When a company develops a culture that differentiates it from other companies and is motivational for attracting creative talent, staff and customers, it provides that company with a competitive advantage and a potential increase in its economic value.

Former Apple leader Steve Jobs quickly fired employees who did not meet his high standards, creating an expectation of excellence and little tolerance for under-performance (Isaacson, 2011). This is an example of the behaviour of leaders becoming enshrined as a practice throughout an organization. Values that Steve Jobs tried to cultivate at Apple were: excellence, creativity, innovation, design elegance and simplicity, attention to detail, secrecy and confrontation where necessary to uphold excellence (Isaacson, 2011; Meyer, 2015; Thomke & Feinberg, 2009). These values became enshrined within the organization and came to define its culture.

WHAT IS ORGANIZATIONAL CULTURE?

One of the most popular and enduring definitions of organizational 'culture' is 'the way we do things around here'

CHAPTER LEARNING OBJECTIVES

At the conclusion of this chapter you will be able to:

- Define organizational culture and describe its characteristics;
- Describe external factors that influence organizational culture;
- Identify internal factors that create and reinforce organizational culture;
- Analyse the way organizations in the creative industries seek to engage with culture, including identifying the difference between espoused and enacted values;
- Critique 'workplace spirituality' and the 'happy family' aspiration.

(Bower, 1966). The Apple example above shows a particular approach and style of working based on shared assumptions, meaning and values. The management theorist Henry Mintzberg has described culture as 'the spirit of the human hive' (Mintzberg, 2013, p. 51). It binds individuals together in the pursuit of objectives.

Great cultures, where most employees sincerely believe in and share the values that the organization is projecting, are both hard to achieve and hard to copy. A popular quote often attributed to management guru Peter Drucker is 'culture eats strategy for breakfast' (Krahle & Gurel-Atay, 2014). You can have great aspirations and fantastic plans, but a dysfunctional culture means that the human resource isn't efficiently deployed at the service of these plans, and energy and focus dissipates. A great culture is important for creative firms to coalesce commitment around their objectives and attract top employees and artists. A great culture internally moderates and reinforces behaviour over and above the actions of any one individual (i.e. very strong cultures will exercise an influence even after a leader is removed).

Organizational studies (Chatman & Jehn, 1994; McClure, 2010) have identified dimensions in which companies differ, such as attitude to risk (in creative organizations, managers are usually comfortable with moderate to high risk); attention to detail (high in the case of Apple); outcome orientation (valuing the end result over the process required to achieve it); people orientation (caring for people and ensuring staff are supported as a priority rather than a secondary consideration); team orientation (placing focus on teams and team performance rather than individuals); aggressiveness (Apple had a more aggressive culture under Jobs); market and consumer orientation (focusing externally on audiences and competitors) (Narver & Slater, 1990); the pursuit of organizational stability and even bureaucracy (with highly formalized processes, rules and structure); or seeking innovation and creativity (Martins & Terblanche, 2003; McClure, 2010). The latter will be a key focus in this chapter.

The values underpinning organizational culture can be both 'espoused' and 'enacted'. 'Espoused values' are what a firm says it values in its speeches and statements, but which it may or may not actually put into practice. 'Enacted values' are what a firm's senior managers actually manifest through their actions, which may have nothing to do with the values that they espouse.

Creative organizations typically aim for the following types of values: professionalism; sympathetic conditions for creative personnel and a supportive environment for creative work; a commitment to artist development; a commitment to quality; a commitment to technological innovation; and a commitment to impacting the broader popular culture (Negus, 1999). For example, Pixar Animation Studios aims for a 'peer culture' where teams help one another to achieve the best outcomes, a culture where communication is direct and informal, and a culture that grants creatives the power and autonomy to drive the creative process (Catmull, 2008). Providing support and autonomy for creative people and giving them encouragement and appropriate resources is vital to their success (McLean, 2005). As we saw in the chapter on structure, structure has implications for organizational culture, as a highly formalized, controlling, centralized organization will have a different (and less creative) culture compared to a more decentralized, informal organization (Martins & Terblanche, 2003). Different companies possess different values. Non-profit arts organizations (e.g. opera, theatre companies, galleries and museums) may additionally prioritize values such as: a collegial and collaborative environment based on mutual respect; sustaining and developing the artform; challenging or stretching audiences and expanding their horizons; building community and connections; enriching the national culture; and upholding artistic and scholarly integrity (Butler, 2000; Camarero & Garrido, 2008; Voss *et al.*, 2000). These values can also influence culture.

There are many external and internal vehicles that influence culture. External factors such as nationality, geographical location, industry, genre and professional specialization all intersect and create a melting pot of cultural influences (Negus, 1999). Internally, cultural values can be introduced and reinforced through staff selection, the behaviour and managerial style of the leadership team, socialization, office environment, dress code, working hours, stories, rituals, symbols, habits of daily interaction, and the artists and stars associated with the company. These will be discussed in greater detail later in the chapter.

As discussed in Chapter 1, an important assumption for workers in creative industries is that the organization will grant artists and creative managers 'creative autonomy'. This is a tradition operating within the creative and cultural industries where artists, creative workers and project teams have been given significant creative freedom. This is due to a number of beliefs: that it intrinsically motivates creative people; that they bring specialized technical and creative expertise which should be trusted and respected; that the tradition of free speech discourages artistic interference and censorship; and that it assists the pursuit of originality, a prized objective (Hesmondhalgh, 2013). Work autonomy is not unique to the creative and cultural industries, but it is crucial to understanding them, due to the tensions it creates in the production process. To fail to grant creative workers/producers autonomy may be perceived by them as a failure to trust them and respect their abilities.

When you join a creative company that works with artists, you must understand this assumption. It is even more true in non-profit organizations: a study examining administrative/artistic directors working in non-profit performing arts organizations recognized 'artistic autonomy' and defined it as 'the artist's right to decide on his/her program irrespective of the customer's needs or other restrictions' (Sorjonen, 2011, pp. 13–14). The arts managers in Sorjonen's study understood artistic autonomy to be an important convention operating in the world of music and performing arts programming.

The former major record company EMI Music (before it was broken up in 2012) provides an example of what can go wrong when business demands are allowed to interfere with creative autonomy. A celebrated instance arose when the band Coldplay's album *X&Y* was delivered later than scheduled. This created company angst, as it impacted the 2004/2005 financial results (the big new hit was budgeted, but never materialized). Chris Martin, the lead singer of Coldplay, resented the implication that his failure to rush the album had cost the company. He commented, 'Deadlines mean nothing to us ... we'll sink the whole company if we have to' (Southall, 2009, p. 173). Even Eric Nicoli, the CEO at the time, later reflected, 'The moment you start to distort the creative process in order to hit fiscal objectives you're asking for trouble' (Southall, 2009, p. 173). Allowing the space for creative autonomy is a vital part of building a 'creative culture'.

WHAT EXTERNAL FACTORS INFLUENCE ORGANIZATIONAL CULTURE?

National identities can influence company cultures (Hofstede *et al.*, 2010). Research has demonstrated that nationalities exhibit distinctive behaviours in dimensions such as: Power Distance (the degree to which people accept that power is not distributed equally – high power distance countries accept hierarchies; lower scoring countries want to spread power); Individualism versus Collectivism (whether more weight is placed on individual achievement or collective achievement); Masculinity versus Femininity (whether traits generally considered male or female receive higher prioritization); Uncertainty Avoidance (the degree to which people are uncomfortable with ambiguity); Long-Term versus Short-Term Orientation (whether the long-term health of the organization or short-term financial achievements are prioritized); and Indulgence versus Restraint (high restraint cultures have stricter norms around the gratification of needs and drives) (Hofstede *et al.*, 2010).

To give an example of the way national influences can infiltrate and inflect values, let's take the confrontation/aggression dimension (related to Masculinity above in the Hofstede research). One of the co-authors was working at a major record company in London in the 1990s and noted a strange semantic battle taking place in a senior management meeting. One female staff member had talked about the need to be more 'assertive' in a particular situation. Another (more senior) male manager corrected her, saying we should be more 'aggressive'. She responded, 'No, I meant what I said: assertive'. And he responded, 'So did I: aggressive'. There may have been a gender basis for the difference (i.e. a woman wanting a more collaborative and conciliatory approach and a man a more aggressive approach, as per Hofstede's model), but it was also a trans-Atlantic battle between London and New York business values. To British executives of that era (and many would still hold the same view today), being 'assertive' means standing up for yourself in a professional way, while 'aggressive' means standing up for yourself but going too far, and subsequently losing one's composure, civility and professionalism. Assertive behaviour strongly puts forward one's case, but not in a way that will necessarily fuel antagonism or a deterioration in the working relationship. However, to managers from New York in the 1990s, the competitive intensity of the marketplace had become so extreme that, whether you liked it or not, 'aggression' was necessary to compete in the corporate bear pit. Industries such as finance had become ferociously aggressive (as captured in books and films such as *Liar's Poker* and *The Wolf of Wall Street*), and the behaviour of Wall Street was beginning to influence the broader New York business culture. Executives from New York began to see 'assertive' as being too polite and too British. It resulted in a cross-cultural tension, with some British managers believing the US influence was negative and 'uncool', and many New York-influenced managers considering the British managers to not be 'hard' enough for the ruthlessness of contemporary commerce.

Different creative industries such as fashion, advertising, movies and music also have their own cultures, with their own stories, symbols, rituals and personalities. Industry culture is reinforced through vehicles such as award ceremonies and the trade press. When seeking to learn an industry culture (e.g. as a job applicant), a good interview strategy is to ask managers which trade and industry media and daily newsfeeds they value. Even if you are unsuccessful in landing the job, you will have demonstrated to the manager your desire to learn about their industry culture, and you will walk away with a clearer understanding of the contemporary reference points for managers working in that industry.

The culture of a given workplace in the creative industries will be influenced by a number of other external factors aside from nationality and industry. The geographical heritage of the organization's parent company can have an influence (e.g. Sony in Japan, Warner in the United States, Universal in Europe). Cities can exert an influence, as one would expect US cities such as New York, Miami and Nashville to exert their own influences on cultural projects. The genre of product can exert an influence (rap, country, Latin and classical music all have different subcultures). Managerial specializations can create their own subcultures, as finance, marketing and artistic personnel can have their own functional perspectives (Dougherty, 1992; Homburg & Jensen, 2007). As we saw in the chapter on conflict, Chapter 5, managers who are responsible for marketing and managers responsible for artistic development may clash due to their different training, perspectives and responsibilities. Other managers such as finance managers, sales managers, HR managers and other specialists will also have their own perspectives (these differences were touched upon in Case Study 3.1 at the conclusion of the chapter on personality).

WHAT SHAPES AND REINFORCES CULTURE INTERNALLY?

As discussed in the introduction to this chapter, culture is created and infused through the organization via a number of internal means. Let us explore these in greater detail:

Staff selection – Companies attempting to generate a strong culture often put rigorous filters on staff selection. The characteristics of the staff who are recruited exercise a profound influence on company culture, and Apple and Netflix have both expressed how seriously they take this (Isaacson, 2011; McCord, 2014).

The behaviour of top management – Nothing is more important in reinforcing culture than the behaviour of the leader and the leadership team. Employees are quick to see the difference between 'espoused' and 'enacted' values, and know that what senior managers do, rather than what they say, is a clearer indication of what is required (Boatright *et al.*, 2018). If a company is attempting to instil an ethical culture, it is insufficient just to publish policy documents on ethical behaviour. That may be important, but far more important is evidence of how this is enacted through the company: what is rewarded? How do the senior managers themselves behave? Only when employees see managers who 'walk the talk' will they be confident that the company is serious about cultivating a certain type of behaviour. The behaviour of top management also defines the 'managerial style' of the company. For example, is the style formal and autocratic, or relaxed and informal (i.e.

not emphasizing hierarchies and 'power distance', in the language of Hofstede)? Many top creative industry managers (such as Richard Branson) deliberately try to act in an inclusive, collaborative, collegial way, trying to reduce power distance to show staff that their managers are approachable, and that they all work as part of a team. Branson will make informal gestures such as not wearing a tie to symbolize this. Virgin has turned informality into a brand value and has achieved enormous success by bringing this value to industries known for stuffiness, formality and bureaucracy.

Socialization – Companies can invest in events and processes that inculcate the organization's values, and make clear the behaviour that is expected. This includes internship programmes, new hire training and induction procedures (i.e. 'onboarding'), celebratory events and company conferences.

Figure 13.2 Creative cultures: Breaking out of suits and becoming more informal. Photo credit: tommaso lizzul / Shutterstock.com.

Office environment – such as location, layout and décor – also says something about the company and its culture. Google's Googleplex facility brings the comforts of home into the office, making 'being in the office' far more attractive. Open plan offices (where all the walls come down) are designed to increase staff communication and are favoured by employers such as Facebook. The idea is that staff in an open plan office will interact more freely and overhear conversations that build their understanding of what is going on. Chance conversations lead to idea generation and greater staff alignment.

Dress code – This also communicates the company values. Do employees wear trainers, jeans, T-shirts and baseball caps, or suits and ties? In the creative industries, the business suit can be perceived as a symbol of people whose focus is financial. It can be used in a derogatory way ('s/he's a suit') to mean that the manager brings a one dimensional financial lens and lacks appreciation and understanding for the creative dimension of the business. A&R executives and advertising creatives can hold this view (see for example Negus (1999)).

Working hours – How much autonomy are staff given towards determining the hours that they work, the location of that work and when they come and go? Are there strict rules or is it a more informal, trusting environment? People in the creative industries tend to work long hours and can be open to stress and overwork (this is discussed further in Chapter 6). Companies such as Netflix are relaxed about the process (the time spent at one's desk), but very focused on the outcomes and what an employee achieves (McCord, 2014).

Habits of daily interaction – Is there a staff canteen where people are encouraged to meet at lunchtime? What staff meetings are scheduled? Are there moments when people get coffee and have a chat together? Do people try to catch up at the end of the week? These moments can strengthen social bonds and create opportunities for 'serendipity', where chance conversations result in important ideas, connections and business outcomes.

Rituals – Rituals are symbolic, repeated events, and they play an important role in reinforcing cultural values. Examples include company conferences, prize-givings, award evenings, staff events and even Friday drinks. Industry events such as festivals and trade fairs can become rituals, and the choice of who from the company will attend is seen to be of great internal significance. The film industry has festivals such as Sundance, Berlin, Cannes and Toronto. The music industry has events such as Coachella and SXSW. The book industry has events such as the Frankfurt Book Fair; the advertising industry, the Cannes Lions awards; and the fashion industry, events in New York, Paris, London and Milan. They are public and trade performances that celebrate and influence industry culture.

Symbols – Dick Hebdige's book *Subculture: The Meaning of Style* (1979) showed how punk subculture used symbols such as safety pins, razor blades, dyed hair, ripped T-shirts and bondage gear to communicate a subversive rejection of society's traditional values. Companies in the creative industries (while criticized by Hebdige for appropriating these symbols for their own purposes) understand the power of symbols. The foyer displays of framed platinum records in music companies are used to symbolize and visually communicate success. Iconic design and advertising work will be displayed in the offices of creative firms to remind staff and visitors of the firm's heritage.

Stories – Organizational stories and even myths can be used to reinforce cultural values. There are many stories that circulate about charismatic leaders such as Steve Jobs and Richard Branson. Anna Wintour, the editor-in-chief of American *Vogue*, has been transformed into a celebrity in her own right, and war stories from a former employee who worked for her became the basis for a fictionalized book and movie, *The Devil Wears Prada* (Weisberger, 2003). Martin Bandier, arguably the world's most successful music publishing executive, provides an example of a 'story' used to communicate something about organizational culture. While head of EMI Music Publishing, he was approached by film executive Jeffrey Katzenberg to license a small piece of music ('Hawaiian War Chant') for the animated film *The Lion King*. Bandier's staff had requested $125,000 for the ten seconds required, which Katzenberg thought was outrageous, so he approached Bandier directly. Bandier responded by asking Katzenberg to name the song, and suggested that if he (Bandier) could correctly hum it, Katzenberg should pay the $125,000. If he couldn't, Katzenberg could have it for $40,000. Katzenberg agreed and gave the name of the song. Bandier hummed it, and told Katzenberg to cut him the cheque for $125,000 (Serwer, 1995). This story has great propaganda value for the company, because it communicates that the company is being run by people who really know music, rather than accountants and 'suits'.

Artists and stars associated with the company – Companies take enormous pride in their association with creative talents, artists and stars, and this can be seen to impact the culture (Negus, 1999). The composition of an artist roster says much about a company's creative strengths and priorities, which can be attractive for other artists as well as employees. Celebrated artists whose sales have waned can be retained on major record companies' rosters, even with minimal financial return, if their legendary status is attractive to younger artists (Negus, 1999).

While charismatic leaders in some sectors of the commercial entertainment industry (such as major record labels) often create the impression of cultural distinctiveness, there have been criticisms that such differences are only superficial (Negus, 1999). The regular movement of top executives between companies and the similarity in fundamental drivers (i.e. inescapable requirements such as profitability for publicly listed companies and the desire to capitalize on changes in consumer trends and preferences) contribute to this. Publicly listed music companies can follow a familiar cycle: as soon as financial results fall below shareholder expectations, there is a round of firings and executive re-shuffles (Negus, 1999; Southall, 2009). A new team is assembled which reinforces familiar platitudes such as the company's commitment to strong artist development, greater cost reduction and increased sales. This team lasts until the next time the sales dip, and then there is another round of firings. Thus new CEOs may provide a veneer of difference, but the underlying strategies and drivers in commercial entertainment remain largely unaltered.

THE 'HAPPY FAMILY' DILEMMA

You may hear an organization describe its culture as a 'happy family'. This seems like a noble aspiration; however, it has proved to be controversial. The argument for creating a 'happy family' is that people like to work in a supported, safe, friendly environment, where people 'have their backs' (i.e. protect them from being stabbed in the back) and trust one another. If people feel like they are expendable commodities who can be quickly and easily dumped on the scrapheap, this undermines their loyalty and their trust in the organization. Organizations that try to achieve a happy family culture can seem more humane and ethical. This style of organization often promotes from within, attempting to maximize the growth and development of those who work for them. They are more likely to ask 'Who among our current staff would be most suitable for this role?' than 'Who is the best person we can hire for this role?'

This type of culture rewards service and loyalty, but can become stale in fast-moving industries. At a certain point in the evolution of the music industry, music companies *shouldn't* have asked, 'Who among our current staff can run our digital business?', but rather, 'Who in companies at the frontier of digital innovation such as Apple and Google can take their knowledge and apply it to our business?' Sometimes it is unrealistic to believe that an organization can generate the internal learning required to keep pace with complex, inter-disciplinary changes to industry practice. Changes in industries lead to changes in required skills, which in turn often means changes in personnel. While there is a responsibility on the part of employers to ensure that staff engage in professional development and keep pace with change so that their skills and employability aren't rendered redundant, sometimes external appointments are critical to infuse the organization with new learning.

The film company Netflix has provided the most public critique of the 'happy family' aspiration (McCord, 2014). They are explicitly trying to cultivate a culture of performance and excellence rather than a 'happy family'. To do this, they want the organization to be like a top sports team, where they have the very best people in their optimal positions. Just as a top sports team wouldn't be a collection of friends, but rather experts at the top of their field, so Netflix rejects the happy family aspiration. Performance cultures bring their own rewards. People enjoy working with other top people, they like the accountability (people being held to account for poor performance), and the superior results which can be generated from a top team lead to higher sales, which in turn allows the firm to offer higher remuneration. Performance cultures see happy family cultures as being poorer performers, as they will not necessarily have the best people and their heightened job security can encourage a sense of slackness and entitlement.

'WORKPLACE SPIRITUALITY'

Another controversial area has been a rise in the concept of 'workplace spirituality' (Robbins & Judge, 2022). In recent years organizations began to realize that to deeply engage employees, they needed to tap into their most profound motivations and drives. These motivations may be centred on making an impact in life, making a positive impact on other people, leaving a legacy through work, or having the opportunity to travel and experience other cultures, among many other motivational factors. Some corporations talk about employee self-actualization and giving consumer goods products 'purpose' to inspire us to have a deep and meaningful relationship with them.

Companies can make an effort to be benevolent, make work meaningful, and conduct themselves ethically, which are all to be applauded. But some organizations, products and organizational missions are inherently more capable of connecting with 'workplace spirituality' and reinforcing the deeper meaning in one's life. Can selling shampoo really deliver self-transcendence and self-actualization in a spiritual sense? Steve Jobs famously said to John Sculley, when he was a Pepsi manager, 'Do you want to spend the rest of your life selling sugared water, or do you want a chance to change the world?' (Isaacson, 2011, p. 141) when offering him the position of Apple CEO in 1983. The good news is that the work of creative and cultural organizations does hold the potential for deeper creative and personal fulfilment, more so than most other products and industries. This is both a blessing and a responsibility, as artists who consider their work to be the 'meaning of their life' will become intensely upset if their creative projects are failing, because so much is at stake.

CONCLUSION

Culture is enormously powerful and valuable for companies, and is influenced in a variety of ways – both unconsciously through external factors, and consciously through the management of internal factors. As an employee you should study the way your organization works with culture. What signals is it sending about the culture that it wants to develop? Is there a gulf between the espoused and enacted values? What machinery does it use to develop culture? What aspects of the culture most resonate with you, and how could you assist in developing the culture? These are all questions that employees should consider when they start working for a company.

Discussion questions and class exercises

1 If a record company's artist roster is part of its culture, how do independent companies expand into different genres without alienating current artists? For example, Big Machine Records is an American independent country music label. Their backing of pop star Taylor Swift saw immense commercial returns, but it changed the perception of the company, especially for country music purists. What are the implications in terms of culture clashes among both staff and artists?

2 Critique the 'happy family' versus 'performance culture' aspiration. Which culture would you rather work in and why?

3 To what degree is 'culture' really just 'brainwashing' (or not)?

4 On his first afternoon as president of former major record company EMI Music, Davitt Sigerson fired 18 senior executives who did not support the creative quality, artist-led culture he wanted to foster (Negus, 1999). To provide greater focus, he put more resources behind fewer releases and cut down the artist roster. Releases went from 64 in the year he took over to 24 the following year. Critique the situation.

5 What is your reaction to the 'workplace spirituality' discussion? Do you find it inspiring? Inappropriate? Why?

CASE STUDY 13 CASABLANCA RECORDS

Figure 13.3 Sunset Boulevard, Los Angeles, the former home of Casablanca Records. Photo credit: trekandshoot / Shutterstock.com.

These excerpts from Fredric Dannen's book Hit Men illustrate extremely dysfunctional organizational culture (although the organization did try to take the theatrical potential of organizational culture to the limit).

If you were cruising along Sunset Boulevard in the late seventies and saw what appeared to be an enormous Mercedes dealership, chances were good that you'd just stumbled upon the parking lot of Casablanca Records. Anyone who subscribed to the American Dream, California style, required a Mercedes convertible. Casablanca, the label of Donna Summer and Kiss and the Village People and synonymous with disco, embodied that dream. …

Its unofficial motto, "Whatever It Takes", became the industry's rallying cry. The idea took hold that *selling* the product was just as important – maybe more important – than the product itself. And it appeared to work. When Casablanca conquered the charts, it did not dawn on the industry, or even PolyGram [its parent company] at first, that the company was losing vast sums of money. Sales were great, but the cost of selling was greater. "Whatever

It Takes" was a recipe for profitless prosperity, and that is what the entire record business suffered in the end. ...

In an industry where excess is a virtue, [label President Neil] Bogart stories are told with awe. He launched Casablanca Records with a $45,000 party in the Century Plaza Hotel's grand ballroom [which would cost nearly ten times that amount in today's dollars], made over as the movie set of *Casablanca*, down to a Dooley Wilson lookalike playing cocktail piano. When the Village People released their hit "In the Navy" Bogart showed up at a record convention dressed as an admiral, with his entire staff in sailor uniforms. When Bogart brought Donna Summer from Germany to New York to promote her first hit album, *Love to Love You Baby*, he had Hansen's of Los Angeles sculpt a life-size cake in her image. The cake was flown to New York in two first-class airlines seats, met by freezer ambulance, and taken to the Penta discotheque for Summer's performance there ...

No one who set foot in Casablanca on Sunset ever forgot it. Asked to describe the ambience, Larry Harris said, "Loud. Real loud. You see these, these are *small* speakers." He pointed to a set that reached his navel. "We were *very* loud." The sonic assault wasn't only from the steady ta-TUM, ta-ta-TUM of booming disco music; Ali DiNoble, the VP of pop promotion, struck an Oriental gong in his office whenever a Casablanca record scored a [radio] station. "Everything was at such a fevered fucking pitch," said PolyGram's Rick Bleiweiss. "You walked into Bruce Bird's office, music was blaring, twelve phones were ringing. You never could talk in that building. You had to shout. I think the average person walking in there would have been floored by the electricity and the volume. Everything in that company was an exaggeration, a caricature".

The interior was patterned after Rick's Café in *Casablanca*. As you walked in the front door, you were greeted by a life-sized stuffed camel and a huge poster of Humphrey Bogart. There were ceiling fans, palm trees, throne-like chairs made of cane, Moroccan rugs and furniture. Joyce Bogart's [Neil's wife and Casablanca exec] mirrored office had fabric draped from the middle of the ceiling to all four corners, to suggest a tent. Neil's office had a fully stocked bar. Gold and platinum albums served as wallpaper. In addition to the exotic décor and head-splitting noise level, there was something else about Casablanca. Said Bruce Bird, "People were *happy*. It was probably one of the happiest record companies I've ever seen".

It was not happy for Danny Davis, however. He was a short, pudgy promotion veteran … "Let me tell you, man. Twelve minutes after I started at Casablanca, almost by actual count, I called my wife and told her I had made the biggest mistake of my life. It's a true story. And I surely wanted to do good. First of all, I was getting more money. Second of all, they had given me a Mercedes 450SEL. But what happened to Casablanca Records was supposed to happen. You can't *do* that twenty-four hours a day. At three o'clock in the afternoon, an adorable little girl would come up and take your *order* for the following day's *drug supply*. You understand what I'm telling you? It was the worst fucking experience of my life".

On a Monday or Tuesday, I'd be looking for [a secretary] and I'd be calling her name. I'd look all over, and there she would be with a credit card in her hand, chopping, chopping the coke on the table.

I would be on the phone with a [radio] program director, and a certain party would come in. And he would run around with a fucking golf club, squashing things off my desk. And as I was on the phone, he would take a match and torch my desk. I would say into the phone, let's say to Jerry Rogers of [radio station] WSGA, Jerry, gonna have to hang up now, my desk is on *fire* …

It is difficult to imagine any record company more unlike Casablanca than PolyGram [its parent company].

Whatever else was wrong with Casablanca, no one would have called it bureaucratic or stodgy, or proposed that it had no discernible chain of command. But that was PolyGram throughout the seventies.

Given the company's origins, it was easy to see why it had turned out that way. PolyGram began as a European classical–music company in 1962 in an exchange of shares between two industrial giants: Siemens AG, a maker of electrical equipment, and Philips, a manufacturer of audio hardware. ...

To say that the Dutch and Germans running PolyGram did not understand the US pop scene would be generous. It is always a mistake to try to buy into a market rapidly, before top management has learned that market. PolyGram assumed that its big acts on the Continent would play in the United States, even though few of them sang in English. Polydor's roster, for example, included a thirteen-year-old Dutch boy named Heintje who sold millions of records in Europe. America greeted him with stony indifference. ...

PolyGram did not return to profitability until 1985, at which point it had lost more than $220 million in the United States. Casablanca was responsible for a major chunk of the deficit. The exact amount has never been disclosed.

Review questions

1 Critique the positive and negative aspects of Casablanca's culture.

2 Compare and contrast the culture of Casablanca with its parent company PolyGram, headquartered in the Netherlands.

References

Boatright, J. R., Smith, J. D. & Patra, B.P. (2018). *Ethics and the Conduct of Business*, 8th Edition. Chennai, India: Pearson India Education Services Pvt. Ltd.

Bower, M. (1966). *The Will to Manage: Corporate Success Through Programmed Management*. New York: McGraw-Hill.

Butler, P. (2000). 'By popular demand: marketing the arts', *Journal of Marketing Management*, Vol. 16, no. 4, pp. 343–364.

Camarero, C. & Garrido, M. J. (2008). 'The influence of market and product orientation on museum performance', *International Journal of Arts Management*, Vol. 10, no 2, pp. 14–26.

Catmull, E. (2008). 'How Pixar Fosters Collective Creativity', *Harvard Business Review*, September 2008, Reprint R0809D.

Chatman, J. A. & Jehn, K. A. (1994). 'Assessing the relationship between industry characteristics and organizational culture: How different can you be?', *Academy of Management Journal*, Vol. 37, no. 3, p. 522–553.

Dannen, F. (1991). 'Casablanca' (Chapter 9), *Hit Men*, Vintage Books. New York: Random House, pp. 161–181.

Dougherty, D. (1992). 'Interpretive barriers to successful product innovation in large firms', *Organization Science*, Vol. 3, no. 2, pp. 179–202.

Hebdige, D. (1979). *Subculture: The Meaning of Style*. London and New York: Methuen.

Hesmondhalgh, D. (2013). *The Cultural Industries*, 3rd Edition. SAGE.

Hofstede, G., Hofstede, J. & Minkov, M. (2010). *Cultures and Organizations: Software of the Mind*. Revised and Expanded 3rd Edition, New York: McGraw-Hill.

Homburg, C. & Jensen, O. (2007). 'The thought worlds of marketing and sales: Which differences make a difference?' *Journal of Marketing*, Vol. 71, July 2007, pp. 124–142.

Isaacson, W. (2011). *Steve Jobs*. London: Abacus.

Krahle, L. R. & Gurel-Atay, E. (eds.). (2014). *Communicating Sustainability for the Green Economy*. New York and London: Society for Consumer Psychology, M. E. Sharpe.

McClure, R. E. (2010). 'The influence of organizational culture and conflict on market orientation', *Journal of Business & Industrial Marketing*, Vol. 25, no. 7, pp. 514–524.

McCord, P. (2014). 'How Netflix reinvented HR', *Harvard Business Review*, January/February 2014. Available at https://hbr.org/2014/01/how-netflix-reinvented-hr (accessed 31 December 2015).

McLean, L. D. (2005). 'Organizational culture's influence on creativity and innovation: A review of the literature and implications for human resource development', *Advances in Developing Human Resources*, Vol. 7, no. 2, pp. 226–246.

Martins, E. C.& Terblanche, F. (2003). 'Building organizational culture that stimulates creativity and innovation', *European Journal of Innovation Management*, Vol. 6., no. 1, pp. 64–74.

Meyer, P. (2015). 'Apple Inc. organizational culture: features and implications', *Panmore Institute*. Available at http://panmore.com/

apple-inc-organizational-culture-features-implications (accessed 29 December 2015).

Mintzberg, H. (2013). *Simply Managing: What Managers Do—and Can Do Better*. San Francisco, CA: Berrett-Koehler Publishers Inc.

Narver, J. C. & Slater, S. F. (1990). 'The effect of a market orientation on business profitability', *Journal of Marketing*, Vol. 54, no. 4, pp. 20–35.

Negus, K. (1999). 'Record company cultures and the jargon of corporate identity' (Chapter 3). In K. Negus (ed.). *Music Genres and Corporate Cultures*. London: Routledge, pp. 63–82.

Robbins, S. P. & Judge, T. A. (2022). *Organizational Behaviour*, 18th Edition. Global Edition. Essex, UK: Pearson Education Limited.

Serwer, A. E. (1995). 'Name that tune for $125,000 Jeffrey', *Fortune Magazine*, 29 May 1995, Time Inc.

Sorjonen, H. (2011). 'The manifestation of market orientation and its antecedents in the program planning of arts organizations', *International Journal of Arts Management*, Vol. 14, no. 1, pp. 4–18.

Southall, B. (2009). *The Rise & Fall of EMI Records*. London: Omnibus Press.

Thomke, S. & Feinberg, B. (2009). *Design Thinking and Innovation at Apple*. Harvard Business School, Case No. 9–609–066.

Voss, G. B., Cable, D. M. & Voss, Z. G. (2000). 'Linking organizational values to relationships with external constituents: A study of non-profit professional theatres', *Organization Science*, Vol. 11, no. 3, pp. 330–347.

Weisberger, L. (2003). *The Devil Wears Prada*. New York: Broadway Books.

Ethics in creative organizations and conclusion

Chapter 14

CONTROVERSIES INVOLVING SUPPLY CHAIN ETHICS

Glamorous fashion brands have often been attacked for the enormous gulf between the aspirational lifestyles they promote, and the wages and conditions of the third world workers who manufacture their products (Klein, 2001). This criticism has led to an overhaul of supply chain practices by big clothing manufacturers such as Nike. In 2012, Apple was attacked over the manufacture of its iPads and iPhones. It was alleged that large companies such as Foxconn Technology, which manufactures iPads and iPhones in China, treat their workers poorly, with reports of multiple suicide attempts, poor factory ventilation and working conditions, excessive overtime required to meet shipment targets, crowded employee dormitories, and workers required to stand up for such long periods their legs swelled (Duhigg & Barboza, 2012). Apple responded that it has a rigorous code of conduct for suppliers, which is audited. The workplace standards that they seek to enforce are generally

DOI: 10.4324/9781003262923-14

Figure 14.1 Ethics are important for supply chains, and the use of Foxconn by Apple has historically attracted criticism. Photo credit: Tada Images / Shutterstock.com.

much more attractive than the standards that prevail in local businesses in these countries.

There is no reason to doubt that Apple managers genuinely care about the ethical treatment of employees, suppliers and contracted workers. However, the situation can become more complex when the company is simultaneously pursuing objectives that clash with this aspiration. Apple is under stock market and competitive pressure to ship large quantities of its products into the marketplace to achieve sales targets. Sales success means higher stock market valuations, more money to invest back into the business, staff praise and commendations, and bonuses paid to some staff. One could argue that pressure placed by Apple on suppliers to meet ambitious targets could contribute to suppliers overworking employees through excessive overtime. Apple can also squeeze supplier margins, which then leads suppliers to take shortcuts to reduce costs and restore some of the lost margin (Duhigg & Barboza, 2012). In one Chinese factory owned by the supplier Wintek, it was found that a chemical called n-hexane could clean iPhone screens three times faster than rubbing alcohol. Making this change increased productivity, but the chemical was found to be toxic, and led to the poisoning of over 100 employees who required medical attention (Duhigg & Barboza, 2012). These observations, of dysfunctional outcomes resulting from the power imbalance between the parties continue to be made (Dong, 2022). So large companies also need to look at the larger structural pressures they place on partners and supplier networks, which may incentivize bad behaviour. Another example of this dynamic is where large movie franchises pressure suppliers such as visual-effects companies, stressing

CHAPTER LEARNING OBJECTIVES

At the conclusion of this chapter you will be able to:

- Identify, define and explain concepts of business ethics;
- Apply theories of business ethics to the creative industries and provide arguments in support of ethical positions.

workers and driving down prices by deploying their superior bargaining power.

Companies and their employees should treat all workers in the supply chain ethically, and in conformance with law, international convention and best practice. However, elevating salaries too far in third world countries may decrease job opportunities and investment, as the very reason companies located manufacturing there in the first place may be lost (Boatright, Smith & Patra, 2018). If companies then leave, local workers may be denied opportunities which they valued more than local options, and which they were happy to undertake voluntarily. Thus, the ethical considerations involved in supply chains are complex.

INTRODUCTION

To what extent do ethical dilemmas actually arise in the day-to-day life of a creative industries manager? Imagine a senior executive in an advertising agency. Studies of senior advertising agency personnel have revealed concerns over: ethical issues regarding charging clients and the legitimacy of mark-ups and re-charges (if there is a cost blowout due to the advertising agency's error, will this be re-charged to the client?); working for clients whose products are unethical and/or unhealthy; seeing their company steal ideas, employees or clients from other advertising agencies; underquoting for a job, knowing that costs will blow out later in the process once the client is committed; and being asked by clients to bundle personal work and costs into the client's bill, or manipulate processes and invoicing

(Hunt & Chonko, 1987). What should be the boundaries in these examples?

It should be stressed that this chapter should be read in conjunction with the discussion of exploitation and toxic criticism presented in Chapter 6, the discussion of harassment and exploiting a power advantage in Chapter 8 and the discussion of diversity, equity and inclusion in Chapter 11. We believe that in order to provide a sound theoretical basis for the discussion it is still worth having a specific chapter devoted to ethics, rather than splitting the content across other chapters. This is also necessary because many of the topics would not find a home adopting that approach.

It is no secret that the music and entertainment industries haven't historically set the highest ethical standards. Pop music historians have revelled in tales of bribery and payola, contractual and tax fraud, extortion, mafia involvement and the exploitation of black artists (Dannen, 1991; Knoedelseder, 1993). The digital transformation and re-invention of these industries provides an opportunity to shake them up and further professionalise them. Market corruption also creates inefficiencies, which in turn create opportunities. The Beatles were one of the pre-eminent acts of the twentieth century, not because they corruptly manipulated the music market, but because they brought great enjoyment to millions of people. Wherever corruption acts as a barrier to connecting great artists with audiences, a commercial opportunity exists to bypass the roadblock, because connecting artists directly with fans who will appreciate their work is commercially lucrative. Technology is facilitating ever greater connection between artists and audiences, which can only strengthen this opportunity.

This chapter focuses on business ethics and ethics in the creative industries workplace. It does not address ethics in non-workplace scenarios and our personal lives. The aim is not to fixate on what is right and wrong in each instance, as the precise factors in each situation will vary. Rather, it is to examine the application of ethical principles and to give you a number of different lenses through which to analyse ethical problems and illuminate issues that arise in the cases that are examined. This will enable you to see more clearly the ethical dimension of situations and be more sophisticated at pulling them apart. It will also help you be more skilled at determining which position to take, and justify the position to others once taken.

Studying ethics is about widening our understanding of the impact of our actions, from a narrow, self-centred perspective to a broader perspective that encompasses the impact on other stakeholders and entities. It is a push for objectivity, because these impacts take place anyway, with or without our awareness. This also has implications for personal 'branding' and reputation, because not considering the outcomes of our actions can gravely injure both of these. Even if your company is forcing you to adopt questionable ethical practices, saying 'I was just following orders' may attract little sympathy, and can leave you personally exposed, both in the court of public opinion and legally.

Even if some of the ethical issues on the following pages don't energize you personally, there are a number of reasons to take them seriously. Firstly, there is a segment of major artists who are enormously energized by ethical matters and will actively campaign and publicly criticize companies who are seen to damage the environment and act unethically. Secondly, there is a segment of consumers who are similarly engaged and will also campaign via social media on instances where they feel companies are failing ethically; this can create media storms in which you may find yourself personally embroiled as a manager. Finally, the volume of company regulation is vast and increasing, and managers as well as their companies can be held personally liable for non-compliance.

ETHICAL CONCEPTS

Let us begin by looking more deeply at underlying ethical concepts and theories, which can help illuminate the topic, and provide tools to analyse the issues that we will discuss later. We will explore in turn each of the following:

- utilitarianism
- Machiavellianism
- deontological theories
- Aristotle's virtue ethics
- The 'Universalizability Principle' of Immanuel Kant

- rights
- ethical relativism

'Utilitarianism' is the belief that the best course of action will produce the greatest balance of pleasure over pain for everyone (Boatright *et al.*, 2018). If I were a concert promoter, shocked and hurt by the terrorist attacks on the Bataclan Theatre in Paris in 2015, I could argue that the torture of terrorists to elicit information is the best course of action, because while it potentially violates the rights of the person being interrogated, it safeguards the majority, which is more important. Irrespective of the rightness or wrongness of this position, it is a utilitarian argument. It is a 'consequentialist' or 'teleological' theory, because it is only concerned with consequences, or the end result, not the way in which we have gone about achieving that result. With utilitarianism, one's actions aren't determined by a set of unchanging ethical principles (i.e. 'it is wrong to torture'); one's position alters depending on what is in the best interests of the majority of people.

'Machiavellianism' is a more extreme example of consequentialism, where the 'end justifies the means'; however, the benefit may not be for the majority of people, but simply the person pursuing the strategy. It is named after the sixteenth-century Italian political writer Niccolò Machiavelli. His famous work *The Prince* (transl. G. Bull, 1961) tried to lay out in no-nonsense terms effective strategies for heads of state to govern in a ruthless, divided world. If murder and devastation will better secure the objective being attempted, then that is what he advocates.

'Deontological' ethical theories (from 'deon', the Greek word for 'duty') contrast with consequentialist or teleological theories by focusing on the way we have gone about securing the end result. They 'attempt to evaluate the *inherent* rightness versus wrongness of various behaviours' (Vitell, 2003, p. 34). They arrive at a set of inflexible ethical principles, whose rightness isn't governed by the outcome in given circumstances (which is seen as irrelevant), but rather the principle being upheld. A study of advertising ethics found that utilitarian ethics was the natural preference of advertising practitioners, but the failure to commit to deontological ethics was resulting in crises and unethical conduct (Pratt & James, 1994).

For example, I could travel internationally to attempt to secure certain commercial rights to a major entertainment festival. In this new country I'm visiting, I discover that bribery is widespread, and I fail to win the contract through my refusal to pay bribes. In this instance I have failed in my commercial objective, but (applying a deontological theory) I consider this irrelevant, because I believe paying bribes is inherently wrong. This points to another dilemma in business ethics, which is that to actually solve systemic problems, these problems may need to be considered at three different levels: the larger system of society and industry practice; at the organizational level in terms of organizational practice and organizational culture; and at the individual level in terms of one's personal ethics. Something such as bribery needs to be addressed at all three levels. I may refuse to personally compromise myself in this way, partly because I don't agree with it ethically and partly because I don't want to open myself up to the personal risk of blackmail and extortion (from someone who threatens to release evidence that I have taken a bribe). But I won't change the overall system in this way.

'Virtue ethics' asks 'what kind of person we should be?' and (as promoted by the Greek philosopher Aristotle) encourages the cultivation of ethical character traits such as honesty, courage and dependability (Boatright *et al.*, 2018). These qualities, embodied in action, build trust among the constituencies that managers need to cultivate to succeed. The German philosopher Schopenhauer was influenced by virtue ethics when he wrote:

> What a person means to themselves, what accompanies them during times of solitude or isolation, and what no other can give or take away, is obviously more important to them than everything they possess or what others may think of them … A virtuous, moderate and placid soul can feel satisfied even in humble circumstances, whereas one who is greedy, envious and evil cannot feel this way no matter how vast their wealth … And yet people are a thousand times more concerned with accumulating wealth than culture, although it

> is obvious that what we are actually contributes more to our happiness than what we own.
>
> (Schopenhauer, 1851, 2000)

Virtue ethics is less concerned with the consequences of specific actions (e.g. making money) than with the intrinsic benefits of behaving virtuously, in and of itself. How we act defines who we are, and being a great and virtuous person is its own reward. Money can come and go, but we always have ourselves. People we admire through the way in which they conduct themselves and the integrity they bring to the workplace, are attractive to work for.

The 'Universalizability Principle' of the philosopher Immanuel Kant (1724–1804) approaches ethical dilemmas by asking, 'What if everyone was to employ the conduct in question as a universal law?' (Boatright *et al.*, 2018). Would that be tenable for society? If not, then advocating it as ethical behaviour is irrational. For example, say I decided to exempt myself from paying for music and movies and instead downloaded them illegally. What would be the implications for the whole system if this was adopted by everyone as a universal principle? The revenue for these industries would collapse, leading to the collapse of the companies within them. The revenue for artists and creative workers would also collapse, meaning they would need to re-direct their energies into other areas to survive. Thus the total professional systems on which we rely for entertainment and enjoyment would also collapse. This is not a sustainable, functional, rational strategy for the consumption of music and movies, because if everyone adopted it, these industries wouldn't exist in any sort of professional form to provide the enjoyment being sought. Thus, individuals who practise this are hypocritical and unethical according to this principle, because they rely upon other people doing something that they are not prepared to do themselves.

'Rights' are important in business life, because laws, regulations or industry practice may require firms and managers to treat people in certain ways, and to be aware of certain entitlements. There are several different kinds of rights, such as 'legal rights', as recognized and enforced by each country's legal system and constitution; 'moral rights', which don't depend on the legal system, but rather are community expectations of what we ought to have; and *specific rights* such as 'contractual rights', which are built into the agreements we sign.

'Ethical relativism' is a controversial concept of particular relevance to international business. It is based on the idea that there is no absolute right or wrong; everything is relative to the culture in which one is living. As each culture has its own rules, 'when in Rome, do as the Romans do'. The advantage of ethical relativism is that it encourages tolerance and respect for other belief systems, and discourages forcing one's own moral views upon others. It is also true that there is moral diversity in the world, and reasonable people can differ on what is morally acceptable. However, a disadvantage to this concept is that many historical cultures conducted practices we would now consider barbaric and unacceptable, but which are uncritically accepted within ethical relativism.

WHY ISN'T THE LAW SUFFICIENT?

In the workplace, you may hear the argument that ethical judgements differ from person to person, and so the only reliable reference point is the law; companies should abide by the law, and everything else is unnecessary, or a personal indulgence. However, there are a number of problems with this viewpoint: (i) if all industry standards or codes of professional ethics were made into law, this would be a negative for business, wrapping industries in even greater quantities of inflexible regulation; (ii) the law is slow to develop and usually lags behind contemporary practice, so being at the forefront of ethical reforms guides the creation of new law and provides a head-start in implementation; (iii) the law actually employs moral concepts that are not legally defined, such as 'good faith', 'best efforts' and 'due care', and even in legal matters that come before a court, courts are often guided by moral considerations that underpin aspects of the law; (iv) many countries have immature legal systems that are not equipped to arbitrate or enforce rulings in commercial matters and so local conventions and ethics are followed; (v) companies can win in legal courts but lose in the court of public opinion, in terms of media coverage, consumer attitudes and sales (Boatright *et al.*, 2018). For these reasons 'just following the law' is insufficient.

CONFLICT OF INTEREST AND BRIBERY

There are many commercial roles we can play in the cultural industries which require us to act on behalf of another entity. If I work for a company, I am acting on behalf of that company, and I need to act in the company's best interests. This is usually stated in my employment contract. Similarly, if I am employed to manage an artist I am required to act in the artist's best interests. Advertising agencies are required to act in their client's best interests. What is a 'conflict of interest'? When self-interest comes into conflict with my ethical and legal duty to best serve the interests of the party I represent who is employing me.

Examine the following examples of conflict of interest in creative and cultural firms:

- You are managing an artist and book them for an engagement that you are not entirely convinced will be best for their career development, but you need the income, and sacrifice their interests for your own;
- An advertising agency learns a great deal of sensitive information about a streaming music company while handling their advertising business. They look like they will be losing this client yet still wish to work in this industry sector. They attract a similar client with the informal suggestion that the information they have acquired working for their competitor may be used to their advantage. Most contracts will have clauses about confidentiality, so this behaviour is betraying the previous client's interests in order to advance the advertising agency's interests (so potentially both a breach of confidentiality and a conflict of interest);
- You are working for an event management company and need to quickly find a catering company. You have a relative who runs a catering company and contact them. Other people in the company subsequently allege that this was personal favouritism and other more reputable suppliers were denied the opportunity to bid for the work which means there is no guarantee the company is obtaining the best service for the best price. They suggest that perhaps you even received a secret 'kickback' from the relative (i.e. a bribe).

There are a number of ways companies can combat conflicts of interest: (i) they can create greater clarity around the issue for managers by publishing codes of conduct, guidelines and policies that provide clear examples of situations that may arise and the way the company expects them to be handled; (ii) they can require managers to refer difficult issues up to the next level of management, or to an internal committee; (iii) they can make structural changes, separating companies or divisions to make it more credible that confidential information will stay within the business unit undertaking the work.

Company directors and entertainment lawyers are 'fiduciaries', which means they are legally entrusted with the care of another's property. Their 'fiduciary duty' is a special legal responsibility that requires them to act solely in the interests of the company or client that has employed them, without gaining any material benefit (except with the knowledge and consent of the owner).

Another area of potential conflict of interest in media industries is where the lines between advertising and editorial begin to blur. Generally, within publications there is a distinction between editorial copy and advertising copy. Editorial material should provide the candid, honest opinion of the publication's editorial staff, and should be independent, so that they can freely criticize and recommend books, music or films, or other products. Advertising material is a paid communication on behalf of an advertiser. The better the quality of the media vehicle (i.e. radio show, blog, magazine, newspaper, etc.), the more they will enforce the distinction, so that they can retain the trust of their audience. When editorial material starts to be corrupted by being bought by advertisers, and there is no disclosure to the readership, there can be a breach of trust. Readers can look to something as independent advice, but find in fact it was simply advertising. Even streaming music has come under this sort of pressure with pay for play influencing the prioritization of tracks, rather than it being editorially driven or audience-driven.

INTELLECTUAL PROPERTY RIGHTS INFRINGEMENT

Intellectual property (IP) rights is a broad category of rights that includes copyright, trademarks, designs and patents (among others). Copyright can apply to many things produced by creative and cultural firms, such as musical, literary, dramatic and artistic works (including photographs), as well as sound recordings, broadcasts and cinematographic works (Simpson & Munro, 2012). A song may have multiple copyrights, such as the copyright in the musical work and sheet music (publishing rights), the copyright in the sound recording and the copyright in the published edition. Intellectual property rights are precisely that: property rights. It is a complex area, and the precise details vary from country to country, but using a creator's copyright can be no different to using other aspects of their personal property, where usage usually requires approvals and/or payment.

It would be fair to say that upholding the principles of copyright and the value of intellectual property is one of the defining challenges of the creative industries in the twenty-first century. If you wish to work in these industries, you have a vested interest in fighting for these rights, as they are the key to your future remuneration.

What are the ethical arguments in support of upholding copyright? One ethical argument was advanced at the outset of this chapter: Kant's 'Universalizability Principle'. If everyone ignored copyright, the entire professional system which generates creative works like books, music and films would collapse. Those who don't pay but enjoy accessing works rely upon other people to do something they are not prepared to do themselves. Because copyright is a property right, a failure to recognize it as such is seen by many in the creative industries as no different to theft.

MORAL RIGHTS

Moral rights apply to many types of artistic work, and are complex, often applying in different countries in different ways. They grant creators and performers three types of rights: the right of attribution (the right to be appropriately credited); the right not to be falsely attributed; and the right of integrity, which means the right not to have the work subjected to 'derogatory treatment' and mutilation (Simpson & Munro, 2012). The latter is about protecting the creator's reputation, which could be impacted negatively by people seeing or hearing the work in a distorted or mutilated form. Even if a creator assigns (i.e. sells) their copyright in a work, they can still retain moral rights. Moral rights protection has historically been stronger in Europe than in the United States, and in the United States it has been stronger in the visual arts than music. So if I am a visual artist whose work was used in a distorted form to advertise a commercial product, I have more grounds to argue that my moral rights have been violated than a pop musician objecting to their music being used by a US Republican candidate at a political rally (Chao, 2015).

In the visual arts, ethical and legal controversy has often existed in relation to resale, publication and use of artistic works (Wood & Rentschler, 2003). This again varies from country to country, but what rights should an artist have in the works they have historically created and sold over the course of their lifetime, as they represent their life's creative output? There can be ethical and legal issues in the traffic of cultural property and ancient artefacts, and cultural sensitivity is needed when working with indigenous art (King & Levin, 2006). Organizations which commission creative work can be accused of censorship if they subsequently seek to edit the work, and sometimes a conflict can appear to arise between estates managing the works of deceased artists and the artist's original intentions.

Although it is not afforded legal protection under moral rights, an ethical issue can arise when artists feel their authenticity as an artist is being undermined through commercial pressures to change their work to make it more marketable to the largest possible audience. It can be a dangerous business to have artists alienated from their work, as they will also be called upon to be passionate advocates and promoters of the work. These pitfalls were discussed in Chapter 4 on attitude and motivation.

UNFAIR DISMISSAL

One concept that arises in the treatment of organizational employees is 'due process', which means that performance management of staff, and decisions taken in relation to staff, fall out of a methodical process in which staff participate. So, for example, employees who have their employment terminated after 'due process' understand the legitimate reasons that have led to the decision (even if they disagree with the decision), have had an opportunity to redress any perceived shortcomings prior to the decision being taken, and have received a fair hearing that would satisfy independent scrutiny. Employees who are terminated do suffer economic and psychological hardship, and do deserve dignity and respect. While enshrined as an employment right in many countries, the United States has a more liberal, flexible approach, which considers employment a mutually agreed contractual undertaking that can be terminated by either party in a more flexible way (Boatright *et al.*, 2018).

Even in countries which have an expectation of due process, employers do have ways around this and can terminate staff with immediate effect. This usually results from an acknowledgement by governments that companies have the right to adapt to changing market environments by altering the structure of their organization, retrenching positions that may be out of date and creating new roles that will drive innovation. In such a situation employees are advised that they are being made redundant due to changing marketplace conditions or technology, that their position is being eliminated, and that they will not be replaced. Such terminated staff may receive some sort of payout governed by legislation or their contractual entitlements.

The issue of just compensation arose in the Apple supply chain case that commenced this chapter in relation to the enormous pay differentials between first world and third world countries. This has been a major issue in the fashion industry, with fashion brands routinely criticized for exploitative third world labour practices, such as the surf brand Rip Curl, which in 2016 was found to have manufactured ski wear labelled 'Made in China' in a North Korean factory with slave-like conditions (Peacock, 2016). This contrasts with fashion brands that have put far more effort into understanding their supply chains, mapping them and making the information public, such as Patagonia (Peacock, 2016). One gripe often raised by employees of large public companies is the remuneration received by top managers compared to the average salary. On the one hand, it may seem obscene that someone can be paid millions of dollars while hardworking staff receive a fraction of that. The logic employed by boards of directors can be summarized as follows. Say a company aims to generate $100 million of turnover per annum. If they employ an amazing CEO who drives the company harder, perhaps they will increase this by $10 million compared to a less capable CEO. What will they pay to secure that $10 million? A $3 million per annum salary might look like a bargain from this perspective.

The Ethical Dilemma of CEO Pay: The Case of Sir Lucian Grainge

Figure 14.2 Lucian Grainge (holding his star on the Hollywood Walk of Fame). Photo credit Kathy Hutchins / Shutterstock.com.

In 2021, Sir Lucian Grainge, Chairman and CEO of Universal Music Group, received payments from his company of over £150 million (around US$200 million at 2021 rates). This was not so much driven by his 'salary' as by bonuses paid to reward him for the way he had grown the value of the company on the stockmarket (that year the company was floated on the stock exchange through an Initial Public Offering). The size of the combined payments created controversy, with many criticizing the payments as obscene, but a case can also be made that it had been earned.

Arguments in favour

To understand the background to this, it is worth reviewing the role Grainge had played over the previous 10 years leading the company, where he had doubled the size of the organization and trebled its profits (Sweney, 2021). He had also personally driven critical and risky bets that had contributed to these results, such as the 2011 acquisition of EMI Music, the home of the Beatles, Pink Floyd and Coldplay. That deal was seen as so risky at the time, that he was seen to be betting his entire career on the outcome (Forde, 2019). He had agreed to cover the risk of the deal being blocked by regulators (which was seen by many as likely) and there were also concerns that he might be overpaying for EMI. The deal was subsequently approved, allowing him to keep key EMI assets. The increased size of his company (the biggest in the world) gave him greater negotiating power with streaming platforms, and their success generated greater revenues, which made the price he paid for EMI Music look like a bargain, and increased the value of Universal. It can be argued that the risky decisions he personally drove helped create billions of dollars for the company. So why should he not receive a relatively small proportion of the wealth he had created? Had his risky bets not paid off he would have lost his job and been ridiculed, so why should he not handsomely benefit from his success? In fact these 'risk and reward' incentives are seen by many as fundamental to entrepreneurialism and capitalism, and vital to ensure that managers are properly motivated to act in the best interests of shareholders, who ultimately own the company and pay the salaries.

Arguments against

To understand the outrage that news of this pay packet caused, it is worth reviewing the music industry context at the time. In the year that this announcement was made, musicians worldwide had seen their incomes plummet as live performance revenue was impacted by pandemic cancellations. Streaming revenue was seen to be paltry for most musicians, generating far less for them than formats like the CD in its heyday. In fact, so disproportionate was Grainge's remuneration, so inequitable, that it exceeded the annual income that *all* songwriters earned in the United Kingdom from streaming and sales combined (2019 data – Beaumont-Thomas, 2021; Smith, 2021). For one corporate 'fat cat' to rake in so much more than people who make the music that audiences value and appreciate, demonstrated to many that the whole system was broken. It shows that the industry places less value on people who devote themselves to musical creativity and beauty than those devoted to deal making. It made many musicians wonder why they even bothered and spurred a call for a complete overhaul in the way musicians are remunerated via streaming platforms.

OCCUPATIONAL HEALTH AND SAFETY (OH&S)

Many creative and cultural industries have significant exposure to OH&S risks, such as event management, touring, TV production and film production. In fact, media commentators and fans delight in keeping track of and listing safety and other problems that arise on entertainment projects, e.g. https://en.wikipedia.org/wiki/List_of_film_accidents. Helicopter crashes have killed actors on the set of *The Twilight Zone* and *Delta Force 2*, as well as the French reality TV series *Dropped*. Workers were killed making the films *For Your Eyes Only* (James Bond), *Top Gun*, *The Bodyguard*, *The Dark Knight* and *The Hangover Part II*. Large stadium concerts and even advertising shoots can create potentially dangerous conditions. Famously, Michael Jackson was filming a Pepsi commercial in 1984 when a faulty pyrotechnic set his hair on fire, inflicting second and third-degree burns.

Companies are responsible for the health and safety of employees and contracted freelance staff who are engaged on these projects. OH&S is heavily regulated, and companies need to be across this legislation. It is insufficient to simply be aware of the legislation and have a few posters in the workplace. Companies need to 'hard wire' and embed health and safety practices into their core operational processes. As an employee you have a duty of care to ensure that the projects you work on are run safely, and you should escalate any concerns. Otherwise you place your own safety at risk, and you may find yourself personally blamed if things go wrong. The safest cultures to work in are the ones where everyone believes they have a role to play in safety.

We also need to understand that this duty of care extends beyond the staff to customers. This topic is too vast to cover in anything more than a cursory way in this book, but from an event and production management perspective we need to follow safe practices such as securing cables, securing the structural integrity of staging, mitigating the risk of piercing audio feedback, even ensuring strobe lighting doesn't trigger epilepsy (which at venues should be at or below four flashes per second) (Hannam, 2015). We need to follow industry regulation and industry best practice with regard to the technical delivery of our events and products.

MARKETING AND ADVERTISING

In the entertainment industry, promotional copywriting can be so hyped it is hard to know what is reality and what is fantasy. It can seem to us sometimes that no one will come to our show unless we state in the advertisement, 'If you don't drop everything immediately and see this show, you will die'. We have all come to expect a degree of hype, and a reasonable person would know that the above claim is intended as an exaggeration. However, legislation does exist around the world to protect consumers from demonstrably false claims that manipulate people into paying money for something on false pretences. While we can say (unsatisfactorily) that deceptive advertising has a tendency to deceive, the Federal Trade Commission in the United States has yet to provide a precise definition (Boatright *et al.*, 2018). But saying that a certain artist will be present at your event, when they have not been invited, have no plans to attend and won't be attending, is false and misleading advertising. Where deceptive advertising begins to make it impossible for people to make rational choices between products in a marketplace, and more likely to suffer significant loss, regulators will be more likely to intervene, particularly if they receive complaints. Look at the litigation that resulted from the Fyre Festival debacle to see the wrath that can fall upon an entrepreneur from disgruntled consumers.

Ethical issues can arise in the promotion of artists, such as artificially boosting social media metrics, artists lip-synching performances for audiences who believe they are paying for a live performance and artists communicating misinformation to the media via their PR agents. Much of this behaviour is driven by the competitive pressures and intensity of the industry rather than a quest to be evil. But careers built on hype and misinformation rarely sustain themselves in the long term, particularly in the internet age, which thrives on puncturing 'hot air', and where audiences can become bored with pure hype.

Privacy protection has increasingly become an issue in marketing, in terms of how we acquire, store and use personal information gained via customer relationship management (CRM) systems. If credit card and personal information is hacked from a company database, it can seriously damage the relationship between the company and its customers, causing practical inconvenience (the cards must be replaced) and leaving customers with a sense of personal violation. In 2011 the Sony PlayStation Network was hacked, leading to confidential details belonging to 77 million users being stolen, such as credit card details, birthdates, addresses and security answers (Stuart & Arthur, 2011).

Staff too have legitimate expectations that personal information gathered on them will be kept confidential (e.g. the results of psychometric or other recruitment tests). This includes keeping it from people in the organization who do not need to know, and not using the information for purposes beyond the originally stated intention.

With regard to pricing, attempts to work with competitors to fix prices or restrict competition can see government regulators intervene, attacking the actions as illegal under 'antitrust' or 'anticompetitive' law. The ideal in a modern, free market economy is to create an open marketplace where buyers and sellers can interact freely. If we don't like one supplier, we are free to look around for an alternative supplier whose prices or product may be more attractive to us. The key take-out for readers of this textbook is that the more significant market power a company wields – think of Apple, Google, Microsoft, etc. – the more alert you should be to antitrust issues, and the more caution you should exercise in entering partnerships with competitors. The point at issue is whether the partnership will negatively impact the free market by restricting consumer choice or artificially inflating prices. The application of antitrust law in the creative industries can be counterintuitive (Saintilan, 2013), and so before entering into partnership agreements with competitors, it is wise to have them vetted by lawyers who are experienced in these matters. Much smaller companies could still be at risk if they attempted to organize a coalition of industry players that had the potential to impact consumer choice and price competition.

GOVERNANCE: PUTTING IN PLACE THE STRUCTURES, PROCESSES AND SYSTEMS TO CATCH AND CORRECT PROBLEMS

Good governance requires systematic monitoring and regulation of the organization's activities (Rentschler, 2015). It needs systematic checks and balances that will catch illegal and unethical conduct. To be effective, it needs to be a systematic solution that is not dependent upon any one person (because any one person may be fallible). The system should have built-in layers that audit and report variances. The system needs to be able to respond effectively to internal complaints and detect criminal behaviour.

The London Philharmonic Orchestra saw itself defrauded by its own finance director, who stole approximately £666,000 from the orchestra between 2005 and 2009 (Charity Commission, UK, 2011). As the regulatory case report published by the UK Charity Commission relates, the actual cost of the fraud was larger, due to the orchestra spending money it thought it had, only to find its budgetary picture was artificially inflated. Had the precise financial situation been understood, the orchestra would have made different decisions. Some of the fraud took place through complex financial manipulation of the accounts, but most of it was simply forging a second signature on cheques. The finance director was eventually sentenced to four years in prison, the stolen money was fully recovered, and much of the consequential losses were also recovered through a range of legal actions (including against a financial institution that honoured the forged cheques). In summary, the organization's governance and systems proved to be weak, but the crisis was handled in decisive fashion by the CEO who minimized the damage. In a financial fraud case in another entertainment organization, unbeknown to shareholders US$381,015 of the company's money was used to purchase its own tickets to artificially boost ticket sales in a production that was transferring to Broadway (Vickery, 2005). They had hoped to use this artificially positive picture to promote the Broadway production, but it was considered accounting and securities fraud by the US Securities and Exchange Commission (SEC).

This points to the necessity (in often under-resourced arts organizations) to keep an eye on the appropriateness of the internal accounting systems, in the midst of all the other operational considerations clamouring for attention. This is even riskier for small start-up organizations, which can expand far quicker than their internal systems can accommodate, requiring constant monitoring and adjustment to bring their size and systems into alignment.

Looking across the full breadth of ethical issues, the types of activities that can be introduced by an organization to provide systematic checks and balances include: introducing ethics filters and strong reference checks in staff recruitment processes; developing codes of ethics to guide employees in matters of sensitivity, which should be tailored to the specific work environment; staff induction processes that communicate the values and policies of the organization; developing an ethics committee to advise on difficult ethical matters; appointing an ethics ombudsman; ensuring policies support 'whistle-blowers' – people who draw management's attention to unethical practices within the organization; conducting ethics audits periodically to assess compliance in high risk areas; and developing ethics education programmes targeted at deeply probing areas of higher risk and complexity (Wood & Rentschler, 2003).

As discussed in the chapter on culture (Chapter 13), it should also be emphasized that in order to create an ethical organization, leaders must not only back the measures verbally and in writing, but also 'walk the talk' and embody the organization's principles in their own conduct (Wood & Rentschler, 2003). Otherwise, they will ring false to staff, who will interpret what is actually rewarded by senior management as revealing the true values of the organization.

ENVIRONMENTAL ETHICS: CONFRONTING THE DESTRUCTION OF THE NATURAL WORLD

> It is unequivocal that human influence has warmed the atmosphere, ocean and land. Widespread and rapid changes in the atmosphere, ocean, cryosphere and biosphere have occurred. The scale of recent changes across the climate system as a whole – and the present state of many aspects of the climate system – are unprecedented over many centuries to many thousands of years. Human-induced climate change is already affecting many weather and climate extremes in every region across the globe. Evidence of observed changes in extremes such as heatwaves, heavy precipitation, droughts, and tropical cyclones, and, in particular, their attribution to human influence, has strengthened since AR5 [the last report]. Global surface temperature will continue to increase until at least mid-century under all emissions scenarios considered. Global warming of 1.5°C and 2°C will be exceeded during the 21st century unless deep reductions in CO_2 and other greenhouse gas emissions occur in the coming decades. Many changes due to past and future greenhouse gas emissions are irreversible for centuries

Figure 14.3 Sustainable Fashion Icon. Photo credit: venimo / Shutterstock.com.

to millennia, especially changes in the ocean, ice sheets and global sea level.

(IPCC, 2021)

The above quotation is drawn from summary statements in a report provided by the Intergovernmental Panel on Climate Change (IPCC), which was established by the United Nations and the World Meteorological Organization as the pre-eminent organization for monitoring climate change. It draws on the work of hundreds of international experts and a vast collection of hard scientific data. The authors of this textbook naturally believe in science and the scientific method, and the evidence is so overwhelming that climate change many years ago stopped being a controversial theory, and became a simple fact of our existence.

Its implications are far reaching, and the most important thing creative and cultural organizations can do is to understand that carbon emissions are driving the problem, and so there is a need to monitor and reduce our carbon footprint. For example, pioneers in 'green theatre' who have prioritized reducing their carbon footprint include the Arcola Theatre in London, the Sydney Theatre Company and the Portland Center Stage, whose Gerding Theater at the Armory is considered one of the greenest buildings in the United States (Gerchak, 2006; Lawler, 2008; Slingerland, 2007). Reducing the carbon footprint of events is becoming a more and more sophisticated practice, and there is now an expectation that when a major event such as the Olympics is staged, it will have a sustainability report published analysing the carbon footprint and waste reduction metrics (see for example the reporting and analysis conducted on the Tokyo 2020 Olympic Games) (TOCOG, 2021).While carbon footprint is related to climate change, it is possible to wreak environmental damage with no carbon footprint impact, such as by pouring poison into a river, or damaging ecosystems through over-population. So, clearly environmental ethics are broader than this one issue. An enormous amount of literature has charted the contribution that business has made to the world's environmental destruction. Rachel Carson's *Silent Spring*, published in 1962, was a seminal work in looking at industrial chemical pollution. Paul Hawken's *The Ecology of Commerce* in

1993 and McDonough and Braungart's *Cradle to Cradle* in 2002 called for a complete re-think in the way that we create products, factoring in their entire lifecycle. It should be noted there were significant environmental concerns in the arts prior to the rise of climate change as an issue (Cless, 1996; Fried & May, 1994). As climate change continues to impact our lives and industries, so will it need to command greater managerial attention, or projects will risk running into legal difficulties or attacks from artists and audiences.

MANAGING YOUR PERSONAL BRAND AND REPUTATION IN THE WORKPLACE

To conclude by returning to themes raised earlier in the book, we encourage readers to look at ethical issues through the lens of their own personal brand and reputation. What do we mean by personal 'brand' and what has this got to do with ethics? We understand personal branding as the impressions people will form about you based on the way you dress, the way you communicate, your behaviour and other considerations. People will form these impressions anyway, and so you will have a 'brand' even without trying. The question is whether you want to consciously manage it. Some people can feel that such a quest is inauthentic, because it involves falsely styling themselves in a fake way. We are not encouraging people to be fake. But we do encourage people to be mindful of the impact they make on others, and to recognize the importance this has on the way they are perceived and treated. In such a theatrical environment as the creative and cultural industries, it can even have implications for your career (unfair as that may sound).

In the academic literature there is a link between ethics and reputation in non-profit cultural leadership (Wood & Rentschler, 2003). We are not advocating that you try to create distinctiveness by only wearing purple velvet clothes and a red beret and carrying a white poodle on a pink satin cushion (which might be distinctive, but could get very boring after a while). Rather we are talking fundamentally about the way you behave in the workforce and the values you espouse in your dealings with those around you, all of which impact the judgements people make about you and the trust they will place in you. This is manifesting ethics in action at a personal level.

If you work for a non-profit organization, the cause or mission that drives your organization can be part of your personal mission, helping to create personal meaning and an authentic underlying purpose to your professional life. There is nothing stopping people working in commercial organizations similarly connecting their work to the deeper meaning in their lives.

CONCLUSION

This chapter has provided a broad survey of ethical issues that can arise in the cultural and creative industries. This encompassed: conflict of interest and bribery; intellectual property right infringement; unfair dismissal; occupational health and safety and product safety; marketing and advertising claims; antitrust/anticompetitive behaviour; and environmental ethics. The way you take this on, or not, has implications for your own personal brand and professional reputation. If we want to build trust with stakeholders and create positive media messages and professional reputations, we need to proactively monitor and manage the issues discussed in this chapter.

DISCUSSION QUESTIONS AND CLASS EXERCISES

Drugs at festivals: Media reports often highlight the dangers of drug use at festivals, a phenomenon that dates back to Woodstock. Is this media overreaction or a legitimate concern? Is it the responsibility of festival organizers to ensure attendees don't die of drug overdoses, or the responsibility of individual concert goers to take care of themselves? (In the event of a drug overdose, who will people blame?)

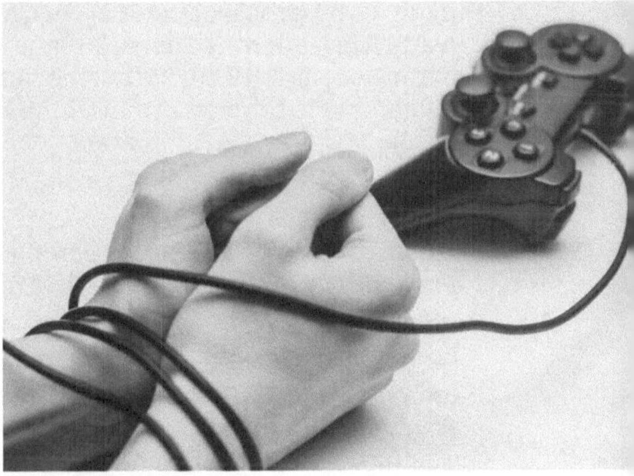

Figure 14.4 Video game addiction. Photo credit: spongePo / Shutterstock.com.

Online game addiction: Online games such as Fortnite, League of Legends and World of Warcraft have attracted criticism for being highly addictive (e.g. see www.gamequitters.com). To what degree do online game manufacturers need to bear in mind the vulnerability of some users to addiction and reduce potential negative outcomes from playing the game?

References

Beaumont-Thomas, B. (2021). 'MPs and music industry bodies criticise pay of Universal head Lucian Grainge', *The Guardian*, published online November 11, 2021. Available at https://www.theguardian.com/music/2021/nov/10/mps-and-music-industry-bodies-criticise-pay-of-universal-head-lucian-grainge (accessed 24 January 2022).

Boatright, J. R., Smith, J. D. & Patra, B. P. (2018). *Ethics and the Conduct of Business*, 8th Edition. Chennai, India: Pearson India Education Services Pvt. Ltd.

Carson, R. (1962). *Silent Spring*. New York: Mariner Books.

Chao, E. (2015). 'Stop using my song: 34 artists who fought politicians over their music', *Rolling Stone*, July 8, 2015. Available at http://www.rollingstone.com/music/lists/stop-using-my-song-34-artists-who-fought-politicians-over-their-music-20150708 (accessed 28 February 2016).

Charity Commission (UK). (2011). *Regulatory Case Report: London Philharmonic Orchestra Ltd*, 20 January. Available at http://webarchive.nationalarchives.gov.uk/20110406065406/http:/www.charity-commission.gov.uk/Library/rcr_london_philharmonic.pdf (accessed 6 March 2016).

Cless, D. (1996). 'Eco-Theatre, USA: The grassroots is greener', *The Drama Review*, Vol. 40, no. 2, pp. 79–102.

Dannen, F. (1991). *Hit Men*. New York: Random House.

Dong, M. (2022). 'Apple and Foxconn: addressing power imbalances in global supply chains', *Business Think*, published 22 February 2022, University of NSW. Available at https://www.businessthink.unsw.edu.au/articles/apple-foxconn-power-imbalances-global-supply-chains (accessed July 4 2022).

Duhigg, C. & Barboza, D. (2012). 'In China, human costs are built into an iPad', *The New York Times*, 25 January 2012. Available at http://www.nytimes.com/2012/01/26/business/ieconomy-apples-ipad-and-the-human-costs-for-workers-in-china.html?_r=0 (accessed 26 February 2016).

Forde, E. (2019). *The Final Days of EMI: Selling the Pig*. London: Omnibus Press.

Fried, L. K. & May, T. (1994). *Greening Up Our Houses: A Guide to a More Ecologically Sound Theatre*. New York: Drama Book Publishers.

Gerchak, K. (2006). 'How green is my theatre?', *American Theatre*, Vol. 23, no. 9, pp. 66–70.

Hannam, C. (2015). *Health and Safety in the Live Music and Event Technical Production Industry: A Guide for Employees and the Self-Employed*. Cambridge: Entertainment Technology Press.

Hawken, P. (1993). *The Ecology of Commerce: A Declaration of Sustainability*. New York: HarperBusiness.

Hunt, S. D. & Chonko, L. B. (1987). 'Ethical problems of advertising agency executives', *Journal of Advertising*, Vol. 16, no. 4, pp. 16–24.

IPCC (2021). 'Summary for policymakers'. In V. Masson-Delmotte, P. Zhai, A. Pirani, et al. (eds). *Climate Change 2021: The Physical Science Basis. Contribution of Working Group to the Sixth Assessment Report of the Intergovernmental Panel on Climate Change*. Switzerland: IPCC.

King, E. A. & Levin, G. (eds.). (2006). *Ethics and the Visual Arts*. New York: Allworth Press.

Klein, N. (2001). *No Logo*. London: HarperCollins.

Knoedelseder, W. (1993). *Stiffed: A True Story of MCA, the Music Business and the Mafia*. New York: HarperCollins.

Lawler, M. (2008). 'Toward a more sustainable theatre', *American Theatre*, Vol. 25, no. 7, pp. 58–61.

Machiavelli, N. & Bull, G. (transl.). (1961). *The Prince*. London: Penguin Classics.

McDonough, W. & Braungart, M. (2002). *Cradle to Cradle: Remaking the Way We Make Things*. New York: North Point Press.

Peacock, B. (2016). 'Rip Curl. When cool is just not cool at all', *B&T Magazine*, 26 February. Available at https://www.bandt.com.au/media/rip-curl-when-cool-is-just-not-cool-at-all (accessed 6 March 2016).

Pratt, C. B. & James, E. L. (1994). 'Advertising ethics: A contextual response based on classical ethical theory', *Journal of Business Ethics*, Vol. 13, pp. 455–468.

Rentschler, R. (2015). *Arts Governance: People, Passion, Performance*. London: Routledge.

Saintilan, P. (2013). 'The Three Tenors antitrust case: What did we learn?', *Journal of the Music & Entertainment Industry Educators Association (MEIEA)*, Vol. 13, no. 1, pp. 13–25.

Schopenhauer, A. (2000). *Schopenhauer's Solace*. Ice Calm Publications, edited by Paul Saintilan, translated by Michael Grunwald (the quoted passages are from *Parerga und Paralipomena*, originally published in 1851).

Simpson, S. & Munro, J. (2012). *Music Business*, 4th Edition. London: Omnibus Press.

Slingerland, A. L. (2007). 'Greening the Greenroom', *Stage Directions*, Vol. 20, no. 11, pp. 44–47.

Smith, D. (2021). 'UMG CEO Lucian Grainge is getting paid $201 million this year—which is more than all UK songwriters combined', *Digital Music News*, published online November 10, 2021. Available at https://www.digitalmusicnews.com/2021/11/10/lucian-grainge-2021-salary/ (accessed 24 January 2022).

Stuart, K. & Arthur, C. (2011). 'PlayStation network hack: Why it took Sony seven days to tell the world', *The Guardian*, 27 April. Available at http://www.theguardian.com/technology/gamesblog/2011/apr/27/playstation-network-hack-sony (accessed 6 March 2016).

Sweney, M. (2021). '"Ruthless but good ears": Lucian Grainge is key architect of music industry revival', *The Guardian*, published online September 21, 2021. Available at https://www.theguardian.com/business/2021/sep/21/key-architect-of-music-industry-revival-lucian-grainge-universal (accessed 24 January 2022).

TOCOG (2021). *Sustainability Post-Games Report, Tokyo 2020*, December 2021. Tokyo: The Tokyo Organising Committee of the Olympic and Paralympic Games (TOCOG).

Vickery, A. (2005). 'Accounting fraud at Live Entertainment Canada, Incorporated, 1993–98', *International Journal of Arts Management*, Vol. 7, no. 2, pp. 15–26.

Vitell, S. J. (2003). 'Consumer ethics research: Review, synthesis and suggestions for the future', *Journal of Business Ethics*, Vol. 43, no. 1/2, pp. 33–47.

Wood, G. & Rentschler, R. (2003). 'Ethical behaviour: The means for creating and maintaining better reputations in arts organisations', *Management Decision*, Vol. 41, no. 5/6, pp. 528–537.

Index

Note: *Italic* page numbers refer to figures.

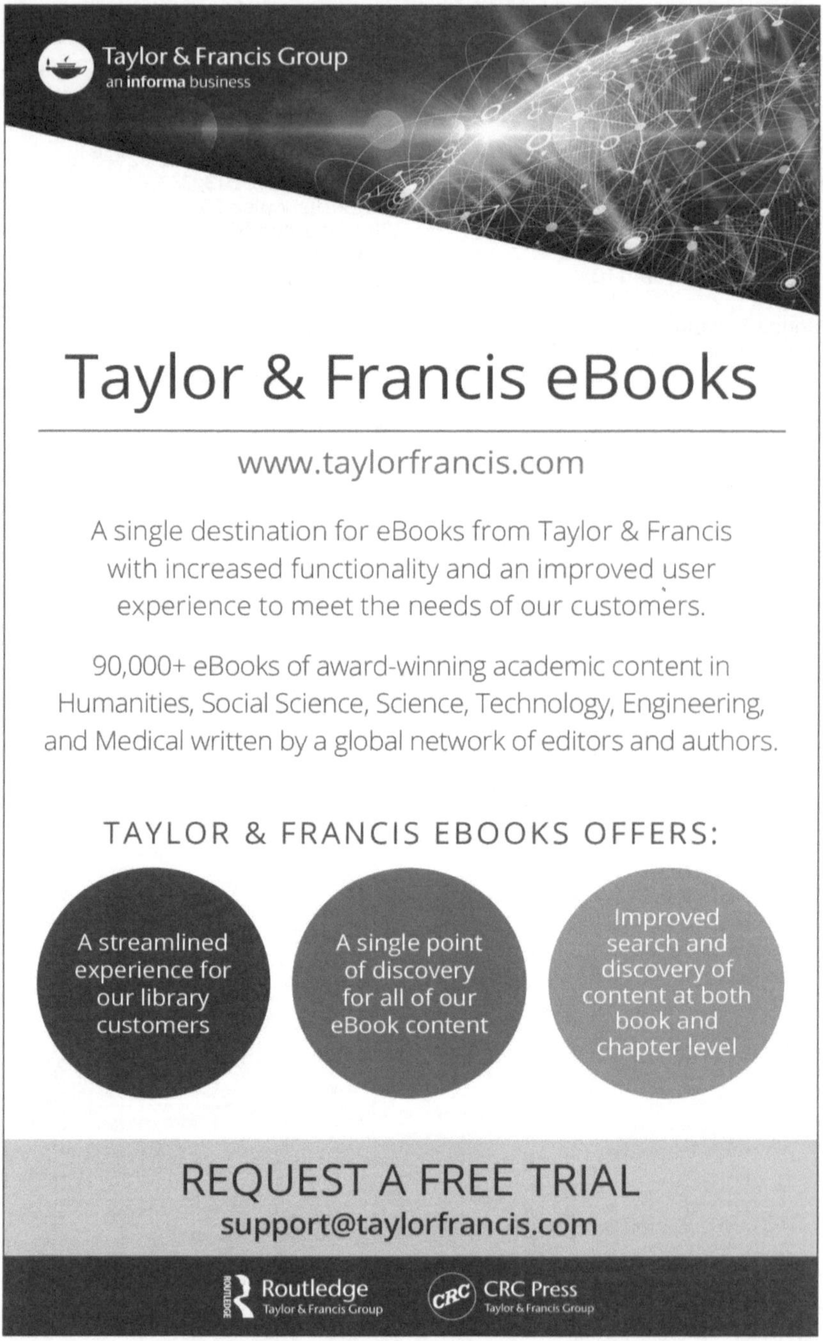
Taylor & Francis Group
an informa business
Taylor & Francis eBooks
www.taylorfrancis.com
A single destination for eBooks from Taylor & Francis with increased functionality and an improved user experience to meet the needs of our customers.
90,000+ eBooks of award-winning academic content in Humanities, Social Science, Science, Technology, Engineering, and Medical written by a global network of editors and authors.
TAYLOR & FRANCIS EBOOKS OFFERS:
A streamlined experience for our library customers
A single point of discovery for all of our eBook content
Improved search and discovery of content at both book and chapter level
REQUEST A FREE TRIAL
support@taylorfrancis.com
Routledge Taylor & Francis Group
CRC Press Taylor & Francis Group